Helen Hershkoff is an assistant professor at New York University School of Law. A 1973 graduate of Radcliffe-Harvard College, she attended Oxford University as a Marshall Scholar and received her law degree in 1978 from Harvard Law School. After working as a litigation associate at the New York law firm of Paul, Weiss, Rifkind, Wharton, and Garrison, she became a staff attorney at the Legal Aid Society of New York, Civil Appeals and Law Reform Unit, where she did welfare test case litigation from 1983 to 1987. From 1987 to 1995, she was an associate legal director of the American Civil Liberties Union.

Stephen Loffredo is an associate professor at the City University of New York Law School, teaching constitutional law, poverty law, and immigrant rights. A 1977 graduate of Yale College, he received his law degree in 1981 from Harvard Law School and then clerked for the New Jersey Supreme Court. From 1982 to 1986, he was a staff attorney at the Legal Aid Society of New York in the South Bronx, where he did neighborhood legal services and welfare test case litigation. He has continued to represent poor people through the clinical program at CUNY Law School and as counsel to the Urban Justice Center (formerly the Legal Action Center for the Homeless). His research and writing focus on the constitutional aspects of poverty law.

ALSO IN THIS SERIES

The Rights of Aliens and Refugees
The Rights of Authors, Artists, and Other Creative People
The Rights of Crime Victims
The Rights of Employees and Union Members
The Rights of Families
The Rights of Indians and Tribes
The Rights of Lesbians and Gay Men
The Rights of Older Persons
The Rights of Patients
The Rights of People Who Are HIV Positive
The Rights of People with Mental Disabilities
The Rights of Prisoners
The Rights of Public Employees
The Rights of Racial Minorities
The Rights of Single People
The Rights of Students
The Rights of Teachers
The Rights of Women
The Rights of Young People
The Right to Protest
The Right to Religious Liberty
Your Right to Government Information
Your Right to Privacy

AN AMERICAN CIVIL LIBERTIES UNION HANDBOOK

THE RIGHTS OF
THE POOR

The Authoritative ACLU Guide to
Poor People's Rights

Helen Hershkoff
Stephen Loffredo

General Editor of the Handbook Series
Norman Dorsen, President, ACLU 1976–1991

SOUTHERN ILLINOIS UNIVERSITY PRESS
CARBONDALE AND EDWARDSVILLE

Library of Congress Cataloging-in-Publication Data
Hershkoff, Helen, 1953–
    The rights of the poor : the authoritative ACLU guide to poor
people's rights / Helen Hershkoff, Stephen Loffredo
        p.   cm. — (An American Civil Liberties Union handbook)
    Includes bibliographical references.
    1. Public welfare—Law and legislation—United States—
Miscellanea.   2. Public welfare—Law and legislation—United
States—Popular works.   3. Poor—Legal status, laws, etc.—United
States—Miscellanea.   4. Poor—Legal status, laws, etc.—United
States—Popular works.   5. Poor—Civil rights—United States—
Miscellanea.   6. Poor—Civil rights—United States—Popular works.
I. Loffredo, Stephen, 1955–   . II. Title. III. Series.
KF3720.Z9H47   1997
362.5′8′0973—dc20   96-41433
                                                              CIP

ISBN 0-8093-2117-3 (cloth : alk. paper)
ISBN 0-8093-2091-6 (pbk. : alk. paper)

For our parents
and for our son, Ben

Contents

Preface   ix
Acknowledgments   xi
Introduction   xiii

I.   Income Support   1
     Aid to Families with Dependent Children   4
     Temporary Assistance for Needy Families Block Grant   32
     Supplemental Security Income   54
     General Assistance   98
     Earned Income Credit   105

II.   Food Assistance   136
     Food Stamp Program   136
     WIC: Special Supplemental Nutrition Program for
       Women, Infants and Children   155
     National School Lunch Program   161
     School Breakfast Program   164
     Summer Food Service Program for Children   167
     Senior Nutrition Programs   168

III.   Health Services   177
     Medicaid   178
     Vaccines for Children   199
     Medicare   200
     State and Local Programs   210
     Public Health Service Act Programs   211
     Hill-Burton   212
     Emergency Care   214

IV.	Housing	222
V.	Education	266
	Preschool Programs	273
	Goals 2000	276
	Title I	277
	Vocational Education	282
	The McKinney Act and Homeless Children	284
	Language-Minority Programs	286
	Education of Children with Disabilities	287
	Pregnant and Parenting Students	296
	Higher Education	297
VI.	Access to Justice	315
VII.	Rights in Public Places	328
VIII.	The Right to Vote	340
	Appendixes	
A.	Supplemental Security Income Worksheet	357
B.	Physician's Report Form Samples	362
C.	Explanation of the "Forty Quarters" Rule	369
D.	Food Stamp Income Worksheets	371
E.	State Guide to an Indigent's Right to Counsel in Civil Cases	383
F.	The Legal System	404

PREFACE

This guide sets forth your rights under present law and offers suggestions on how they can be protected. It is one of a continuing series of handbooks published in cooperation with the American Civil Liberties Union (ACLU).

Surrounding these publications is the hope that Americans, informed of their rights, will be encouraged to exercise them. Through their exercise, rights are given life. If they are rarely used, they may be forgotten and violations may become routine.

This guide offers no assurances that your rights will be respected. The laws may change, and in some of the subjects covered in these pages, they change quite rapidly. An effort has been made to note those parts of the law where movement is taking place, but it is not always possible to predict accurately when the law *will* change.

Even if laws remain the same, their interpretation by courts and administrative officials often varies. In a federal system such as ours, there is a built-in problem, since state and federal laws differ, not to speak of the variations among states. In addition, there is much diversity in the ways in which particular courts and administrative officials interpret the same law at any given moment.

If you encounter what you consider to be a specific abuse of your rights, you should seek legal assistance. There are a number of agencies that may help you, among them ACLU affiliate offices, but bear in mind that the ACLU is a limited-purpose organization. In many communities, there are federally funded legal service offices that provide assistance to persons who cannot afford the costs of legal representation.

In general, the rights that the ACLU defends are freedom of inquiry and expression; due process of law; equal protection under the law; and privacy. The authors in this series have discussed other rights (even though they sometimes fall outside the ACLU's usual concern) in order to provide as much guidance as possible.

These books have been planned as guides for the people directly affected: thus the question-and-answer format. (In some areas, there are more detailed works available for experts.) These guides seek to raise the major issues and inform the nonspecialist of the basic law on the subject. The authors of these books are themselves specialists who understand the need for information at "street level."

If you encounter a specific legal problem in an area discussed in one of these handbooks, show the book to your attorney. Of course, he or she will not be able to rely exclusively on the handbook to provide you with adequate representation. But if your attorney hasn't had a great deal of experience in the specific area, the handbook can provide helpful suggestions on how to proceed.

NORMAN DORSEN, *General Editor*
Stokes Professor of Law
New York University School of Law

The principal purpose of this handbook, as well as others in this series, is to inform individuals of their legal rights. The authors from time to time suggest what the law should be, but their personal views are not necessarily those of the ACLU. For the ACLU's position on the issues discussed in this handbook, the reader should write to Public Education Department, ACLU, 125 Broad Street, New York, NY 10004.

ACKNOWLEDGMENTS

This book reflects the help of many individuals and groups, and we would like to express our appreciation to as many of them as possible (we list organizational affiliations for identification purposes only).

We are enormously grateful for the assistance, support, and collegiality of Jane Perkins of the National Health Law Program; Fred Fuchs of Legal Aid of Central Texas; Maura Kelly, Eileen Ordover, and Bernard Lee (together with Kathleen Boundy, Lauren Jacobs, and Margot Rogers) of the Center for Law and Education; Carrie M. Lewis and Geri Henchy of the Food Research and Action Center; and Christopher A. Hansen of the ACLU.

We thank David B. Bryson of the National Housing Law Project for permission to rely extensively on *HUD Housing Programs: Tenants' Rights* (2d ed. 1994) as the basis for the housing chapter; Timothy J. Casey of the Center on Social Welfare Policy and Law for permission to adapt materials coauthored with Adele M. Blong on the AFDC program; Michael Stoops of the National Coalition for the Homeless for permission to use materials on the right of homeless persons to vote; Marion Nichols for reviewing the General Assistance section; Katherine Castro and Katherine Bishop for materials and advice on the housing chapter; Jodie Levin Epstein for information on Learnfare; Gina Mannix for materials about AFDC benefit levels; and Ellen Teller for information on food programs.

We thank many legal services and legal aid lawyers who offered suggestions, gave advice, and shared their expertise. In particular, we thank Steven Godeski and David Udell for reviewing the Supplemental Security Income section; and Christopher D. Lamb for reviewing the Earned Income Credit section.

We thank a number of ACLU attorneys. We are grateful to Arthur N. Eisenberg for reviewing the chapters on access to justice, rights in public places, and the right to vote; Laughlin McDonald for reviewing the chapter on the right to vote; and Philip Tegeler for materials on the Section 8 program.

We thank Holly Maguigan for advice on criminal procedure; Nancy Morawetz for discussions about the "welfare reform" act; Joseph Rosenberg for information on supplemental needs trusts; and Florence Wagman Roisman for general advice.

We thank Martin O'Connell of the Census Bureau for information on the demographics of voting patterns; and David A. Price of the Center for Public Policy Studies for permission to adapt materials coauthored with Steven Weller on the right to counsel in civil cases.

We thank Arthur Lubow for general advice. We thank Rossiya Fajardo for checking hundreds of footnotes.

We thank the American Civil Liberties Union, the Bureau of the Census (Population Division), the Center on Budget and Policy Priorities, the Center for Law and Education, the Center for Law and Social Policy, the Center for Public Policy Studies, the Center on Social Welfare Policy and Law, the Children's Defense Fund, the Food Research and Action Center, the Low Income Housing Information Service, the Main Street Legal Services of the City University of New York Law School, the National Center on Women and Family Law, Inc., the National Coalition for the Homeless, the National Consumer Law Center, the National Health Law Program, the National Housing Law Project, the National Law Center on Homelessness and Poverty, the New York University School of Law, the San Francisco Coalition for Low Income Housing, the Urban Institute, and the University of Pennsylvania Public Service Program for materials and support.

We thank the students and legal volunteers who provided research and technical assistance: Sameer Ashar, Lesley Carver, Leslie Cooper, Timothy Corbett, Kara Finck, Jennifer Friedman, Jill Hasday, Geri Henchy, John Hlinko, Diana Hortsch, Hunter S. Labovitz, Yuanchung Lee, Michael Lisi, Cornelius O'Connell, Andrew Perlman, Szerina Perot, Keri Powell, Darren Rosenblum, Ellen Ross, Jason Sanders, Tracy Schneider, Elizabeth Shapiro, Daniel Simon, Sharon Telford, Robert Vincent, David Weinstein, Glenna Wyman, and especially Wendy Stryker.

We thank Sylvia Law and Burt Neuborne for launching this project with their original version of *The Rights of the Poor*. We thank Norman Dorsen for encouragement and inspiration. We thank Margaret Hale and Richard Kelsey for secretarial assistance and for seeing the project to the end. Errors that remain, and opinions expressed, are those of the authors alone.

INTRODUCTION

Twenty years have passed since the ACLU first published *The Rights of the Poor* (written by Sylvia A. Law with a chapter by Burt Neuborne).[1] During this time, life has become increasingly hard for the nation's poor. More than one-fifth of America's children now live in poverty[2]—the highest child poverty rate in thirty years[3]—and the gap between rich and poor has become greater than in any other industrialized nation.[4] The income of the average poor family with children is only $5.40 per person per day, and even working full time at the minimum wage no longer lifts a family out of poverty.[5]

While the United States leads the industrialized world in infant mortality, in child poverty, and in income inequality, it trails in social spending.[6] Indeed, government cutbacks to the social programs described in the first edition of this book contributed heavily to the impoverishment of America.[7] Although more children are now poor, total spending on AFDC[8]— until 1996 the major source of subsistence payments for poor families with children—dropped in real terms by nearly 20 percent from 1973 to 1989.[9] And the value of an average AFDC grant declined over the last two decades by nearly half, reaching less than 40 percent of the federal poverty line in 1995.[10]

Numerous polls show that the majority of Americans believe our society has a moral obligation to end poverty.[11] Yet our social policies have moved far from a politics of compassion. The War on Poverty, declared by President Lyndon Baines Johnson thirty years ago, has become instead a war on the poor, who are routinely blamed for the nation's social problems and effectively banished from mainstream life.[12] And the "welfare reform" frenzy that President Bill Clinton ignited with his 1992 campaign pledge to "end welfare as we know it" has produced federal legislation that by even the government's account will make the plight of America's poor immeasurably worse.[13]

In the present political climate, it has never been more urgent for poor people to have information about rights that the law continues to guarantee. This book thus has a dual purpose.

First, this book explains how poor people can use the law to help obtain services needed for basic living: cash income support, food assistance, health care, housing, and education. Under some programs (for example, food stamps), poor people have an entitlement to assistance if they apply for benefits and meet eligibility requirements. Under other programs (for example, housing), poor people do not have an entitlement to assistance and not every applicant who is eligible actually receives help. The eligibility rules of all programs for the poor are very complex. They also change frequently. Passage of the 1996 "welfare reform" act has further complicated the legal scene. This book is only a starting point in learning about the rights that poor people have to government-provided benefits. If you need assistance, it is very important to talk to a legal services lawyer, to a community organization, or to a welfare office about the eligibility requirements that apply where you live.

Second, this book describes civil rights and civil liberties that all Americans, including the poor, possess under law and explains how the poor can use these rights to participate more fully in political life and in community activities. In the 1994 national election, barely one-fifth of the population with incomes of less than $5,000 voted, in contrast to over 60 percent of those with incomes of more than $50,000.[14] Voting alone may not enhance the political power of the poor. But voting combined with nonelectoral strategies—mobilization, organization, and demonstration—has historically been an effective means of giving the poor a greater voice in public affairs. Essential to this constituency-building approach is the First Amendment right to protest and to association—civil liberties that are guaranteed by the Bill of Rights and immune from majoritarian abuse.[15] This book thus explains the constitutional rights that Americans have in public places: the right to speak out, to use parks and libraries, and to participate in a community's public life. In addition, the book describes how poor people can use the courts to help enforce the rights that the law guarantees. And, finally, this book discusses the right to vote and to run for office, in the hope that poor people will register to vote and will exercise their right to vote in elections at every level of government.[16]

More than a half century ago, President Franklin Delano Roosevelt spoke to the nation of the integral connection between liberty and material well-being. "We have come to a clearer realization," President Roosevelt said, "that true individual freedom cannot exist without economic security and independence." Seeking to establish "a new basis of security and prosperity . . . regardless of station or race or creed," FDR called for "a second Bill of Rights" that would guarantee:

the right to a useful and remunerative job . . . ;
the right to earn enough to provide adequate food and clothing and recreation;
the right . . . to a decent home;
the right to adequate medical care and the opportunity to achieve and enjoy good health;
the right to adequate protection from the economic fears of old age and sickness and accident and unemployment; and . . .
the right to a good education.[17]

Social policy in the United States has never approached this vision. As a nation, we remain at a great distance from the system of economic justice advocated by President Roosevelt fifty years ago. Yet the rights of the poor have increased during the intervening years, and largely because of the struggles of poor people themselves. As this book goes to press, these hard won gains have never been in greater jeopardy. For the rights of the poor to survive, we must remain vigilant in their defense.

NOTES

1. Sylvia A. Law, with a chapter by Burt Neuborne, *The Rights of the Poor* (1973).

2. *See* Staff of House Comm. on Ways and Means, 103d Cong., 2d Sess., *Overview of Entitlement Programs: 1994 Green Book, Background Material and Data on Programs Within the Jurisdiction of the Committee on Ways and Means* 1154, 1156 (Comm. Print 1994)(hereinafter, *1994 Green Book*).

3. *See* Margaret L. Usdansky & Patricia Edwards, *In 1993, Child Poverty Levels Hit 30-year High*, USA Today, Nov. 14, 1994, 2A.

4. *See* Steven A. Holmes, *Income Disparity Between Poorest and Richest Rises*, N.Y. Times, June 20, 1996, A1; Keith Bradsher, *Gap in Wealth in U.S. Called Widest in West*, N.Y. Times, Apr. 17, 1995, A1; *Inequality: For Richer, for Poorer*, The Economist, Nov. 5–11, 1994, at 19; Kevin Phillips, *The Politics of Rich and Poor* 8 (1990). Between 1973 and 1992, the income of the poorest 20 percent of the population declined, while the income of the richest 20 percent of the population rose. *See 1994 Green Book, supra* note 2, at 1189–1211.

5. *See* Arloc Sherman, *Wasting America's Future: The Children's Defense Fund Report on the Costs of Child Poverty* xvi (1994).

6. *See* Gary Burtless, *Public Spending on the Poor: Historical Trends and Economic Limits,* in Sheldon Danziger, Gary Sandifur & Daniel Weinberg eds., *Confronting Poverty: Prescriptions for Change* 80–83 (1994).

7. *See, e.g.,* Center on Social Welfare Policy and Law, *1991: The Poor Got Poorer as Welfare Programs Were Slashed* (Publ. No. 165, Feb. 1992).

8. AFDC refers to the Aid to Families with Dependent Children program, 42 U.S.C.A. § 601 *et seq.* (West 1996), described in chapter 1 of this book. The Personal Responsibility and Work Opportunity Reconciliation Act of 1996, Pub. L. No. 104-193, 110 Stat. 2105 (1996), repealed the AFDC program effective July 1997.

9. Based on AFDC expenditures of $20.7 billion in 1973 and $16.7 billion in 1989, in constant 1990 dollars. *See* Jason DeParle, *Fed by More Than Slump, Welfare Caseload Soars,* N.Y. Times, Jan. 10, 1992, A1, A16. By contrast, in 1990 alone, the federal government gave $39 billion in tax breaks to the richest 1 percent of Americans. *See* Sherman, *supra* note 5, at xxv.

10. *1994 Green Book, supra* note 2, at 325, 366–67.

11. *See, e.g., What to Do about Welfare?,* 6 Public Perspective: A Roper Center Review of Public Opinion and Polling (Feb./Mar. 1995); Steven Kull, *Fighting Poverty in America: A Study of American Public Attitudes* (Center for the Study of Policy Attitudes, 1994); Paul Toro & Manuel Manrique, *National Public Opinion Poll* (Wayne State Univ., 1994).

12. *See* David Savage, *Budget Ax Hangs Heavily over Legal Aid Services for the Poor,* L.A. Times, Feb. 15, 1995, A5 (quoting Alexander D. Forger, president of the Legal Services Corporation, that "[t]he War on Poverty has turned into a war against those in poverty"); Bob Herbert, *Scapegoat Time,* N.Y. Times, Nov. 14, 1994, A19.

13. *See* Alison Mitchell, *Two Clinton Aides Resign to Protest New Welfare Law,* N.Y. Times, Sept. 12, 1996, A1; Robert Pear, *Budget Agency Says Welfare Bill Would Cut Rolls by Millions,* N.Y. Times, July 16, 1996, A12.

14. *See* Bureau of the Census, Current Population Reports, Series 1–20, No. 466, *Voting and Registration in the Election of November 1992* 56 at Table 13 (U.S. Government Printing Office, 1993); Adam Clymer, *Poor Losers: Class Warfare? The Rich Win by Default,* N.Y. Times, Aug. 11, 1996, § 4, 1; *Low Income Voters Turnout Fell in 1994 Census Reports,* N.Y. Times, June 11, 1995, § 1, at 28; *see generally* Frances Fox Piven & Richard A. Cloward, *Why Americans Don't Vote* (1989).

15. *But see Clark v. Community for Creative Non-Violence,* 468 U.S. 288, 314 n.14 (1984)(Marshall, J., dissenting)("judicial administration of the First Amendment, in conjunction with a social order marked by large disparities in wealth . . . tends systematically to discriminate against efforts by the relatively disadvantaged to convey their political ideas").

16. *But see* Legal Services Corporation Act of 1974, 42 U.S.C.A. § 2996f(a)(6)(A)–(C) (West 1996)(prohibiting legal services attorneys from engaging in "political activity," "voter registration activity," or provision of "voters with transportation to the polls"); Pub. L. No. 104-134, 110 Stat. 1321 (1996)(prohibiting legal services attorneys from participating in class action litigation).

17. Franklin Delano Roosevelt, "January 11, 1944," *Fireside Chats* (1995).

THE RIGHTS OF THE POOR

1

Income Support

What is poverty?

In its most basic sense, poverty means not having enough money to meet subsistence needs, such as food, clothing, medicine, and housing. Poverty can also refer to a relative state of deprivation. A person is poor in this sense if she or he possesses substantially fewer goods and services, or has significantly reduced access to goods and services, than the average individual.[1] In the United States, poverty also has an official definition, meaning the federal government's income threshold for who is poor, taking into account family size, total income, and inflation.[2] As originally designed, the federal poverty index measured how much income a household needed to purchase the U.S. Department of Agriculture's least costly food plan (designed for temporary, emergency use) and multiplied that number by three.[3]

In its current form, the poverty index bears little relation to how much income a person actually needs for subsistence.[4] Some social scientists criticize the poverty index on the ground that it is too low and seriously understates the number of persons who are really poor.[5] Other commentators contend, however, that the index overstates rates of poverty because it excludes in-kind benefits (such as public housing or Medicaid) from its definition of income.[6] Whatever its limitations, the federal poverty index remains the benchmark for participation in many social programs and is widely used by policymakers and others in discussions about poverty. It is thus the definition of poverty typically used throughout this book.[7]

Who is poor in the United States?

In 1996, a family of four was officially poor if its income was less than $15,600.[8] Rates of poverty for all Americans reached a thirty-year high in 1993, when over 15 percent of the nation lived below the poverty line.[9] Women and members of racial and ethnic minorities are hardest hit by poverty,[10] and in 1995, 29.3 percent of African Americans and 30.3 percent of Latinos had household incomes below the poverty line.[11]

Can a person work and still be poor?

Yes. Working even a full-time job outside the home does not guarantee that a family or individual will be lifted out of poverty.[12] In 1993, more than half of the poor, or 22 million persons, lived in households in which at least one person worked.[13] That year, an individual who worked full-time, year-round at the minimum wage of $4.25 per hour had a gross income that was little more than half of the poverty line for a family of four.[14] Many individuals who receive welfare also work, although often only at part-time jobs for the minimum wage or less.[15] As a general matter, working people were more likely to have been poor in 1990 than they were a decade earlier, and this was especially true of female-headed households.[16] Low wages, racial and gender discrimination, and inadequate educational and job opportunities are some of the reasons that the working poor stay poor.[17]

Is poverty greater in the United States than in other industrialized countries?

Yes. Many studies indicate that an important reason for high poverty rates in the United States is the inadequacy of government antipoverty efforts. To take one example, AFDC grants to poor families in 1994 left participating households with income that was on average only 38 percent of the federal poverty line. And close to 40 percent of the children living in poverty in the United States received no assistance at all.[18] Indeed, the United States devotes a smaller percentage of its Gross Domestic Product to social spending than any other advanced industrialized nation. It is of course difficult to compare income distribution patterns across economic systems. But as numerous commentators contend, "[W]ith comparable patterns of economic growth, other nations reduced poverty to a far greater extent. The difference . . . is that other countries have more generous and effective social policies." A social scientist concludes, "America has high poverty rates not because it must, but because it chooses to."[19]

Is there a federal constitutional right to welfare?

No. The United States Supreme Court has held that the federal Constitution does not create a right to welfare.[20]

Almost thirty years ago, the Court recognized that "[w]elfare, by meeting the basic demands of subsistence, can help bring within the reach of the poor the same opportunities that are available to others to participate meaningfully in the life of the community."[21] And throughout the 1960s, courts considered whether poverty should be deemed a suspect classification for purposes of equal protection analysis and whether a right to welfare—also called a "right to live"—could be located in the Fourteenth Amendment to the federal Constitution.[22] At the time, many commentators believed that the Court would and should assume a special role in the protection of the poor.[23] By the early 1970s, however, the Court had rejected the view that the federal Constitution guarantees any right to minimal subsistence, declaring instead that "the intractable economic, social, and even philosophical problems presented by public welfare assistance programs are not the business of this Court."[24]

The Court has since consistently declined to find a general right to affirmative government services in the federal Constitution.[25] In this respect, the Court's poverty jurisprudence diverges significantly from that of international human rights law, which recognizes, at least as a matter of aspiration, a right to subsistence and its essential connection to individual freedom and political dignity.[26] Many legal scholars continue to believe that the federal Constitution should be read to establish a right to welfare as a foundational aspect of our democratic order.[27] As one respected scholar predicts, "[D]espite its difficulties a doctrine will ultimately emerge that recognizes . . . constitutional rights to decent levels of affirmative governmental protection in meeting the basic human needs of physical survival and security, health and housing, employment and education."[28]

Is there a state constitutional right to welfare?

It depends. Unlike the federal Constitution, some state constitutions contain explicit clauses recognizing the power and responsibility of state and local government to provide assistance to the poor.[29]

The New York Constitution, for example, imposes on the state an affirmative duty to provide for "[t]he aid, care and support of the needy."[30] The Mississippi Constitution creates a state duty to "provide homes or farms as asylums for those persons who, by reason of age, infirmity, or misfortune, may have claims upon the sympathy and aid of society."[31] And the Oklahoma Constitution authorizes "the Legislature and the people . . . to provide . . . for the relief and care of needy aged persons who are unable to provide for themselves, and other needy persons who, on account of immature age, physical infirmity, disability, or other cause, are unable to provide or care for themselves."[32] Whether a state court will interpret a state constitution to establish a right to welfare depends on the language of its poverty clause, the constitutional history, the purposes it is meant to serve, and the principles guiding the court in its decisionmaking.[33]

The rest of this chapter describes the major federal and state statutory programs that provide income support to the poor. For the last generation, the two most important federal subsistence programs have been Aid to Families with Dependent Children (AFDC) and Supplemental Security Income (SSI). In 1996, Congress repealed AFDC, effective July 1997, and replaced it with "block grants" that states can use to provide "temporary assistance for needy families." As this book goes to press, states are first beginning to design their new "block grant" programs.

This chapter explains a poor person's rights under the AFDC and SSI programs and also sets forth the federal law that governs establishment of the new block grant programs. The chapter also includes a section on General Assistance programs, which exist in about one-third of the states and are funded entirely by state and local governments without any federal contribution. Finally, the chapter provides information about the Earned Income Credit, which uses the federal tax system to provide income support to low-wage workers.

AID TO FAMILIES WITH DEPENDENT CHILDREN

What is Aid to Families with Dependent Children?

For the last sixty years, Aid to Families with Dependent Children (AFDC) has been the federal government's most important income support program for indigent families with dependent children, providing cash assistance as an entitlement to all eligible applicants.[34] The federal Department of Health and Human Services (HHS) creates many of the AFDC program's rules and regulations, but the program is administered at the local level by state and local agencies. The federal government funds 50 to 80 percent of the program's costs.

In August 1996, Congress and the President agreed to repeal the AFDC program and to replace it with block grant funding that states can use to establish new assistance programs for indigent families (the next section of this book discusses these new assistance programs). Under the 1996 law, Congress eliminated any federal entitlement to AFDC as of October 1996, and it is generally expected that the AFDC program will stop in July 1997. Nevertheless, even after the federal AFDC program ends, you may still have a right to AFDC benefits under state law or because of "waivers" that your state obtained from the federal government. If you currently receive AFDC, it is important to check with a local legal services attorney, a community organization, or with a welfare agency to find out how long the AFDC program will continue to operate where you live.

The President has called the AFDC program "fundamentally broken." But unless the nation substantially invests in improved education, job, and child care opportunities for the poor, AFDC's repeal will mark a major step backward in our nation's commitment to low-income Americans. The federal government first provided needy children with cash assistance during the Great Depression, when the Social Security Act of 1935 created the Aid to Dependent Children (ADC) program. In establishing the program, the federal government's goal was to allow poor children to live at home with their families instead of in orphanages and other public institutions. The program grew slowly. Originally, only children whose fathers were dead or absent from the household were eligible for aid, but later amendments to the Social Security Act extended assistance to children with a disabled or unemployed parent. By 1945, almost every state had established a state ADC agency. In 1962, parents or caretaker relatives of poor children became eligible for aid, and the name of the program was changed to Aid to Families with Dependent Children.[35]

Who receives AFDC?

At the program's peak in 1994, more than 14.36 million people, in 5.08 million families, received AFDC benefits.[36] That same year, one in seven children lived in a household that participated in the AFDC program.[37] But many families that were eligible for assistance received no benefits at all.

There are many common misperceptions about the families who do receive AFDC.[38] For instance, many people believe that these families are unusually large. In fact, in 1992, 72.7 percent of all AFDC families had only one or two children. Families receiving AFDC are also often perceived to be uneducated. Yet in 1992, more than half of the mothers receiving AFDC whose educational history was known had at least a high school diploma.[39]

Another misconception is that most AFDC recipients are members of racial or ethnic minorities. While minorities are disproportionately represented among AFDC families, 55.2 percent of the people who enter the

AFDC program are white.[40] Lastly, many people imagine that a very large percentage of the people who receive AFDC are dependent on these benefits for long periods of time. On the contrary, 48 percent of the people who enter the AFDC program receive benefits for under two years. Only 17 percent of AFDC recipients remain in the program for eight years or more.[41]

Can poor families get AFDC after 1997?

It depends on where you live. The Personal Responsibility and Work Opportunity Reconciliation Act of 1996, signed by President Bill Clinton on August 22, 1996, repealed AFDC as of July 1997 and eliminated any federal right to AFDC benefits as of October 1996.[42] Nonetheless, even after the federal AFDC program ends, you may still have a right to AFDC under state law or because of "waivers" that allow a state to continue the program for a period of time. If you currently receive AFDC, it is important to check with your local welfare agency, or with a legal services attorney, to find out whether AFDC will continue to be available to poor people where you live. The rest of this chapter describes the AFDC rules that are generally in effect until the program ends.

Who is eligible for AFDC?

To get AFDC, a family must be needy and (1) have at least one child; (2) have a caretaker relative living in the same house as the child; and (3) the child must be "deprived of parental support or care," which means that at least one parent does not support or care for the child because the parent is deceased, physically or mentally incapacitated, absent from the home, or an unemployed wage earner.[43]

Who is a child?

The AFDC program considers all people under age 18 to be children. In some states, an 18-year-old who is a full-time student at a high school or a vocational school and will graduate by age 19 is also considered to be a child. States have the option of giving aid to pregnant women if the fetus, were it a child, would be eligible for AFDC. Women in this situation can receive benefits starting in the sixth month of pregnancy.[44] A teenage parent may also qualify as a child.

Who is considered a "caretaker relative" of a needy child?

A caretaker relative is a relative who takes care of and lives with a needy child. The relative does not have to be the needy child's biological mother or father, and the child does not have to be in a traditional family to receive AFDC. The only requirement is that the caretaker be related to the child—by blood, marriage, or adoption—within a certain degree of kinship. The relative does not have to have legal custody or guardianship of the child.

If a parent is living with and caring for the child, then the parent is the caretaker relative. If not, other relatives may serve as caretakers, as long as they live with the child. An AFDC caretaker relative may thus be a parent, grandparent, sister, brother, stepparent, stepsister, stepbrother, uncle, aunt, first cousin, nephew, niece, persons of older generations as denoted by prefixes of grand-, great-, or great-great-, the spouse of any of the previously mentioned relatives even if the marriage has ended, or any other relation by blood, marriage, or adoption within the "fifth degree of kinship," such as first cousin once removed.[45]

A child is considered to be living with the caretaker relative even if the child is temporarily absent from the caretaker's home, as long as the caretaker retains responsibility for the child's care and control.[46] A child may also qualify as living with a caretaker relative even if the child and caretaker are homeless.[47]

Can a child have more than one designated caretaker?

Unless a child is needy because of parental incapacity or unemployment, only one relative can receive AFDC as a child's caretaker, even if there is more than one adult relative living in the home. When a child is needy because a parent is disabled or unemployed, both parents, whether or not married to each other, or a parent and stepparent can be considered caretakers and receive AFDC.[48]

When is a child deprived of the support or care of a parent?

A child is deprived of parental support or care if at least one parent is (1) deceased; (2) physically or mentally incapacitated; (3) absent from the home; or (4) an unemployed "principal earner."[49]

When is a parent too disabled to support a child?

A needy child is eligible for AFDC if at least one parent's ability to support or care for the child has been substantially reduced by a physical or mental defect, illness, or impairment that is expected to last for at least thirty days. A parent can be employed and still be considered incapacitated, as long as the parent's medical condition substantially reduces his or her ability to support the child.[50]

When is a parent absent from the home?

A parent is considered absent from the home when he or she is continuously out of the home for any reason except solely for military service.[51] Not living with the child is enough to constitute absence. However, an AFDC agency may decide that a parent who is not living at home, but who has frequent and substantial contact with the child, is not absent. A convicted prisoner permitted to live at home while serving a sentence may qualify as absent.

When is a parent an unemployed "principal earner"?

Needy two-parent families are eligible for AFDC if the parent who is the principal earner is unemployed and has a "work history." The principal earner is the parent who earned more money in the twenty-four-month period before the family applied for aid.[52] To be considered unemployed, the principal earner must (1) be working less than one hundred hours a month; and (2) have a work history.[53]

The principal earner has a "work history" if she or he was *eligible* for unemployment compensation benefits at any point during the twelve months before the family applied for AFDC. If this requirement is met, the parent has a work history even if she or he never actually *received* unemployment benefits. The parent also has a work history if she or he would have qualified for unemployment compensation but for the fact that her or his work was not covered under the unemployment compensation law.[54]

For all other principal-earner parents, the regulations for determining who has a work history are somewhat complicated. The AFDC program divides the year into four calendar quarters: January through March; April through June; July through September; and October through December. A principal earner who has worked in at least six calendar quarters during any thirteen calendar quarter period that ended less than a year before the family applied for AFDC has a work history. The six quarters of work do not have to be consecutive. Any quarter in which the principal-earner parent earned $50 or more, or got credit for a quarter of coverage under the Social Security program, or participated in a work program run by the AFDC agency counts as a quarter of work. In some states, participation under the Job Training Partnership Act (JTPA) or full-time attendance at an elementary or high school or in a vocational or technical course also counts as work,[55] but only four quarters of JTPA participation or school attendance can count toward the six-quarter work-history requirement.[56]

Can someone who is not a United States citizen receive AFDC?

Maybe. Before Congress passed the 1996 welfare act, federal law clearly stated that aliens lawfully admitted for permanent residence and aliens permanently residing in the United States under color of law were eligible for AFDC.[57] The 1996 welfare act bars noncitizens who are not "qualified aliens" (the term is defined below) from receiving public assistance that is provided "by an agency of the United States or by appropriated funds of the United States."[58] Since the AFDC program is administered by state agencies and funded with both state and federal money, it is unclear whether this new anti-immigrant eligibility restriction applies. If a state decides that the new restrictions do apply, it will provide AFDC only to those noncitizens who are "qualified aliens," defined by federal law as immigrants who

- are lawful permanent residents ("green card" holders);
- have obtained political asylum;[59]
- have been granted refugee status;[60]
- have been granted "withholding of deportation";[61]
- have been "paroled" into the United States for a period of at least one year;[62] or
- are "Cuban-Haitian conditional entrants."[63]

In addition, noncitizens who are or have been victims of domestic violence may qualify for benefits. Federal law provides that a noncitizen who has been "battered or subjected to extreme cruelty" in the United States by a spouse or parent, or by a member of the spouse or parent's family living in the same household, may qualify for benefits if (a) the individual has applied for or received lawful permanent resident status or suspension of deportation status based on the relationship with a spouse or parent who is a United States citizen or a lawful permanent resident; (b) the person responsible for the battering or cruelty no longer lives with the individual; and (c) the Attorney General determines that "there is a substantial connection between such battery or cruelty and the need for the benefits."

The parent of a battered or abused child may also qualify for benefits if the criteria above are met and the parent did not "actively participate in [the] battery or cruelty."

As this book goes to press, the Attorney General has yet to issue regulations describing how the government will decide whether battered or abused immigrants qualify for particular federal benefits.[64]

Finally, it is important to note that a needy child who is a United States citizen is entitled to AFDC benefits even if his or her caretaker relative is ineligible for benefits because of immigration status.[65]

Can a family that just moved to a state receive AFDC?

Yes. The United States Supreme Court ruled over twenty-five years ago in a case called *Shapiro v. Thompson* that it is unconstitutional to deny welfare benefits to needy families who are newcomers to a state.[66] In addition, current AFDC regulations prohibit states from imposing any length-of-residence requirement on eligible families.[67] Nevertheless, some states have recently attempted to pay reduced benefits to new residents, and these restrictions have been challenged in court under the *Shapiro* test.[68] Such practices violate the guarantee of equal protection of law. They should also be found to violate Article IV, section 2 of the federal Constitution, which provides that the "citizens of each state shall be entitled to all Privileges and Immunities of Citizens in the Several States," and Article I, section 8, which regulates "Commerce . . . among the several States," and has been repeatedly interpreted to prohibit states from inhibiting the interstate movement of persons, including the poor.[69]

Can migrant workers receive AFDC?

Yes. Migrant workers are considered residents of the state in which they currently live and are eligible for AFDC even if they are unemployed.[70]

Can homeless people who do not have an address receive AFDC?

Yes. Homeless families are eligible for and can receive AFDC in the state in which they currently live.[71]

Can workers who are on strike receive AFDC?

It depends. An individual is ineligible for AFDC in any month in which he or she is participating in a strike on the last day of the month. If a caretaker relative who is a parent participates in a strike, his or her children are also ineligible for AFDC.[72]

AFDC should be provided to a striking worker unless it is reasonable to expect that he or she will still be striking on the last day of the month.[73] If a participant receives AFDC while on strike and is still on strike at the end of the month, the aid provided is considered an "overpayment." If aid is denied and the participant is not striking on the last day of the month, he or she is entitled to compensation for an "underpayment."

What is an "essential person" under the AFDC program?

An essential person is someone who is (1) living in the home of a person receiving AFDC; (2) not personally eligible for assistance; and (3) essential for the AFDC recipient's well-being.[74] For instance, in some states, if a working mother with young children has a sister or a friend living in the house to help care for the children, the family may be able to get money under the AFDC program to provide for the sister or friend as an "essential person."

The AFDC agency considers the income and resources of an essential person when determining if a family is eligible for aid and how much aid the family should receive.[75] In addition, if an essential person receives a large sum of money, the AFDC agency may count this sum as income to the family and deny the family aid for a number of months.[76] An AFDC agency cannot name someone as an essential person unless the AFDC family agrees.[77]

Can states add their own requirements for getting AFDC?

Sometimes. Federal law gives states some flexibility in setting eligibility requirements for AFDC. However, federal law also prohibits states from excluding certain families from their AFDC programs or from imposing certain eligibility restrictions and requirements.[78] For instance, states may not deny AFDC to a family simply because the caretaker relative is an unmarried mother with a boyfriend who sometimes visits overnight at her home.[79] Nor, as discussed above, may a state require that a family live in the state for a certain period of time in order to receive benefits.

What is an "assistance unit"?

An AFDC assistance unit is the group of household members who are part of an application for AFDC. An assistance unit typically includes a caretaker relative and one or more dependent children. In general, all parents and siblings living with a child applying for AFDC *must* be included in the AFDC assistance unit—which means that their income, resources, and needs *must* be considered in determining AFDC eligibility and grant amount.[80] Caretaker relatives other than parents generally may choose whether to be included in the assistance unit. The advantage of inclusion is that the caretaker's needs are considered in determining the maximum grant level available to the unit, and the caretaker is automatically entitled to Medicaid. The potential disadvantage is that the caretaker's income and resources are considered in setting the grant level and may result in a lower benefit. Before deciding who should be in a family's assistance unit for AFDC, the applicant can ask to have his or her benefit level calculated with and without the caretaker in the assistance unit.

How much income can a family have and still be eligible for AFDC?

To be financially eligible for AFDC, a family must meet two income requirements: (1) the family's "countable income" must be less than its monthly "payment standard"; and (2) the family's "gross income" cannot exceed 185 percent of its monthly "need standard."[81]

What is income?

AFDC agencies consider any cash that a family receives to be income, whether or not this money is earned. However, cash that does not represent a gain for the family is not considered income.[82] For example, if a family receives cash from the sale of property, the proceeds do not count as income.

Some states also count as income goods and services the family receives. The dollar value assigned to goods and services cannot exceed the amount that the state's need or payment standard includes for those items.[83] For example, if a family of four is given a year's worth of clothing from a church, and the state's standard of need includes $200 per year for clothing for a family of that size, the state can count the clothes as income, but only up to $200 of income.

What is countable income?

Countable income is all income received by a family for a given month, less any income that is disregarded or exempted by law, and (1) is actually available to meet the basic needs of family members in the AFDC assistance unit or (2) legally belongs to a member of the assistance unit and that person has the legal ability to make the income available to meet the family's basic needs.[84]

What is gross income?

Gross income is a family's countable income plus (1) any child support payments that were not included in the family's countable income and

(2) any earnings that were not included in the family's countable income, *except* the Earned Income Credit and a dependent child's earned income under the Job Training Partnership Act in those states that exclude JTPA income from countable income. In addition, some states exclude from gross income the earnings of a dependent child who is a full-time student for up to six months of every year.[85]

What types of income are not countable income?

The following types of income are either disregarded or exempted and therefore not included in a family's countable income:

    1. Income of dependent children if the children are students and do not work full time;[86]

    2. In some states, earned or unearned income under the Job Training Partnership Act that a dependent child receives;[87]

    3. In some states, the earnings of dependent children who are full-time students if the state also does not count these earnings when calculating gross income;[88]

    4. Up to $200 worth of unpaid child care for children under age two;

    5. Up to $175 worth of unpaid child care for children over age two;

    6. If the family has earned income and has not received AFDC in at least one of the preceding four months, two-thirds of all money earned after the first $30;[89] otherwise, the first $90 of earnings received, then $30 plus one-third of earnings during the next four months, and $30 during the next eight months;[90]

    7. An Earned Income Credit and other tax refunds;[91]

    8. The first $50 of a monthly child support payment;[92]

    9. Loans and grants;[93]

    10. Fruits and vegetables grown at home;

    11. Some AFDC payments to dependent children;

    12. In some states, small one-time gifts worth no more than $30 per recipient per calendar-quarter;[94]

    13. In some states, aid from other agencies or organizations;

    14. In some states, money used to support people who do not receive aid from AFDC;[95]

    15. The value of U.S. Department of Agriculture donated foods;

16. Benefits received from child nutrition programs (such as WIC) or nutrition programs for the elderly (such as meals on wheels);

17. Payments to VISTA workers;

18. Certain payments to members of Indian tribes;

19. Payments for supportive services such as child care or reimbursement of out-of-pocket expenses made to volunteers serving as foster grandparents, senior health aides, or senior companions; and

20. Payments made under the Agent Orange litigation settlement.[96]

Is the income of people who are not part of an AFDC assistance unit ever considered in determining a family's AFDC eligibility and benefit level?

Yes. The government assumes that certain people will help support families applying for AFDC, estimates how much support can be expected, and considers that amount to be part of the family's countable income. This is known as "deeming of income," because income of a person who is not a part of the AFDC assistance unit is "deemed" to be available for the support and maintenance of the household. The people whose income is always subject to deeming are (1) parents of a dependent child who live in the home but are ineligible for AFDC;[97] (2) grandparents of a dependent child who live in the home, if the child's parent is under age 18 and is the child's caretaker;[98] (3) a dependent child's stepparent who lives at home, but is not personally applying for aid;[99] (4) the sponsor of an immigrant-applicant or recipient who entered the United States within the past three years;[100] and (5) an AFDC "essential person."[101] The income of the spouse of a caretaker relative who lives in the AFDC household may be deemed available if the caretaker relative decides to be a part of the assistance unit.[102] The only exception to the deeming rules is that the income of a Supplemental Security Insurance recipient who falls into one of the above categories is never considered.[103]

What is a state's need standard?

The need standard is the amount of money that a state says a family requires each month to meet basic needs such as food, clothing, shelter, fuel and utilities, personal care items, and essential household supplies. Each state AFDC agency sets its own need standard for families of different sizes and may take into account a variety of factors, such as differences in housing costs. A family is not eligible for AFDC if its gross income exceeds 185 percent of the appropriate standard of need.[104]

Unfortunately, federal law does not require states to set realistic need standards that actually afford recipients enough money for subsistence or even to meet the federal poverty level.[105] Indeed, in January 1994, the AFDC benefit payable to a family of three with no countable income was less than the poverty level in all states and less than two-thirds the poverty level in all but three states. Even including food stamps, benefits for a family of three were below 75 percent of the poverty level in thirty-eight states and below the poverty level in all states but Alaska and Hawaii.[106]

What is the payment standard?

The AFDC payment standard is the percentage of a state's need standard that the state actually pays to an eligible household of a certain size. Most states do not pay AFDC benefits at 100 percent of the need standard. As of January 1994, the payment standard in only eleven states was equal to a state's need standard for a family with no countable income. These states are: Connecticut, Delaware, Kansas, Massachusetts, Minnesota, Nebraska, New Mexico, New York, North Dakota, Oregon, and Rhode Island. Even in these states, however, the maximum benefit that was payable did not necessarily meet the need standard.[107] And in the remaining states, AFDC benefits are only a fraction of what the state itself claims an indigent family needs for subsistence.

Here is an example of how the payment standard works in those states that do not pay benefits at 100 percent of a family's need standard:

Hypothetical need standard for family of four with no income	$400
Hypothetical payment standard of 80 percent of need	$320
Hypothetical benefit to family	$320

In addition, states are allowed to cap their AFDC payments at a "payment maximum."[108] For example, in a state that has a need standard of $320 for a family of four, the need standard for a family of six might be $450. If the state has capped its benefits at a payment maximum of $400, then the larger family will receive benefits of no more than $400 a month.

TABLE 1-1

**1995 AFDC State Need and Maximum Benefits for a One-Parent,
Two-Child Family with No Countable Income**

State	100% of Need Standard	Maximum Benefits
Alabama	$ 673	$164
Alaska	1,022	923
Arizona	964	347
Arkansas	705	204
California	715	607
Colorado	421	356
Connecticut	872	680
Delaware	338	338
District of Columbia	712	420
Florida	991	303
Georgia	424	280
Hawaii	1,140	712
Idaho	991	317
Illinois	936	377
Indiana	320	288
Iowa	849	426
Kansas	429	429
Kentucky	526	228
Louisiana	658	190
Maine	553	418
Maryland	517	373
Massachusetts	579	579
Michigan		
(Washtenaw County)	587	489
(Wayne County)	551	459
Minnesota	532	532
Mississippi	368	120
Missouri	846	292
Montana	530	416
Nebraska	364	364
Nevada	699	348
New Hampshire	1,674	550
New Jersey	985	424
New Mexico	381	381

TABLE 1-1 continued on next page

TABLE 1-1 *continued*

State	100% of Need Standard	Maximum Benefits
New York		
(Suffolk County)	$ 703	$703
(New York City)	577	577
North Carolina	544	272
North Dakota	431	431
Ohio	901	341
Oklahoma	645	324
Oregon	460	460
Pennsylvania	614	421
Rhode Island	554	554
South Carolina	440	200
South Dakota	507	430
Tennessee	500	185
Texas	751	188
Utah	568	426
Vermont	1,148	650
Virginia	393	354
Washington	1,176	546
West Virginia	991	253
Wisconsin	647	517
Wyoming	674	360

Source: Congressional Research Service, *AFDC Program Parameters by State, 1988–1995*
(Washington, D.C., June 13, 1995).

Table 1-1 sets forth the AFDC need standard and maximum benefit that is payable in each of the fifty states and the District of Columbia as of 1995.

What is the smallest AFDC grant a family will receive in a month?

A family will receive aid if it is eligible for an AFDC grant of at least $10 or more in a given month.[109]

Do need and payment standards ever change?

Sometimes. Under federal law, every state has to reevaluate its need and payment standards at least every three years.[110] However, these reevaluations do not necessarily lead to increases in the standards.

Do families with special needs have higher need and payment standards?

Sometimes. States may give extra aid to families that have a "special need," namely, a need that the state recognizes as basic, but that only some families have. Special needs include pregnancy, special dietary requirements, training or educational expenses, and expenses caused by catastrophe or eviction.[111]

What are "child only" standards?

In some families, the dependent children qualify for AFDC, but the caretaker relative either has not applied or is not eligible for aid. States with a "child only" standard give these children less money than an AFDC family of the same size in which an adult also receives AFDC.[112] In other words, under a "child only" standard, an assistance unit of three dependent children with a caretaker who does not receive AFDC receives a smaller AFDC payment than an assistance unit of two children and a caretaker relative who does receive AFDC.

What are "prorated" standards?

States that use prorated standards set AFDC payments for smaller families by looking at the payment a larger family gets and giving the smaller family a proportionately smaller grant. For instance, if a five-person AFDC family receives $500 a month, or $100 per person, then a state with prorated standards might give a three-person family three times $100, or $300 a month. Prorated standards can hurt smaller families because some of their costs may be as high as those for larger families. For example, both the five-person and three-person family might have to pay about the same amount of rent. The federal government allows states to have prorated standards only in limited circumstances.[113]

Can a family own any assets and still receive AFDC?

Yes, but subject to strict limits. To be eligible for AFDC for a given month, a family can own no more than $1,000 worth of certain resources, called "countable resources," on the first day of that month. States can set a lower resource limit than this, but all states currently use the $1,000 cap. The resources requirement affects only eligibility and does not affect the amount of aid a family receives.[114]

What is a "resource"?

Under the AFDC program, a resource is any property that a family owns, including savings.

What is a "countable resource"?

A countable resource is property that is (1) owned by members of the assistance unit, and, in some cases, by other persons legally responsible for members of the assistance unit; (2) available for the AFDC family's use;[115] and (3) not exempted or disregarded under law.

What types of resources do not count?

The following are exempted or disregarded resources and generally do not count towards the $1,000 resource limit:

1. A home that is the family's usual residence, regardless of its value;

2. Other real property that a family is making a good-faith effort to sell (this attempt to sell may continue in most states for no longer than six months, and in some states, nine);

3. A burial plot;

4. The value of a funeral agreement up to $1,500 per person or a lower limit set by the state;

5. An Earned Income Credit (but only in the month of receipt and the month after);

6. Loans and grants;

7. In some states, items essential to daily living and of limited financial value, such as clothing or furniture;

8. A car with an equity value (actual value minus the amount owed on the car), up to a limit that differs state by state but which currently cannot exceed $1,500;[116]

9. Payments or assistance provided under certain federal programs, including, but not limited to: (a) supplemental food assistance; (b) U.S. Department of Agriculture donated foods; (c) payments made to volunteer foster grandparents, senior health aides, senior companions, or VISTA volunteers; (d) Low Income Home Energy Assistance; and (e) disaster assistance;[117]

10. Certain cash payments and stock distributed to members of Indian tribes;[118] and

11. Payments made under the Agent Orange litigation settlement or the Radiation Exposure Compensation Act.[119]

If the value of a resource exceeds the exemption limit set by the AFDC agency, the excess value is counted toward the $1,000 countable resource limit. For example, if a car has an equity value of $2,200, it exceeds the exemption limit of $1,500 by $700. Seven hundred dollars are thus included as countable resources.

Whose resources count in determining eligibility?

The resources of all persons in the AFDC assistance unit are considered in determining AFDC eligibility. As noted earlier, the general rule is that all household members who are parents or siblings of a child applying for AFDC *must* be included in the assistance unit.[120] At the caretaker's option, the following people may also be counted: (1) caretaker relatives who are not parents and (2) children who live in the same house but are not full or half brothers or sisters.

In addition, an essential person's resources, while not directly counted, are considered through the "deeming" process already described.[121] Also considered through the deeming process are the resources of an alien's sponsor during the alien's first three years of lawful residence. But the resources of a Supplemental Security Income recipient are never deemed available to an AFDC applicant or recipient.[122]

What happens if a family receives a "lump sum payment," such as an inheritance, a lottery prize, or a personal injury award?

If a member of an AFDC assistance unit receives a lump sum payment in a month in which the family is applying for or receiving AFDC and the lump sum is "countable income" then the family may be disqualified from receiving AFDC for a period of time. How long a period can be determined by dividing the lump sum, plus any other countable income received in the month, by the family's need standard.[123] Here is an example of how the lump sum income rule works: If a family receives an inheritance of $900 and its need standard is $300 per month, the lump sum will disqualify the family from receiving AFDC for three months ($900 divided by $300 equals three). States can resume a family's AFDC benefits before the disqualification period ends if (1) something happens that changes the family's need standard and thus the amount of aid for which the family is eligible; (2) the family cannot use the lump sum payment because of circumstances beyond its control; or (3) the family incurs, becomes responsible for, and pays medical expenses that offset the lump sum payment in a month in which the AFDC agency is denying it aid.

Even if a family is denied AFDC for a period of time because of the lump sum income rule, it may still be eligible for food stamps or Medicaid. There is no lump sum rule for these programs, and a family can receive assistance as long as its resources do not exceed program limits and the family meets all other requirements.

Is there any way to avoid application of the lump sum income rule?

Yes. A person who expects to receive money in a lump sum payment can avoid application of the lump sum income rule by withdrawing from the AFDC program before the month in which he or she will receive the payment. Some people, usually caretakers, can withdraw from AFDC individually. Others, usually children, have to withdraw with their entire families. A person or family that withdraws from AFDC because of a lump sum payment can reapply for AFDC in a later month as long as it is not the month in which the lump sum was received. (If the family still has some of the proceeds of the lump sum payment when it reapplies for AFDC, those moneys will count as a resource. A family in this situation should consider spending that portion of the lump sum exceeding the $1,000 resource limit to repay debts, to pay down a mortgage (the value of the family's home does not count as a resource) or to purchase some other exempt resource.) Avoiding application of the lump sum rule can result in more total aid for a family.[124]

How does a family apply for AFDC?

In order to apply for AFDC, a family must (1) complete an application form; (2) be interviewed; (3) provide evidence of the family's financial situation; and (4) in some cases, let an AFDC interviewer come to the family's home. The AFDC agency is supposed to accommodate the special needs of sick or disabled people who would like to apply for AFDC.

The application will ask for the Social Security numbers of all members of the assistance unit. If someone in the assistance unit does not have a Social Security number, he or she will have to apply for one at a Social Security Administration office (the AFDC agency can help the family do this). As long as the caretaker relative cooperates in applying for Social Security numbers for herself and for all dependent children, the agency cannot deny, delay, or discontinue benefits for lack of a number.[125]

When do AFDC benefits begin?

Federal law requires state AFDC agencies to make a decision on an AFDC application, and—if the decision is favorable—to mail the first AFDC payment within forty-five days of the date of the application.[126] Some states have set even shorter deadlines for processing AFDC applications.

States may pay AFDC benefits back to the date of the family's application. At the least, states must pay benefits back to the date it approved an AFDC application or to thirty days after the date the family applied, whichever is earlier.[127]

If a family needs immediate assistance, can it get aid before the application process is completed?

In some emergency situations, states can provide immediate aid, even before the application process is complete. Emergencies include natural disasters such as floods, fires, and storms; evictions; potential evictions; foreclosures; homelessness; utility shut-off or loss of heating fuel or equipment; violent crimes; child or spousal abuse; loss of employment or strike; health hazards; emergency medical needs; illness; accident; or injury.[128] If a family faces one of these emergencies and needs immediate assistance, it should tell the AFDC worker who takes the application about its special circumstances.

What other benefits do AFDC families receive?

Families receiving AFDC are automatically eligible for Medicaid. Most AFDC families are also eligible for food stamps. Food stamp benefits are not counted in determining AFDC eligibility, but the Food Stamp program considers AFDC payments to be countable income.[129]

Once a family starts to receive AFDC, how often will its eligibility be redetermined?

A family's ongoing eligibility for assistance must be redetermined by the state at least every six months. And every twelve months, someone from the state AFDC agency will meet with the caretaker in person. These interviews are officially called "eligibility redetermination interviews."[130] A state may have additional reporting or interview requirements to determine a family's on-going eligibility, and families should check with their caseworkers to learn about their obligations.

Is the AFDC benefit check paid directly to the family's caretaker relative?

It depends. Usually benefits are paid directly to a family's caretaker relative with no restrictions on their use. However, some or all of a family's benefit can go directly to vendors or can be issued as a two-party check if the caretaker prefers this arrangement or if the AFDC agency believes that the caretaker cannot manage the benefits in the children's best interests. Vendors are people such as landlords, mortgage companies, or utility companies that provide goods and services to the AFDC family. Two-party checks are made out to both the caretaker and a vendor and require the signature of both to be cashed.[131]

Benefits can also be paid to a "protective payee," a responsible adult who spends the grant on behalf of the needy family. This may happen when the caretaker is ineligible for aid because he or she has violated program requirements relating to work, provision of Social Security numbers, cooperation in collecting child support, striking, or fraud, or where the caretaker cannot manage the benefits on his or her own.[132]

Is the information that a family provides to the AFDC agency kept confidential?

Only the AFDC agency and other federal or federally assisted programs can have information about AFDC recipients.[133] However, states can disclose the current address of an AFDC recipient to a law enforcement agency that knows the person's correct Social Security number and demonstrates that the person is a fugitive felon.[134]

What information does the AFDC program receive from other government agencies about a family?

An AFDC agency can get information about a family from a number of government sources. In particular, it can get wage and other information furnished by employers, as well as income tax return information with respect to unearned income from the Internal Revenue Service. In most states, an AFDC agency can also get quarterly wage information from the unemployment compensation program.[135]

What are work programs?

All states are required to establish work programs for AFDC recipients, called Job Opportunities and Basic Skills (JOBS) programs.[136] JOBS programs include high school education, basic and remedial education, English as a second language instruction, job skill training, job readiness activities, and job development and job placement activities.

Are AFDC recipients required to participate in a JOBS program?

If state resources are available, AFDC recipients must participate in a work program unless federal rules exempt them. Recipients who are exempt from the work program requirement do not have to join, but can participate if they choose. The following people are exempt:

1. Children below age 16;

2. Children age 16 or 17 who are full-time students, but not in college;

3. Children age 18 who are full-time, noncollege students if the state considers 18-year-olds who are expected to complete their schooling before age 19 to be dependent children;[137]

4. People too ill or incapacitated to participate;

5. People over age 59;

6. People needed at home to care for an incapacitated or ill household member;

7. People too far from the work program site;

8. Women more than three months pregnant;

9. Full-time VISTA volunteers;

10. Some people already working over thirty hours a week;[138]

11. A caretaker relative who is personally caring for a child below age three (or younger in some states);

12. A caretaker relative who is personally caring for a child under age six, unless the state guarantees child care (caretakers personally caring for a child under age six cannot be required to participate in a work program for more than twenty hours a week).[139]

Generally, only one parent in a family receiving AFDC because of unemployment is eligible for the child care exemption, and in some states, no parent is eligible. Moreover, if a caretaker is going to school, the AFDC agency may decide that she or he is not personally caring for the child.[140]

Caretaker parents under age 20 who have not graduated from high school may have to be full-time students in high school or a high school equivalency program to be exempt.[141]

Can AFDC recipients choose which work program to join?

Recipients will not always be able to choose a program and may have to accept any job that is offered. However, before anyone is assigned to a work program or told to apply for a particular job, the state AFDC agency must assess his or her job skills and employment prospects and develop an individual "employability plan."[142] While this assessment is taking place, the AFDC recipient can be required to spend up to three weeks looking for a job.

Special rules apply to caretakers who are under age 20 and have not yet completed high school. Generally, such individuals can be required to participate only in an educational program unless an educational assessment determines that education is inappropriate for them. A caretaker who is age 20 or older and has not completed high school can be required to participate in a noneducational placement only if she or he demonstrates basic literacy or the agency determines that the most appropriate job is one that does not require a high school education.[143]

Do JOBS participants receive any special services?

Yes. State AFDC agencies must provide JOBS participants with supportive services to enable them to participate in or apply for work programs and approved educational or training programs.[144] Services include child care and transportation.[145] Services must also be provided to recipients who are exempt from the JOBS program, but who choose to participate. In addition, AFDC agencies must provide child care to AFDC recipients who could not accept or keep a job without this help. Recipients can choose which type of child care they want if more than one arrangement is available and can refuse (or accept) an informal child care arrangement, such as child care by a relative or neighbor.

What if an AFDC recipient refuses to participate in a work program or violates the program rules?

AFDC recipients who are required to participate in a work program and refuse or fail to follow work program rules without "good cause" may be "sanctioned" and denied aid. The first time a recipient violates the work program requirement, the sanction will last until the requirement is met. The second time, the sanction will last until the requirement is met or three months, whichever is longer. The third time, the sanction will continue until the requirement is met or six months, whichever is longer.[146]

Special rules apply to two-parent households in which the unemployed principal earner is sanctioned. In that case, the other parent, who is also living with the child, must participate in a work program or also be sanctioned.[147] Despite the sanction, the children in the assistance unit will continue to receive aid.

What is "good cause" for not fulfilling the work program requirement?

"Good cause" for not fulfilling the requirement includes (1) a failure by the AFDC agency to provide necessary supportive services, such as child care; (2) a failure by the AFDC agency to assign the recipient to an appropriate work program; (3) a work program assignment that violates the AFDC program's rules; and (4) circumstances beyond the recipient's control that prevented participation.

In addition, a recipient should not be sanctioned if his or her failure to meet the work program requirement was not deliberate.[148] For instance, if a recipient was not told of an appointment with a work program officer, she should not be sanctioned for not keeping the appointment.

What rights does a recipient facing a work program sanction have?

Anyone about to be sanctioned has the right to "conciliation" and, if that does not resolve the issue, the right to a "fair hearing" to challenge the agency's unfavorable decision.[149] The conciliation procedure gives the recipient an opportunity—before any sanction is imposed—to explain any valid reason he or she had for not meeting the work program requirement. It also gives the recipient the chance to avoid sanctions by agreeing to begin fulfilling the requirement. "Fair hearing" rights are described later in this section.

What is the child support collection requirement?

To get AFDC, a caretaker must agree that all child support owed to the family (and spousal support if the caretaker also receives AFDC) will go directly to the AFDC agency. This means that the AFDC program receives all support payments due or paid while a family is receiving aid. However, as explained below, the agency must give the family the first fifty dollars of support payments received for any month.[150]

Where necessary, a caretaker relative must cooperate in establishing the child's paternity and in getting child support payments from the father, unless the caretaker has good cause for not cooperating.[151] Cooperation includes (1) providing information about the identity and location of the absent father; (2) appearing for interviews and court hearings; and (3) turning over to the AFDC program support payments received directly from the absent father.[152] A caretaker who fails to cooperate without good cause is ineligible for aid as long as the noncooperation persists.[153] A caretaker has good cause not to cooperate if she fears that doing so will subject her family to physical or emotional harm or if her child is the product of a rape or incest. The AFDC agency may decide that a caretaker has good cause not to cooperate during certain stages of the process (for example, the caretaker might be required to provide information about the identity of the father but not have to appear at interviews).[154] Even if the AFDC agency finds good cause, the state may still try to obtain support payments if it believes that its efforts will not be harmful to the family.

Does a family get to keep any of the support payments that the AFDC agency collects?

Yes. A family getting AFDC keeps the first fifty dollars of any monthly support payment that the AFDC agency collects. The AFDC agency can use the rest of the money to reimburse itself for the aid it has given the family.[155] This fifty dollars does not affect the family's eligibility for AFDC or the size of the AFDC grant the family receives.

If the support payments collected are large, they may disqualify the family from AFDC (but the family would keep the support payments).[156] If a family leaves the AFDC program for this or any reason, it can choose to have the state continue to collect support payments on its behalf, rather than collect payments directly from the absent parent. Under these circumstances, the AFDC agency can keep any payments due before or while the family was receiving AFDC, up to the total amount of benefits paid,[157] but must promptly forward all other payments to the family.[158]

What is an overpayment?

An overpayment is an improperly large AFDC payment made to a family. Overpayments can happen if a family makes a mistake or the AFDC agency makes a mistake, if a family experiences changed circumstances, or if a family engages in fraud.

Except in fraud cases, the state has authority not to collect an overpayment if it is less than thirty-five dollars or if the cost of collection exceeds the amount of the overpayment.[159] The AFDC agency must otherwise try to recover overpayments, including those made because of agency mistakes, even if the person who received the overpayment is no longer getting AFDC.[160] The state can get the overpayment back by having the family that received the overpayment repay the money or by reducing the amount of monthly aid the family receives by up to ten percent or both.[161]

What is an underpayment?

An underpayment is an improperly small AFDC payment made to a family. Underpayments may be caused by some of the same factors that cause overpayments. An AFDC agency is required to correct all underpayments.[162] However, former recipients of AFDC who are no longer eligible for aid may have some difficulty collecting such payments.[163]

What happens if a member of a family receiving AFDC commits program fraud?

States have the option of disqualifying recipients from the AFDC program if a judicial or administrative hearing finds that the person (1) "intentionally" (2) "made a false or misleading statement or misrepresented, concealed, or withheld facts or committed any act intended to mislead, misrepresent, conceal, or withhold facts or propound a falsity" (3) "for the purpose of establishing or maintaining a family's eligibility . . . or of increasing (or preventing a reduction)" in the amount of aid.[164] Individuals found guilty of committing fraud will be disqualified for six months for the first violation, twelve months for the second, and life for the third.

How are families notified about decisions affecting their participation in the AFDC program?

AFDC agencies must provide a family with written notice of any decision it makes about the family's case.[165] The notice must describe the agency's decision, state the reasons and legal authority for the decision, and explain the family's right to appeal the decision. In addition, if the agency intends to reduce or terminate a family's benefits, it must mail a written notice at least ten days in advance of the date that the reduction or termination is scheduled to become effective.[166] As explained below, advance notice is required so that the family will have a chance to appeal the decision before any benefits are reduced or terminated.

What can a family do if the AFDC agency makes a harmful decision about its case?

If a family disagrees with a decision made by the AFDC agency, it may appeal the decision through a state agency hearing called a "fair hearing."[167] This right was established over twenty-five years ago in a case called *Goldberg v. Kelly*,[168] where the United States Supreme Court held that a welfare recipient has a constitutional right to a full and fair hearing before the government reduces or terminates his or her benefits. Families whose AFDC applications are denied also have a right to a fair hearing.

The notice of the AFDC agency's decision contains an explanation of these appeal rights and how to request a fair hearing, including the number of days the family has from the notice date to appeal.[169] Families should not be reluctant to ask for a hearing. *Most AFDC families win their hearings.* In 1983, AFDC families in New York City won three out of every four hearing decisions.[170] In some states, families can also request a fair hearing if workers at the AFDC agency harass or treat them poorly.

Can a family's benefits be reduced or terminated before the hearing?

In almost all cases, if an AFDC agency decides to reduce, suspend, or end benefits and the family appeals the decision within a set period of time, the family is entitled to have its benefits continue unchanged until the case is decided by a hearing judge.[171] However, if a family's benefits are continued at their original level and the family loses the fair hearing, then the AFDC agency may attempt to recover any benefits to which the family was not entitled.[172]

What rights does a family have at a fair hearing?

Families that request a fair hearing have a number of important rights. These include the right to examine the entire case record in advance of the hearing; the right to be shown, in advance of the hearing, all of the documents that the AFDC agency plans to use at the hearing; the right to be represented at the hearing by a lawyer or by another person, such as a friend or community advocate; the right to present evidence and witnesses; the right to make any arguments without undue interference; and the right to confront and cross-examine witnesses for the other side.[173] The state must decide a family's appeal based only on the evidence presented at the hearing. The hearing decision must be in writing and must be issued and implemented within ninety days of when the family requested the hearing.[174]

How should a family prepare for the fair hearing?

Before the hearing, the family should gather evidence to support its case. Evidence can be documents, such as a rent receipt, and it can be witnesses, such as a landlord who will testify about how many dependent children live in the household. If a witness cannot come to the fair hearing, the family can take a letter from that witness to the hearing explaining what the witness knows about the case. If requested, the hearing judge can order witnesses who do not want to testify to come to the hearing.

In addition, it is a good idea for the family to ask for its case record and to review it, along with any documents the agency plans to use, before the hearing actually takes place. The case record may contain evidence that helps the family's case. Examining these papers in advance will help the family or its representative prepare questions or arguments for the hearing and decide what other evidence to gather.

What happens at the fair hearing?

At the hearing, there will be at least three people: the caretaker relative, a representative of the AFDC agency, and the administrative law judge (ALJ) who will decide the issue. As discussed before, a family may also bring witnesses and someone to represent it. (Even if a family does not have a lawyer, it is often a good idea to bring along a friend for support.) The hearings are taped. It is important that everyone speak loudly and clearly and that no one start speaking until the tape recorder is on. This is because the tape of the hearing becomes very important if the family loses the hearing and wants to appeal.

The ALJ will open the hearing by naming all the people present and by explaining what the hearing is about. If the ALJ does not list all the reasons why the family requested the hearing, the caretaker relative or her representative should say so. Otherwise, the ALJ will not deal with those problems.

The representative from the AFDC agency will tell the agency's side of the story first. When the representative is finished, the caretaker relative or her representative can ask questions that the government is required to answer.

The family will then have a chance to present its side of the case. The caretaker should give the ALJ any documents the family would like to use as evidence and should tell the judge her story. The family may also present any witnesses it has at this point. When the caretaker and the caretaker's witnesses are done speaking, the AFDC representative may ask them questions.

Before the hearing closes, the ALJ must give the family an opportunity to explain why the agency's action was wrong and to make any other relevant statement or argument that has not already been made.

What happens if a family wins its hearing?

Within a few weeks of the fair hearing, the family will receive a written decision from the state. If the decision is in the family's favor, the AFDC agency must comply by issuing the benefits or services that were wrongfully withheld. Normally, a family will get back any money it lost if benefits were reduced or cut off in violation of the law. The decision should be implemented within ninety days of the date that the family first requested the hearing.[175]

What happens if a family loses its fair hearing?

If the fair hearing decision does not give the family all that it asked for, the family may want to appeal the decision in court. Families in this position should seek assistance from a legal aid or legal services office as soon as possible because in most states a lawsuit must be started within a relatively short period of time after receipt of the fair hearing decision.

What if a family wins its hearing, but the AFDC agency does not comply with the hearing judge's decision?

If the agency does not comply with the hearing judge's decision, the family should complain. Complaints may be made in person, by going to the welfare office, or by telephone, but it is good to keep a record of all conversations. If the agency still will not comply, the family should contact a legal aid or legal services office for help and advice on whether it should bring a lawsuit against the AFDC agency in court.

Does a family receive any benefits once it leaves the AFDC program?

Yes. States must provide transitional Medicaid benefits for twelve months to families that lose AFDC eligibility because of increased hours of

employment or increased income from employment. States also have to provide transitional child care for up to twelve months to families that are not
receiving AFDC if the adults in the family will not be able to work without
such help and the family will otherwise be at risk of becoming eligible for
AFDC.[176]

TEMPORARY ASSISTANCE FOR NEEDY FAMILIES BLOCK GRANT

**What is the Personal Responsibility and Work Opportunity
Reconciliation Act of 1996?**

On August 22, 1996, President Clinton "end[ed] welfare as we know
it"[177] by signing the Personal Responsibility and Work Opportunity Reconciliation Act of 1996, passed earlier that summer by a Republican-domi-
nated Congress.[178] The 1996 act "reformed" welfare by abolishing the Aid
to Families with Dependent Children program, thus ending the federal government's sixty-one-year-old guarantee of public assistance to the nation's
poorest children. The 1996 welfare act instead gives states fixed amounts of
federal money (called "block grants") to establish new programs of "temporary assistance for needy families." The act also cuts tens of billions of dollars from food stamps and federal disability assistance under the Supplemental Security Income program.[179]

A broad national consensus seemed to favor reform of the welfare system. But many commentators predict that the new act will inflict severe
hardship on large numbers of poor families with children.[180] The Urban Institute, a respected research organization, estimates that the abolition of the
AFDC program will quickly drive an additional 1.1 million children into
poverty and deepen the destitution of the millions who are already impoverished. By the year 2001, the new law will bar 3.5 million poor children
from any federal cash assistance; by 2005, 4.86 million poor children will
be excluded.[181]

What is the Temporary Assistance for Needy Families block grant?

The Temporary Assistance for Needy Families (TANF) block grant,
authorized by the Personal Responsibility and Work Opportunity Reconciliation Act of 1996, replaces the former Aid to Families with Dependent
Children program. Congress has stated that the goals of the TANF block
grant are (1) to provide temporary assistance to needy families with children
subject to tough work requirements and time-limited eligibility; (2) to dis-

courage poor women from having children out of wedlock and encourage the formation of marital families; and (3) to ensure that needy adults work so their families can become self sufficient. The act does not require states to provide cash benefits to the poor, and the new assistance programs that will be put in place can differ from city to city and state to state in terms of type of benefits, eligibility, application processes, and reporting requirements.[182]

Proponents of the act believe that it has the capacity to lift poor families out of the welfare system and into the labor market. But the act has many strong and well-informed critics. Senator Daniel Patrick Moynihan, for example, a long-time expert on welfare policy, has characterized the act's reliance on block grants in place of entitlements as a dangerous experiment that "mak[es] cruelty to children an instrument of social policy," with "absolutely no evidence" that its radical approach will work.[183]

Indeed, the 1996 welfare act rests on three untested and doubtful assumptions. The first is that states can address child poverty more effectively through capped federal block grants than through the AFDC program, even though the block grants could leave states with billions less in federal antipoverty dollars than AFDC provided, especially during periods of recession. The second assumption is that eliminating the AFDC program's guarantee of assistance will significantly reduce teen pregnancies and out-of-wedlock births to poor women—an assumption repeatedly shown to be false.[184] And the third assumption is that the parents of poor children will find jobs once they have been cut from welfare. But numerous studies, including government reports, have concluded that there are not nearly enough jobs for all the parents of needy children who currently receive AFDC.[185]

The 1996 welfare act does not mandate that states provide any specific kinds of assistance to the poor. The new law does, however, establish a framework for the block grant programs that states will set up to replace AFDC. The rest of this section describes the new act's major provisions and how they are expected to affect the new temporary assistance programs. If you are in need of cash assistance or other services, it is important to check with your local welfare agency, or with a legal services attorney, about the block grant program that operates where you live.

When do programs under the TANF block grant begin?

States that accept block grants under the 1996 welfare act must begin operating programs of temporary assistance for needy families no later than July 1, 1997.[186] These programs replace a state's AFDC, Emergency Assistance, and JOBS programs. Some states may decide to continue to run their AFDC programs after July 1, 1997, but they need special permission (called a "waiver") from the U.S. Department of Health and Human Services.[187]

States can elect to start their TANF programs sooner than July 1, 1997. Some states may want an earlier implementation date because it will work to increase the size of their federal block grant. In any event, the 1996 welfare act states that as of October 1, 1996, poor people no longer have any federal right to AFDC benefits.[188] An indigent family with children may, however, continue to have a right to AFDC under state law. If you are in need of cash assistance after that date, you should consult a legal services or legal aid attorney for information about the TANF program that operates where you live. You can also try to get information from the agency that implements your town's TANF program (in many areas, it may be the same agency that ran the AFDC program).

How do programs established under the Temporary Assistance to Needy Families block grant differ from the Aid to Families with Dependent Children program that Congress and the President abolished?

The TANF block grant differs from the AFDC program in a number of important ways—all of which are potentially harmful to the health and well being of poor families with children.[189]

The first difference is that AFDC was an entitlement program, which means that the government guaranteed public assistance to all eligible families that applied for benefits. By contrast, the TANF block grant is designed to deprive poor families of any "individual entitlement" to federally funded assistance and to relieve states of any federal obligation to provide cash assistance (though there may be constitutional defects to this approach).[190] In addition, federal law imposes strict durational limits on how long an eligible family can receive federally funded benefits, even if the head of the household cannot find work.[191]

The second major difference flows from the first. Under the AFDC program, the federal government guaranteed that public money would be available to provide benefits for all eligible families that applied for assistance.[192] Thus, during periods of recession or economic downturn, when poverty levels rose, AFDC costs increased (for example, AFDC costs increased $5 billion in a three-year period of economic trouble in the early 1990s). By contrast, under the TANF block grant, each state receives a fixed amount of federal funding, based on its past AFDC expenditures, to run a temporary assistance program.[193] Although there is a limited contingency fund, federal funding essentially does not increase to meet increased rates in poverty that result from rising unemployment or other structural factors.

Finally, under the AFDC program, states had financial incentives to spend state dollars for poor people's benefits. This is because the federal and state governments shared the cost of AFDC payments under a complex financial formula that gave the state up to four dollars of federal money every time it added one dollar of state money to the program. The TANF block grant, by contrast, does not include any of these financial incentives to encourage state contribution. Indeed, states can divert funds from the TANF block grant to other social purposes that do not necessarily assist the truly needy, thus further reducing the amount of funding available for poor families' benefits.[194]

How large is the TANF block grant?

The U.S. Department of Health and Human Services estimates that the total block grant for "temporary assistance for needy families" programs will be $16.4 billion for each year from 1996 to 2003. Each state will receive a fixed allotment, based on prior expenditures for the state's AFDC, Emergency Assistance, and JOBS programs. The state grant is equal to the greater of: (1) the average of federal payments for these three programs in 1992 through 1994; (2) federal payments in 1994; or (3) federal payments in 1995.

Will every state receive a TANF block grant?

A state will receive a TANF block grant only if it chooses to accept federal funding for authorized social purposes. The federal government does not require a state to accept this money.

Can a state's TANF block grant be increased?

Somewhat. A state may receive additional federal funds if it fulfills some of the major purposes of the block grant, such as reducing out-of-wedlock births or moving poor people into the job market. In particular, the federal government will provide up to five eligible states with "bonus" payments of $20 million ($25 million if fewer than five are eligible) for reducing out-of-wedlock births. Another source of special money is available if the state's population increases so that per capita spending on poor people would otherwise decrease. In this circumstance, a state may receive a supplemental grant of up to 2.5 percent of the state's block grant (subject to an across-the-board cap of $800 million for fiscal years 1998–2001). Finally, so-called high performing states, with high percentages of recipients who become "engaged in work," are eligible for "bonus" payments of up to 5 percent of their block grants (capped overall at one million dollars for fiscal years 1999–2003).[195]

Can a state's TANF block grant be reduced?

Yes. The state is subject to financial penalties if it fails to achieve some of the federal law's goals. These include ensuring that fixed percentages of the assistance caseload become "engaged in work," which in certain circumstances can include educational activities and community service. These penalties are discussed later in this section.[196]

What happens if a state's TANF block grant runs out and poor families still need assistance?

States may use state and local money to assist needy families. Federal law also creates a "contingency" fund of two billion dollars that can be paid to the states in special situations over the next five years.[197] The Center for Budget and Policy Priorities predicts, however, that the "contingency fund is almost certain to run out part way through the next recession." Finally, the act also allows the federal government to make loans, not exceeding $1.7 billion, to the states for assistance purposes.[198]

How will states go about designing their new "temporary assistance for needy families" programs?

If a state chooses to accept a TANF block grant, it must submit a plan to the U.S. Department of Health and Human Services outlining how it will design certain features of its temporary assistance program. Before submitting the plan to the federal government, the state is required to consult with local governments and "private sector organizations" and to allow at least a 45-day comment period.[199] A state's development of its TANF plan provides an important opportunity for the poor and their advocates to attempt to influence the terms and conditions of the state's new family assistance program.[200]

Among the features that the plan must address are:

- How the state plans to conduct an assistance program that serves all political subdivisions (but not necessarily in a uniform way), provides assistance to needy families with children, and enables such families to become self-sufficient through work;[201]

- How the state plans to require adult recipients to engage in work, once the state determines that they are ready for work or after they have received assistance for twenty-four months (the months do not have to be consecutive), whichever is earlier;[202]

- How the state plans to require parents receiving assistance to engage in work activities;[203]

- How the state plans to ensure that adult recipients perform community service once they have received assistance for two months or more (states may opt out of this provision);[204]

- How the state plans to prevent and reduce the number of out-of-wedlock pregnancies and to establish numerical goals for reducing nonmarital births in the period 1996 through 2005;[205] and

- How the state plans to conduct an educational and training program on statutory rape that will expand teen pregnancy programs to include men.[206]

In addition, and perhaps most importantly, the state's plan must set forth "objective," "fair," and "equitable" criteria for determining TANF eligibility, and must describe how families denied assistance may appeal from the government's adverse decision.[207]

Finally, the state must make a number of certifications to the federal government. These include, for example, that the state will continue to operate child support enforcement, foster care, and adoption assistance programs. The state must also certify which state agencies will administer and supervise its new assistance programs.[208]

Under the AFDC program, states were also required to submit a plan of operation to the federal government. Both the federal government and beneficiaries could go to court to enforce the plan if the state violated any of its terms. The 1996 welfare act, by contrast, purports to limit even the federal government's right to compel compliance with a state plan if, for example, the state fails to follow the requirements of "fair" and "objective" eligibility criteria.[209] The constitutionality of these provisions may be open to challenge.

Are states required to provide cash public assistance under their TANF block grants?

No. Unlike the AFDC program, which required participating states to provide cash public assistance, the TANF block grant contains no such mandate. While the federal government has imposed strict work requirements and time limits on aid, it does not require that states provide cash assistance to any child, individual, or family. States have discretion to use their grants for any activity that is reasonably designed to achieve the purposes of the block grant.[210] Federal law explicitly provides that the TANF block grant can be used to provide low-income households with assistance in meeting heating and cooling expenses, and in any other way that has previously been authorized under the state's AFDC program as of September 30, 1995. The act also allows states to use their TANF block grants to provide job placement vouchers or payments to state-approved public and private job placement agencies that give employment placement services to recipients of TANF-funded assistance.[211]

A state can use up to 30 percent of its TANF block grant to implement programs under the Child Care and Development block grant and the Title XX Social Services block grant. No more than one-third of the funds can be transferred to Title XX purposes and must be used for children and families whose income is less than 200 percent of the federal poverty line.[212]

In addition, a state can spend up to 15 percent of its block grant for administrative purposes. An additional portion of the TANF block grant can be used for information technology and computerization to establish monitoring or tracking systems called for by the TANF block grant.[213] Still more of the grant can be used to establish an electronic benefit transfer system.[214]

How large are cash benefits payable under a TANF block grant program?

Each state has discretion to decide whether to provide cash payments under its TANF block grant program and how large those cash payments will be. Moreover, the level of benefits does not have to be uniform throughout the state. Some commentators have predicted that states will engage in a "race to the bottom," cutting cash payments to extremely low levels in the expectation that poor people will leave the state.[215] Other commentators contend that states with more reasonable welfare payments will become "magnets" that attract poor people from low-benefit states (the empirical evidence, however, does not support this view).[216]

Can TANF benefits include medical services?

No. A state cannot use its TANF block grant to provide medical services to needy families with children. Medical services do not include prepregnancy family planning services.[217] For more information about how the Personal Responsibility and Work Opportunity Reconciliation Act of 1996 affects your ability to obtain free medical services, please see the chapter on health services in this book.

What is an "individual development account"?

A state may use a portion of its TANF block grant to fund "individual development accounts" for eligible individuals to allow them to save earned income for designated purposes. An account is essentially a trust that is created and funded by the United States, with matching funds from other sources. The account can be used only for qualified purposes that are defined by federal law:

- to pay for post-secondary educational expenses;
- to purchase a first home; or
- to capitalize a business.

An eligible individual will contribute earned income to his or her individual development account but may not withdraw funds except for qualified purposes. Funds in the account shall be disregarded for purposes of other benefit programs, so the eligible individual will not suffer a reduction in benefits.[218]

If a state's TANF block grant program provides for cash public assistance, are all needy families eligible for benefits?

No. Federal law bars certain categories of needy families with children from assistance. In addition, states have discretion to exclude other categories of families from its TANF assistance program. Some states may choose to exclude two-parent families from eligibility. Others may choose to exclude teen mothers. Still others may exclude families that become poor because an employed parent is on strike due to a labor-management dispute. In addition to deciding which kinds of families are "categorically" eligible for assistance under TANF programs, each state will have to establish how much income and resources a family can have and still be financially eligible for benefits under the TANF block grant. A state will have to define what counts as income in determining eligibility and whether any payments received by the family can be disregarded in assessing the household's basic needs. Some states may decide to count in-kind goods and services that a family receives in its definition of income. Other states may decide to "deem" the income of people who are not immediate relatives to be available to an applicant family in determining financial eligibility.

Federal law does not define many of these terms, leaving it to the states to fill in the details subject to a few procedural requirements (for example, the requirement that states must include in their plans "objective criteria" for the "determination of eligibility").[219] Although the 1996 welfare act gives states broad flexibility in designing their assistance programs, that discretion is limited by state and federal constitutional guarantees. For example, state programs that deny all assistance to entire categories of poor people, or that draw irrational distinctions among groups of poor people may violate the constitutional guarantees of due process and equal protection of law.

The state's broad discretion to define eligibility—and thus to prevent many poor families with children from receiving needed relief—contrasts with earlier federal AFDC requirements, which mandated relief to all poor families with children that met financial eligibility guidelines, as long as the child lived in the same house with his or her caretaker relative and was deprived of parental support. The AFDC statute and implementing regulations were also interpreted by the courts to prevent the states from imposing additional, arbitrary eligibility restrictions on poor families.

Can childless families receive benefits under the Temporary Assistance for Needy Children block grant?

No. Federal law prohibits states from using their TANF block grants to provide benefits to poor childless families, unless the family includes a pregnant woman.[220] Benefits are thus available only to families in which a poor minor child lives with a custodial parent or other adult caretaker relative. The act defines "child" to include an individual who is under age 18, or under age 19 if he or she is a full-time student in secondary school or in vocational or technical training.[221] An "adult" is an individual who is not a child.[222] The act does not define "caretaker relative."

Can a family receive benefits for a child who is temporarily living away from home?

It depends. Under federal law, a state may not use its TANF block grant to give a family benefits for a minor child who has been, or is expected to be, absent from the home for a period of forty-five consecutive days. A state has authority to reduce the period to not less than thirty consecutive days, or increase it to not more than 180 consecutive days, if it specifies this in its state plan. A parent will lose benefits if he or she fails to report a child's absence from the home within five days of "the date that it becomes clear to the parent (or relative) that the minor child will be absent for [the number of days that would disqualify him or her from receiving TANF at home]." States have discretion to establish good cause exceptions to this federal prohibition, but must include these exceptions in the state plan.[223]

Can poor immigrant families with children receive benefits under the Temporary Assistance for Needy Children block grant?

It depends. The 1996 welfare act contains many anti-immigrant provisions that exclude—or authorize states to exclude—large numbers of low-income immigrant families from TANF programs. Although President Clinton signed this law, he and other politicians have called for modification or repeal of the anti-immigrant provisions, so that by the time you read this book, the law may have changed. Also, the constitutionality of the anti-immigrant provisions is an open question and these provisions may be challenged in court.[224] As this book goes to print in October 1996, however, the law stands as follows.

In general, the 1996 welfare act gives each state discretion to decide whether and under what circumstances immigrants can receive TANF benefits.[225] The law does, however, impose several significant rules that states must follow.

No TANF benefits for undocumented or non-"qualified" immigrants. A state may not use federal TANF funds to provide assistance to any immigrant who is not a "qualified alien" as defined by the 1996 welfare act.[226] A "qualified alien" is an immigrant who

1. is a lawful permanent resident ("green card" holder);
2. has obtained political asylum;[227]
3. has been granted refugee status;[228]
4. has been granted "withholding of deportation";[229]

5. has been "paroled" into the United States for a period of at least one year;[230] or

6. is a "Cuban-Haitian conditional entrant."[231]

In addition, federal law gives the Attorney General discretion to include certain victims of domestic violence in the definition of "qualified aliens" who may receive TANF assistance. Specifically, a noncitizen who has been "battered or subjected to extreme cruelty" in the United States by a spouse or parent, or by a member of the spouse or parent's family living in the same household, may receive TANF benefits if

1. the individual has applied for or received lawful permanent resident status or suspension of deportation status based on the relationship with a spouse or parent who is a United States citizen or lawful permanent resident;

2. the person responsible for the battering or cruelty no longer lives with the individual; and

3. the Attorney General determines that "there is a substantial connection between such battery or cruelty and the need for the benefits."

The parent of a battered or abused child may also qualify for benefits if the criteria above are met and the parent did not "actively participate in [the] battery or cruelty."

As this book goes to press, the Attorney General has yet to issue regulations describing how the government will decide whether battered or abused immigrants qualify for particular federal benefits.[232]

Immigrants who are not "qualified aliens" may not receive assistance funded by a TANF block grant. States may, however, elect to use state funds to assist immigrant families who are not eligible for TANF benefits.

New immigrants disqualified for first five years in the U.S. Most immigrants who enter the United States after August 22, 1996, are barred from federally funded TANF benefits for a period of five years from the date they become a "qualified alien" (as defined above).[233] There are a few exceptions to this rule. The five-year bar does not apply to immigrants who are refugees or political asylees or have been granted "withholding of deportation." Nor does the five-year bar apply to active-duty members of the United States armed forces or honorably discharged veterans, or to their spouses or un-married dependent children.[234]

States must include specified immigrants in TANF program. A state may not exclude certain categories of immigrants from its TANF program. Immigrants in the following categories qualify for TANF benefits if otherwise eligible:

• Refugees, political asylees, and immigrants whose deportation has been withheld[235] qualify for TANF during their first five years in the United States.[236]

• Lawful permanent residents who have worked in the United States for the equivalent of forty qualifying quarters in the Social Security system or can be credited with forty quarters based on the work of a spouse or parents qualify for TANF.[237] Quarters of work creditable to an immigrant's parents while the immigrant was a minor and quarters creditable to the immigrant's spouse during their marriage count toward the forty required.[238] (Appendix C to this book sets forth a fuller explanation of the forty quarters rule.)

• Active-duty members of the U.S. armed forces and honorably discharged veterans, their spouses, or unmarried dependent children qualify for TANF if they are lawfully residing in the United States.[239]

"Deeming" of sponsor income and resources to the immigrant. The 1996 welfare act may be interpreted to require that all the income and resources of an immigrant's sponsor (and the sponsor's spouse) be added to the immigrant's own income and resources for purposes of determining TANF eligibility and grant amount.[240] "Deeming" of sponsor income in this manner would deny TANF benefits to many needy families, even when the immigrant family and the sponsor both have sub-poverty incomes; the addition of two incomes—even inadequate ones—will likely place the immigrant family above the TANF income limits.

This new "deeming" rule applies (if it applies at all to TANF) only to immigrants whose sponsors signed the special affidavit of support prescribed by the 1996 welfare act.[241] The law requires that the new affidavits be used starting sometime between October 1996 and February 1997.[242] If an immigrant is subject to the new deeming rule, sponsor income and resources will be deemed to the immigrant until he or she becomes a U.S. citizen unless one of the following exceptions applies.

First, sponsor income will not been deemed to an immigrant who can be credited with forty quarters of covered employment, as described above.

Second, sponsor income will not be deemed to an immigrant who is unable to afford food and shelter without TANF benefits. In such cases, the deeming rules are suspended for a period of twelve months. After the twelve months expire, however, all sponsor income will be deemed even if that disqualifies the immigrant's family from TANF and leaves it with no means of securing food or shelter.

Third, sponsor income will not be deemed for a period of twelve months if the immigrant or her child has been battered or subjected to "extreme cruelty" in the United States by a spouse or parent (or by a member of the spouse or parent's family residing in the same household) and the state decides that there is a "substantial connection" between the need for TANF assistance and the battering or cruelty. In addition, the batterer's income will never be deemed to the immigrant (even after twelve months) if the battering or cruelty has been recognized in an administrative or judicial order (e.g., an order of protection from family court) or in a determination by the Immigration and Naturalization Service (e.g., approval of a battered spouse waiver or self-petition), as long as the batterer is not living with the immigrant.[243]

Immigrants who currently receive AFDC will continue to receive aid until January 1, 1997, after which they will be evaluated for eligibility under the new law.[244]

Can teen parents receive benefits?

It depends. Federal law allows states to use their TANF block grants to provide assistance to teen parents, but if the parent is under 18 and unmarried, then certain restrictions apply. First, an unmarried parent under 18 years of age who does not have a high school diploma must attend high school or an equivalent training program unless his or her child is under 12 weeks old.[245] Second, the parent must live in an "adult supervised setting," which means either with a parent, guardian, or adult relative or in a "supportive living arrangement," such as a "maternity home" or "second chance home." (States must help teen parents locate an appropriate "adult supervised" living arrangement.)[246] The states have the option of exempting teen parents whose parents are dead and who lack an appropriate adult relative.

The states can also make exceptions for other teen parents in three situations:

1. The teen parent is being or has been subjected to serious physical or emotional harm, sexual abuse, or exploitation in the home of the parent or responsible adult.
2. Substantial evidence exists that the teen parent will be in imminent or serious harm because of acts or omissions if forced to live with a parent or responsible adult.
3. The state determines that it is in the best interest of the teen parent to have living arrangements other than with his or her parents.[247]

Can convicted criminals receive benefits?

It depends on the nature of the crime.

Drug related convictions. Under federal law, persons convicted of a drug-related felony after the enactment of the Personal Responsibility and Work Opportunity Reconciliation Act of 1996 are prohibited for life from receiving benefits, although the family is eligible to receive assistance reduced by the ineligible household member's pro rata share. Pregnant women and individuals participating in a drug treatment program are exempted. States have authority to opt out of this federal prohibition.[248]

Welfare fraud. A state may not use its TANF block grant to provide assistance to any person convicted of fraudulently misrepresenting his or her residence in order to obtain assistance in two or more states, unless the conviction is at least ten years old.[249]

Fugitive felons and parole and probation violators. A state may not use its TANF block grant to provide assistance to any fugitive felon or convicted criminal who is in violation of parole or probation terms.[250]

Can a needy family that has just moved to a state receive benefits?

The 1996 welfare act allows states the option of treating "families moving into the state from another state differently than other families" for the first twelve months of residence.[251] The state is required, however, to indicate in its plan of operation whether it intends to engage in differential treatment and what the treatment will entail. The state may choose, for example, to treat "interstate immigrants" under the program requirements of their prior state of residence. If a newcomer's home state provides a lower level of assistance, he or she may be limited to that amount for the first year.[252]

Discrimination against new residents, even when authorized by Congress, raises a number of disturbing constitutional problems. An outright denial of benefits, as well as certain two-tier systems of public assistance that effectively discriminate against newcomers, should be found to violate the equal protection guarantee of the Fourteenth Amendment to the United States Constitution. Indeed, almost thirty years ago, the Supreme Court ruled that the Fourteenth Amendment prohibits state discrimination against new state residents who apply for AFDC.[253] Such discrimination in state TANF programs would be equally unconstitutional under Article IV, section 2, of the federal Constitution, which protects the privileges and immunities of citizens,[254] and raises questions under the commerce clause, which has been repeatedly interpreted to prohibit states from burdening the interstate movement of poor persons.[255]

How long can an eligible family receive benefits?

The 1996 welfare act imposes strict time limits on TANF benefits. It bars states from using federal TANF funds to assist any family that includes an adult who has received TANF benefits for sixty months (the months do not have to be consecutive).[256] The federal bar applies even if the parent of needy children is unable to find an adequate job. This will likely cause widespread hardship, since numerous studies make clear that there are not nearly enough jobs to supply employment for all the families that will lose public assistance because of the new law's time limits.[257]

In determining whether the sixty-month limit has been reached, TANF assistance that an adult received while a minor child does not count unless the child was the head of household or married to the head of household. Receipt of AFDC benefits or other non-TANF benefits does not count toward the sixty-month limit. Nor does the sixty-month cap include any month in which no adult member of the family received assistance (for example, when a grandparent is caring for a grandchild and assistance is obtained only for the child). Moreover, TANF assistance received on an Indian reservation or Alaskan native village does not count toward the sixty-month cap if the reservation or village has at least one thousand residents and an unemployment rate of at least 50 percent.[258]

The sixty-month limit applies very broadly to any assistance that the family receives that is funded by the TANF block grant. This might include in-kind benefits such as child care, counseling, or vouchers. The cap is thus not limited to cash assistance. (However, as noted above, a family's prior receipt of AFDC benefits—or any non-block grant assistance—does not count toward the sixty-month cap.) Thus, receipt of cash benefits or other assistance that is solely state-funded, such as General Assistance payments, does not count toward the sixty-month limit.

It is important to recognize that the sixty-month cap is a federal mandate. States have authority to impose even shorter durational limits on recipients. States could thus choose to cap benefits at thirty-six months, or forty-eight. The U.S. Department of Health and Human Services estimates that if all states were to adopt a two-year, rather than a five-year, time limit, 5.5 million children would be denied needed assistance by 2006.[259]

Can states make exceptions to the sixty-month cap on benefits?

Yes, but these exceptions are subject to strict federal limits. A state may exempt up to 20 percent of its caseload from the sixty-month cap on TANF benefits. Exemptions may be given in cases of "hardship" and in cases where the family includes an individual who has been battered or subjected to extreme cruelty.[260] Federal law does not define "hardship." "Battery" and "extreme cruelty" are defined as follows:

    1. physical acts that resulted in, or threatened to result in, physical injury to the individual;

    2. sexual abuse;

    3. sexual activity involving a dependent child;

    4. being forced as the caretaker relative of a dependent child to engage in nonconsensual sexual acts or activities;

    5. threats of, or attempts at, physical or sexual abuse;

    6. mental abuse;

    7. neglect or deprivation of medical care.[261]

If a family does not meet one of these exceptions, can it receive any benefits after the sixty-month limit has been reached?

Yes, but not if the benefits are funded by the TANF block grant.[262] Federal law contains a specific "rule of interpretation" to make clear that states can use state funds to provide benefits to children or families that become ineligible for TANF block grant assistance because of the sixty-month limit.[263] Needy families can therefore receive assistance under any residual General Assistance program that the state operates. Assistance, including vouchers, may also be available under the Title XX Social Services block grant.

Are there mandatory work requirements in the TANF program?

Yes. Federal law generally requires states to ensure that recipients of TANF assistance are engaged in work or educational activities, and each state must describe in its plan of operation how it intends to implement the federal work requirement.[264] In meeting the work requirements, federal law prohibits the states from using TANF recipients to displace jobs that become vacant due to layoffs, involuntary reduction of workforce, or termination. The state must provide a grievance process to deal with displacement issues, and state law protecting against displacing must remain in force. In addition, states have authority to excuse the victims of domestic violence and single parents of very young children from these requirements (these exceptions are discussed below).

Are there community service requirements for poor families that receive assistance under the TANF block grant?

Maybe. A state may, at its option, require any parent or caretaker who receives TANF assistance for more than two months to participate in community service employment.[265] States may not require community service, however, from recipients who are already working or who are exempt from work requirements. Each state that elects to have a community service requirement has authority to determine the kinds of service that recipients may do and how many hours they must perform. States may opt out of the community service requirement by notifying the Secretary of the U.S. Department of Health and Human Services.

What counts as work?

Federal law sets out a very narrow definition of work. Essentially, it provides for nine categories of work activities that will count in meeting the *basic* work-hours requirements for receipt of TANF-funded benefits:

1. Unsubsidized employment;
2. Subsidized private sector employment;
3. Subsidized public sector employment;

4. Work experience (including refurbishment of publicly assisted housing) if private sector employment is not available;

5. On-the-job training;

6. Job search and job readiness assistance;[266]

7. Community service programs;

8. Vocational educational training (not to exceed twelve months for any individual); and

9. Provision of child care services to an individual who is participating in a community service program.

In addition to these activities, which satisfy the basic work-hours requirement, federal law also sets out three other kinds of work activities that count in meeting the act's *total* work-hours requirements:

1. Job skills training directly related to employment;

2. Education directly related to employment; and

3. Satisfactory attendance at secondary school or in a G.E.D. program.[267]

How many hours does a parent or caretaker have to work to get assistance for his or her family under the TANF block grant?

Federal law states very precisely how many hours a parent or caretaker has to work to get assistance for his or her family under the TANF block grant. The number of hours depends on whether the head of the household is a single parent or part of a two-parent household. It also depends on the parent's age and the ages of his or her children. Recipient work hours are calculated on a monthly basis using the average number of hours of work per week during that month.[268]

In general, the minimum number of hours that a single parent must work is 20 hours per week in fiscal year 1997, and this requirement increases to 30 hours in fiscal year 2000 (though the work requirement remains at 20 hours per week for single parents with a child under 6 years of age.)[269] Two-parent households face heavier work burdens. For these families, the minimum number of hours is 35 hours per week.[270] Table 1-2 sets forth the mandatory work hours for different categories of recipients.[271]

TABLE 1-2
Mandatory Work Requirements

Type of Recipient	Total Work				Basic Work			
	1997	1998	1999	2000+	1997	1998	1999	2000+
All Families	20	20	20	25	20	20	20	30
Two-Parent Families	35	35	35	35	30	30	30	30
Single Parent with Child under 6	20	20	20	20				

Source: Personal Responsibility and Work Opportunity Reconciliation Act of 1996, Pub. L. No. 104–193, 110 Stat. 2105 (Aug. 22, 1996).

What are the penalties if a parent or caretaker fails to meet his or her work requirements?

Federal law generally requires a participating state to sanction families in which the parent or caretaker "refuses" to meet his or her work requirements. The state must reduce the family's assistance by at least the pro rata share of the assistance attributable to the parent or caretaker. The state has authority to reduce the family's benefit by an even greater amount or to terminate the family's assistance entirely. However, the state need not reduce assistance if the family member can show "good cause" for failing to satisfy his or her work requirement or if the family meets some other exception that the state has established.[272]

What happens if a parent or caretaker cannot find child care and is therefore unable to meet his or her work requirements?

Special rules apply to single parents who care for children younger than six if appropriate child care is not available. Families in this situation may not be sanctioned for failure to meet work requirements if they show that appropriate child care cannot be obtained for one or more of the following reasons:

- The parent cannot obtain appropriate child care within a reasonable distance from the individual's home or work site;

- Informal child care is either unavailable or unsuitable;
- Formal child care is either unavailable or unaffordable.[273]

Are any other families exempt from the work requirements?

It depends upon the state. The federal law gives states the option of exempting certain families from TANF work requirements, including:

1. Single-parent families that include a child under 12 months old;[274]
2. Families that have been victimized by domestic violence;[275] and
3. Families with a single teen parent attending high school or "education directly related to employment."[276]

Can the state's block grant be reduced if not enough recipients meet the mandatory work requirements?

Yes. Federal law requires participating states to ensure that an increasing percentage of families receiving assistance under the TANF block grant participate in work activities. The minimum rate for all families in fiscal year 1997 is 25 percent, which rises to half the caseload in fiscal year 2002. The minimum rate is higher for two-parent families. Here, the state must ensure that at least 75 percent of families receiving assistance participate in work activities, and the rate rises to 90 percent in fiscal year 1999. States have discretion to exclude certain families from these calculations, including single parents who are caring for children younger than 12 months.[277] Even so, many government officials have admitted that it will be nearly impossible for any state to approach the law's employment targets.[278] Despite these constraints, a state's TANF block grant can be reduced from 5 to 21 percent if it fails to meet these minimum percentages.[279]

Can a family lose benefits if the parent or children do not attend school?

Yes. Federal law allows (but does not require) a state to sanction a family if any child under 18 does not attend school. Before the repeal of the AFDC program, a number of states had imposed "Learnfare" programs that conditioned the receipt of welfare benefits on a dependent child's regular school attendance.[280] Empirical studies show, however, that these programs did not improve student achievement or their subsequent entry into the labor market.[281]

In addition, the 1996 welfare act allows states to sanction families with an adult member older than age 20 and younger than 51 who does not have a high school diploma and who is not working toward attaining a diploma. Sanctions cannot be imposed, however, on individuals who are found to lack "the requisite capacity" to complete a course of study after assessment by a medical, psychiatric, or other appropriate professional.[282]

Federal law also prohibits states from providing TANF block grant benefits to a custodial parent who is under 18 years and whose child is at least 12 weeks, unless the parent has successfully completed or is pursuing a high school diploma or participating in an alternative education or training program approved by the state.

What happens if a family receives child support or alimony?

Federal law requires families receiving assistance funded by the TANF block grant to assign to the state any rights that it may have to alimony, child support, or any other third-party support. States must deny TANF assistance to any family that fails to assign its support rights. States may not, however, take any support payments that exceed the amount of TANF benefits given to the family. Nor may a state ask a family to assign any support payment that becomes due after the family stops receiving TANF benefits.[283]

Does an unwed mother have to tell the state the name of her child's biological father?

Yes. Federal law requires the state to sanction a family in which the mother does not cooperate in establishing the paternity of an out-of-wedlock child. Penalties are also imposed if the mother refuses to cooperate in establishing, modifying, or enforcing a child support order. The state can withhold a pro rata share of the family's assistance of at least 25 percent or can eliminate benefits altogether.[284]

How does a family apply for TANF block grant assistance?

The federal law does not say how a family applies for assistance under programs funded by the TANF block grant. Each state has authority to design its own application procedures. In some states, the application process that was in place for the AFDC program may continue in effect. Other states may redesign their application processes. You will have to check with the local agency administering the TANF program in your community to find out how to apply.

What is an Individual Responsibility Plan?

The 1996 welfare act is premised on the idea that poor people will be able to move from welfare to work in strictly limited time periods. Federal law thus requires that every applicant for TANF assistance receive an initial assessment of his or her skills, prior work experience, and employability. Based on this assessment, the state may then prepare an Individual Responsibility Plan that the recipient must follow. If the recipient fails to comply with the terms and conditions of his or her Individual Responsibility Plan, the state has authority to sanction the recipient's household by a pro rata reduction in benefits.[285]

Is the state required to respect the confidentiality of information that a family includes in its application for assistance?

In order to receive a TANF grant, a state has to tell the federal government how it will protect the confidentiality of information that it collects about families applying for or receiving assistance. Specifically the law says that the state must outline in its plan how it will "take such reasonable steps as the state deems necessary to restrict the use and disclosure of information about individuals and families receiving assistance under the program attributable to funds provided by the federal government."[286]

What happens if the state denies the applicant's request for assistance?

In order to receive a TANF grant, a state must tell the federal government what kind of administrative appeal and hearing procedures it intends to establish as part of its new assistance program. Specifically, federal law requires the state to include in its TANF plan "an explanation of how the state will provide opportunities for recipients who have been adversely affected to be heard in a state administrative or appeal process."[287] Under the law governing the AFDC program, states must give families advance notice of any proposed reduction or termination of benefits and must offer families an opportunity to contest the proposed action at a hearing *before* any benefits may be reduced or denied. Applicants for AFDC are also entitled to a written notice describing the state's action on their case and a chance to contest the action at a hearing. These requirements came about as a result of the landmark Supreme Court decision in *Goldberg v. Kelly*, which held that the Constitution's due process guarantee gives welfare recipients the right to written notice and an opportunity to be heard before benefits may be reduced or terminated.[288] The 1996 welfare act does not impose any specific duties on states to provide adequate notice and hearing rights to TANF applicants and recipients. Of course states may choose to provide such rights in their TANF programs, but, failing that, courts should hold that the Constitution mandates them. Although the welfare act claims to create no federal entitlement to TANF benefits, federal law does require that states operate their TANF programs in accordance with "fair" and "objective" written eligibility standards,[289] and some states may retain specific entitlement status for cash assistance in their state laws. In either event, the legal interest created by these federal and state laws should be found sufficient to trigger constitutional due process protections; and impoverished families' critical interest in receiving subsistence benefits should be held to require full notice and hearing rights for TANF applicants and recipients.

Supplemental Security Income

What is Supplemental Security Income?

Supplemental Security Income (SSI) is a federal welfare program that makes monthly cash payments to poor people who are disabled or blind or have reached age 65. Congress created the SSI program in 1972 to replace a patchwork of state-administered programs for the aged, blind, and disabled.[290] Because the federal government funds all but a small part of SSI benefits and sets minimum national benefit levels, SSI grants are generally larger than payments made under state-administered family assistance or general assistance programs. About six million people currently receive SSI.[291]

Who runs the SSI program?

The SSI program is run by the federal Social Security Administration.[292] The Social Security Administration maintains over a thousand local offices throughout the United States. These are known as district offices and are the places where individuals can obtain information and forms, submit applications for benefits, and file appeals. You can find the Social Security District Office closest to you by checking the blue pages (government listings) of a local telephone book under "Social Security Administration." You can also call the Social Security Administration's toll-free service and information number, 1-800-772-1213.

Are there any other state or federal programs for disabled people?

Yes, there are a number of programs other than SSI that make cash payments to disabled persons. Most states have short-term disability programs that provide workers a portion of their salary during brief periods of disability. States also require all employers to participate in the Workers Compensation program, which provides payments to workers who receive injuries, including disabling injuries, on the job. The federal Social Security disability program provides cash payments to disabled workers and, in certain circumstances, to disabled spouses and disabled children of workers who have paid Social Security taxes over a sufficient period of time. None of these programs, however, are specifically for poor people, and this book does not discuss them.

Who is eligible for Supplemental Security Income?

You are eligible to receive SSI payments if you meet all four of the following requirements:

1. You must be a member of one of the groups covered by the SSI program. You must be either (a) age 65 or older, or (b) legally blind, or (c) disabled.
2. Your income must be within the SSI program limits.
3. Your assets must be within the SSI program limits.
4. You must live in one of the fifty states, the District of Columbia, or the Northern Mariana Islands[293] and be (a) a citizen of the United States; (b) a legal permanent resident of the United States who has worked in the United States the equivalent of forty qualifying quarters in the Social Security system, or can be credited with forty quarters based on the work of a spouse and/or parent (appendix C to this book explains the forty quarters rule in greater detail); (c) a noncitizen lawfully residing in the United States who is an active-duty member of the U.S. armed services or an honorably discharged veteran, or the spouse or unmarried dependent child of such a person; or (d) an immigrant

granted refugee, asylee, or "withholding of deportation" status, but only during the first five years after receiving that status.

Before Congress enacted the Personal Responsibility and Work Opportunity Reconciliation Act in August 1996, any lawful permanent resident could qualify for SSI. The anti-immigrant restrictions in the 1996 welfare act cut an estimated 500,000 elderly and disabled individuals from the SSI program, leaving many of them with no means of subsistence.[294] As this book goes to press, President Clinton and other politicians have called for the repeal of these new restrictions on immigrant eligibility for SSI, and by the time you read this book, SSI eligibility of lawful permanent residents may have been restored.

How does an individual prove eligibility for SSI as an aged person?

To receive SSI as an aged person, you must prove that you are age 65 or older. The best evidence of your age is a birth certificate or religious record of your birth recorded before your fifth birthday.[295] If no such document is available, the Social Security Administration will consider other proof of your age, including a school record, census record, Bible or other family record, church record of baptism or confirmation made in youth or early adult life, an insurance policy, a marriage record, an employment record, a labor union record, fraternal organization record, military record, voting record, delayed birth certificate, birth certificate of your child, physician's or midwife's record of your birth, immigration record, naturalization record, or passport.[296] If you are age 68 or older, the Social Security Administration will accept any document that is at least three years old and shows your age.[297]

How does an individual prove eligibility for SSI as a blind person?

You can receive SSI payments as a blind person if (1) your vision is 20/200 or less in the better eye with the use of glasses or (2) you have tunnel vision in the better eye that reduces your field of vision to 20 degrees or less.[298] You may receive SSI payments as a blind person even if you are able to work and even if you are in fact working. The amount of your earnings, however, will be considered as income to you in determining your financial eligibility for SSI and the amount of your payment. If you are not legally blind, but have eye problems that prevent you from working, you may still be eligible for SSI as a disabled person.

How does the Social Security Administration decide if an adult is eligible for SSI as a disabled person?

To receive SSI as a disabled adult, you must have a long-term medical condition that makes it impossible for you to work regularly at a paying job. In the language of the Social Security Act, you must be "unable to engage in any substantial gainful activity by reason of any medically determinable physical or mental impairment which can be expected to result in death or which has lasted or can be expected to last for a continuous period of not less than twelve months."[299] "Substantial gainful activity" means work that requires significant physical or mental activities and is done for pay or profit.[300]

The rules for determining whether an individual is disabled under the SSI program are complicated. If you believe that you may qualify for SSI as a disabled person, you should consider seeking the assistance of a legal aid or legal services lawyer or other experienced advocate who can work with your doctor, medical clinic, and/or hospital to present the medical and other information needed to show that you are disabled. This section will describe some of the basic rules for deciding whether an individual is disabled under the SSI program. But, because of the volume and complexity of this area of law, a complete presentation of the subject is not practicable.

The Social Security Administration (SSA) uses a five-part test to determine whether an adult is disabled under the SSI program. SSA sometimes refers to this test as its "sequential evaluation" of disability.

1. *Is the individual currently working?* If you are currently engaged in "substantial gainful activity" (substantial work for pay or profit), the Social Security Administration will conclude that you are not disabled. To determine if work is substantial gainful activity, the Social Security Administration will consider whether the work requires "significant physical or mental activities";[301] whether the worker is able to perform the job satisfactorily "without more supervision or assistance than is usually given other people doing similar work";[302] and whether the work is done under "special conditions," for example, work performed in a sheltered workshop.[303] Work that involves minimal duties and is of little use to the employer will not be considered substantial gainful activity.[304]

Work that results in average earnings of less than $300 per month ($500 per month if earned in a sheltered workshop) ordinarily will not be considered substantial gainful activity. Conversely, work that results in average earnings of more than $500 per month ordinarily will be considered substantial gainful activity.[305] In deciding whether your work pays enough to be considered substantial gainful activity, the Social Security Administration will not count any part of your wages that are subsidized[306] and will subtract the cost to you of services and items that enable you to work despite your medical condition.[307]

If you are *not* currently engaged in substantial gainful activity, go to step two.

2. *Is the individual's medical condition "severe"?* To be considered disabled for SSI purposes, you must suffer from a "severe" medical condition. A physical or mental condition, or a combination of such conditions, is "severe" if it significantly limits your ability to do basic work activities. Basic work activities include lifting; carrying; pulling; pushing; reaching; handling; standing; sitting; walking; seeing; hearing; speaking; understanding; carrying out and remembering instructions; using judgment; responding appropriately to supervision, coworkers, and usual work situations; and dealing with changes in a routine work setting.[308] If your medical conditions do not significantly limit your ability to do one or more of these basic work activities, the Social Security Administration will conclude that you are not disabled.[309]

If your medical condition does significantly limit your ability to do basic work activities, go to step three.

3. *Does the individual's medical condition appear on the Social Security Administration's "listing" of disabling conditions?* The Social Security Administration maintains a list of physical and mental conditions that the agency has determined to be disabling, irrespective of the sufferer's age, education, and work experience.[310] The list is called the "Listing of Impairments" and is published in Title 20 of the Code of Federal Regulations, part 404, subpart P, appendix 1. It is available for viewing at any Social Security office.[311] If your medical condition is on this list, or is as severe as a condition on the list, then the Social Security Administration will conclude that you are disabled.[312]

If your medical condition is not on the list or as severe as a condition on the list, go to step four.

4. *Does the individual's medical condition prevent performance of his or her past work?* If your medical condition is not on the Social Security Administration's listing of disabling conditions, the next question is whether your medical problem prevents you from doing the kind of work that you have done in the past fifteen years.[313] To answer this ques-

tion, the Social Security Administration will first determine which basic work activities you can still do despite your medical conditions. This is called your "residual functional capacity." The Social Security Administration will then compare your residual functional capacity to the physical and mental activities required to do your usual work. If your medical condition does not prevent you from doing your previous work, the Social Security Administration will conclude that you are not disabled.[314] If your medical condition does prevent you from doing your previous work, go to step five.

5. *Is there other work that the individual can do despite his or her medical conditions?* Once you show that your medical condition prevents you from doing your previous work, the next question is whether you can do any other job that exists in large numbers in the national economy. If you can do other work despite your medical condition, then you will be found "not disabled." On the other hand, if there are no other jobs that you can do, you will be found "disabled"[315] and entitled to SSI.

To determine whether you are able and qualified to do some job other than your usual work, the Social Security Administration must consider four factors: (1) your age, (2) your educational background, (3) your past work experience, and (4) your residual functional capacity (the work activities you can still do despite your medical conditions).[316]

If your medical condition causes only "exertional limitations" (i.e., limitations on your ability to sit, stand, walk, lift, carry, push, or pull), the Social Security Administration will use a series of charts, known as the Medical-Vocational Guidelines or "the grids," to determine whether there are jobs you can do.[317] (The Medical-Vocational Guidelines are published in Title 20 of the Code of Federal Regulations, part 404, subpart P, appendix 2, and are available for viewing at any Social Security office.) For each combination of age, educational background, work skills, and residual functional capacity,[318] there is an entry in the guidelines that says "disabled" or "not disabled." Reproduced in table 1-3 are the Medical-Vocational Guidelines for individuals with a residual functional capacity limited to sedentary work (i.e., individuals whose medical conditions prevent them from doing work more strenuous than sedentary work).

Example: Mary Green is 53 years old, completed high school, has worked only in unskilled jobs, and suffers from medical conditions that limit her to sedentary work. Guideline rule 201.12 applies because it describes a person with Ms. Green's age, education, work experience, and

TABLE 1-3

Residual Functional Capacity: Maximum Sustained Work Capability Limited to Sedentary Work as a Result of Severe Medically Determinable Impairment(s)

Rule	Age	Education	Previous Work Experience	Decision
201.01	Advanced age (55 and over)	Limited or less	Unskilled or none	Disabled
201.02	Advanced age	Limited or less	Skilled or semiskilled; skills not transferable	Disabled
201.03	Advanced age	Limited or less	Skilled or semiskilled; skills transferable	Not disabled
201.04	Advanced age	High school graduate or more; does not provide for direct entry into skilled work	Unskilled or none	Disabled
201.05	Advanced age	High school graduate or more; provides for direct entry into skilled work	Unskilled or none	Not disabled
201.06	Advanced age	High school graduate or more; does not provide for direct entry into skilled work	Skilled or semiskilled; skills not transferable	Disabled
201.07	Advanced age	High school graduate or more; does not provide for direct entry into skilled work	Skilled or semiskilled; skills transferable	Not disabled
201.08	Advanced age	High school graduate or more; provides for direct entry into skilled work	Skilled or semiskilled; skills not transferable	Not disabled
201.09	Nearing advanced age (50–54)	Limited or less	Unskilled or none	Disabled

TABLE 1-3 continued on next page

TABLE 1-3 *continued*

Rule	Age	Education	Previous Work Experience	Decision
201.10	Nearing advanced age	Limited or less	Skilled or semiskilled; skills not transferable	Disabled
201.11	Nearing advanced age	Limited or less	Skilled or semiskilled; skills transferable	Not disabled
201.12	Nearing advanced age	High school graduate or more; does not provide for direct entry into skilled work	Unskilled or none	Disabled
201.13	Nearing advanced age	High school graduate or more; provides for direct entry into skilled work	Unskilled or none	Not disabled
201.14	Nearing advanced age	High school graduate or more; does not provide for direct entry into skilled work	Skilled or semiskilled; skills not transferable	Disabled
201.15	Nearing advanced age	High school graduate or more; does not provide for direct entry into skilled work	Skilled or semiskilled; skills transferable	Not disabled
201.16	Nearing advanced age	High school graduate or more; provides for direct entry into skilled work	Skilled or semiskilled; skills not transferable	Not disabled
201.17	Younger individual (45–49)	Illiterate or unable to communicate in English	Unskilled or none	Disabled
201.18	45–49	Limited or less; at least literate and able to communicate in English	Unskilled or none	Not disabled

TABLE 1-3 continued on next page

TABLE 1-3 *continued*

Rule	Age	Education	Previous Work Experience	Decision
201.19	45–49	Limited or less	Skilled or semiskilled; skills not transferable	Not disabled
201.20	45–49	Limited or less	Skilled or semiskilled; skills transferable	Not disabled
201.21	45–49	High School graduate or more	Skilled or semiskilled; skills not transferable	Not disabled
201.22	45–49	High School graduate or more	Skilled or semiskilled; skills transferable	Not disabled
201.23	Younger individual (18–44)	Illiterate or unable to communicate in English	Unskilled or none	Not disabled
201.24	18–44	Limited or less; at least literate and able to communicate in English	Unskilled or none	Not disabled
201.25	18–44	Limited or less	Skilled or semiskilled; skills not transferable	Not disabled
201.26	18–44	Limited or less	Skilled or semiskilled; skills transferable	Not disabled
201.27	18–44	High School graduate or more	Unskilled or none	Not disabled
201.28	18–44	High School graduate or more	Skilled or semiskilled; skills not transferable	Not disabled
201.29	18–44	High School graduate or more	Skilled or semiskilled; skills transferable	Not disabled

residual functional capacity. Rule 201.12 is applicable to individuals, like Ms. Green, who (1) are between 50 and 54 years old, (2) have a formal education through at least high school, but have not "recently completed education which provides a . . . direct entry into skilled sedentary work,"[319] (3) have no work skills that are readily transferable to other occupations, and (4) are limited to sedentary work by medical conditions. The rules state that a person with these characteristics (who cannot do his or her customary work) is disabled.[320]

The Medical-Vocational Guidelines represent the Social Security Administration's findings about the types of jobs that exist in the national economy and the ability of individuals with certain physical restrictions and skill levels to do those jobs. The older an individual, the less education he or she has, and the lower his or her skill level and residual functional capacity, the greater the likelihood that the guidelines will direct a finding of disability. Conversely, the younger an individual, the more advanced her or his educational background and skill level, the more likely it is that the guidelines will direct a finding of nondisability. Indeed, as a general rule, individuals who are under age 50 will not be found disabled when the guidelines are applied.[321] This does not mean that people under age 50 will never be found disabled. For one thing, a person under age 50 might have a medical condition that appears on the listing of conditions presumed to be disabling at step three.

In addition, there are three situations in which the Social Security Administration may not use the Medical-Vocational Guidelines to reject a claim of disability.

First, the guidelines may not be used to find you "not disabled" if your medical condition prevents you from performing even "sedentary" work on a regular basis. Sedentary work requires the worker to lift and carry up to ten pounds at a time, be able to sit at a work station for approximately six hours in an eight-hour workday, and occasionally stand and walk.[322] Extended periods of continuous sitting are required and workers usually cannot alternate sitting and standing at will.[323] If your medical condition precludes even this degree of physical exertion, then the guidelines may not be used against you.

Second, the guidelines may not be used to deny benefits if you suffer from one or more "non-exertional" limitations that "significantly" reduce your ability to work. A non-exertional limitation is any limitation that "does not directly affect the ability to sit, stand, walk, lift, carry, push or pull." This includes limitations that "affect the mind, vision, hearing, speech and use of the body to climb, balance, stoop, kneel, crouch, crawl, reach, handle and use of the fingers for fine manipulations."[324] So, for example, the guidelines may not be used to deny SSI disability benefits to an individual with a psychological limitation, such as nervousness, anxiety, or depression, that makes it difficult to function in a job.[325] Nor may the guidelines be used to deny disability where the individual has difficulty maintaining attention or concentration, or understanding or remembering instructions. Other examples of situations where the guidelines may not be used to deny benefits include individuals whose medication causes drowsiness and precludes climbing or working with machines; individuals who do not have full use of their hands and fingers; individuals who have difficulty tolerating dust, fumes, or other features of certain workplaces; individuals with hearing, seeing, or speaking problems; and individuals who have difficulty crawling, stooping, or crouching.[326]

If your medical condition causes only non-exertional limitations, the guidelines do not apply at all.[327] If you suffer from both exertional and non-exertional limitations, the guidelines will be consulted to see if your exertional limitations warrant a finding of disability. If not, then the guidelines may be used as a "framework" for considering whether there are jobs that you can perform.[328] It is important to remember that the Medical-Vocational Guidelines represent the government's assessment of whether a person of a certain age, educational background, skill level, and exertional ability can perform the tasks required by any job that exists in large numbers in the national economy. The guidelines do not take into account restrictions on ability to work that result from non-exertional limitations; to the contrary, the guidelines assume that the individual has no limitation on his or her ability to see, hear, speak, reach, climb, perform fine manipulations with hands, understand instructions, concentrate, use machinery, etc. If your medical condition does cause any such limitation, the guidelines may not be used to deny disability benefits. In such cases, the Social Security Administration may consult a vocational expert to determine whether there are jobs that a particular individual can perform despite specific exertional and non-exertional limitations.

Third, the guidelines may not be used to deny your claim for SSI if you have worked for 35 years or more at arduous, unskilled physical labor, you are unable to perform such labor because of your medical condition, and you have only a "marginal education" (generally sixth grade or less). Under such circumstances, the Social Security Administration will conclude that you are disabled.[329]

Can a person who is disabled due to alcoholism or drug addiction qualify for SSI?

An individual with an alcohol or drug addiction can receive SSI disability benefits, but only if the person (1) is disabled because of a medical condition other than alcohol or drug addiction and (2) would be disabled even if he or she stopped using drugs or alcohol.[330] Alcoholism and drug addiction are medical conditions that may cause severe disability and, until recently, individuals suffering from these conditions could qualify for SSI. Benefits were paid through a responsible third party, and recipients were required to participate in drug or alcohol treatment programs. Congress terminated SSI eligibility for this group of people as part of the Contract with America Advancement Act of 1996.[331] After March 29, 1996, new applicants for SSI disability no longer qualify on the basis of alcoholism or drug addiction. And effective January 1, 1997, existing SSI recipients disabled only by drug addiction or alcoholism were dropped from the program.

Can a disabled child qualify for SSI?

A child under 18 years of age can qualify for SSI disability benefits if he or she "has a medically determinable physical or mental impairment, which results in marked and severe functional limitations, and which can be expected to result in death or which has lasted or can be expected to last for a continuous period of not less than 12 months."[332] This definition of child disability was imposed by the 1996 welfare bill enacted by the Republican-controlled Congress and signed by President Clinton in August 1996. The purpose of the new definition is to cut costs by reducing the number of disabled children who qualify for SSI. Approximately 300,000 disabled children will be expelled from the SSI program as a result of the new law.

Before Congress enacted the 1996 welfare law, a disabled child could qualify for SSI if his or her medical condition was comparable to one that would prevent an adult from working. Under the old law, the Social Security Administration would assess the severity of the child's medical condition, and, if necessary, perform an "individualized functional assessment" to determine whether the child's condition was comparable to one that would be considered disabling in an adult.[333] The new law prohibits the Social Security Administration from considering the actual functional capabilities of children under 18 years of age and instead appears to require that disability determinations be based solely on the child's medical diagnosis, signs, and symptoms. As a result, many functionally disabled children will be excluded from the SSI program and denied assistance.

Are premature and low birthweight infants ever considered disabled?

Yes. The Social Security Administration considers two categories of premature and low birthweight babies to be disabled and therefore eligible for SSI. First, infants born at thirty-seven weeks or earlier who weigh less than

1,200 grams at birth are deemed to be disabled at least until age one.[334] In addition, infants born at thirty-seven weeks or earlier who weigh at least 1,200 grams but less than 2,000 grams *and* who are at least four weeks small for gestational age are deemed to be disabled at least until age one.[335]

What kind of evidence is used to decide whether a person is disabled?

The Social Security Administration must consider any information that you provide about your medical conditions and how those conditions limit your ability to do work-related activities.[336] Usually the most important kind of evidence is medical evidence, including reports, test results, and other medical records from doctors, hospitals, or clinics that have treated you. You should therefore do your best to obtain a complete report from the medical professionals who have treated you. Also important are your own statements to the Social Security Administration about how your medical conditions—including pain and the side effects of medications—limit your daily activities and your ability to work. You may also provide statements from other people (e.g., relatives, neighbors, former employers, clergy, social workers, etc.) who have observed your medical conditions and can comment on how they restrict your daily activities and your ability to do work-related activities.[337]

Must the Social Security Administration consider the effects of pain and other symptoms in determining whether or not an individual is able to work?

Yes. The Social Security Administration must consider the symptoms of your medical conditions, such as pain, weakness, dizziness, fatigue, and nervousness, when deciding whether you are disabled.[338] Symptoms need not be considered, however, if there is no objective medical evidence that you suffer from a medical condition that might produce the symptoms you say you have.[339] (Objective medical evidence means test results or physical or psychological abnormalities observed by a doctor.) If there is objective medical evidence of a physical or psychological condition that can produce the symptoms you complain of, the Social Security Administration will consider your statements about the severity and persistence of the symptoms and the effect that the symptoms have on your ability to engage in ordinary daily activities and work-related activities. In many cases, pain or other symptoms can be disabling. For instance, severe, persistent back pain that can only be relieved by frequent changes in position and lying down every thirty minutes would likely prevent the sufferer from doing any job.

How important is it for an SSI applicant to submit a thorough report from his or her doctor?

In most cases, complete information from an SSI applicant's treating physician is the most important and convincing evidence of disability. A thorough report from your treating physician is therefore critical. The report from your doctor should give a medical history and fully describe all of your medical conditions. The report should include a description of all physical and/or psychological abnormalities observed by your doctor, the symptoms that you have reported to the doctor, the results of any medical tests or laboratory diagnostic techniques (e.g., x-rays, CAT scans, electrocardiograms, blood tests, psychological tests, etc.), the treatment prescribed, and the prognosis. In addition, the report should state the degree to which your medical conditions—including symptoms like pain and the impact of medications—limit your ability to do work-related activities.[340] Sample report forms that your doctor can fill out are included in appendix B of this book.

Your treating physician is the health professional most familiar with your medical conditions. For this reason the Social Security Administration is required to give great weight to a thorough report from your treating doctor or doctors.[341] It is important that your doctor's report contain the information listed above because the Social Security Administration will not give very much weight to an incomplete report or a brief note stating only that you are under treatment and cannot work. Test results and medical observations included in your doctor's report can establish that your medical condition meets or equals a condition on the Social Security Administration's listing of disabling conditions. Your physician's assessment of the physical and/or mental limitations caused by your medical conditions can also show that you are no longer able to work. Your doctor should be informed of the Social Security Administration's disability rules and the medical information required to show disability. This is best done by a legal aid or legal services lawyer or other advocate familiar with the SSI program. At the least, your doctor should review the Social Security Administration's listing of disabling conditions, because very specific test results and/or clinical findings must be reported for there to be a finding of disability.

What happens if an individual applying for SSI cannot get a report from his or her treating doctor or clinic?

If you cannot get medical records or reports from your doctor, clinic, or other health care provider, the Social Security Administration must "make every reasonable effort" to obtain medical records and reports from these sources.[342] If the Social Security Administration is unable to get sufficient information from your health care providers to determine whether you are disabled, it may arrange for you to be examined and/or tested by a doctor or psychologist at the government's expense.[343]

Can the Social Security Administration require an SSI claimant to be examined by a doctor other than his or her own doctor?

The Social Security Administration may ask you to have one or more physical or psychological tests or examinations if the medical information obtained from your treating physician, clinic and/or hospital is not sufficient to make a decision about whether you are disabled.[344] The government will pay for any such test or examination. If you fail or refuse to have the test or examination without a good reason, the Social Security Administration may decide, based on the evidence it has, that you are not disabled, and may deny your claim for SSI.[345] You can decline to have a particular examination or test if your doctors advise you that you should not have that test or examination.[346] If this is the case, you must tell the Social Security Administration immediately about your doctor's advice. You may also object to the particular doctor chosen by the Social Security Administration to perform the examination.[347] Good reasons for objecting to a particular doctor include (1) the doctor examined you in connection with a previous disability application that was denied; (2) the doctor previously assisted an opponent of yours, such as your employer in a contested workers compensation claim; (3) you cannot easily get to the doctor's office; (4) you and the doctor do not speak the same language and translation is not available; or (5) the doctor "lacks objectivity," which means that the doctor is in some way biased against your claim.[348] The Social Security Administration will usually assign a different doctor when you make such an objection.

You may also request that your own doctor be selected to perform whatever additional tests or examinations are required to decide whether you are disabled. The Social Security Administration will choose your doctor to perform the needed tests or examinations if your doctor is qualified, is willing and able to perform the test or examination for the fee offered by the government, and generally furnishes complete and timely reports.[349]

Does an SSI claimant have to accept and follow prescribed treatment in order to receive SSI disability benefits?

In order to receive SSI, you must follow treatment prescribed by your doctor if the treatment can improve your condition sufficiently to enable you to work.[350] If you refuse such treatment without a good reason, the Social Security Administration may deny your application for SSI, or, if you are already receiving benefits, it may cut off your payments.[351] The Social Security Administration has given the following as examples of good reasons for refusing prescribed treatment that could enable you to walk:

1. The treatment is contrary to your religious beliefs;

2. The treatment is cataract surgery for one eye when there is a severe, untreatable loss of vision in the other eye;

3. The prescribed treatment is surgery that was previously performed for the same medical condition with unsuccessful results;

4. The treatment is "very risky" to you because of its "enormity (e.g., open heart surgery), unusual nature (e.g., organ transplant), or other reason"; or

5. The treatment involves amputation of a limb or major part of a limb.[352]

Does a disabled person have to accept vocational rehabilitation services in order to receive SSI disability benefits?

The Social Security Administration may refer an SSI recipient between ages 16 and 65 to a state agency that provides vocational rehabilitation services if such services may restore the recipient's ability to work.[353] If you refuse without a good reason to accept vocational rehabilitation services, the Social Security Administration may deny or suspend your SSI benefits.[354] The Social Security Administration has given the following as some examples of good reasons for refusing vocational rehabilitation services:

1. The services offered are not designed to restore your ability to work;

2. You are already in either a government or a private program that is expected to restore your ability to work;

3. You are regularly attending a school, college, university, or course of technical or vocational training or rehabilitation and the program is designed to restore your ability to work;

4. You are physically or mentally unable to participate in the program offered;

5. The services offered would interfere with a medical program provided to you;

6. The services would require you to be away from home and your absence would be harmful to the health and welfare of your family;

7. You are presently working or will be working within three months; or

8. Accepting such services would be contrary to your religious beliefs.[355]

Can a person who lives in a homeless shelter or a public institution receive SSI payments?

Maybe. In general, you may not receive an SSI payment for a given month if you were a resident of a "public institution" during that entire month.[356] A "public institution" for these purposes is a government-operated or government-controlled establishment that provides food, shelter, and some treatment or other services to four or more persons.

There are several important exceptions to this rule:

1. *Public shelters for the homeless.* You may receive SSI payments as a resident of a public homeless shelter for up to six months in any nine-month period.[357] For example, if you lived in a public shelter for an entire year, you could receive SSI for the first six months. You would then be ineligible for months seven, eight, and nine, but you could begin receiving SSI again in month ten for another six months. If you do not live in a public shelter throughout an entire month, the SSI payment you receive for that month does not count toward the six-month limit.[358] If you live in a homeless shelter that is *not* operated or controlled by the government, there is no limit on your eligibility for SSI payments.

2. *Medical care facilities.* If you reside in a public medical or psychiatric facility, or a public or private facility where Medicaid pays more than fifty percent of the cost of your care, you may continue to receive

your full SSI grant for up to two months after entering the institution, as long as the institution agrees that the SSI benefits will not be used to pay for the cost of institutional care.[359] In addition, if a physician certifies that your stay in the facility is not likely to last over three months, and you need your SSI payments to pay the rent or otherwise maintain your home, you may receive benefits for the first three months that you are in the medical facility.[360] If you do not qualify for full SSI payments, you may still receive a reduced payment, sometimes referred to as a "personal needs allowance." (In 1996, the SSI personal needs allowance was thirty dollars per month for an individual, and about half the states added a state supplement to those payments.)[361]

3. *Educational or vocational facilities.* If you live in a public educational institution and receive training, knowledge, or skills to prepare for gainful employment, you may receive SSI payments.[362]

4. *Community residence serving no more than sixteen people.* If you live in a publicly operated community residence that is designed for and serves no more than sixteen residents, you may receive SSI payments.[363]

Can a person who lives outside of the United States receive SSI payments?

No. SSI benefits are not available to persons living outside of the fifty states, the District of Columbia, or the Northern Mariana Islands.[364] This means you may not receive SSI if you live in Puerto Rico, Guam, the U.S. Virgin Islands, or any other United States territory, or in any foreign country. (By contrast, Social Security disability, retirement, and survivors' benefits may be received by eligible individuals regardless of their place of residence.) Normally, a home address within the fifty states, the District of Columbia, or the Northern Marianas will be sufficient proof of residency for SSI eligibility. However, if the Social Security Administration suspects that you do not reside in the United States, it may require you to submit evidence, such as telephone or utility bills, lease, rent receipts, or documents that show you participate in a social service or educational program in the United States.[365]

Can an SSI recipient travel outside of the United States and still receive SSI checks?

An SSI recipient may travel outside of the fifty states, the District of Columbia, and the Northern Mariana Islands for up to twenty-nine consecutive days without any loss of benefits. If, however, a recipient remains outside of these locations for thirty consecutive days or more, the Social Security Administration will suspend the SSI benefits.[366] Benefits will resume after the individual has returned and remained in the fifty states, the District of Columbia, or the Northern Mariana Islands for thirty consecutive days.[367]

Can a person who is not a United States citizen receive SSI payments?

Maybe. The 1996 welfare bill enacted by the Republican-controlled Congress and signed by President Clinton in August 1996 disqualified most disabled and elderly immigrants from the SSI program.[368] The anti-immigrant provisions of the new law cut approximately half a million aged and severely disabled legal immigrants from SSI, leaving many with no means of support whatever. President Clinton has stated that he will seek new legislation to restore eligibility for legal immigrants, so the law as described below may have changed by the time you read this book. As of January 1997, however, eligibility for SSI was limited to the following individuals:

1. United States citizens;

2. Lawful permanent residents who have accumulated forty calendar quarters of work covered by the Social Security system or can be credited with forty quarters based on the work of a spouse or parent (appendix C explains the forty-quarters rule in greater detail)[369]

3. Noncitizens lawfully residing in the United States who are active duty members of the U.S. armed forces or honorably discharged veterans or the spouse or unmarried dependent children of such individuals;[370] or

4. Immigrants granted refugee, asylee, or "withholding of deportation" status (under sections 207, 208, or 243(h), respectively, of the Immigration and Naturalization Act), but eligibility lasts only for five years from the date the immigrant gained the status.[371]

In light of these restrictions, legal immigrants who are elderly or disabled should consider applying for U.S. citizenship. Immigrants may apply for U.S. citizenship after five years as a lawful permanent resident (a "green card" holder) or after three years if the immigrant received a green card through a citizen spouse.[372]

Who qualifies for SSI as a United States citizen?

To qualify for SSI as a U.S. citizen, you must show that you were born in one of the fifty states, the District of Columbia, Puerto Rico, Guam, the United States Virgin Islands, American Samoa, Swain's Island, or the Northern Mariana Islands or that you are a naturalized citizen of the United States or acquired U.S. citizenship by virtue of a parent's American citizenship.[373]

How much is the SSI benefit payment?

SSI benefits are paid monthly. The amount of the monthly SSI payment depends upon several factors, including (1) whether the state you live in provides a supplement to the basic federal benefit, (2) the amount of any other income you may have, (3) your living arrangements, and (4) whether an "essential person" lives with you.

In 1997, the basic federal SSI benefit is $484 per month for an eligible individual and $726 per month for an eligible couple (husband and wife both eligible for SSI) living together.[374] The payment you actually receive may be higher than the basic federal benefit if your state adds a "state supplement" or if there is an "essential person" living with you. Conversely, if you have income or receive support and maintenance in cash or in kind, your SSI payment may be reduced by an amount equal to some portion of your income. The effect of income on SSI eligibility and grant amount is discussed later in this section.

Are SSI payments increased when there is inflation?

Yes. The federal portion of the SSI grant is tied to the Consumer Price Index (CPI). Cost-of-living adjustments are added to the federal SSI payment each year in proportion to increases in the CPI.[375] Nevertheless, in 1996, the federal benefit rate for an individual was less than 73 percent of the federal poverty level.[376]

What is a state supplement?

States may make additional payments to SSI recipients to "supplement" the basic federal benefit.[377] The amount of the state supplement varies from state to state, and some states have elected to make no supplemental payments at all. In 1996, twenty-six states and the District of Columbia provided supplemental payments. The median state supplement in 1994 was thirty-one dollars per month for an individual.[378]

States that make supplemental payments to SSI recipients usually vary the amount of the supplement depending upon the individual's circumstances, including one or more of the following: (1) living arrangements (e.g., living alone, living with spouse, living in a congregate care facility), (2) geographic location within the state (if cost of living varies widely within the state), and (3) basis for SSI eligibility (i.e., aged, disabled, or blind).[379]

How much income can an individual receive and still be eligible for SSI?

Because SSI is a need-based program, the amount of an individual's income is a key factor affecting both eligibility for SSI and the size of the SSI benefit payment. "Income" means "anything you receive in cash or in kind that you can use to meet your needs for food, clothing or shelter."[380]

To be eligible for SSI, your *countable* income must not exceed the maximum SSI grant that a person in your category may receive. Your "countable income" is your total income minus allowable exclusions and deductions. If your countable income is more than the maximum SSI grant, you are ineligible for SSI. If your countable income is less than the maximum SSI grant, then you are eligible for an SSI grant equal to the difference between your countable income and the maximum benefit.

Total Income − *Exclusions and Deductions* = Countable Income

Maximum SSI Benefit − *Countable Income* = SSI Grant Payment

Example: Mr. Smith has a total income of $500 per month, and the allowable deductions and exclusions under the SSI program for Mr. Smith turn out to be $200 per month. This means that Mr. Smith's countable income is $300 per month ($500 minus $200). Mr. Smith lives alone in a state with no SSI supplement, so his maximum SSI benefit in 1997 would be $484 per month (the federal benefit for an individual). Since Mr. Smith's countable income is less than his maximum SSI grant, he is eligible for benefits. His grant amount will be $184 per month, the maximum grant level reduced by his countable income ($484 − $300 = $184).

What is income for purposes of the SSI Program?

There are three kinds of "income" that the Social Security Administration considers when determining your eligibility for SSI and the amount of your grant: (1) cash income received by you, including gross wages and net self-employment income; (2) "in-kind income," which means food, clothing, or shelter given to you or some other thing given to you that you can use to obtain food, clothing, or shelter; and (3) income that is received by another person but that the Social Security Administration "deems" available to you (usually income of a relative who is legally responsible for you).[381]

"Earned income" refers to cash or goods that you receive in return for work and includes gross income from wages, net earnings from self-employment, and payments for services performed in a sheltered workshop.[382] "Unearned income" refers to other cash or goods that you receive (for example, interest on a savings account).[383]

What is not considered income?

Cash or goods that are not food, clothing, or shelter and cannot be used to obtain food, clothing, or shelter are not "income" for purposes of the SSI program.[384] In addition, cash or goods that you receive from the sale or exchange of your property are not considered income, although they may be considered "resources." Social Security Administration regulations also exclude a number of other items from the definition of income,[385] including:

1. *Medical care and services.* This exclusion applies to (a) medical care and services that you receive free or at reduced rate, including room and board during any medical confinement; (b) cash you receive under a medical program or health insurance policy to repay you for health services you have already purchased; (c) medical program or health insurance payments that can be used only for medical services; (d) direct payments of your health insurance premiums by someone else; (e) assistance in cash or in kind that you receive from a government program designed to provide medical or vocational care or services; (f) in-kind assistance, other than food, clothing, or shelter, that you receive from a nongovernmental program designed to provide medical or vocational care or services.

2. *Social services.* These include (a) assistance in cash or in kind that you receive from a governmental program designed to provide social services; (b) in-kind assistance, other than food, clothing, or shelter, that you receive from a nongovernmental program designed to provide social services; (c) cash assistance that you receive from a nongovernmental

social services program to pay for services (e.g., homemaker services) other than food, clothing, or shelter.

3. *Income tax refunds.* Refunds of taxes that you have already paid are not considered income. (Also, as explained below, the federal Earned Income Credit is not countable income for SSI purposes.)

4. *Payments by credit life or credit disability insurance.* This exclusion applies, for example, to mortgage payments made by a credit disability policy after you become disabled. Such payments are not income, and neither is the increased equity in your home.

5. *Proceeds of a loan.*

6. *Bills paid for you.* If a friend, relative, or other person pays a bill for you, the payment is not income. However, if the paid bill was for food, clothing, or shelter, those goods will be considered in-kind income and may affect the amount of your SSI grant. If the paid bill was for something other than food, clothing, or shelter, the payment does not count as income at all and does not affect your SSI grant amount.

7. *Replacement of lost, stolen, or destroyed income.*

8. *Weatherization assistance.* Examples include insulation, storm doors, and storm windows.

9. *Payments from the Department of Veterans Affairs resulting from unusual medical expenses.*

10. *Interest or other earnings from retroactive SSI payments made to a child under 18.* Earnings from retroactive SSI payments made to a child under 18 do not count as income if the payments are placed in an account used only for the child's educational and training expenses, medical expenses, and certain expenses related to the child's disability, including personal needs assistance, special equipment, housing modification, and therapy or rehabilitation. These earnings are not counted as income even after the child reaches age 18.[386]

11. *Payments from a crime victim's compensation fund.*[387]

12. *State relocation assistance.*[388]

How is the amount of an individual's SSI grant calculated?

As discussed above, eligibility for SSI and the amount of your grant are determined by comparing your countable income to the maximum SSI grant that a person in your category may receive. "Countable income" means total income minus exclusions and deductions. One set of exclusions and deductions applies to earned income and a different set of exclusions and deductions applies to unearned income. A worksheet with instructions that you can use to compute your SSI grant amount is provided in appendix A of this book.

What is an approved plan for achieving self-support?

If you are blind or disabled, you may ask the Social Security Administration to help you design a "plan for achieving self-support," also known as a PASS plan.[389] PASS plans are a wonderful and largely unused way for blind or disabled individuals to keep and accumulate income and savings while receiving SSI benefits. The goal of a PASS plan is to enable you to work again. For example, it might be possible that additional education, training, therapy, or resources would enable you to work and support yourself. If the Social Security Administration approves a PASS plan for you, it will allow you to set aside income or resources to carry out your plan (e.g., to pay tuition or set up a business). Income or resources set aside and used to fulfill an approved PASS plan are not counted in determining SSI eligibility or grant amount.

The Social Security Administration has set out several requirements for a plan to achieve self-support. A PASS plan will be approved only if it (a) is in writing; (b) is designed especially for you; (c) is designed for an initial period of no more than eighteen months (although the Social Security Administration may allow you to extend the program to a maximum of forty-eight months); (d) states your specific occupational goal (i.e., explains what job or work you hope to perform at the end of the plan); (e) states what income and/or resources you have and how they will be used to fulfill your plan; and (f) shows how the money used for the plan will be kept separate from your other funds.[390]

If an individual receives food, clothing, or shelter from a friend or relative, does that affect his or her eligibility for SSI?

If you receive food, clothing, or shelter that is paid for by another person, the Social Security Administration will count the value of those items as "in-kind income" in determining your eligibility for SSI and the amount of your grant.[391] ("Shelter" for these purposes includes room, rent, mortgage payments, property taxes, water, energy costs, sewerage, and garbage collection fees.)[392] There are two rules for determining the dollar value of food, clothing, or shelter that is given to you: the "one-third reduction rule" and the "presumed value rule."

The one-third reduction rule. The one-third reduction rule applies, with the important exceptions noted below, if you are living in the household of a person who pays for both your food *and* your shelter.[393] If the one-third reduction rule applies, the Social Security Administration will not attempt to calculate the actual dollar value of the food, clothing, and shelter given to you but will instead deem those items to be worth one-third of the federal benefit level and reduce your SSI grant by that amount.[394] In 1997, the federal benefit rate for an individual covered by the one-third reduction rule is $323 per month (the federal benefit level for an individual, $484 per month, minus one-third of that amount).

If the Social Security Administration uses the one-third reduction rule in your case, it will not count any other in-kind support or maintenance that you receive in calculating your SSI benefit.[395] This means that you can receive any amount of in-kind support and maintenance and there will be no additional effect on your eligibility for SSI or the size of your grant. However, cash that you receive will still be counted as income after application of the regular exclusions and deductions.[396]

Exceptions: The one-third reduction rule does *not* apply if the person who pays for your food and shelter is (a) your spouse; (b) a minor child; (c) your parent, if you are a minor and your parent is ineligible for SSI; or (d) another person who is ineligible for SSI and whose income may be "deemed" to you (e.g., a sponsor of a resident alien or an "essential person").[397] The one-third reduction rule also does not apply if (1) all members of the household in which you live receive some form of public cash assistance payments;[398] (2) you live in a "noninstitutional care situation" (e.g., foster care, family care, etc.);[399] (3) you pay at least a pro rata share of household operating expenses;[400] or (4) you, a spouse who lives with you, or any person whose income is deemed to you has an ownership interest in the home or is liable to the landlord for any part of the rent.[401]

The presumed value rule. The "presumed value rule" will be used if you receive in-kind support or maintenance (food, clothing, or shelter) and the "one-third reduction rule" does not apply to you.[402] Under the presumed value rule, the Social Security Administration assumes that the in-kind support or maintenance (food, clothing, or shelter) you receive is worth one-third of the federal benefit rate plus twenty dollars.[403] This amount is called the "presumed value." In 1997, one-third of the federal benefit rate is $161 per month, making the "presumed value" $181 ($161 plus $20).

If you agree that the in-kind support or maintenance you receive is worth at least as much as the presumed value, then that amount will be considered unearned income to you and used to determine your eligibility for SSI and the amount of your SSI grant. However, if you can show that the actual value of the food, clothing, and shelter you receive is less than the presumed value, the Social Security Administration will count only the actual value as income to you.[404]

You can show that the actual value of the food, clothing, and shelter you receive is less than the presumed value (1) by showing that the current market value of those items, minus any amount you paid for them, is less than the presumed value or (2) by showing that the actual amount someone else paid for your food, clothing, or shelter is less than the presumed value.[405]

Does the Social Security Administration ever count income received by a person's family members in determining the person's eligibility for SSI?

Under certain circumstances, the Social Security Administration will assume that another person's income is available for your support and maintenance and will count some of that person's income as though it were your own. This is called "deeming of income." Income that is "deemed" to you is considered in determining your eligibility for SSI and your grant amount.[406]

Income may be deemed to you in any of the following situations.

1. *Your spouse or "common law spouse" lives with you.* If your spouse lives with you, is ineligible for SSI, and has income other than public assistance, the Social Security Administration will look at the amount of your spouse's income to decide whether some of it must be deemed to you. For these purposes, "spouse" includes a person "who lives with you as your husband or wife" even if you are not formally married.[407]

2. *Your parent lives with you.* If you are under age 18 and you live with a parent who is ineligible for SSI and has income other than public assistance, the Social Security Administration will look at the amount of your parent's income to decide whether some of it must be deemed to you.[408] *Exception*: Your parents' income will not be deemed to you if (a) you previously received a reduced SSI benefit (i.e., a "personal needs allowance") while residing in a medical facility where more than 50 percent of the cost of your care was paid for by Medicaid; (b) you are eligible for Medicaid benefits for home care; and (c) deeming of your parents' income would make you ineligible for SSI or eligible for less than the SSI personal needs allowance (thirty dollars per month in 1996) plus any state supplement. If this exception applies, you are eligible for an SSI payment equal to the personal needs allowance plus any state supplement, reduced by your own countable income, if any.[409]

3. *You are an immigrant who has a sponsor.* If you are a lawful permanent resident of the United States (i.e., have a "green card") and an individual "sponsored" your application for permanent residence by signing
an affidavit agreeing to support you, the Social Security Administration
may "deem" some or all of your sponsor's income to be your income for
purposes of determining your eligibility for SSI. If your sponsor signed
an affidavit of support before the 1996 welfare act took effect,[410] the
sponsor's income may only be deemed to you during the first three years
that you have your green card[411] and will not be deemed to you at all if
(a) you became blind or disabled *after* your admission to the United
States;[412] (b) you were granted political asylum or refugee status;[413] or (c)
your sponsor was an organization, not an individual.[414] If your sponsor
signed the new kind of affidavit of support required by the 1996 welfare
act (the new affidavits must be used starting sometime between October
1996 and February 1997)[415] and your sponsor is an individual (not an
organization), all the income of your sponsor and his or her spouse will
be deemed to you until you become a United States citizen unless one of
the following exceptions applies.

First, your sponsor's income will not be deemed to you if you have
worked in the United States for the equivalent of forty qualifying quarters in the Social Security system, or if you can be credited with forty
quarters of coverage based on your work plus the work of your spouse
and/or parents. (Appendix C describes the forty-quarters rule in greater
detail.)

Second, your sponsor's income will not automatically be deemed to
you if you would be unable to afford food and shelter without SSI
benefits. In that case, the Social Security Administration will not use the
deeming rules for a period of twelve months and will only count the
income that your sponsor actually gives you. After twelve months, however, all of your sponsor's income will be deemed to you.

Third, sponsor income will not be deemed to you for a period of
twelve months if you or your child have been battered or subjected to
"extreme cruelty" in the United States by your spouse or parent (or by a
member of your spouse or parent's family while residing with you), and
the Social Security Administration decides that there is a "substantial
connection" between your need for public assistance and the battering
or cruelty. In addition, the batterer's income will never be deemed to you
(even after twelve months) if the battering or cruelty has been recognized in an administrative or judicial order (e.g., an order of protection

from family court) or in a determination by the Immigration and Naturalization Service (e.g., approval of a "battered spouse" waiver or self-petition), as long as the batterer is not now living with you.[416]

4. *You live with an "essential person."* If your SSI grant has been increased to meet the needs of an "essential person," the Social Security Administration will look at the amount of the essential person's income to decide whether some of it must be deemed to you.[417]

How much income can be deemed to an SSI claimant and used to determine his or her eligibility?

The Social Security Administration has adopted very technical rules for computing the amount of another person's income that may be deemed to you and used to determine your eligibility for SSI. If the Social Security Administration has deemed another person's income to you, either you or your representative should look at the full text of the deeming rules. These rules appear in Title 20 of the Code of Federal Regulations at sections 416.1160 through 416.1169 and are available for viewing at any Social Security office.

How much money or other resources can an individual have and still be eligible for SSI?

In order to qualify for SSI: the value of your countable resources may not exceed the maximum amounts set by law. In 1996 a single person could own countable resources worth up to $2,000 and still qualify for SSI. A married couple could own countable resources worth up to $3,000.[418]

"Resources" means cash, other liquid assets, and any other property that you or your spouse own and can convert to cash.[419] Cash or other property is considered "income" in the month you receive it and as a "resource" in later months that you own it. As discussed below, not all resources are counted in determining your eligibility for SSI. Certain items, such as your home, a car, and a burial fund of up to $1,500, are excluded. Any resources that are not excluded are countable resources.

What resources are excluded in determining eligibility for SSI?

The following items are not counted as resources in determining your eligibility for SSI:

1. *Your home.* Your home is not counted as a resource, regardless of how much it is worth.[420] Your home for these purposes is the house (or

co-op or condominium) that is your principal place of residence; you need not be living there currently, as long as you intend to return. If you are living in a nursing home or other institution, your house will not be counted as a resource, whether or not you intend to return, if your spouse or any other dependent lives there.

2. *Household goods and personal effects.* Up to $2,000 worth of household goods (e.g., furniture) and personal effects (e.g., clothing) is not counted as resources.[421] (In determining the worth of household goods and personal effects, the Social Security Administration looks at the equity value of those items. Equity value is the amount you could receive by selling an item, minus any amount you still owe for the item.) Also not counted as resources are one wedding ring and one engagement ring and any items "required because of a person's physical condition" (e.g., wheelchair, dialysis machine, hospital bed).[422]

3. *Automobile or other motor vehicle.* An automobile does not count as a resource, regardless of its value, if you or a member of your household (a) needs it for employment; (b) needs it to obtain medical treatment; (c) needs it (or another vehicle) for essential transportation because distance, terrain, climate, or similar factors make other forms of transportation impractical; or (d) are handicapped and the vehicle is modified for operation by or transportation of a handicapped person.[423]

An automobile not needed for one of the purposes described above is counted as a resource only if its current market value exceeds $4,500. The amount by which the value of the automobile exceeds $4,500 is counted as a resource.[424]

4. *Property used for self-support.* Up to $6,000 of your equity in property used to produce income (e.g., land, equipment, tools) is not counted as a resource.[425] In addition, up to $6,000 of your equity in property used to produce goods or services for your household (e.g., land, livestock, and equipment used to produce food for home consumption) is not counted as a resource.[426]

5. *Resources used for a plan to achieve self-support.* If you are blind or disabled, resources used to fulfill an approved plan to achieve self-support are not counted as resources.[427]

6. *Life insurance.* Life insurance policies do not count as resources if the total face value (the amount paid at death) for any insured person does not exceed $1,500. Term insurance and burial insurance are not considered in determining face value. If the life insurance you own exceeds this limit, the cash surrender value (the amount the insurance

company will pay you on cancellation of the policy) will be counted as a resource.[428]

7. *Burial plots and funds.* The value of burial spaces, crypts, headstones, containers, and similar items and services for you or members of your immediate family is not counted as a resource. Up to $1,500 per person, set aside from your other money and clearly designated for burial expenses for yourself or your spouse, will not count as a resource. If you set up a burial fund, the interest earned on that money does not count as a resource (even if the interest pushes the fund above $1,500), as long as you leave the interest in the burial fund.[429]

8. *Retroactive Social Security or SSI payments.* Retroactive Social Security or SSI payments are not counted as resources for six months from the date of receipt. In order to take advantage of this exclusion, you must keep records that allow you to distinguish your retroactive payments from your other money. At the end of six months, any part of the retroactive payments that you have not spent will count as a resource. Also, things that you purchase with the retroactive payments may immediately be counted as a resource if they are not exempt. For example, if you purchase stocks or bonds with your retroactive money, they will immediately count as resources.[430]

Retroactive SSI payments to a child under 18, and interest earned on those funds, are not counted as resources at all if the payments are placed in an account used solely for the child's educational and training expenses, medical expenses, and certain expenses related to the child's disability, including personal needs assistance, special equipment, housing modification, and therapy or rehabilitation. These funds are not counted as resources even after the child reaches age 18.[431]

9. *Certain benefit payments from other programs.* There are many programs that provide income or benefits to individuals and specify that such income or benefits may not be considered for determining SSI eligibility.[432] A list of benefits and payments that are not counted as resources for SSI purposes appears in Title 20 of the Code of Federal Regulations, at regulation 416.1236. The following are some examples of benefits and payments that do not count as resources. Note, however, that benefits and payments must be kept separate from your other money in order to be excluded as a resource.[433]

a. Food stamps;
b. WIC (Women, Infants and Children) food coupons;

   c. Federally donated foods;

   d. Meals provided under the School Lunch Program;

   e. Home Energy Assistance payments;

   f. Federal housing assistance;[434]

   g. Certain grants or loans to undergraduates made or insured through a program administered by the U.S. Secretary of Education;

   h. Distributions made to Native Americans from certain claim funds, judgments, and land trusts;

   i. Payments from the Agent Orange Settlement Fund;

   j. Payments made under section 6 of the Radiation Exposure Compensation Act;

   k. Assistance received on account of a major disaster.[435]

10. *Indian lands.* If you are a member of a federally recognized Indian tribe, land allotted to you that you cannot sell without the permission of other individuals, the tribe, or the federal government does not count as a resource.[436]

11. *Replacement of lost, damaged, or stolen excluded resources.* Cash or goods that you receive to replace or repair an excluded resource (e.g., cash received to repair your home) do not count as resources.[437]

Can an individual reduce his or her countable resources in order to qualify for SSI?

Yes. If you have countable resources that exceed the SSI program's limits, you can still become eligible for SSI by reducing the value of those resources. There are several ways to do this.

1. *Transfer the resources.* You may give away cash and/or other property in order to bring your countable resources within the SSI program limits.[438] Note, however, that giving away resources to your spouse or to your parent (if you are a minor child) will not make you eligible for SSI because the resources of spouses are deemed available to each other and the resources of a parent are deemed available to his or her minor children. You should also bear in mind that giving away resources may result in your being temporarily disqualified from receiving Medicaid for nursing home or other long-term care. (This is discussed in the Medicaid section of chapter 3 of this book.) Finally, you should keep records

of the resources that you give away because the Social Security Administration may ask you to prove that you no longer own them.

2. *Spend the resources or convert them into excluded resources.* Another way to bring your countable resources within the SSI limits is to spend them on things that do not count as resources. You may, for instance, spend countable resources on living expenses, educational expenses, or to repay debts. You may also become eligible for SSI by using countable resources to purchase other resources that are not counted in determining SSI eligibility. For instance, cash in a bank account (a countable resource) may be used to purchase a motor vehicle, or to purchase a home, or to pay down a mortgage on your existing residence. Since your home and an automobile are generally not considered countable resources, purchasing these items reduces your countable resources and can bring you within the SSI limit. Again, make sure to keep receipts or other records of the resources you spend, because the Social Security Administration may ask for such proof.

3. *Transfer the resources into a "supplemental needs trust."* You may also transfer resources into a discretionary trust established solely for your benefit. This type of trust is commonly known as a "supplemental needs trust" and is usually designed to pay for goods and services not covered by government benefits. A supplemental needs trust would thus pay for needs other than food, clothing, and shelter (covered by SSI) or medical care (covered by Medicaid). The trust could also pay for basic necessities—such as shelter costs—but this might result in a one-third reduction of your SSI grant. Money placed in a qualifying trust does not count as a resource for purposes of SSI eligibility.[439]

There are several advantages to transferring your excess resources into a trust instead of giving the money away. If the money is placed into a supplemental needs trust, it will be used to purchase goods and services that benefit you directly and improve your quality of life. In addition, transferring excess resources into a properly structured trust not only allows you to qualify for SSI, but also may allow you to qualify for Medicaid.[440] By comparison, if you simply give away your excess resources, you may become ineligible for Medicaid for a period of time.

There are a few disadvantages to transferring resources into a supplemental needs trust. First, a trust document must be drafted, which normally requires the assistance of a legal professional. Second, a trustee is needed to manage the trust property and the trustee should not give you cash directly from the trust—since this would count as income and reduce your SSI grant—but should instead purchase the goods and services that you need. Finally, if the trust is established so that you can qualify for Medicaid, any amount remaining in the trust at your death will be used first to repay the Medicaid program for medical assistance received during your lifetime.

4. *Sell your nonliquid resources.* The Social Security Administration counts resources differently depending upon whether the resources are "liquid" or "nonliquid." Liquid resources means cash or other resources that you can convert to cash within twenty days. All other resources are nonliquid (real estate, machinery, and buildings are some examples of nonliquid resources).

If your liquid countable resources do not exceed one-quarter of the SSI resource limit, you can receive SSI payments even though your *total* countable resources (liquid plus nonliquid) are more than the SSI limit.[441] The catch is that you must agree to sell the nonliquid countable resources that exceed the SSI limit and use the proceeds to repay the SSI benefits you received during the months you owned excess resources.[442] If you choose this option, you will be given three to six months to sell personal property and an unlimited time to sell real estate, as long as you are making "reasonable efforts" to sell.[443] (Remember, though, that real estate used as your primary residence does not count as a resource, regardless of its value. The value of your primary residence may never be the reason for denying you SSI, and you may not be required to sell your primary residence.) If you are unable to sell your real estate within nine months despite reasonable efforts, you can continue receiving SSI payments and the Social Security Administration will make you repay only nine months of SSI benefits when the real estate is finally sold.[444]

Do the resources of other persons ever count in determining an individual's eligibility for SSI?

Yes. Under certain circumstances, the Social Security Administration will assume that another person's resources are available for your support and maintenance and will count those resources as though they were your own. This is called "deeming of resources." Resources that are "deemed" to you are considered in determining your eligibility for SSI.[445]

Resources may be deemed to you in any of the following situations. In all of these situations, only "countable resources" can be deemed available to you. "Excluded resources" are never considered in determining SSI eligibility.

1. *Your spouse lives with you.* If your spouse lives with you and is ineligible for SSI, all of your spouse's countable resources, except any pension funds he or she may own, will be deemed to you.[446] For these purposes, "spouse" includes a person who lives with you as your husband or wife, even if you are not formally married.[447]

2. *Your parent lives with you.* If you are under age 18 and you live with a parent who is ineligible for SSI, some of your parent's countable resources may be deemed to you. If you live with one parent, the amount by which your parent's countable resources exceed the SSI limit for an individual will be deemed to you. (In 1996 the SSI resource limit for an individual was $2,000.) If you live with two parents, the amount by which your parents' countable resources exceed the SSI limit for a couple will be deemed to you. (In 1996 the SSI resource limit for a couple was $3,000.) Note, however, that any pension funds your parents own do not count as resources for deeming purposes and may not be deemed to you.[448] Your parents' resources will not be deemed to you if (a) you previously received a reduced SSI benefit (i.e., a personal needs allowance) while residing in a medical facility where more than 50 percent of the cost of your care was paid for by Medicaid, (b) you are eligible for Medicaid benefits for home care, and (c) deeming of your parents' resources would result in your being ineligible for SSI. If this exception applies, you are eligible for an SSI payment equal to the personal needs allowance plus any state supplement, reduced by your own countable income, if any.[449]

3. *You are an immigrant who has a sponsor.* If you are a lawful permanent resident of the United States (i.e., have a "green card") and an individual "sponsored" your application for permanent residence by signing an affidavit agreeing to support you, then some or all of the sponsor's resources may be deemed to you.[450] If your sponsor signed the affidavit of support before the deeming provisions of the 1996 welfare act took effect sometime between October 1996 and February 1997,[451] then any countable resources the sponsor owns in excess of the SSI limit may be deemed to you during the first three years that you have your green card[452] but will not be deemed to you at all if (a) you became blind or disabled after your admission to the United States,[453] (b) you were

granted political asylum or refugee status,[454] or (c) your sponsor was an organization, not an individual.[455] If your sponsor signed the new kind of affidavit of support required by the 1996 welfare act (the new affidavits must be used starting sometime between October 1996 and February 1997)[456] and your sponsor is an individual (not an organization), then any resources owned by your sponsor and his or her spouse will be deemed to you until you become a U.S. citizen unless one of the following exceptions applies.

First, your sponsor's resources will not be deemed to you if you have worked in the United States for the equivalent of forty qualifying quarters in the Social Security system or if you can be credited with forty quarters of coverage based on your work plus the work of your spouse and/or parents. (Appendix C describes the forty-quarters rule in greater detail.)

Second, your sponsor's resources will not automatically be deemed to you if you would be unable to afford food and shelter without SSI benefits. In that case, the Social Security Administration will not use the deeming rules for a period of twelve month and will only count the resources that your sponsor actually gives you. After twelve months, however, all of your sponsor's resources will be deemed to you.

Third, sponsor resources will not be deemed to you for a period of twelve months if you or your child have been battered or subjected to "extreme cruelty" in the United States by your spouse or parent (or by a member of your spouse or parent's family while residing with you), and the Social Security Administration decides that there is a "substantial connection" between your need for public assistance and the battering or cruelty. In addition, the batterer's resources will never be deemed to you (even after twelve months) if the battering or cruelty has been recognized in an administrative or judicial order (e.g., an order of protection from family court) or in a determination by the Immigration and Naturalization Service (e.g., approval of a "battered spouse" waiver or self-petition), as long as the batterer is not now living with you.[457]

4. *You live with an essential person.* If your SSI grant has been increased to meet the needs of an "essential person," the Social Security Administration will deem your countable resources to include the countable resources of that essential person.[458] If the resources deemed from the essential person make you ineligible for SSI, the Social Security Administration will remove the person from consideration, so that the extra resources will not be counted and you can qualify for benefits.

How do I apply for SSI?

To apply for SSI, you must fill out and sign an application form, and the form must be filed at a Social Security Administration office. Application forms can be obtained at any Social Security office. To locate the office nearest you or to arrange for an appointment, you may call the Social Security Administration's toll-free teleservice number, 1-800-772-1213. Local Social Security offices may also be found in the government listings of the telephone book.

If the person applying for SSI is under age 18, mentally incompetent, or physically unable to sign the application, the Social Security Administration will accept an application signed by a responsible relative or other responsible person. You do not have to go to the Social Security office yourself in order to file an application; a relative, friend, or other person can bring the completed form to the Social Security office for you.[459] You may also mail your completed application form to the Social Security Administration, but it is generally better to have your application submitted by hand in order to avoid any problem with lost or misplaced mail.

Does the date of an SSI application affect the amount of benefits the applicant receives?

Yes. If you are eligible for SSI, you will be paid benefits starting the first day of the month after the date you filed your application. If you did not meet all the eligibility criteria for SSI on the first day of the month after you applied, you will be paid benefits beginning on the day you first became eligible.[460]

Normally, the date used for determining the month that your SSI benefits begin is the date your application is filed at a Social Security office. However, there are some important exceptions:

Mailed applications. If you mail your application to the Social Security Administration, the postmark counts as the application date.[461]

Oral or written inquiries. If you, your spouse, or other responsible relative or person calls or writes to the Social Security Administration to ask about your eligibility for SSI, the Social Security Administration will send a notice explaining the need to file an application form. If you file an application form within sixty days of the date on this notice, the date of your original call or letter counts as the date of your application.[462]

Deemed application date based on misinformation. If you failed to file an application for SSI because of incomplete, misleading, or inaccurate information provided by an employee of the Social Security Administration, the date you received the misinformation can count as your date of application.[463] For this to happen, you must notify the Social Security office that you did not apply earlier because an agency employee gave you or your representative misinformation about your eligibility.

How long does it take the Social Security Administration to make a decision on an SSI application?

The law does not set any limit on the amount of time the Social Security Administration can take to decide a claim for SSI disability benefits. A wait of two to four months, or more, from application to initial decision is not unusual.

Can an applicant receive SSI benefits while his or her application is being processed?

In cases where it is readily apparent that an SSI applicant is disabled or blind, the Social Security Administration may find the individual "presumptively disabled" and pay benefits for up to six months while the application is being processed.[464] Some examples of the many medical conditions that may warrant a finding of "presumptive disability" include AIDS or symptomatic HIV infection, amputation of two limbs, total deafness or blindness, and severe mental deficiency.[465]

How does the Social Security Administration notify an SSI claimant when it makes a decision on his or her case?

The Social Security Administration must give you written notice of any action it takes on your case. If the Social Security Administration decides to deny your application, it must give you a written notice stating the reasons for the denial and explaining your right to appeal.[466] If the Social Security Administration decides that your SSI payments should be reduced or terminated, it must give you advance written notice so that you will have an opportunity to appeal the decision before any reduction or termination of your benefits.[467] This notice must also state the reason for the proposed action and tell you how to appeal.

Is there a right to appeal decisions that affect eligibility for SSI?

Yes. You have a right to appeal any negative action that affects your eligibility for SSI or the amount of your SSI payment.[468] In most cases it is worthwhile to file an appeal. The Social Security Administration is a large bureaucracy and it frequently makes mistakes. In 1993, for instance, nearly

68 percent of the people who appealed their claims to an administrative law judge were awarded benefits.[469] Keep in mind that there are time limits for making an appeal. In general, you must file your appeal within sixty days of the date you receive written notice of a negative action. The appeals process is described more fully below.

How does the appeals process work?

There are three levels of appeal within the Social Security Administration.

First, if your application is denied, or your benefits are reduced or terminated, you may ask the agency to reconsider its decision; this is called a "request for reconsideration."

Second, if the decision after reconsideration is still against you, you may request a hearing before an administrative law judge.

Third, if the administrative law judge does not decide in your favor, you may appeal to the Social Security Administration's Appeals Council.

If you win at any level of appeal, that is the end of the appeal process; you will be given the benefits you requested, and there is no need to proceed to the next level of appeal. If you lose at all three levels, you are entitled to appeal your case to federal court.

How is an appeal filed?

To file an appeal at any level—reconsideration, administrative law judge hearing, or appeals council—you must submit a written request for the appeal to a Social Security office. All Social Security offices have forms that you can fill out to request an appeal and you should use those forms if possible.[470] If that is not possible, you may request an appeal by letter. When filing an appeal by letter, be sure to include your Social Security number and a description of the decision that you wish to appeal.

What is the time limit for filing an appeal?

In general, you have sixty days from the date you receive an unfavorable decision to file an appeal. This is true whether you are requesting reconsideration, a hearing before an administrative law judge, or an appeals council review. If you are a current SSI recipient and you appeal a decision to reduce, suspend, or terminate your benefits within ten days of receiving notice of the proposed action, you will receive full benefit payments without interruption while the appeal is being decided.[471]

It is assumed that you receive a written notice from the Social Security

Administration five days after the date on the notice, unless you are able to prove that you actually received the notice on a later date.[472] *To be safe, therefore, you should make sure to file your appeal no later than sixty-five days (the sixty-day limit plus the five-day presumed mailing time) from the date on the notice of an unfavorable decision.* Indeed, it makes sense to file your appeal well in advance of the sixty-day limit to avoid any dispute about timeliness. If at any level of the appeal process, you receive an unfavorable decision and you do not file an appeal to the next level within the sixty-day time limit, you will lose your right to any further administrative appeal (and may lose the right to take your case to federal court) unless you can show that you had a good reason for not filing on time.

Can an appeal be filed after the sixty-day time limit is over?

You should make every possible effort to file your appeal on time because in most cases failure to do so means that you will lose your right to appeal. Under limited circumstances, however, appeals may be filed after the sixty-day deadline if you can show that you had good cause for not filing an appeal on time.[473] Examples of good reasons for missing the appeal deadline include: (1) you had a serious illness that kept you from filing on time; (2) there was a death or serious illness in your immediate family; (3) the Social Security Administration did not give you accurate information about when and how to file an appeal; (4) you asked the Social Security Administration for more information about a decision within the sixty-day limit and delayed filing your appeal until after receiving a response; (5) there were other "unusual or unavoidable circumstances" that prevented you from filing an appeal on time; or (6) other factors, such as physical or mental incapacity or limited ability to read, write, or understand English, "prevented you from filing a timely [appeal] or from knowing or understanding the need to file a timely [appeal]."[474]

Your request for additional time to appeal must be made in writing and must describe your reason for not filing an appeal within the sixty-day limit.

What happens at the reconsideration level of appeal?

Reconsideration is the first level of appeal. The Social Security Administration has established four procedures for deciding reconsideration requests: case review, informal conference, formal conference, and disability hearing. The procedure used in your case depends upon the type of decision that you are appealing. If you are an applicant for SSI and your application is denied on medical grounds (e.g., it is decided that you are not disabled), you receive a case review.[475] If you are an applicant for SSI and you request reconsideration on a non-medical issue (e.g., a decision that your countable income is above the SSI limit), you may choose either a case review or an informal conference.[476] If you already receive SSI and are appealing a decision to reduce, suspend, or terminate your benefits, you may choose a case review, an informal conference, or a formal conference.[477] If the reason given for stopping your benefits is that you are no longer blind or disabled for medical reasons, you may also choose to have a disability hearing.[478]

Case review. In a case review, you will be given a chance to examine your Social Security Administration files, to provide any additional written evidence you have, and to discuss your case with the SSA official who will do the reconsideration. That official will then make a decision based on any information that you provide and the information already in your file.[479]

Informal conference. At an informal conference, you will be given a chance to examine your file, to present any additional written evidence you may have, and to bring witnesses to testify on your behalf. The official conducting the informal conference must make a written record of the proceeding and include that record in your file. The official who conducts the conference will make a decision based on the evidence presented and any information already in the file.[480]

Formal conference. A formal conference works the same way as an informal conference, except that you may also ask the Social Security Administration to subpoena (i.e., to order the appearance of) witnesses and documents to help you prove your case, and you will be given a chance to cross-examine any witnesses whose testimony is not favorable to you.[481]

Disability hearing. If you request a disability hearing, the Social Security Administration must review your file and make sure that the medical evidence is complete and up-to-date. You may request that the Social Security Administration assist you in obtaining any relevant medical information and may also submit whatever additional evidence you have.[482] A hearing will then be conducted by a "disability hearing officer," a government employee who has been trained to examine and evaluate medical evidence. At the hearing, you have all the procedural rights of a formal conference, including the right to have the Social Security Administration subpoena documents and witnesses.[483]

Can an unfavorable reconsideration decision be appealed?

Yes. If you are not satisfied with the reconsideration decision, you may request a hearing before an administrative law judge (ALJ). As discussed

above, you have sixty days from the date you receive a reconsideration decision to file a request for a hearing.

How are claimants notified of the time and place of the hearing?

If you request a hearing before an administrative law judge, the Social
Security Administration will mail you a notice announcing the time and
place of the hearing. The notice will be mailed at least twenty days before
the hearing is scheduled.[484] Hearings are usually scheduled two to four
months after a request for a hearing is filed. You may request that the time
and/or place of the hearing be changed, and the request should be granted
if you have a good reason. For instance, the ALJ should grant a request to
postpone the hearing if you need more time to find a representative, or if
you recently located a representative and she or he needs more time to prepare for the hearing, or if a witness with important evidence is unable to
attend the hearing at the scheduled time.[485]

What happens at a hearing before an administrative law judge?

The ALJ is a lawyer employed by the Social Security Administration's
Office of Hearings and Appeals. He or she will conduct your hearing and is
required by law to pursue and develop all of the evidence that is relevant to
deciding your appeal.[486] ALJ hearings typically take place in small hearing
rooms equipped with microphones and tape machines to record the proceedings. Typically, the only people present at the hearing are the ALJ, the
ALJ's clerk, you, your representative (if you have one), and any witnesses. In
almost all cases, the ALJ will ask you a series of questions about the facts
relating to your claim.

You have a number of important procedural rights at this stage of the
appeals process. As always, you have the right to examine and make copies
of your file and any evidence that the Social Security Administration relied
upon in deciding your case. You have the right to submit additional evidence and to have that evidence included in your file and considered by the
ALJ. You have the right to bring witnesses to the hearing and to have them
testify on your behalf. You have the right to question any witness who gives
testimony unfavorable to your claim. You are entitled to make a statement
at the hearing, or submit a written statement, explaining your position. If
the Social Security Administration plans to have a medical expert or vocational expert testify at your hearing, it should notify you of that fact in
advance. If you make a request at least five days before your hearing, the

Social Security Administration will issue subpoenas ordering witnesses with relevant information (e.g., a doctor who treated you) to testify, and/or ordering that relevant documents (e.g., hospital records) be delivered to the hearing. You are entitled to bring an attorney or other person to the hearing to represent you. The Social Security Administration must tape record the hearing so that there will be a complete and accurate record of the testimony and statements made. At the conclusion of the hearing, you may ask the ALJ for time to obtain and submit additional evidence to support your claim.[487] The ALJ will prepare a written decision and mail a copy of the decision to you. The ALJ must issue the decision within ninety days of your request for a hearing unless you requested a postponement of the hearing or the question to be decided was whether you are disabled.[488]

What should be done to prepare for a hearing before an Administrative Law Judge?

Although Social Security hearings are set up so that individuals can present their own cases, you should make every effort to obtain an attorney or other experienced advocate to represent you at the hearing. Such advocates can work with your doctors or other medical care providers to obtain persuasive evidence of your disability. They are very familiar with the rules governing SSI eligibility and the kinds of evidence you need to win your case. Most legal aid and legal services offices have attorneys and paralegals who are experts at representing SSI claimants. You should seek assistance from the office in your area right away. If assistance is not available from a legal aid or legal services office, those offices should be able to give you a referral list of other agencies or individuals who may be able to help. Because the process of finding an advocate to represent you may take some time, you should start looking for one as soon as you decide to request a hearing before an administrative law judge. If you have not located an advocate by the time you receive the notice announcing the date of your hearing, you may ask the ALJ to postpone the hearing to give you more time to find a representative.[489]

At the same time you are looking for an advocate, there are things that you should do to prepare for the hearing in case you must represent yourself. You should immediately begin to gather evidence to support your claim. For instance, if the question to be decided at the hearing is whether or not you are disabled, you should obtain reports from the doctors who have treated you to prove that your medical condition prevents you from working. The

Social Security Administration is required to give great weight to a thorough report from your treating physician. Sample report forms that your doctor can use are included in appendix B of this book.

You should also review the file that the Social Security Administration has compiled for use at your hearing. This file should be available for viewing and copying at the Social Security Hearing office where your hearing will be held. The file contains the evidence that the Social Security Administration relied on to deny your claim. If the file is missing important evidence—records of a hospitalization, for instance—you should immediately request in writing that the ALJ issue a subpoena requiring the holder of the missing evidence to provide you and the judge with copies.[490] (Requests for subpoenas must be made in writing no later than five days before the hearing.) In addition, you may want to obtain other evidence or locate witnesses for the hearing to contest any unfavorable evidence that is in your file. You should meet with any witnesses well in advance of the hearing, both to discuss their testimony and to determine if they will come to the hearing voluntarily. If you believe that an important witness may not come to the hearing willingly, you should ask the ALJ in writing to issue a subpoena ordering the witness to appear. (When a subpoena is issued, the Social Security Administration will pay the witness the same fees and transportation expenses that would be paid by a federal court.)[491]

Finally, you should think carefully about your own testimony. The ALJ will ask you a series of questions at the hearing and your answers may provide some of the most important evidence in your case. For instance, if the issue to be decided is whether or not you are disabled, the ALJ will ask you about your medical conditions and how those conditions limit your ability to function. You will also be asked to describe your daily activities, whether you are able to do household chores, shop for groceries, take public transportation, engage in hobbies, etc. The ALJ asks about your daily activities to determine whether you are able to function sufficiently to hold a job. You should be ready to describe in detail all the symptoms of your illness, including pain and any side effects of medication or treatment, and how those symptoms have limited your regular activities. Be prepared to describe how your medical conditions limit your ability to do basic work activities, such as like lifting, carrying, pulling, pushing, reaching, handling, standing, walking, seeing, hearing, speaking, understanding, carrying out and remembering instructions, and working with others in a regular job setting.

You should also be prepared to explain in detail how your illness prevents you from doing any of the jobs that you have held in the past.

Can an unfavorable administrative law judge decision be appealed?

Yes. If you disagree with the ALJ's ruling, you have sixty days from receipt of the ALJ's decision to request review by the appeals council. A form for requesting appeals council review is available at any Social Security office and your request for review may be submitted to any Social Security office. If you have any additional evidence that you want the appeals council to consider, you may submit it with your request for review.[492]

The appeals council is based in Arlington, Virginia, and is composed of administrative law judges employed by the Social Security Administration. The appeals council accepts only a very small percentage of cases for review and usually rules against the claimant. Nevertheless, with a few exceptions discussed in the next question, you must file a timely request for appeals council review and receive an unfavorable decision before you can take your case to federal court.

Can an unfavorable appeals council decision be challenged in court?

Yes. You may file an action in the federal district court within sixty days of receiving an unfavorable decision from the appeals council. It is best to have the assistance of an attorney to file the lawsuit, but many claimants bring their cases to court without the help of a lawyer. Many federal district courts have a clerk's office with staff whose job is to help unrepresented individuals file their cases in court (this is sometimes called the "pro se" office). You should seriously consider appealing your case to federal court even if you do not have a lawyer because the courts frequently overturn decisions of the Social Security Administration. Indeed, the federal courts have criticized the Social Security Administration on many occasions for denying or terminating SSI benefits in violation of federal law.

As noted above, the general rule is that you may not bring your SSI claim to court until after you have received an adverse initial decision and have gone through all three levels of administrative appeal (reconsideration, ALJ hearing, and appeals council review). However, an exception to this rule may be made if you are claiming that a regulation, policy, or procedure of the Social Security Administration is illegal or unconstitutional or that a provision of the Social Security Act violates the federal Constitution. In these circumstances, it may be possible to file an action directly in federal court without first going through the administrative appeals process.[493] Contact a legal aid or legal services office if you believe that the Social Security Administration has violated a federal law or the federal Constitution in your case.

Do SSI claimants receive benefits during an appeal?

Maybe. If you apply for SSI and your application is denied, you will not receive SSI payments while you appeal the denial. (You may, however, be eligible for other cash benefits, such as Temporary Assistance to Needy Families or General Assistance.) If you win the case on appeal, you will receive benefits retroactive to the date of your application. If you appeal a decision to reduce, suspend, or terminate your SSI benefits, you have the right to continue receiving your full SSI payment while your appeal is being decided, but you must act quickly to claim this right. To continue receiving your regular SSI payment, you must appeal within ten days of receiving a notice of intent to reduce or terminate your benefits.[494]

GENERAL ASSISTANCE

What is General Assistance?

General Assistance is cash assistance provided to poor individuals who are not eligible for federal relief such as AFDC, Temporary Assistance for Needy Families block grant benefits, or SSI. It is a residual program of last resort and funded completely by state and local government. Some states call their General Assistance programs by other names—for example, Home Relief (New York); Poor Relief (Indiana); and Emergency Aid to the Elderly, Disabled, and Children (Massachusetts). States and localities have broad discretion in the design and administration of their General Assistance programs, but must comply with the equal protection and due process guarantees of the United States Constitution. How to apply for benefits and how much assistance a poor person receives depend on where the applicant lives and how the local program is administered.[495]

Because of the repeal of the AFDC program and its replacement with the Temporary Assistance for Needy Families block grant, as well as cut backs to the SSI and food stamp programs, many impoverished persons may find themselves over the coming years without any federal source of subsistence support. This situation will create extreme pressure on states and localities to provide General Assistance to poor people who are unable to find jobs or are unable to work. Vigorous advocacy is essential to ensure that states meet their moral and political responsibilities to impoverished residents.[496]

Do all states have General Assistance programs?

No. Statewide General Assistance programs exist in only twenty-two states.[497] Ten states do not have statewide programs but require every county to have a General Assistance program.[498] In ten other states, General Assistance programs exist in at least one county.[499] Eight states have no General Assistance program in any county or any part of the state.[500]

Even before passage of the 1996 federal welfare act, many states had cut back their General Assistance programs, by eliminating the program entirely, reducing benefit levels, or denying benefits to certain categories of needy applicants. For example, in 1996 Pennsylvania ended its General Assistance program for able-bodied, childless individuals.[501]

States frequently try to justify cutbacks in General Assistance programs on the ground that relief deters employable people from working. The empirical evidence, however, shows that individuals who are barred from General Assistance programs often are not able to obtain long-term employment despite serious efforts to find work. A 1989 study of General Assistance cuts in Pennsylvania, for example, found that a majority of those who had lost relief because of caseload reductions could not find a job within twelve months of termination of their benefits.[502] Similarly, a 1992 study of General Assistance cuts in Cleveland, Ohio found that only 17.3 percent of former recipients were able to find jobs three to six months after losing benefits.[503] Those who advocate slashing General Assistance and forcing the poor to work do not take sufficient account of the realities of the current labor market.[504]

Loss of General Assistance can mean extreme hardship for impoverished individuals left without any safety net.[505] A study of Pennsylvania's General Assistance program found that many persons who were cut for budget reasons from the relief rolls became homeless.[506] A similar analysis of Michigan's program found that 36 percent of the poor people dropped from General Assistance—20,000 individuals—were evicted because they could not pay rent.[507] In addition, some of the elderly poor faced extreme medical emergencies because they did not have money to buy medicine.[508] Many policy analysts have questioned whether the private, nonprofit sector will be able to fill the gap created by the government's withholding of subsistence support.

Who can apply for General Assistance?

Anyone can apply for General Assistance, but relief is generally limited to narrow categories of poor people who are not eligible for federal welfare. A poor person who needs to apply should check with a legal services or legal aid lawyer to find out what the specific application procedures are in his or her locality. The local welfare office is required to provide an application and also assistance in answering the questions.

Despite differences in procedures at the local level, the application process in most states shares many features. Based on rights derived from the Fourteenth Amendment to the federal Constitution, all General Assistance applicants and recipients are entitled to equal treatment and fair procedures. State law may also provide additional protection.

The right to equal treatment means that similarly situated individuals have to be treated the same, and a welfare officer cannot deny benefits for arbitrary reasons that are unrelated to the applicant's economic needs. In particular, an applicant cannot be denied relief because of race, sex, color, or religion. The right to fair procedure also affords many different protections. An applicant has a right to know the rules that govern the General Assistance program in his or her region, and these rules should be determinate and in writing.[509] The applicant has a right to have the welfare office take his or her application and give a decision within a reasonable time.[510] And if the application is denied or benefits are reduced or terminated, the agency has to give a written explanation of its decision and afford an opportunity for the applicant or recipient to challenge the action at a fair hearing.[511]

Who is eligible for General Assistance?

General Assistance is a residual program of last resort for individuals who are destitute but not eligible for federal assistance. Whether a poor person receives General Assistance depends on the specific eligibility requirements that govern the program in his or her region. As in all welfare programs, eligibility is limited to individuals who meet strict income requirements. In statewide programs, the income limits are generally fixed. In many countywide programs, there is no set income limit, and eligibility is instead determined on a case-by-case basis. Income tests vary considerably from state to state and county to county. In Delaware, for example, the income limit for an individual is $123; in Washington, the limit is $339.[512]

In addition to an income test, most General Assistance programs limit the assets that a person can own while receiving relief. As a general rule, assets include all bank accounts, but exclude (though sometimes only partially) the value of a home, car, or personal belongings. In almost half the states, a recipient is allowed to own fewer assets for the General Assistance program than for AFDC.

Some states also limit eligibility to individuals who meet special requirements. All General Assistance programs provide payments to disabled individuals who are waiting for their SSI applications to be approved. Some programs also provide payments to persons who are temporarily disabled or to unemployable individuals who have no skills. Still other programs provide only emergency relief, limited to families facing an urgent crisis, such as a flood or fire.

Persons with Disabilities. In all forty-two states that have some kind of General Assistance program, persons with disabilities are eligible for benefits. The disability must be verified by a doctor. Some states, however, limit the benefits that even persons in this category can receive. There are two major limitations.

- Benefits are provided only to persons whose disability is expected to last for a certain period of time.[513]
- Benefits are provided only to persons who are waiting for their SSI applications to be decided. It often takes a long time for an SSI application to be processed. In all states with General Assistance programs, benefits are provided to disabled persons who have applied for SSI but who are waiting for their benefits to start.[514]

Families with Children. Twenty-five states provide General Assistance (either statewide or in specific counties) to families with children that are not eligible for AFDC. In general, these programs have been limited to families and children that are not eligible for AFDC. With the repeal of the AFDC program, General Assistance for families with children may become an extremely important source of subsistence relief for thousands of indigent households.[515]

Pregnant Women. Some states and counties provide General Assistance under certain conditions to pregnant women. The pregnancy must be verified by a doctor. In general, relief has been limited to women who are not eligible for AFDC. Arizona, for example, has provided benefits to pregnant women in their final trimester who are not eligible for AFDC. Other states, such as Maryland, have provided General Assistance pending determination of the pregnant woman's AFDC application. Still other states have made relief available to any pregnant woman who is not eligible for AFDC. It is likely that restrictions of this sort will continue with respect to benefits under the federally funded Temporary Assistance for Needy Families block grant.

Employable Adults. Unemployed adults without children are eligible for General Assistance in eight statewide programs and eleven county programs.[516]

Can noncitizens receive General Assistance?

Maybe. Twenty-five years ago, in a case called *Graham v. Richardson*, the United States Supreme Court invalidated state laws that barred legal immigrants from public assistance programs.[517] The Court ruled that state discrimination against legal immigrants violates the equal protection guarantee of the Fourteenth Amendment to the United States Constitution. Thus, before passage of the Personal Responsibility and Work Opportunity Reconciliation Act of 1996—the so-called welfare reform act—it was settled law that a state had to make General Assistance available to lawful permanent residents ("green card" holders) and to certain other legal immigrants on the same basis as U.S. citizens.

The 1996 welfare act has made this question more complicated. Among the many anti-immigrant provisions of the law is a section that authorizes states to disqualify most legal immigrants from state General Assistance programs.[518] Immigrant categories that states may *not* bar from General Assistance are:

1. Refugees, political asylees, and immigrants whose deportation has been withheld,[519] but only during their first five years in the United States.[520]

2. Lawful permanent residents who have worked in the United States for the equivalent of forty qualifying quarters in the Social Security system or who can otherwise be credited with forty quarters because

of work done by a spouse or parents.[521] Quarters of work creditable to an immigrant's parents while the immigrant was a minor and quarters creditable to the immigrant's spouse during their marriage count toward the forty required.[522] (Appendix C to this book describes in greater detail how the forty quarters rule works.)

3. Active-duty members of the U.S. armed forces and honorably discharged veterans and their spouses or unmarried dependent children if lawfully residing in the United States.[523]

4. Any other category of immigrant that is not barred from federal programs comparable to General Assistance. Federal law does not specify which federal programs are to be considered "comparable" to General Assistance, but advocates should argue that this provision of law requires states to include in their General Assistance programs any category of immigrant that qualifies for SSI, Temporary Assistance for Needy Families benefits, or food stamps.[524]

The 1996 welfare act allows states to deny General Assistance to all other immigrants, including long-term legal residents. Even with federal authorization, though, state laws that bar legal immigrants from General Assistance should be ruled unconstitutional. Indeed, the Supreme Court addressed this very issue in *Graham v. Richardson*, ruling that states may not discriminate against legal immigrants in ways that violate the Constitution's equal protection guarantee, even if Congress has authorized such discrimination.[525]

The 1996 welfare act also permits states to use federal "sponsor deeming" rules in determining new immigrants' eligibility for General Assistance.[526] "Sponsor deeming" means that all the income and resources of the immigrant's sponsor (and the sponsor's spouse) are added to the immigrant's own income and resources for purposes of assessing eligibility and grant amount—whether or not the immigrant actually receives any financial support from his or her sponsor. In most instances, this form of deeming will result in the immigrant being declared ineligible for relief, since the addition of two incomes—even very inadequate ones—will normally exceed the General Assistance program's eligibility limits. Federal law authorizes states to apply this deeming rule only in cases of immigrants whose sponsors signed the special affidavit of support prescribed by the 1996 welfare act.[527] (The law requires that the new affidavits be used starting sometime between

October 1996 and February 1997.)[528] Federal law also appears to require that states offer the same exceptions to the deeming rule as appear in "comparable" federal programs, such as SSI and Temporary Assistance for Needy Families.[529] (These exceptions are described in earlier sections of this chapter dealing with the Temporary Assistance for Needy Families Block Grant and with Supplemental Security Income.)

The "sponsor deeming" rule will likely face constitutional challenges. Before the passage of the 1996 welfare act, several courts held that sponsor deeming in General Assistance programs amounts to unconstitutional discrimination against legal immigrants.[530] Now that federal law authorizes states to practice this sort of discrimination, courts will likely be called upon to address the issue again and should find that these measures violate the constitutional guarantee of equal protection. Moreover, in states where courts have ruled that legal immigrants have a state constitutional right to subsistence benefits, federal authorization to impose deeming rules or other discriminatory eligibility restrictions should be held to be without any force whatever.[531]

Can a poor person who has just moved to a state still receive General Assistance?

Yes. Twenty-five years ago, in the landmark case of *Shapiro v. Thompson*,[532] the United States Supreme Court struck down a state law that denied welfare assistance to applicants who had not lived in the state for one year. Although *Shapiro* involved AFDC, its principle was subsequently extended to county medical assistance in *Memorial Hospital v. Maricopa County*.[533] Under the *Shapiro* rule, states and localities may not deny welfare benefits of any kind to new residents.

Recently, some states have tried to limit the welfare payments new residents can receive, typically capping benefits at the level the family would have received in its prior state of residence.[534] These newer forms of durational residence restrictions should be struck down under the *Shapiro* test as a violation of equal protection and the right to travel.[535] Such practices should also be found to conflict with both Article IV, section 2, of the federal Constitution, which provides that the "Citizens of each State shall be entitled to all Privileges and Immunities of Citizens in the several States" and Article I, section 8, which regulates "Commerce . . . among the several States" and has been repeatedly interpreted to prohibit states from inhibiting the interstate movement of persons, including the poor.[536]

How long can a poor person receive General Assistance?

How long a poor person may receive General Assistance depends on where he or she lives and the rules that govern the state or county relief program. In many states, time limits have been linked to the period it takes to have an SSI or AFDC application approved. In some states, eligible individuals can receive General Assistance without any durational limit but must periodically reapply for benefits. Other states, however, impose strict length-of-time limits on General Assistance recipients. A few states limit benefits to a maximum of six months out of twelve.

How much money do General Assistance recipients receive?

General Assistance grants are not generous and often fall far below the federal poverty level. The average individual maximum monthly grant is currently only 33 percent of the federal poverty level.[537] The amount of General Assistance relief that an individual can receive depends on the rules governing his or her state or county program. Some states determine payment levels on a case-by-case basis; others have schedules of relief depending on income and assets. Still other states have different schedules of relief depending on whether the applicant is disabled, pregnant, or has other special characteristics.

Maximum monthly benefits vary considerably from state to state and county to county. Table 1-4 sets forth 1992 grant levels in those states that had statewide benefit levels.

EARNED INCOME CREDIT

What is the Earned Income Credit?[538]

The Earned Income Credit (EIC)[539] was enacted in 1975 and is a federal tax benefit for families and individuals who work full- or part-time but have low income. The EIC reduces the amount of taxes that a low-income worker would otherwise have to pay to the federal government for income earned in a given year. If the worker does not owe any taxes, he or she is still eligible for the EIC and will receive a cash payment, either from the Internal Revenue Service after filing a tax return, or from the employer during the course of the year. Before 1995 came to a close, more than nineteen million families claimed EICs, with an average credit of $1,239 per family.[540] Many thousands of other poor workers were eligible for EICs but did not apply.[541] Low-income workers who receive EICs generally have earnings at or near

TABLE 1-4
General Assistance Maximum Benefit Levels (1992)

	One Person	*Three Persons*
Alaska	$120	$360
Arizona	$173	**
Connecticut*	$356	$680
Delaware	$123	$224
District of Columbia	$258	**
Hawaii	$407	$693
Kansas	$196	$403
Maryland	$154	**
Massachusetts	$339	$522
Michigan	$246	$459
Minnesota	$203	$510
Missouri	$ 80	$240
New Jersey	$210	$390
New Mexico	$192	**
New York	$352	$577
Ohio	$115	$193
Oregon	$268	**
Pennsylvania	$215	$421
Rhode Island	$327	$554
South Carolina	$ 27	**
Utah	$233	**
Washington	$339	$531

Source: Marion Nichols, Jon Dunlap & Scott Barkan, *National General Assistance Survey, 1992*
(Center on Budget and Policy Priorities, 1992).

* In Connecticut, an able-bodied General Assistance recipient received $314, not $356, in FY 1992.
The higher amount obtained only for disabled General Assistance recipients.

** General Assistance programs in Arizona, the District of Columbia, Maryland, New Mexico, South
Carolina, and Utah do not cover families.

the minimum wage (for most of 1996, the minimum wage was only $4.25, and full-time work produced an annual income for a family of three that was 27 percent below the poverty line). Reports indicate that although the EIC has helped offset some of the decline in the value of the minimum wage, low-income wages, even adjusted for the EIC, are still below their value in 1979.[542]

Who is eligible for an EIC?

The EIC is available to any low-income working taxpayer. (Immigrant workers must have valid employment authorization in order to qualify for the EIC.)[543] In 1993, the EIC was specifically expanded to include childless workers. An individual who receives AFDC or other public assistance can take an EIC, as long as he or she has some earned income during the tax year, files the proper federal income tax forms (1040 or 1040A and Form EIC), and meets certain income restrictions. Income limits for the EIC depend on the size of the household, and beginning in 1996 there is also a cap on the amount of income from investments that an otherwise eligible worker can have. In addition, childless families have to meet age requirements. For tax year 1996, a worker can claim an EIC if he or she satisfies these requirements:[544]

- *Families without Children.* An individual who is not raising any children in the home can claim an EIC if he or she is over age 25 and below age 65 the last day of the tax year, i.e., December 31. Family income cannot exceed $9,500 (with no more than $2,200 of income from investments); the individual must have lived in the United States for at least half of the year; and he or she cannot have been claimed as a dependent by any other taxpayer.[545]
- *Families with One Qualifying Child.* An individual who is raising one qualifying child in the home can claim an EIC if family income is below $25,078 (with no more than $2,200 of income from investments).[546]
- *Families with Two or More Qualifying Children.* An individual who is raising two or more qualifying children in the home can claim an EIC if family income is below $28,495 (with no more than $2,200 of income from investments).[547]

What is a "qualifying child" for purposes of the EIC?

A qualifying child has to satisfy four requirements:

- *Residence.* The child must live with the worker in a home located in the United States for at least half of the taxable year (except that an "eligible foster child" must live with the worker the entire year).[548]
- *Relationship.* The child can be the worker's biological child or de-

scendant (for example, a grandchild), adoptive child, foster child, or stepchild. (For purposes of the EIC, a foster child is a child the worker cares for as his or her "own child," and who lives with the worker the entire year.)[549] A married child can be a qualifying child only under limited circumstances.[550]

• *Age and disability.* The child must be under age 19 at the end of the tax year; or a student under age 24 at the end of the tax year; or of any age if permanently and totally disabled at any time during the tax year.[551]

• *Social Security number.* If the child was born before the tax year for which the worker is claiming an EIC, the worker must provide the child's Social Security number. If the child does not have a Social Security number, the worker can apply for one by filing Form SS-5 with the local Social Security Administration.

How large is the EIC?

The EIC is a percentage of a family's total wages up to a maximum dollar amount.

For tax year 1996, a worker without children can claim a credit of 7.65 percent of earnings up to about $4,100, with a maximum credit of $323. At incomes above $5,000, the maximum credit begins to phase down and reaches zero at incomes above $9,500.

A worker with one qualifying child can claim a credit of 34 percent of earnings up to about $6,000, with a maximum credit of $2,152. At incomes above $11,500, the maximum credit begins to phase down and reaches zero at incomes above $25,078.

A worker with two qualifying children can claim a credit of 40 percent of earnings up to about $8,500, with a maximum credit of $3,556. At incomes above $11,500, the maximum credit begins to phase down and reaches zero at incomes above $28,495.[552]

Table 1-5 lists EIC benefits for taxable year 1996 at different household income levels.

Can a worker receive welfare and still claim an EIC?

Yes. A worker can currently claim an EIC even if he or she receives welfare. This has been the rule since 1991 (for tax years through 1990, a worker could not claim an EIC if his or her welfare benefits were more than his or her wages). Over 7 percent of families receiving AFDC also had simultaneous wage earnings in 1992.[553] Indeed, in 1993, more than half of the poor,

TABLE 1-5
Earned Income Credit, Tax Year 1996

1996 Income	No Child	One Child	Two or More Children
$ 500	$ 40	$ 179	$ 210
$ 1,000	$ 78	$ 349	$ 410
$ 3,000	$231	$1,029	$1,210
$ 4,000	$308	$1,369	$1,610
$ 7,000	$189	$2,152	$2,810
$ 9,000	$ 36	$2,152	$3,556
$11,000	0	$2,152	$3,556
$13,000	0	$1,926	$3,258
$15,000	0	$1,606	$2,837
$20,000	0	$ 807	$1,784
$25,000	0	$ 8	$ 731

Sources: 26 U.S.C.A. § 32 (West 1996); *The 1997 Earned Income Credit Campaign,* A Project of the Center on Budget and Policy Priorities (Dec. 1996).

or twenty-two million individuals, lived in households that included at least one worker.[554]

The EIC does not count as income in determining whether an individual is eligible for AFDC and is disregarded in determining whether gross income is below 185 percent of his or her state's standard of need.[555] The EIC is also excluded from income in calculating the amount of an AFDC grant.[556] The Medicaid, SSI, food stamp, and federal housing programs also exclude the EIC from countable income for eligibility and grant purposes.

The EIC does not count as a resource for two months under the AFDC, Medicaid, SSI, and federal housing programs. After the second month that an individual receives the EIC, the credit payment will count as a resource unless he or she has already spent it or converted it to an exempt resource.[557] The food stamp program excludes the EIC as a resource for one year after it is received.[558]

Can a worker get an EIC if he or she is not a United States citizen?

Yes, but only if the worker is a resident alien for tax purposes.[559] To meet this requirement he or she must be a legal permanent resident with a green card (I-551). In 1994, a noncitizen also met this requirement if she or he lived in the United States for at least six months during the tax year, or for an average of four months each year in the last three years, and her or his main home was the United States. Qualifying children must live with the worker in the United States for more than six months out of the year.

The following categories of immigrants may also qualify for the EIC:

- Amnesty temporary residents and amnesty family members granted "Family Fairness" or "Family Unity" status;
- Refugees, asylees, and those granted Temporary Protected Status; and
- Applicants for these and other immigration statuses who have legal work authorization.

Receiving an EIC does not make an individual a "public charge" for immigration purposes and does not indicate inability to provide financial support to himself or herself or the family.[560]

How does the EIC work?

The EIC is a tax credit. If a worker would otherwise have to pay federal income tax, the credit reduces the amount of the tax obligation. If the credit exceeds the tax obligation, even if the tax obligation is zero, the worker will receive a cash refund.[561]

Consider the following examples:

- John Romero has three children and earned $16,000 in tax year 1994. His federal income tax was $90, which was withheld from his wages throughout the year. He applies for an EIC and is eligible for a credit of $1,639. The Internal Revenue Service will pay back the $90 of taxes already withheld and issue an additional check of $1,549.
- Berta Brite has no children and worked part-time in tax year 1995, earning $4,900. Because of her low wages, Ms. Brite had no taxes withheld and does not owe the Internal Revenue Service any tax. She claims an EIC and receives a check for $314.
- June Smith is raising two foster children in her home. She earned $25,000 in tax year 1995 and owes the Internal Revenue Service $400 more in income taxes than were withheld throughout the year. She claims an EIC and is eligible for a $333 credit, which reduces the additional tax owed to $67.

How is an EIC claimed?

To claim an EIC, an individual must file a federal income tax form, even if he or she would not otherwise be required to file a return because income is so low. Married couples must file jointly.

If the worker did not raise children during the tax year, he or she can file any tax form, i.e., Form 1040, 1040A, or 1040EZ. The worker can write "EIC" on the Earned Income Credit line of the return, and have the Internal Revenue Service calculate the amount of the credit. The worker can also calculate the credit and list the amount claimed on the EIC line.

If the worker raised at least one child during the tax year, he or she has to file either Form 1040 or 1040A and fill out and attach Schedule EIC. The worker can choose to fill out only the first side of Schedule EIC, and the Internal Revenue Service will calculate the amount of the credit.

If the worker is self-employed, he or she needs to fill out a special series of forms: Schedule C, Schedule SE (if self-employment income is more than $400), Form 1040, and Schedule EIC (if he or she was raising children in the home).

Is an EIC given only at end of the tax year?

No. Under certain circumstances a worker can get an "advance" EIC payment. In 1997, advance EIC payments are available to any worker raising at least one child at home who has income that year of less than $25,750. Childless families are not currently eligible for an advance EIC. Advance EICs cannot be claimed by farm workers getting paid day by day or by workers who do not have Social Security or Medicare taxes withheld from their pay.

Under the advance payment system, the worker receives a portion of the EIC in every paycheck and the remainder of the EIC after filing a year-end income tax return. If a worker elects an advance payment and earns between $490 and $1,450 a month, he or she can expect $50 extra in each biweekly paycheck.

How is an advance EIC claimed?

Eligible workers must fill out a W-5 form called the "Earned Income Credit Advance Payment Certificate" and give the bottom part to their employer. If a worker marries during the year or gets a large increase in income, he or she should consider filing a new W-5 form to stop receiving advance EIC payments. Otherwise, he or she may face a large tax obligation at the end of the year.

Can a worker file for a back refund?

Yes. A worker can claim an EIC credit as far back as three years. The individual does not have to be currently eligible for an EIC as long as he or she received income during the years for which a refund is claimed.[562] To apply, the individual needs to file a number of different forms with the Internal Revenue Service: Form 1040X for the year for which an EIC is claimed, as well as a copy of that year's income tax form and Schedule EIC.

Are there ways to get help in claiming an EIC?

Yes. Workers can get free help with tax preparation through a federal program called Volunteer Income Tax Assistance (VITA). VITA is administered by the Internal Revenue Service, which sponsors local tax clinics at community churches, shopping malls, libraries, and other public places. The clinics are open from late January or early February through April 15. To find out where a VITA clinic is located in your community, call the Internal Revenue Service at 1-800-TAX-1040. If the IRS phone line is busy, you can also call the IRS worker education coordinator for your region, whose telephone number should be listed in a local phone book.

What documents are needed to have taxes prepared?

The following documents may be needed in preparing taxes and should be brought to a VITA clinic:

- Last year's tax return;
- This year's W-2 forms from all jobs;
- This year's 1099-G form if unemployment insurance benefits were received;
- This year's 1099-INT forms if bank interest was received;
- The Social Security numbers of all household members over age one;
- This year's mortgage statements.

Do any states provide tax credits to poor families that work?

Yes. New York, Wisconsin, Minnesota, and Vermont have established state EICs that supplement the federal credit. In New York, for example, the additional state EIC is 7.5 percent of the federal EIC claimed, and by 1997 is expected to rise to 20 percent.[563] Other states are working to establish their own tax credit programs, and they are extremely important to poor families; in most states, low-income households pay a larger share of their earnings in state and local taxes than the more affluent.

Notes

1. *See* Lee Rainwater, *What Money Buys: Inequality and the Social Meanings of Income* (1974).

2. *See* Staff of House Comm. on Ways and Means, 103d Cong., 2d Sess., *Overview of Entitlement Programs: 1994 Green Book, Background Material and Data on Programs Within the Jurisdiction of the Committee on Ways and Means* 1154, 1156 (Comm. Print 1994) (hereinafter, *1994 Green Book*).

3. *See* Mollie Orshansky, *The Measure of Poverty: Technical Paper I, Documentation of Background Information and Rationale for Current Poverty Matrix* 233–83 (U.S. Dep't of Health, Education, and Welfare, 1977).

4. *E.g.*, Kathryn A. Lavin & Kathryn H. Porter, *Enough to Live On: Setting an Appropriate AFDC Need Standard* (Center on Budget and Policy Priorities, 1992).

5. *E.g.*, John E. Schwarz & Thomas L. Volgy, *The Forgotten Americans* 61–63 (1992); S. M. Miller & Else Oyen, *Remeasuring Poverty*, 5 Poverty & Race Action Council 1 (Sept./Oct. 1996); Robert Pear, *Experts' Concept of Poverty Makes More People Poor*, Des Moines Register, Apr. 30, 1995, 7.

6. *See* U.S. Bureau of the Census, *Alternative Methods of Valuing Selected In-Kind Transfer Benefits and Measuring Their Effect on Poverty* (Technical Paper No. 50, 1982) (discussing impact of in-kind exclusion on levels of poverty).

7. For a discussion of alternative economic and social measures, *see* Cass R. Sunstein, *Well-Being and the State*, 107 Harv. L. Rev. 1303 (1994).

8. *See* 61 Fed. Reg. 10720, 10721 (Mar. 15, 1996).

9. David Dahl, *Census Portraits Show Blacks Losing Ground*, Capital Times, Feb. 23, 1995, 1B.

10. Harrell R. Rodgers, Jr., *Poor Women, Poor Children: American Poverty in the 1990s* (3d ed. 1996).

11. *See* Steven A. Holmes, *For Hispanic Poor, No Silver Lining*, N.Y. Times, Oct. 13, 1996, § 4, at 5; Ramon G. McLeod, *Poverty Fell, Income Rose in U.S. in 1995, But Latinos Lagging, Census Report Shows*, San Francisco Chronicle, Sept. 27, 1996, A1.

12. *See* U.S. General Accounting Office, Testimony Before the Comm. on Governmental Affairs, U.S. Senate, *Low-income Families: Comparison of Incomes of AFDC and Working Poor Families* (Jan. 1995).

13. *See* Isaac Shapiro, *Four Years and Still Falling: The Decline in the Value of the Mini-*

mum Wage (Center on Budget and Policy Priorities, 1995); Robyn Meredith, *Minimum Wage, Minimum Effect*, N.Y. Times, Oct. 1, 1996, D1.

14. *See* Joel F. Handler, *Two Years and You're Out*, 26 Conn. L. Rev. 857, 861 (1994).

15. In 1990, 15.6 percent of female-headed households, with the equivalent of three-fourths or more persons working full-time, were poor, compared to 12.7 percent in 1980. *See* Staff of House Comm. on Ways and Means, 103d Cong., 1st Sess., *Overview of Entitlement Programs: 1993 Green Book, Background Materials and Data on Programs Within the Jurisdiction of the Committee on Ways and Means* 1135–26 (Comm. Print 1993).

16. *See* Martha Minow, *The Welfare of Single Mothers and Their Children*, 26 Conn. L. Rev. 817 (1994).

17. 1994 Green Book, *supra* note 2, at 366–67.

18. *Id.* at 399.

19. Jason DeParle, *In Debate on U.S. Poverty, 2 Studies Fuel Argument on Who Is to Blame*, N.Y. Times, Oct. 29, 1991, at A20; Rodgers, *supra* note 10, at 240.

20. *Dandridge v. Williams*, 397 U.S. 471 (1970).

21. *Goldberg v. Kelly*, 397 U.S. 254, 264 (1970).

22. *See* Aryeh Neier, *Only Judgment: The Limits of Litigation in Social Change* 127–40 (1982).

23. *See* Edward V. Sparer, *The Right to Welfare, in The Rights of Americans: What They Are—What They Should Be* 65, 83 (Norman Dorsen ed. 1971); Frank Michelman, *The Supreme Court, 1968 Term—Foreword: On Protecting the Poor Through the Fourteenth Amendment*, 83 Harv. L. Rev. 7 (1969); *but see* Robert H. Bork, *The Constitution, Original Intent, and Economic Rights*, 23 San Diego L. Rev. 823 (1986); Ralph K. Winter, Jr., *Poverty, Economic Equality, and the Equal Protection Clause*, 1972 Sup. Ct. Rev. 41.

24. *Dandridge v. Williams*, 397 U.S. at 487.

25. *DeShaney v. Winnebago County Dep't of Social Servs.*, 489 U.S. 189, 196 (1989).

26. *E.g.*, International Bill of Human Rights, G.A. Res. 217A, U.N. GAOR, 3d Sess., 183 mtg. at 76, U.N. Doc. A/810 (1948) ("Everyone has the right to a standard of living adequate for the health and well-being of himself and of his family.").

27. *See, e.g.*, Stephen Loffredo, *Poverty, Democracy and Constitutional Law*, 141 U. Pa. L. Rev. 1277 (1993); Akhil Reed Amar, *Forty Acres and a Mule: A Republican Theory of Minimal Entitlements*, 13 Harv. J.L. & Pub. Pol'y 37 (1990); Peter B. Edelman, *The Next Century of Our Constitution: Rethinking Our Duty to the Poor*, 39 Hastings L.J. 1 (1987).

28. Laurence H. Tribe, *Unraveling National League of Cities: The New Federalism and Affirmative Rights to Essential Government Services*, 90 Harv. L. Rev. 1065, 1065–66 (1977).

29. State constitutional provisions that deal explicitly with poverty are collected in Burt Neuborne, *Foreword: State Constitutions and the Evolution of Positive Rights*, 20 Rutgers L.J. 881, 893–95 & nn. 60–82 (1989).

30. N.Y. Const. art. XVII, § 1.

31. Miss. Const. art. XIV, § 252.

32. Okla. Const. art. XXV, § 1.

33. Sarah Ramsey & Daan Braverman, *"Let Them Starve"—Government's Obligation to Children in Poverty*, 68 Temple L. Rev. 1607 (1995).

34. The information in this section is drawn largely from Adele M. Blong & Timothy J.

Casey, *AFDC Program Rules for Advocates: An Overview*, 27 Clearinghouse Rev. 1164 (1994); and the *1994 Green Book, supra* note 2.

35. Letter from the White House (Oct. 9, 1996). For a history of welfare programs in the United States *see* Robert H. Bremner ed., *Children and Youth in America: A Documentary History* 519–20, vol. 3 (1974); and Murray Levine & Adeline Levine, *Helping Children: A Social History* 198 (2d ed. 1992).

36. Jennifer Dixon, *U.S. Welfare Rates Fall After Years of Growth*, Com. Appeal, Nov. 4, 1995, A1.

37. *1994 Green Book, supra* note 2, at 401.

38. *See* Center on Social Welfare Policy and Law, *Welfare Myths: Fact or Fiction? Exploring the Truth about Welfare* (1996); M. Brinton Lykes, Ali Banuazizi, Ramsay Liem & Michael Morris eds., *Myths about the Powerless: Contesting Social Inequalities* (1996); Janice Hamilton Outtz, *Shattering Stereotypes: A Demographic Look at Children in the United States* (Center for Demographic Policy, 1994).

39. *1994 Green Book, supra* note 2, at 401–2 (*citing* Office of Family Assistance, Administration for Children and Families, and Congressional Budget Office).

40. *Id.* at 440–47 (*citing* David T. Ellwood, *Targeting Would-Be Long-Term Recipients of AFDC,* table IV-1).

41. *Id.* at 441.

42. Pub. L. No. 104-193, 110 Stat. 2105 (1996).

43. 42 U.S.C.A. §§ 606(a), 607 (West 1996); *see also* 45 C.F.R. § 233.90 (1996).

44. 42 U.S.C.A. § 606(b) (West 1996); 45 C.F.R. § 233.90(c)(2)(iv) (1996).

45. 42 U.S.C.A. § 606(a) (West 1996); 45 C.F.R. § 233.90(c)(1)(v)(A) (1996); U.S. Dep't of Health and Human Servs., HHS Action Transmittal ACF-AT-91-33 (1991).

46. 45 C.F.R. § 233.90(c)(1)(v)(B) (1996).

47. U.S. Dep't of Health and Human Servs., HHS Action Transmittal, FSA-87-7 (1987).

48. 42 U.S.C.A. § 606(b) (West 1996); 45 C.F.R. § 233.10(b)(2)(ii)(B) (1996).

49. 45 C.F.R. § 233.90(a)(1) (1996).

50. *Id.* at § 233.90(c)(1)(iv) (1996).

51. 42 U.S.C.A. § 606(a) (West 1996); 45 C.F.R. § 233.90(c)(1)(iii) (1996).

52. 42 U.S.C.A. § 607 (West 1996); 45 C.F.R. § 233.101 (1996).

53. *Id.*

54. 42 U.S.C.A. § 607(b)(1)(A)(iii)(d)(3) (West 1996); 45 C.F.R. § 233.101(a)(3)(v) (1996).

55. 42 U.S.C.A. § 607(d)(1) (West 1996); *1994 Green Book, supra* note 2, at 332–33.

56. 42 U.S.C.A. § 607(b)(1)(A)(iii)(I) (West 1996).

57. *See* 8 U.S.C.A. § 1255a(h) (West 1996); 42 U.S.C.A. § 602(f) (West 1996); 42 U.S.C.A. § 602(a)(33) (1996); 45 C.F.R. § 233.50 (1996).

58. Pub. L. No. 104-193, 110 Stat. 2105, § 401 (1996).

59. *See* Immigration and Nationality Act § 207.

60. *See id.* at § 207.

61. *See id.* at § 243(h).

62. *See id.* at § 212(d)(5).

63. *See id.* at § 203(a)(7), as in effect prior to April 1, 1980.

64. *See* 8 U.S.C.A. § 1641(c) & (c)(2) (West 1996).

65. *See Doe v. Reivitz,* 830 F.2d 1441 (7th Cir. 1987).

66. 394 U.S. 618 (1968).

67. 45 C.F.R. § 233.40 (1996).

68. *See Anderson v. Green,* 115 S. Ct. 1059 (1995).

69. *See Zobel v. Williams,* 457 U.S. 55 (1982)(privileges and immunity clause); *Edwards v. California,* 314 U.S. 160 (1941)(commerce clause); Stephen Loffredo, *"If You Ain't Got the Do, Re, Mi": The Commerce Clause and State Residence Restrictions on Welfare,* 11 Yale L. & Pol'y Rev. 147 (1993).

70. 45 C.F.R. § 233.40(a)(1)(ii) (1996).

71. U.S. Dep't of Health and Human Servs., HHS Action Transmittal, FSA-87-7 (1987).

72. 42 U.S.C.A. § 602(a)(21) (West 1996); 45 C.F.R. § 233.106 (1996).

73. *See* 45 C.F.R. § 233.31(b)(1) (1996).

74. 42 U.S.C.A. §§ 602(a)(7)(A), 606(b) (West 1996).

75. *Id.* at § 602(a)(7) (1996).

76. *Id.* at § 602(a)(17) (West 1996); 45 C.F.R. § 233.20(a)(3)(ii)(F) (1996).

77. 45 C.F.R. § 233.20(a)(2)(vi) (1996).

78. *See* 42 U.S.C.A. §§ 602, 603 (West 1996); 45 C.F.R. § 233.90(a)(1) (1996).

79. *See King v. Smith,* 392 U.S. 309 (1968) (invalidating "man in the house" rule).

80. *See* 42 U.S.C.A. § 602(a)(38) (West 1996); 45 C.F.R. § 206.10(a)(1)(vii) (1996).

81. 42 U.S.C.A. § 602(a)(18) (West 1996).

82. *See Mangrum v. Griepentrog,* 702 F. Supp. 813 (D. Nev. 1988); *see also Lukhard v. Reed,* 481 U.S. 368 (1987).

83. U.S. Dep't of Health and Human Servs., HHS Quality Control Manual § 3565(B) (Jan. 1, 1989); *see also* 45 C.F.R. § 233.20(a)(ii)(E) (1996).

84. 45 C.F.R. § 233.20(a)(3)(ii)(D) (1996).

85. 42 U.S.C.A. § 602(a)(18) (West 1996); 45 C.F.R. § 233.20(a)(3)(xiii) (1996).

86. 42 U.S.C.A. § 602(a)(8)(A)(i) (West 1996).

87. *Id.* at § 602(a)(8)(A)(v) (West 1996).

88. *Id.* at § 602(a)(8)(A)(vii) (West 1996).

89. *Id.* at § 602(a)(7), (a)(8)(B) (West 1996).

90. *Id.* at § 602(a)(8)(A)(ii–iv), (B)(ii) (West 1996).

91. *Id.* at § 602(a)(8)(A)(viii) (West 1996).

92. *Id.* at §§ 602(a)(8)(vi), 657(b)(1) (West 1996).

93. 45 C.F.R. § 233.20(a)(3)(iv)(B), (xxi) (1996).

94. *Id.* at § 233.20(a)(3)(iv) (1996).

95. *Id.* at § 233.20(a)(3)(ii)(C) (1996).

96. *1994 Green Book, supra* note 2, at 327–28, 334.

97. U.S. Dep't of Health and Human Services, HHS Action Transmittal FSA-AT-91-4 (Feb. 25, 1991).

98. 42 U.S.C.A. § 602(a)(39) (West 1996); 45 C.F.R. § 233.20(a)(3)(xviii) (1996).

99. 42 U.S.C.A. § 602(a)(31) (West 1996); 45 C.F.R. § 233.20(a)(3)(xiv) (1996).

100. 42 U.S.C.A. § 615 (West 1996); 45 C.F.R. § 233.51 (1996).

101. 42 U.S.C.A. § 602(a)(7) (West 1996).

102. 45 C.F.R. § 233.20(a)(3)(vi) (1996).

103. 42 U.S.C.A. § 602(a)(24) (West 1996).

104. 45 C.F.R. § 233.20(a)(3)(ii) (1996).

105. *See* 45 C.F.R. § 233.20(a)(2)(ii) (1996); *Shea v. Vialpando,* 416 U.S. 251 (1974); *Jefferson v. Hackney,* 406 U.S. 535 (1972); *Dandridge v. Williams,* 397 U.S. 471 (1970); *Rosado v. Wyman,* 397 U.S. 397 (1970)

106. *See 1994 Green Book, supra* note 2, at 366–67 (*citing* table prepared by Congressional Research Service from information provided by a telephone survey of the states).

107. *Id.*

108. *See* Center on Social Welfare Policy and Law, *An Explanation of Fill the Gap Budgeting as Used in the AFDC Program,* 23 Clearinghouse Rev. 153 (1989).

109. 42 U.S.C.A. § 602(a)(32) (West 1996).

110. *Id.* at § 602(h) (West 1996).

111. *See* 45 C.F.R. § 233.20(a)(2)(v) (1996).

112. *See* 42 U.S.C.A. § 612 (West 1996).

113. *Id.*

114. *Id.* at § 602(a)(7)(B) (West 1996).

115. 45 C.F.R. § 233.20(a)(3)(ii)(D) (1996).

116. 42 U.S.C.A. § 602(a)(7)(B) (West 1996); 45 C.F.R. §233.20(a)(3)(i)(B), (iv) (1996).

117. For a full listing of exempt resources, *see* 45 C.F.R. §§ 233.20(a)(3)(i)(B), 233.20(a)(4)(ii) (1996).

118. *Id.* at § 233.20(a)(4)(ii).

119. *Id.*

120. 42 U.S.C.A. § 602(a)(38) (West 1996); 45 C.F.R. § 206.10(a)(1)(vii) (1996).

121. 42 U.S.C.A. § 602(a)(7) (West 1996).

122. *Id.* at § 602(a)(24) (West 1996).

123. *Id.* at § 602(a)(17) (West 1996); 45 C.F.R. § 233.20(a)(3)(ii)(F) (1996).

124. *See* Gina Mannix, *The AFDC Lump Sum Rule: How It Works and How to Avoid It,* 26 Clearinghouse Rev. 271 (1992).

125. 42 U.S.C.A. § 1320b-7(a)(1) (West 1996); 45 C.F.R. § 205.52 (1996).

126. 45 C.F.R. § 206.10(a)(3) (1996).

127. *Id.* at § 206.10(a)(6) (1996).

128. *1994 Green Book, supra* note 2, at 360–61.

129. *Id.* at 334.

130. 45 C.F.R. § 206.10(a)(9) (1996).

131. 42 U.S.C.A. § 606(b) (West 1996); 45 C.F.R. § 234.60 (1996).

132. 42 U.S.C.A. §§ 602(a)(19)(G), 602(a)(26)(B), 606(b) (West 1996).

133. *Id.* at § 602(a)(9) (West 1996).

134. *1994 Green Book, supra* note 2, at 437.

135. *Id.* at 438.

136. *See* 42 U.S.C.A. §§ 681–87 (West 1996).

137. *Id.* at § 602(a)(19)(C)(v) (West 1996); 45 C.F.R. § 250.30(b)(1) (1996).

138. 42 U.S.C.A. § 602(a)(19)(C) (West 1996); 45 C.F.R. § 250.30(b) (1996).

139. 42 U.S.C.A. § 602(a)(19)(C)(iii) (West 1996); 45 C.F.R. § 250.30(b)(9) (1996).

140. 42 U.S.C.A. § 602(a)(19)(C)(iii), (D), (E) (West 1996); 45 C.F.R. § 250.30(b)(9), 250.32 (1996).

141. 42 U.S.C.A. § 602(a)(19)(E) (West 1996); 45 C.F.R. § 250.32 (1996).

142. 42 U.S.C.A. § 682(b)(1) (West 1996); 45 C.F.R. § 250.41(b) (1996).

143. 42 U.S.C.A. § 682(d)(2) (West 1996); 45 C.F.R. § 250.32(b) (1996).

144. 42 U.S.C.A. § 602(g)(1) (West 1996).

145. *Id.*; 45 C.F.R. § 255.2(a), (e) (1996).

146. 42 U.S.C.A. § 602(a)(19)(G) (West 1996); 45 C.F.R. § 250.34 (1996).

147. 42 U.S.C.A. § 602(a)(19)(G)(i)(II) (West 1996); 45 C.F.R. § 250.34(c)(2) (1996).

148. 42 U.S.C.A. § 602(a)(19)(G) (West 1996); 45 C.F.R. § 250.35 (1996).

149. 42 U.S.C.A. § 682(h) (West 1996); 45 C.F.R. § 250.36 (1996).

150. 42 U.S.C.A. § 602(a)(26)(A) (West 1996); 45 C.F.R. §§ 232.11 and 302.51(f) (1996).

151. 42 U.S.C.A. § 602(a)(26)(B) (West 1996); 45 C.F.R. § 232.12 (1996); *see also* 42 U.S.C.A. § 1396k (West 1996) and 42 U.S.C.A. § 602(a)(26)(C) (West 1996).

152. 45 C.F.R. § 232.12(b) (1996).

153. 42 U.S.C.A. § 602(a)(26)(B) (West 1996).

154. *Id.*; 45 C.F.R. §§ 232.40–.49 (1996).

155. 42 U.S.C.A. § 657(b) (West 1996); 45 C.F.R. § 302.51 (1996).

156. 42 U.S.C.A. § 654(5) (West 1996); 45 C.F.R. §§ 232.20, 302.32 (1996).

157. *1994 Green Book, supra* note 2, at 336–37.

158. 42 U.S.C.A. § 657(c) (West 1996); 45 C.F.R. §§ 302.32(f), 302.33, 302.51(e),(f) (1996).

159. 42 U.S.C.A. § 233.20(a)(13)(vi) (West 1996).

160. *Id.* at § 602(a)(22) (West 1996).

161. 45 C.F.R. § 233.20(a)(13)(i)(A) (1996).

162. 42 U.S.C.A. § 602(a)(22) (West 1996).

163. *See* U.S. Dep't of Health and Human Servs., HHS Information Memorandum FSA-IM-89-4 (1989) for a discussion of the rights of people in this situation.

164. 42 U.S.C.A. § 616 (West 1996); 45 C.F.R. §§ 235.111–.113 (1996).

165. 45 C.F.R. §§ 205.10(a)(4), 206.10(a)(4) (1996).

166. *Id.* at § 205.10(a)(4) (1996).

167. *See* 42 U.S.C.A. § 602(a)(4) (West 1996); 45 C.F.R. § 205.10(a)(5) (1996).

168. 397 U.S. 254 (1970).

169. 45 C.F.R. §§ 205.10(a)(3)–(4), 206.10(a)(4) (1996).

170. *See* New York City Legal Aid Society, Community Advocate Project, *The People's Guide to Fair Hearings* 34 (1985).

171. 45 C.F.R. § 205.10(a)(13), (6) (1996); *see also Goldberg v. Kelly*, 397 U.S. 254 (1970).

172. 45 C.F.R. § 205.10(a)(7) (1996).

173. *Id.* at § 205.10(a)(1), (2), (12)–(17) (1996).

174. *Id.* at § 205.10(a)(16) (1996).

175. *Id.*

176. *1994 Green Book, supra* note 2, at 333–34, 343, 364–65.

177. *See* Joel Handler, *"Ending Welfare As We Know It"—Wrong for Welfare, Wrong for Poverty*, 2 Geo. J. on Fighting Poverty 3, 4 (1994).

178. Pub. L. No. 104-193, 110 Stat. 2105 (1996).

179. This section relies on a number of reports issued shortly after enactment of the Personal Responsibility and Work Opportunity Reconciliation Act of 1996: Mark Greenberg & Steve Savner, *A Detailed Summary of Key Provisions of the Temporary Assistance for Needy Families Block Grant of H.R. 3734, The Personal Responsibility and Work Opportunity Reconciliation Act of 1996* (Center for Law and Social Policy, 1996); Isabel V. Sawhill ed., *Welfare Reform: An Analysis of the Issues* (Urban Institute, 1996); David A. Super, Sharon Parrott, Susan Steinmetz & Cindy Mann, *The New Welfare Law* (Center on Budget and Policy Priorities, 1996); and U.S. Department of Health and Human Servs., Office of the Assistant Secretary for Planning and Evaluation, *Personal Responsibility and Work Opportunity Reconciliation Act of 1996 (104 H.R. 3734), Summary of Provisions* (Last rev., Aug. 13, 1996).

180. *See* Robert Pear, *Budget Agency Says Welfare Bill Would Cut Rolls by Millions*, N.Y. Times, July 16, 1996, A12; Editorial, *Ducking the Truth about Welfare Cuts*, N.Y. Times, June 26, 1996, A18; Alison Mitchell, *Greater Poverty Toll Is Seen in Welfare Bill*, N.Y. Times, Nov. 10, 1995, A27.

181. *See* Sawhill, *supra* note 179.

182. Title I of the act provides, "No individual entitlement. This part shall not be interpreted to entitle any individual or family to assistance under any state program funded under this part." Pub. L. No. 104-193, 110 Stat. 2105, § 103(a)(1) (adding new § 401(b)(1996) to Title IV of the Social Security Act).

183. *Excerpts from Debate in the Senate on the Welfare Measure, Remarks of Mr. Moynihan*, N.Y. Times, Aug. 2, 1996, A16; *see* Robert Pear, *Senators Vote to Cut Off Benefits for Legal Aliens*, N.Y. Times, July 20, 1996, 7.

184. *See, e.g.*, Linda McClain, *"Irresponsible" Reproduction*, 47 Hastings L. J. 339, 381–85 (1996) (citing studies).

185. *See, e.g.*, Office of Management and Budget, *Potential Poverty and Distributional Effects of Welfare Reform Bills and Balanced Budget Plans* (Nov. 9, 1995); Christopher Jencks & Katherine Edin, *Do Poor Women Have a Right to Bear Children*, American Prospect 45–46 (1995); Katherine Newman & Chauncey Lennon, *The Job Ghetto*, American Prospect 66–67 (1995); Gordon Lafer, *The Politics of Job Training: Urban Poverty and the False Promise of JTPA*, 22 Politics & Society 353 (1994); William Julius Wilson, *When Work Disappears*, N.Y. Times, Aug. 18, 1996, § 6, at 26; David T. Ellwood, *Welfare Reform in Name Only*, N.Y. Times, July 22, 1996, A19; Peter T. Kilborn, *Up from Welfare: It's Harder and Harder*, N.Y. Times, Apr. 16, 1995, § 4, at 1 (citing study showing that in Harlem "14 people chase every $4.25-an-hour fast-food job").

186. Pub. L. No. 104-193, 110 Stat. 2105, § 116 (1996); *see* Ronald Smothers, *Farewell, Welfare State*, N.Y. Times, Oct. 13, 1996, § 4, at 5 (describing state plans establishing assistance programs under the block grant).

187. States that received permission from the U.S. Department of Health and Human Services to run experimental programs under the AFDC law may, in some circumstances, continue to operate those programs beyond July 1, 1997. Pub. L. No. 104-193, 110 Stat. 2105, § 103 (adding new § 415 (1996) to Title IV of the Social Security Act).

188. *See* Pub. L. No. 104-193, 110 Stat. 2105, § 103(a)(1) (adding new § 401(b)(1996) to Title IV of the Social Security Act).

189. *See* Super et al., *supra* note 179, for a more detailed discussion of the differences between the AFDC program and the TANF block grant.

190. *See* Pub. L. No. 104-193, 110 Stat. 2105, § 103(a)(1) (adding new § 401(b)(1996) to Title IV of the Social Security Act).

191. *See id.* at § 103(a) (1996) (adding new § 408 (1996) to Title IV of the Social Security Act).

192. *See* 42 U.S.C.A. §§ 601 *et seq.* (West 1996).

193. *See* Pub. L. No. 104-193, 110 Stat. 2105, § 103 (1996) (adding new § 403(a) (1996) to Title IV of the Social Security Act).

194. *See id.* (adding new §§ 404(d) & (e) (1996) to Title IV of the Social Security Act); *see generally* Super et al., *supra* note 179, at 6–7.

195. *See* Pub. L. No. 104-193, 110 Stat. 2105, § 103 (1996) (adding new § 403(a) (1996) to Title IV of the Social Security Act).

196. *See id.* (adding new § 409(a)(3) (1996) to Title IV of the Social Security Act).

197. *See* U.S. Department of Health and Human Servs., Office of the Assistant Secretary for Planning and Evaluation, *Personal Responsibility and Work Opportunity Reconciliation Act of 1996 (104 H.R. 3734), Summary of Provisions* (Last rev., Aug. 13, 1996).

198. Pub. L. No. 104-193, 110 Stat. 2105, § 103 (1996) (adding new § 406(a) (1996) to Title IV of the Social Security Act).

199. *Id.* (adding new § 402 (1996) to Title IV of the Social Security Act).

200. *See State Cash Assistance under a Block Grant: Preparing for Advocacy,* Welfare News 6–7 (Aug. 20, 1996).

201. Pub. L. No. 104-193, 110 Stat. 2105, § 103 (1996) (adding new § 402(a)(1)(A)(i) (1996) to Title IV of the Social Security Act).

202. *Id.* (adding new § 402(a)(1)(A)(ii) (1996) to Title IV of the Social Security Act).

203. *Id.* (adding new § 402(a)(1)(A)(iii) (1996) to Title IV of the Social Security Act).

204. *Id.* (adding new § 402(a)(1)(B)(iv) (1996) to Title IV of the Social Security Act).

205. *Id.* (adding new § 402(a)(1)(A)(v) (1996) to Title IV of the Social Security Act).

206. *Id.* (adding new § 402(a)(1)(A)(vi) (1996) to Title IV of the Social Security Act).

207. *Id.* (adding new § 402(a)(1)(B)(iii) (1996) to Title IV of the Social Security Act).

208. *Id.* at § 104.

209. *Id.* (adding new § 417 (1996) to Title IV of the Social Security Act).

210. *Id.* at § 103 (adding new § 404(a)(1)(2) (1996) to Title IV of the Social Security Act).

211. *Id.* (adding new § 404(f) (1996) to Title IV of the Social Security Act).

212. *Id.* (adding new § 404(d)(3) (1996) to Title IV of the Social Security Act).

213. *Id.* (adding new § 404(b) (1996) to Title IV of the Social Security Act).

214. *Id.* (adding new § 404(g) (1996) to Title IV of the Social Security Act).

215. Note, *Devolving Welfare Programs to the States: A Public Choice Perspective*, 109 Harv. L. Rev. 1984, 1985 (1996)(contending that block grants will produce "a substandard welfare system that worsens the plight of the nation's poor").

216. *See* Center on Social Welfare Policy and Law, *Welfare Myths: Fact or Fiction? Exploring the Truth about Welfare*, *supra* note 38, at 25–26 (citing empirical studies).

217. Pub. L. No. 104-193, 110 Stat. 2105, § 103 (1996) (adding new § 408(a)(6) (1996) to Title IV of the Social Security Act).

218. *Id.* (adding new § 404(h)(1)–(3) (1996) to Title IV of the Social Security Act).

219. *Id.* (adding new § 402(a)(1)(B)(iii) (1996) to Title IV of the Social Security Act).

220. *Id.* (adding new § 408(a)(1)(A) (1996) to Title IV of the Social Security Act).

221. *Id.* (adding new § 419(2) (1996) to Title IV of the Social Security Act).

222. *Id.* (adding new § 419(1) (1996) to Title IV of the Social Security Act).

223. *Id.* (adding new § 408(a)(10) (1996) to Title IV of the Social Security Act).

224. The new act raises the important legal question of whether the Constitution allows states to exclude immigrants from programs established with TANF grants. Section 402(b) of the 1996 welfare act, Pub. L. No. 104-193, 110 Stat. 2105, § 402(b) (1996), gives states the option to exclude certain legal immigrants from the state's TANF program. This part of the law appears to be unconstitutional because it authorizes states to discriminate against lawful permanent resident aliens (immigrants with "green cards") in the administration of a public assistance program. The United States Supreme Court has previously ruled that such discrimination by states violates the equal protection clause of the Fourteenth Amendment, even if the federal government has authorized the discrimination. *Graham v. Richardson*, 403 U.S. 365 (1971). The drafters of the 1996 welfare act apparently recognized this constitutional flaw and attempted to avoid it with a legislative "finding" that any restrictions placed by a state on immigrant eligibility for public assistance are the "least restrictive means" of achieving "compelling" national immigration policies. Pub. L. No. 104-193, 110 Stat. 2105, § 400 (1996). (Unlike the states, the federal government may discriminate against immigrants in the exercise of its constitutional power to regulate immigration. *See Mathews v. Diaz*, 426 U.S. 67 (1976).) The statute is unconvincing on this point, though, because it does not mandate any particular federal policy toward immigrants. Rather, it delegates broad authority to fifty state governments to adopt fifty different, uncoordinated, and inconsistent state policies toward immigrants, policies over which the federal government has no control. For this reason alone, it cannot credibly be maintained that the law is necessary to the achievement of national immigration policy. Therefore, state laws that treat legal immigrants more harshly than federal law *requires* should be held unconstitutional on the authority of *Graham v. Richardson*.

225. Pub. L. No. 104-193, 110 Stat. 2105, § 402(b) (1996).

226. *Id.* at § 401(a).

227. *See* Immigration and Nationality Act § 207.

228. *See id.* at § 208.

229. *See id.* at § 243(h).

230. *See id.* at § 212(d)(5).

231. *See id.* at § 203(a)(7), as in effect prior to April 1, 1980.

232. 8 U.S.C.A. § 1641(c) & (c)(2) (West 1996).

233. Pub. L. No. 104-193, 110 Stat. 2105, § 403(a) (1996).

234. *Id.* at § 403(b).

235. *See* Immigration and Nationality Act § 243(h) (withholding of deportation).

236. For refugees, the five-year eligibility period begins on the date the immigrant was admitted to the United States as a refugee. For asylees and immigrants whose deportation has been withheld, the five-year period begins on the date that political asylum or withholding of deportation was granted. Pub. L. No. 104-193, 110 Stat. 2105, § 402(b)(2)(A) (1996).

237. *Id.* at §§ 402(b)(2)(B) & 435 (1996).

238. *Id.* at § 435 (1996).

239. *Id.* at § 402(b) (1996).

240. The new federal statute is not clear on this point. Section 421 of the Personal Responsibility and Work Opportunity Reconciliation Act of 1996, Pub. L. No. 104-193, 110 Stat. 2105 (1996), requires that sponsor income and resources be deemed to an immigrant "in determining the eligibility and the amount of benefits of an alien for any federal means-tested public benefits program." The question is whether a program established under the Temporary Assistance for Needy Families block grant is a "federal means-tested public benefits program" for purposes of the deeming provision. The act does not specifically include TANF in the definition, and it may be argued that TANF, a state-administered program that receives federal and state funds, is outside the statutory provision. In addition, section 402(b) of the act gives states broad discretion to set standards governing immigrant eligibility for TANF, and does not refer to the sponsor-deeming requirements.

241. Pub. L. No. 104-193, 110 Stat. 2105, § 421 (1996). An immigrant's "sponsor" for these purposes is the individual who files an application seeking lawful permanent resident status (a "green card") for the immigrant and who signs an affidavit agreeing to support the immigrant financially. For the effective date of the new sponsor affidavit, *see id.* at § 423(c) (1996).

242. 8 U.S.C.A. § 1631(e) (West 1996).

243. *Id.* at § 1631(f) (West 1996).

244. Pub. L. No. 104-193, 110 Stat. 2105, § 103 (1996) (adding new § 402(b)(2)(D) (1996) to Title IV of the Social Security Act).

245. *Id.* (adding new § 408(a)(4) (1996) to Title IV of the Social Security Act).

246. *Id.* (adding new § 408(a)(5) (1996) to Title IV of the Social Security Act).

247. *Id.* (adding new § 408(a)(5)(B) (1996) to Title IV of the Social Security Act).

248. *Id.* at § 115.

249. *Id.* at § 103 (adding new § 408(a)(8) (1996) to Title IV of the Social Security Act).

250. *Id.* (adding new § 408(a)(9) (1996) to Title IV of the Social Security Act).

251. *Id.* (adding new § 404(c) to Title IV of the Social Security Act).

252. *Id.* (adding new § 402(a)(1)(B)(i) (1996) to Title IV of the Social Security Act).

253. *Shapiro v. Thompson*, 394 U.S. 618 (1969); *see also Green v. Anderson*, 26 F.3d 95 (9th Cir. 1994), *vacated on other grounds sub nom. Anderson v. Green*, 115 S. Ct. 1059 (1995).

254. States will argue that limiting newly arrived families to the benefit amount available in their state of origin does not violate equal protection because (1) the federal statute explicitly authorizes such discrimination and (2) the discrimination does not deny newcomers *all* benefits but merely leaves them in the same position they would have been in had they not

migrated. The Supreme Court rejected the first argument in *Shapiro* and in several later cases, holding that Congress may not authorize states to take actions that would otherwise violate the Fourteenth Amendment. *See Graham v. Richardson*, 403 U.S. 365 (1971). The second argument was considered and rejected in 1994 by the federal Court of Appeals for the Ninth Circuit, in *Green v. Anderson*, 26 F.3d 95 (9th Cir. 1994), *vacated on other grounds sub nom. Anderson v. Green*, 115 S. Ct. 1059 (1995).

255. *See* Stephen Loffredo, *"If You Ain't Got the Do, Re, Mi": The Commerce Clause and State Residence Restrictions on Welfare*, 11 Yale Law & Pol'y Rev. 147 (1993).

256. Pub. L. No. 104-193, 110 Stat. 2105, § 103 (1996)(adding new § 408(a)(7) (1996) to Title IV of the Social Security Act).

257. *See, e.g.*, Lafer, *supra* note 185, at 353; Newman & Lennon, *supra* note 185, 66–67; Jencks & Edin, *supra* note 185, at 45–46; Ellwood, *supra* note 185, at A19.

258. *Id.* (adding new § 408(a)(7)(D) (1996) to Title IV of the Social Security Act).

259. *See* Super et al., *supra* note 179, at 6.

260. Pub. L. No. 104-193, 110 Stat. 2105, § 103 (adding new § 408(a)(7)(C) (1996) to Title IV of the Social Security Act).

261. *Id.* (adding new § 408(a)(7)(C)(iii) (1996) to Title IV of the Social Security Act).

262. Some states may have waivers from this requirement that predate passage of the 1996 welfare act. *See id.* (adding new §§ 415(a)(1) & (2) (1996) to Title IV of the Social Security Act).

263. *Id.* (adding new § 408(a)(7)(F) (1996) to Title IV of the Social Security Act).

264. *Id.* (adding new § 407 (1996) to Title IV of the Social Security Act).

265. *Id.* (adding new § 402(a)(1)(B)(iv) (1996) to Title IV of the Social Security Act).

266. Job search activity is not "work" if a recipient engages in it for longer than six weeks, or for twelve weeks in states with an unemployment rate that is at least 50 percent greater than the national unemployment rate, or for longer than four consecutive weeks. *Id.* (adding new § 407(c)(2)(A)(i) (1996) to Title IV of the Social Security Act).

267. *Id.* (adding new § 407(d) (1996) to Title IV of the Social Security Act).

268. *Id.* (adding new § 407(b) (1996) to Title IV of the Social Security Act).

269. *Id.* (adding new § 407(c)(2)(B) (1996) to Title IV of the Social Security Act).

270. *Id.* (adding new § 407(c) (1996) to Title IV of the Social Security Act).

271. *See id.* at § 407 (1996). Teen heads of households may meet work requirements by maintaining satisfactory attendance at a secondary school or equivalent or by participating in education directly related to employment. *See id.* at § 407(c)(2)(C) (1996).

272. *Id.* (adding new § 407(e)(1) (1996) to Title IV of the Social Security Act).

273. *Id.* (adding new § 407(e)(2) (1996) to Title IV of the Social Security Act).

274. *Id.* (adding new § 407(b)(5) (1996) to Title IV of the Social Security Act).

275. *Id.* (adding new § 402(a)(7) (1996) to Title IV of the Social Security Act). This provision allows states to "waive, pursuant to a determination of good cause, other program requirements . . . in cases where compliance with such requirements would make it more difficult for individuals receiving [TANF benefits] to escape domestic violence or [would] unfairly penalize such individuals who are or have been victimized by such violence, or individuals who are at risk of further domestic violence."

276. *Id.* (adding new § 407(c)(2)(C) (1996) to Title IV of the Social Security Act).

277. *Id.* (adding new § 407(b)(5) (1996) to Title IV of the Social Security Act).

278. *See, e.g.,* David Firestone, *New York Losing Millions for Lack of Welfare Plan,* N.Y. Times, Oct. 9, 1996, A1; David T. Ellwood, *Welfare Reform in Name Only,* N.Y. Times, July 22, 1996, A19.

279. Pub. L. No. 104-193, 110 Stat. 2105, § 103 (adding new § 409(a)(3) (1996) to Title IV of the Social Security Act).

280. *Id.* (adding new § 404(i) (1996) to Title IV of the Social Security Act).

281. *See, e.g.,* John Pawasarat & Lois Quinn, *The Impact of Learnfare on Milwaukee County Social Service Clients* 2 (Univ. of Wisconsin-Milwaukee, 1990).

282. Pub. L. No. 104-193, 110 Stat. 2105, § 103 (1996) (adding new § 404(j) (1996) to Title IV of the Social Security Act).

283. *Id.* (adding new § 408(a)(3) (1996) to Title IV of the Social Security Act).

284. *Id.* (adding new § 408(a)(2) (1996) to Title IV of the Social Security Act).

285. *Id.* (adding new § 408(b)(1996) to Title IV of the Social Security Act).

286. *Id.* (adding new § 402(a)(1)(iv) (1996) to Title IV of the Social Security Act).

287. *Id.* (adding new § 402(a)(1)(B)(iii) (1996) to Title IV of the Social Security Act).

288. *Goldberg v. Kelly,* 397 U.S. 254 (1970).

289. Pub. L. No. 104-193, 110 Stat. 2105, § 103 (1996) (adding new § 402(a)(1)(B)(iii) (1996) to Title IV of the Social Security Act).

290. Pub. L. No. 92-603 (1972 amendments to the Social Security Act), *codified at* 42 U.S.C.A. §§ 1381, 1383 (West 1996).

291. *1994 Green Book, supra* note 2, at 207.

292. The federal law governing the Supplemental Security Income program can be found in Title 42 of the United States Code (U.S.C.A.) at sections 1381 through 1383. The Social Security Administration's regulations regarding the SSI program are published in Title 20 of the Code of Federal Regulations (C.F.R.) at part 416. The Social Security Administration (SSA) publishes several manuals that contain the rules and procedures for programs administered by the agency. These include the "Program Operations Manual System" (POMS), the "Social Security Handbook," and the "Supplemental Security Income Handbook." SSA also issues "Social Security Rulings" that explain the agency's interpretation of laws governing the SSI program. You may review these materials at any Social Security District Office or Branch Office. 20 C.F.R. § 422.430 (1996).

293. *Id.* at § 416.1603(c) (1996).

294. *See* Pub. L. No. 104-193, 110 Stat. 2105, §§ 400 *et seq.* (1996).

295. 20 C.F.R. § 416.802 (1996).

296. *Id.* at § 416.803 (1996).

297. *Id.* at § 416.801 (1996).

298. *Id.* at § 416.981 (1996). Social Security Administration regulations state: "An eye which has a limitation in the field of vision so that the widest diameter of the visual field subtends an angle no greater than 20 degrees is considered to have a central visual acuity of 20/200 or less." *Id.* You can also receive SSI as a blind person if in December 1973 you were receiving state Aid to the Blind benefits under Title X or Title XVI of the Social Security Act and if you are still blind as defined by the state program. *Id.* at § 416.982 (1996).

299. 42 U.S.C.A. § 1382c(a)(3)(A) (West 1996); 20 C.F.R. § 416.905 (1996).

300. 20 C.F.R. § 416.972 (1996).

301. *Id.*

302. *Id.* at § 416.973 (1996).

303. *Id.* at § 416.973(c) (1996).

304. *Id.* at § 416.973(b) (1996).

305. *Id.* at § 416.974(b) (1996).

306. *Id.* at § 416.974(a)(2) (1996).

307. *Id.* at § 416.976(a) (1996).

308. *Id.* at § 416.921(b) (1996).

309. *Id.* at § 416.921(a) (1996). The Social Security Administration has stated that a physical or mental impairment "can be considered as not severe only if it is a slight abnormality which has such a minimal effect on the individual that it would not be expected to interfere with the ability to work irrespective of age, education, or work experience." Social Security Ruling 85-28.

310. 20 C.F.R. § 416.925 (1996).

311. Federal law requires that the Social Security Administration make copies of its regulations available for public inspection at all of its district branch offices. 20 C.F.R. § 422.430 (1996).

312. The Social Security Administration will conclude that a medical condition is as severe as a condition on the list if it is "at least equal in severity and duration" to the most similar medical condition that appears on the list. 20 C.F.R. § 416.926(a) (1996).

313. *Id.* at §§ 416.920(e), 416.960(b), 416.961 (1996).

314. *Id.* at § 416.920(e) (1996).

315. *Id.* at § 416.920(f) (1996).

316. *Id.*

317. *Id.* at § 416.969a(b) (1996).

318. For purposes of the Medical-Vocational Guidelines, the Social Security Administration has defined four categories of residual functional capacity: heavy work, medium work, light work, and sedentary work. A residual functional capacity for heavy work means that the individual can lift up to one hundred pounds at a time, frequently lift and carry fifty pounds, walk and stand most of the work day, and push and pull arm and leg controls on machinery. 20 C.F.R. § 416.967(d) (1996). At the other end of the spectrum, a residual functional capacity for only sedentary work means that the individual can lift up to ten pounds, sit for most of the work day, and occasionally walk or stand. 20 C.F.R. § 416.967(a) (1996). These residual functional capacity categories are described more fully in Social Security Ruling 83-10.

319. 20 C.F.R. pt. 404, subpt. P, app. 2, § 201.00(d) (1996).

320. *Id.* at app. 2, table 1, rule 201.12 (1996).

321. The one exception to this rule is that an individual between ages 45 and 49 who is (1) restricted to sedentary work, (2) has no transferable work skills, (3) is unable to perform her prior work, and (4) is illiterate or unable to communicate in English is considered disabled. 20 C.F.R. pt. 404, subpt. P, app. 2, § 201.00(h) (1996).

322. 20 C.F.R. § 416.967(a) (1996); Social Security Ruling 83-10.

323. Social Security Ruling 83-12.

324. 20 C.F.R. § 416.969a (1996); Social Security Ruling 83-10, glossary.

325. *See* Social Security Ruling 85-15 ("The basic mental demands of competitive, re-munerative, unskilled work include the abilities (on a sustained basis) to understand, carry out and remember simple instructions; to respond appropriately to supervision, co-workers and usual work situations; and deal with changes in a routine work setting. A substantial loss of ability to meet any of these basic work-related activities . . . would justify a finding of disability [even for young, well-educated and highly skilled individuals].").

326. 20 C.F.R. § 416.969a (1996); Social Security Ruling 83-12.

327. 20 C.F.R. § 416.969a(c)(27) (1996); 20 C.F.R. pt. 404, subpt. P, app. 2, § 200.00(e)(1) (1996).

328. 20 C.F.R. § 416.969a(d) (1996); 20 C.F.R. pt. 404, subpt. P, app. 2, § 200.00(e)(2) (1996); Social Security Ruling 83-11.

329. 20 C.F.R. § 416.962 (1996).

330. Social Security Administration Office of Disability, Disability Notes, Pub. L. No. 64-040 (No. 16) July 30, 1996.

331. Pub. L. No. 104-121, § 105 (1996). This provision amends the Social Security Act by inserting the following: "An individual shall not be considered disabled for purposes of [the SSI program] if alcoholism or drug addiction would (but for this subparagraph) be a contrib-uting factor material to the Commissioner's determination that the individual is disabled."

332. 42 U.S.C.A. § 1382c(a)(3) (West 1996), as amended by Pub. L. No. 104-193, 110 Stat. 2105, § 211 (1996).

333. *See Sullivan v. Zebly*, 493 U.S. 521 (1990).

334. 20 C.F.R. §§ 416.924b(c)(1), 416.926a(d)(10) (1996).

335. *Id.* at §§ 416.924b(c)(2), 416.926a(d)(11) (1996).

336. *See generally id.* at § 416.912 (1996).

337. *Id.* at § 416.913(e) (1996).

338. *Id.* at § 416.929 (1996).

339. *Id.*

340. *Id.* at § 416.913(c) (1996).

341. *Id.* at § 416.927 (1996).

342. *Id.* at § 416.912(d) (1996).

343. *Id.* at § 416.917 (1996).

344. *Id.* and 20 C.F.R. § 416.919a (1996).

345. *Id.* at § 416.918 (1996).

346. *Id.* at § 416.918(c) (1996).

347. *Id.* at § 416.919j (1996).

348. *Id.*

349. *Id.* at § 416.919h (1996).

350. *Id.* at § 416.930(a) (1996).

351. *Id.* at § 416.930(b) (1996).

352. *Id.* at § 416.930(c) (1996).

353. *Id.* at § 416.1710 (1996).

354. *Id.* at §§ 416.212, 416.1715 (1996).

355. *Id.* at § 416.1715(b) (1996).

356. *Id.* at § 416.211 (1996).

357. *Id.* at §§ 416.201, 416.211(d) (1996).

358. *Id.* at §§ 416.211(a)(2), 416.211(d) (1996).

359. 61 Fed. Reg. 10274 (Mar. 13, 1996).

360. *Id.*; *1994 Green Book, supra* note 2, at 211, 219.

361. 20 C.F.R. § 416.211(b) (1996); *see also 1994 Green Book, supra* note 2, at 219.

362. 20 C.F.R. § 416.211(c)(ii) (1996).

363. *Id.* at § 416.211(c) (1996).

364. *Id.* at §§ 416.1600–.1603 (1996).

365. *Id.* at § 416.1603(a) (1996).

366. *Id.* at § 416.1327 (1996).

367. *Id.*

368. Pub. L. No. 104-193, 110 Stat. § 2105, Title IV (1996).

369. *Id.* at § 402(a)(2)(B) (1996).

370. *Id.* at § 402(a)(2)(C) (1996).

371. *Id.* at § 402(a)(2)(A) (1996).

372. Immigration and Nationality Act, §§ 316(a), 319.

373. 20 C.F.R. § 416.1610 (1996).

374. 61 Fed. Reg. 55346 (Oct. 25, 1996).

375. Social Security Amendments of 1983 (Pub. L. No. 98-21); 20 C.F.R. § 416.405 (1996).

376. *See* 61 Fed. Reg. 8286 (Mar. 4, 1996).

377. 20 C.F.R. § 416.2001 (1996).

378. *1994 Green Book, supra* note 2, at 222–23; *see* 61 Fed. Reg. 18529 (Apr. 26, 1996).

379. 20 C.F.R. § 416.2030 (1996).

380. *Id.* at § 416.1102 (1996).

381. *Id.*

382. *Id.* at § 416.1110 (1996).

383. *Id.* at § 416.1120 (1996).

384. *Id.* at § 416.1103 (1996).

385. *See id.* (1996). Please note that the list of items excluded from income frequently changes.

386. 42 U.S.C.A. §§ 1382a(b)(21); 1383(a)(2)(F) (West 1996).

387. 61 Fed. Reg. 1711 (Jan. 23, 1996).

388. *Id.*

389. 20 C.F.R. §§ 416.1180–.1182 (1996).

390. *Id.* at §§ 416.1181, 416.1226 (1996).

391. *Id.* at §§ 416.1130–.1148 (1996).

392. *Id.* at § 416.1130(b) (1996).

393. *Id.* at § 416.1131 (1996).

394. *Id.*

395. *Id.* at § 416.1131(c) (1996).

396. *Id.* at § 416.1131(b) (1996).

397. *Id.*

398. *Id.* at § 416.1132(c)(5) (1996). If every member of a household receives some form of public assistance payments, every member is considered to be living in his or her own household, and the one-third reduction rule does not apply. *Id.* at § 416.1142 (1996). The "presumed value rule" might still apply, but only if food, clothing, or shelter is received from someone outside of the household. *Id.*

399. *Id.* at § 416.1132(c)(3) (1996). You are living in a "noninstitutional care situation" if an agency responsible for your care places you in a private household licensed or approved by the agency to provide care under a specific program (such as foster care) and you, the agency, or someone else pays for your care. *Id.* at § 416.1143 (1996).

400. *Id.* at § 416.1132(c)(4) (1996). Your "pro rata share of household operating expenses" is equal to the total operating expenses paid for by members of your household divided by the number of persons living in the household. Household operating expenses are the expenditures made by household members for food, rent, mortgage, property taxes, home energy, water, sewerage, and garbage collection. (Expenses paid for by persons outside the household are not counted for these purposes.) *See id.* at § 416.1133 (1996). The one-third reduction rule does not apply if you are paying a pro rata share of household operating expenses. *Id.* The "presumed value rule" might still apply to you, but only if you receive food, clothing, or shelter from someone outside of your household. *Id.*

401. *Id.* at § 416.1132(c)(1)–(2) (1996).

402. *Id.* at § 416.1141 (1996).

403. *Id.* at § 416.1140 (1996).

404. *Id.* at § 416.1140(a)(2) and (b)(2) (1996).

405. *Id.* at § 416.1140(a)(2) (1996).

406. *Id.* at § 416.1160 (1996).

407. *Id.* at §§ 416.1160(a)(1) and (d), 416.1161, 416.1163 (1996).

408. *Id.* at §§ 416.1160(a)(2), 416.1161, 416.1165 (1996).

409. *Id.* at §§ 416.415, 416.1165(i) (1996); 60 Fed. Reg. 360 (Jan. 4, 1995).

410. The deeming provisions of the Personal Responsibility and Work Opportunity Reconciliation Act of 1996, Pub. L. No. 194-193, 110 Stat. 2105 (1996), apply only to immigrants whose sponsors sign the new type of affidavit of support required by section 423 of the act (adding a new section 213A to the Immigration and Nationality Act). The new affidavits must be used beginning on a date, to be designated by the Attorney General, that is no earlier than 60 days and no later than 180 days from the date of enactment (August 22, 1996). *See* Pub. L. No. 104-193, 110 Stat. 2105, § 423(c) (1996).

411. Pub. L. No. 103-152, 107 Stat. 1576, § 7(b) (1995).

412. 20 C.F.R. § 416.1166a(d)(3) (1996).

413. *Id.* at § 416.1166a(d)(1) and (2) (1996). You were granted "refugee status" for these purposes if you were admitted to the United States as a refugee under section 207(c)(1) of the Immigration and Nationality Act or you were "paroled" into the United States as a refugee under section 212(d)(5) of that act. *Id.*

414. *Id.* at § 416.1160(d) (1996).

415. Pub. L. No. 104-193, 110 Stat. 2105, § 423(c) (1996).

416. *Id.* at § 421 (1996) (exception for forty qualifying quarters); 8 U.S.C.A. § 1631(e) (West 1996) (exception for financial hardship); *id.* at § 1631(f) (West 1996) (exception for battering or "extreme cruelty").

417. 20 C.F.R. §§ 416.1160(a)(4), 416.1161, 416.1168 (1996). If you received benefits under the Aid to the Aged, Blind and Disabled (AABD) program in December 1973 and the state considered the needs of an individual living with you to determine the amount of your AABD grant, that individual may be an "essential person." The individual is an essential person only if he or she (1) has been living with you since December 1973; (2) was ineligible for AABD benefits in December 1973; (3) has never been eligible for SSI; and (4) had his or her needs included in the calculation of your AABD grant in December 1973. 20 C.F.R. §§ 416.220–.222 (1996). If one or more essential persons currently live with you, you may ask the Social Security Administration to include any or all of them in the calculation of your SSI grant. For every essential person included in your grant, your SSI payment will be increased by one "essential person increment." *Id.* at § 416.223(c)(2)(ii) (1996). In 1996, the essential person increment was $235 per month. The potential downside to including an essential person in your SSI grant is that the Social Security Administration will consider any income received by the essential person to be available to you. *Id.* at § 416.223(b) (1996). If the essential person has significant income, this may result in a net reduction of your SSI payment.

418. 20 C.F.R. § 416.1205 (1996); *1994 Green Book, supra* note 2, at 215.

419. 20 C.F.R. § 416.1201 (1996).

420. *Id.* at § 416.1212 (1996).

421. *Id.* at § 416.1216(a) (1996).

422. *Id.* at § 416.1216(c) (1996).

423. *Id.* at § 416.1218(b)(1)(i)–(iv) (1996).

424. *Id.* at § 416.1218(b)(2) (1996).

425. *Id.* at § 416.1222 (1996).

426. *Id.* at § 416.1224 (1996).

427. *Id.* at § 416.1225 (1996).

428. *Id.* at § 416.1230 (1996).

429. *Id.* at § 416.1231 (1996).

430. *Id.* at § 416.1233 (1996).

431. 42 U.S.C.A. §§ 1382b(a)(12), 1383(a)(2)(F) (West 1996).

432. *See generally* 20 C.F.R. § 416.1236–.1238 (1996).

433. *Id.* at § 416.1236(b) (1996).

434. This includes assistance paid under the United States Housing Act of 1937, the National Housing Act, Section 101 of the Housing and Urban Development Act of 1965, Title V of the Housing Act of 1949, or section 202(h) of the Housing Act of 1959. *See* 20 C.F.R. § 416.1238 (1996).

435. *Id.* at § 416.1237 (1996).

436. *Id.* at § 416.1234 (1996).

437. *Id.* at § 416.1232 (1996).

438. *Id.* at § 416.1246(f) (1996).

439. Program Operations Manual System (POMS) § SI 01120.200 (1994). This POMS transmittal, issued by the Social Security Administration in March 1994, is entitled "Trust Property" and discusses how resources held in trusts are dealt with in determining SSI eligibility. Unfortunately, trusts are treated somewhat differently under the SSI and Medicaid programs, depending on the structure of the trust and how it is treated under the relevant

state law. Consult a lawyer or other trained advocate if you plan to transfer resources into a supplemental needs trust.

440. If you are under age 65 and disabled, you may place assets into a supplemental needs trust in order to become eligible for Medicaid, and there is no period of disqualification. 42 U.S.C.A. § 1396p(d)(4)(A) (West 1996). However, the trust must be established by your parent, grandparent, legal guardian, or a court, and the amount remaining in the trust when you die will be used first to repay the state for Medicaid that your received. *Id.* Other types of trusts that can qualify individuals of any age for Medicaid are discussed in the Medicaid section of chapter 3 of this book.

441. 20 C.F.R. § 416.1240(a)(1) (1996).

442. *Id.* at § 416.1240(a)(2) (1996).

443. *Id.* at § 416.1242 (1996).

444. *Id.* at § 416.1245(b) (1996).

445. *See generally id.* at § 416.1202 (1996).

446. *Id.* at § 416.1202(a) (1996).

447. *Id.* and at §§ 416.1806, 416.1811 (1996).

448. *Id.* at § 416.1202(b) (1996).

449. *Id.*; 60 Fed. Reg. 360 (Jan. 4, 1995).

450. 20 C.F.R. § 416.1204 (1996).

451. The deeming provisions of the Personal Responsibility and Work Opportunity Reconciliation Act of 1996, Pub. L. No. 104-193, 110 Stat. 2105 (1996), apply only to immigrants whose sponsors sign the new type of affidavit of support required by section 423 of the act (adding a new section 213A to the Immigration and Nationality Act). The new affidavits must be used beginning on a date, to be designated by the Attorney General, that is no earlier than 60 days and no later than 180 days from the date of enactment (August 22, 1996). *See* Pub. L. No. 104-193, 110 Stat. 2105, § 423(c) (1996).

452. Pub. L. No. 103-152, 107 Stat. 1516 (1996).

453. *Id.*; 20 C.F.R. § 416.1166a(d)(3) (1996).

454. *Id.* at §§ 416.1204, 416.1166a(d)(1) and (2) (1996). You were granted "refugee status" for these purposes if you were admitted to the United States as a refugee under section 207(c)(1) of the Immigration and Nationality Act or you were "paroled" into the United States as a refugee under section 212(d)(5) of that act. *Id.*

455. *Id.* at §§ 416.1204, 416.1160(d) (1996).

456. Pub. L. No. 104-193, 110 Stat. 2105, § 423(c) (1996).

457. *Id.* at § 421 (1996) (exception for forty qualifying quarters); 8 U.S.C.A. § 1631(e)(West 1996)(exception for financial hardship); *id.* at § 1631(f)(West 1996)(exception for battering or "extreme cruelty").

458. "Essential person" is defined *supra*, note 417.

459. *See generally* 20 C.F.R. §§ 416.301–.320 (1996).

460. 42 U.S.C.A. § 1382(c)(7) (West 1996).

461. 20 C.F.R. § 416.335 (1996).

462. *Id.* at §§ 416.340, 416.345 (1996).

463. *Id.* at § 416.351 (1995).

464. *Id.* at §§ 416.931–.933 (1996).

465. *Id.* at § 416.934 (1996).
466. *Id.* at §§ 416.1404, 416.1422, 416.1453, 416.1479 (1996).
467. *Id.* at § 416.1336 (1996).
468. *Id.* at § 416.1402 (1996).
469. *1994 Green Book, supra* note 2, at 57.
470. 20 C.F.R. § 422.525 (1996).
471. *Id.* at § 416.1336 (1996).
472. *Id.* at § 416.1401 (1996).
473. *Id.* at §§ 416.1409(b), 416.1433(c), 416.1468(b) (1996).
474. *Id.* at § 416.1411(b) (1996); Social Security Ruling 91-5.
475. 20 C.F.R. § 416.1413a(b) (1996).
476. *Id.* at § 416.1413a(a) (1996).
477. *Id.* at § 416.1413b (1996).
478. *Id.*
479. *Id.* at § 416.1413(a) (1996).
480. *Id.* at § 416.1413(b) (1996).
481. *Id.* at § 416.1413(c) (1996).
482. *Id.* at § 416.1413(d) (1996).
483. *See generally id.* at § 416.1414–.1418 (1996).
484. *Id.* at § 416.1438 (1996).
485. *Id.* at § 416.1436(d) (1996).
486. *Id.* at § 416.1444 (1996).
487. *Id.* at § 416.1429 (1996).
488. *Id.* at § 416.1453 (1996).
489. *Id.* at § 416.1436(b)–(d) (1996).
490. *Id.* at § 416.1450(d) (1996).
491. *Id.* The witness fee in 1996 was $40 per day plus the actual cost of transportation by common carrier at the most economical rate reasonably available. If the witness uses an automobile, mileage plus the actual cost of tolls and parking will be paid. *See* 28 U.S.C.A. § 1821 (West 1996).
492. 20 C.F.R. § 416.1468(a) (1996).
493. *See, e.g., Mathews v. Eldridge,* 424 U.S. 319 (1976).
494. 20 C.F.R. § 416.1336(b) (1996).
495. The information in this section is drawn largely from Marion Nichols, Jon Dunlap & Scott Barkan, *National General Assistance Survey, 1992* (Center on Budget and Policy Priorities, 1992); and Iris J. Lav et al., *The States and the Poor: How Budget Decisions Affected Low Income People in 1992* (Center on Budget and Policy Priorities, 1992).
496. *Cf.* "State Cash Assistance Programs Under a Block Grant," *Welfare News* 6–7 (Aug. 20, 1996) (discussing the need for advocacy at the local level).
497. The states are Alaska, Arizona, Connecticut, Delaware, the District of Columbia, Hawaii, Kansas, Maryland, Massachusetts, Michigan, Minnesota, Missouri, New Jersey, New Mexico, New York, Ohio, Oregon, Pennsylvania, Rhode Island, Utah, Vermont, and Washington. Although South Carolina has a statewide General Assistance program, in early 1992 it served only five cases a month. *See* Telephone conversation with Marion Nichols,

Center on Budget and Policy Priorities, Aug. 23, 1996; S.C. St. § 43-5-310, Code 1976 § 43-5-310 (1995).

498. The states are California, Idaho, Illinois, Indiana, Iowa, Maine, Montana, Nebraska, New Hampshire, and Wisconsin.

499. The states are Colorado, Florida, Georgia, Kentucky, Nevada, North Carolina, North Dakota, South Dakota, Texas, and Virginia.

500. The states are Alabama, Arkansas, Louisiana, Mississippi, Oklahoma, Tennessee, West Virginia, and Wyoming.

501. 1996 Pa. Legis. Serv. Act 1996-35 (S.B. 1441) (Purdon's 1996).

502. *See* Anthony Halter, *Homeless in Philadelphia: A Qualitative Study of the Impact of State Welfare Reform on Individuals*, 19 J. Sociology and Social Welfare 7 (1989).

503. *See* Clitia J. Coulton, *General Assistance Program Reductions in Cuyahoga County* (Case Western Reserve Univ., Nov. 1992).

504. *See* Sandra K. Danziger & Sheldon Danziger, *Will Welfare Recipients Find Work When Welfare Ends?* in Isabel V. Sawhill ed., *Welfare Reform: An Analysis of the Issues* 41–44 (Urban Institute, 1996).

505. *See* Sandra Hauser & Henry Freedman, *Jobless, Penniless, Often Homeless: State General Assistance Cuts Leave "Employables" Struggling for Survival* (Center on Social Welfare Policy and Law, Feb. 1994).

506. *See* Halter, *supra* note 502.

507. *See* Knud L. Hansen, *The Impact of Elimination of the General Assistance Program in Michigan* (Wayne State Univ., Aug. 1992).

508. *See* Jason DeParle, *The Sorrows, and Surprises, after a Welfare Plan Ends*, N.Y. Times, Apr. 14, 1992, at A1.

509. *See Carey v. Quern*, 588 F.2d 230, 232 (7th Cir. 1978).

510. *See Publicover v. Golden*, Civ. No. 77-110-D (D.N.H. 1977), reprinted in Henry A. Freedman, *Seminar in Welfare Law* (Columbia Univ. School of Law, Spring 1986).

511. *See Goldberg v. Kelly*, 397 U.S. 254, 264 (1970).

512. As of 1992.

513. States that have this limit include Connecticut, Kansas, Maryland, Michigan, and Ohio.

514. The states include Connecticut, Delaware, the District of Columbia, Massachusetts, and Minnesota.

515. The states include Connecticut, Delaware, Hawaii, Kansas, Massachusetts, Michigan, Minnesota, Montana, Nebraska, Rhode Island, Vermont, and Wisconsin.

516. The states are Alaska, Connecticut, Minnesota, New Jersey, New York, Ohio, Pennsylvania, and Utah. In Montana and Nebraska, the programs are statewide, but in some places, county-based. In Wisconsin, the program is statewide and throughout the state, county-based.

517. *Graham v. Richardson*, 403 U.S. 365 (1971).

518. Pub. L. No. 104-193, 110 Stat. 2105, § 412 (1996).

519. *See* Immigration and Nationality Act § 243(h) (withholding of deportation).

520. For refugees, the five-year eligibility period begins on the date the immigrant was

admitted to the United States as a refugee. For asylees and immigrants whose deportation has been withheld, the five-year period begins on the date that political asylum or withholding of deportation was granted. *See* Pub. L. No. 104-193, 110 Stat. 2105, § 402(b)(2)(A) (1996).

521. *Id.* at §§ 402(b)(2)(B) & 435 (1996).

522. *Id.* at § 435 (1996).

523. *Id.* at § 402(b) (1996).

524. Illegal Immigration Reform and Immigrant Responsibility Act of 1996, § 553.

525. *Graham*, 403 U.S. 365 (1971). The authors of the 1996 welfare act recognized this constitutional flaw and attempted to avoid it with a legislative "finding" that any restriction imposed by a state on immigrant eligibility for public assistance is the "least restrictive means" of achieving "compelling" national immigration policies. Pub. L. No. 104-193, 110 Stat. 2105, § 400 (1996). (Unlike the states, the federal government may discriminate against immigrants in the exercise of its constitutional power to regulate immigration. *See Mathews v. Diaz*, 426 U.S. 67 (1976).) But the statute is unconvincing on this point because it does not mandate any particular federal policy towards immigrants. Rather, it delegates broad authority to fifty state governments to adopt fifty different, uncoordinated and inconsistent state policies toward immigrants—policies over which the federal government has no control. For this reason alone, it cannot credibly be maintained that the law is necessary to the achievement of national immigration policy. Therefore, state laws that treat legal immigrants more harshly than federal law *requires* should be held unconstitutional on the authority of *Graham v. Richardson*.

526. Pub. L. No. 104-193, 110 Stat. 2105, § 422 (1996)

527. *Id.* at § 422(a)(1). An immigrant's "sponsor" for these purposes is the individual who files an application seeking lawful permanent resident status (a "green card") for the immigrant and who signs an affidavit agreeing to support the immigrant financially.

528. *Id.* at § 423(c) (1996).

529. Illegal Immigration Reform and Immigrant Responsibility Act of 1996, § 553.

530. *See Barannikova v. Town of Greenwich*, 643 A.2d 251 (Conn. 1994).

531. *See Minino v. Perales*, 581 N.Y.S.2d 162 (Ct. Apps. 1992), *aff'g* 562 N.Y.S.2d 626 (App. Div. 1st Dept. 1991).

532. 394 U.S. 618, 627 (1969).

533. 415 U.S. 250, 251 (1974).

534. *See, e.g.*, Minn. Stat. § 256D.065 (1995); Wis. Stat. § 49.19 (1995).

535. *See Mitchell v. Steffen*, 487 N.W.2d 896 (Minn. 1992) (invalidating Minnesota two-tier welfare system); *see also Anderson v. Green*, 115 S. Ct. 1059 (1995) (vacating, on ripeness grounds, lower court decision invalidating California law that capped newcomers' AFDC grants at benefit level available in state of origin); *but see Jones v. Milwaukee County*, 485 N.W.2d 21 (Wisc. 1992) (upholding sixty-day length-of-residence requirement for Wisconsin general relief program). *See generally* Loffredo, *supra* note 255.

536. *Zobel v. Williams*, 457 U.S. 55, 71 (O'Connor, J. concurring) (1982) (privileges and immunity clause); *Edwards v. California*, 314 U.S. 160, 174 (1941) (commerce clause).

537. Telephone conversation with Marion Nichols, Center on Budget and Policy Priorities, Aug. 23, 1996 (basing percentage on 1996 Congressional Budget Office estimates).

538. The information in this section is drawn largely from materials distributed by the

1997 Earned Income Credit Campaign, A Project of the Center on Budget and Policy Priorities. Other useful sources include Henry A. Freedman & Christopher D. Lamb, *The Earned Income Credit Can Help Families Receiving AFDC and Other Benefits* (Center on Social Welfare Policy and Law, Jan. 1995); *1994 Green Book, supra* note 2, at 699–704.

539. 26 U.S.C.A. § 32 (West 1996).

540. *See* Center on Budget and Policy Priorities, *The 1997 Earned Income Credit Campaign,* unpaginated (Dec. 1996); *see also 1994 Green Book, supra* note 2, at 704, table 16-13 (estimating that in 1994, eighteen billion households claimed EICs).

541. *See* U.S. General Accounting Office, *Tax Administration: Earned Income Credit— Data on Noncompliance and Illegal Alien Recipients,* Report to the Hon. William V. Roth, Jr., U.S. Senate 3 (Oct. 1994) (hereinafter, *1994 GAO Report*)(reporting that in 1990, only between 75 and 86 percent of eligible families claimed the EIC).

542. Based on 1995 estimates. *See* Isaac Shapiro, *Four Years and Still Falling: The Decline in the Value of the Minimum Wage* 6, 10–13 (Center on Budget and Policy Priorities, 1995). In 1996, Congress amended the minimum wage, with a phase-in increase of fifty cents beginning Oct. 1, 1996. *See* Pub. L. No. 104-188, 110 Stat. 188 (1996).

543. *See* Pub. L. No. 104-193, 110 Stat. 2105, § 451 (1996) (amending 26 U.S.C. § 32(c)(1) (1996).

544. 26 U.S.C.A. § 32(b)(2)(B), (c)(l)(A) (West 1996).

545. *Id.* at § 32(b) (West 1996).

546. *Id.*

547. *Id.* at § 32(c)(3)(A) (West 1996).

548. *Id.* at § 32(c)(3)(B)(iii) (West 1996).

549. *Id.* at § 32(c)(3)(A), (B) (West 1996).

550. *Id.* at § 32(c)(3)(C) (West 1996).

551. *See* 26 U.S.C.A. § 32(b)(1)(A), (2) (West 1996); Center on Budget and Policy Priorities, *The 1997 Earned Income Credit Campaign,* unpaginated (Dec. 1996).

552. Center on Budget and Policy Priorities, *The 1997 Earned Income Credit Campaign,* unpaginated (Dec. 1996).

553. *See 1994 Green Book, supra* note 2, at 402. Some reports estimate that 39 percent of single women receiving AFDC also work. *See* Heidi Hartmann & Roberta Spalter-Roth, *Reducing Welfare's Stigma: Policies That Build upon Commonalities among Women,* 26 Conn. L. Rev. 901, 908 (1996), *citing* Roberta M. Spalter-Roth et al., *Combining Work and Welfare: An Alternative Anti-Poverty Strategy* (1992).

554. *See* Shapiro, *supra* note 542; *see also* U.S. General Accounting Office, *Low-Income Families: Comparison of Incomes of AFDC and Working Poor Families,* Testimony before the Comm. on Governmental Affairs, U.S. Senate, Statement of Jane L. Ross, Director, Income Security Issues, Health, Education, and Human Services Division (Jan. 25, 1995); N.Y.C. Human Resources Admin., *Project Bulletin: Work and Public Assistance: Employment Outcomes for a Cohort of AFDC Cases* (Aug. 1988).

555. 42 U.S.C.A. § 602(a)(18) (West 1996).

556. *Id.* at § 602(a)(8)(A)(viii) (West 1996).

557. *Id.* at § 602(a)(7)(B)(iv) (West 1996) (AFDC rule on exclusion of EIC).

558. 7 U.S.C.A. § 2014(g)(3) (West 1996).

559. *See* 26 U.S.C.A. § 32(c)(1)(E) (West 1996). The welfare act of 1996 specifically amends the Internal Revenue Code to deny the Earned income Credit to "individuals not authorized to be employed in the United States." *See* Pub. L. No. 104-193, 110 Stat. 2105, § 451 (1996).

560. *See* Center on Budget and Policy Priorities, *The 1997 Earned Income Credit Campaign*, unpaginated (Dec. 1996).

561. According to press reports, the Internal Revenue Service is not quick in issuing EIC refund checks. *See* Maria O. Howard, *IRS Scrutiny Slows Rapid Refunds*, Richmond Times Dispatch, Feb. 8, 1995, at A-1. The refund process is delayed by the IRS' investigation of EIC requests. For example, the IRS verifies taxpayer Social Security numbers and also ensures that workers are not claiming any specific child more than once as a dependent. *See* Center on Budget and Policy Priorities, *The 1996 Earned Income Credit Campaign*, unpaginated (1996).

562. *See* Christopher D. Lamb, *Helping Low-Income Families Use the Earned Income Credit*, 28 Clearinghouse Rev. 1266 (1995).

563. *See* N.Y.S. Dep't of Social Servs., Informational Letter 95 INF-3 (Feb. 6, 1995).

11

Food Assistance

Does the federal Constitution guarantee a right to food?

The United States Supreme Court has never directly decided whether a starving person has a constitutional right to food, but the Court has ruled more generally that the federal Constitution does not create a right to subsistence.[1] It is therefore unlikely that the Court as currently composed will recognize a federal constitutional right to food. The Court has held, however, that once the government establishes a food assistance program, the Constitution requires that the program be administered fairly and prohibits the government from excluding needy individuals or groups for arbitrary reasons.[2]

Is there a state constitutional right to food assistance?

Maybe. More than a dozen state constitutions create affirmative rights to subsistence. Some of these provisions may provide the basis for establishing a positive right to food assistance for the hungry.[3] At present, however, no court has expressly recognized such a right.

FOOD STAMP PROGRAM

What is the food stamp program?[4]

The food stamp program is the federal government's most important effort in the fight against hunger. The program serves two independent but interrelated goals: to improve the nutritional status of poor persons and to provide indirect economic support to farmers. The food stamp program dates back to the Great Depression, with a limited program in effect from 1939 to 1943. President John F. Kennedy revived the food stamp program on a pilot basis in 1961 after witnessing shocking conditions of hunger in West Virginia during his presidential campaign of the previous year.

Congressional research subsequently confirmed that the program was an effective weapon in the war against hunger, and in 1964 Congress passed the Food Stamp Act establishing the program on a permanent basis. The program was extended nationwide in 1974.

The United States Department of Agriculture administers the food stamp program. The federal government pays the full cost of benefits and shares administrative expenses with the states. In 1995, 26 million Americans—almost 10 percent of the population—participated in the food stamp program and received an average per person benefit of $71 a month.[5] Many more poor people are eligible for assistance but do not apply. Indeed, federal studies show that the food stamp program serves less than 60 percent of the income-eligible population.[6]

The food stamp program has improved the health and diet of poor people who receive assistance. Together with other government programs that provide poor people with nutrition support, food stamps have resulted in:

- A decline in the rate of low birth weight among newborns, from 8.3 to 7 percent;
- A decline in the rate of stunting among preschoolers by almost 65 percent; and
- A decline in the rate of anemia among preschoolers by 5 percent or more depending on race and ethnicity.[7]

Studies further show that participation in the food stamp program substantially improves the diet of poor families by 20 to 40 percent and that food stamp shoppers, compared to all other shoppers, obtain 7 to 29 percent more of eleven key nutrients for every dollar spent on food.[8]

What are food stamps?

Generally, food stamps are government coupons that can be spent just like money to buy food at stores. In some states, the program uses an electronic benefits system instead of paper coupons.[9] Food stamps do not count as income or resources for any other public benefit program.[10]

Who can receive food stamps?

Food stamps are an entitlement, and before enactment of the Personal Responsibility and Work Opportunity Reconciliation Act of 1996—the "welfare reform" act—almost all poor people could receive food stamps if they applied for assistance. Under the 1996 act, which amends the law that governs the food stamp program, most legal immigrants are barred from receiving benefits. The new act also severely limits the right of able-bodied, childless individuals between the ages of 18 and 50 to receive food stamps.[11] Nevertheless, food stamps remain available to many people in need of assistance. You do not have to live with children to get food stamps. You do not have to be elderly or disabled. And you do not have to be on welfare or be unemployed. A recipient does, however, have to meet strict income, resource, and work registration requirements that are described later in this chapter.

What can you buy with food stamps?

You can use food stamps to buy any food except alcohol and pet food. You cannot use food stamps to buy soap, diapers, paper products, toothpaste, toilet paper, tobacco, or anything else that is not food.[12] You can, however, use food stamps to buy seeds and plants to grow food, and in Alaska you can use food stamps to buy some hunting and fishing equipment.

Can you use food stamps to buy prepared meals?

It depends. Food stamps generally cannot be used to buy hot food or prepared meals.[13] There are, however, exceptions to this rule:

> • If you are homebound, you can use food stamps to pay for "meals-on-wheels" that are delivered to your home.[14]
> • If you receive treatment at a public or private residential drug or alcohol program, you can use food stamps to buy meals at the center.[15]
> • If you live in a group home for the disabled or a shelter for battered women, you can use food stamps to pay for meals at your residence.[16]
> • If you are age 60 or over or disabled, you and your spouse can use food stamps to buy meals at approved group-meal sites.[17]
> • If you are age 60 or older, you can use food stamps to pay for meals at approved restaurants.[18]
> • If you are homeless, you can use food stamps to pay for food at shelters and soup kitchens, but you have the right to eat these meals without giving any food stamps for them.[19] In some places, homeless individuals can also use food stamps to buy meals at restaurants.[20]

Do all grocery stores accept food stamps?

No, but many grocery stores, supermarkets, and co-ops around the country do. Check to see if the stores in your neighborhood accept food stamps. Frequently, a store that participates in the program will post a sign that says, "We accept food stamps." Stores that accept food stamps have to be approved by the federal government, and must be fair and polite to food stamp customers. They cannot make a food stamp recipient wait in a separate line, charge more than the regular price for groceries, or discriminate against food stamp customers in any way.[21] The store also cannot charge sales tax on food bought with food stamps.[22]

Do food stamps have to be used all at once?

No. A food stamp household does not have to spend its entire food stamp allotment in one transaction. You can spend just the amount you need for what you want to buy. If the change from your transaction is more than one dollar, the store will give you food stamps. If the change is less than one dollar, you will receive coins.[23]

What is a household?

Food stamps are given to households.[24] A household for food stamp purposes is an individual living alone, an individual living with others who does not buy food or make meals with them, or a group of individuals who live, buy food, and make meals together.[25] Members of a food stamp household do not have to be related, and a household is not necessarily the same as all the people who live with you.

Applying for food stamps as a separate household from other people living with you can help you in several ways. Two households generally receive more food stamps than one large household with the same number of members. Also, you will not be cut off food stamps if a member of another household fails to meet program requirements or begins to earn too much to qualify for assistance. However, the food stamp program has specific rules to determine which persons must be a part of your food stamp household. In particular, under the 1996 welfare act, children under age 22 who live with their parents cannot apply as a separate household even if they themselves have children, are married, or purchase and prepare their own food.[26]

Who is in a food stamp household?

Under the food stamp program, a "household" is a functional unit. Generally, your food stamp household includes the people with whom you live and with whom you customarily purchase and prepare food. But there are important exceptions to this general rule. To figure out who is in your food stamp household, you can consider these three questions:

1. Do you live together?
    • If the answer is no, the person does not belong to your food stamp household.
    • If the answer is yes, go on to the next question.
2. Do you live with your spouse, your child who is under age 22, or a child under your control?
    • If the answer is no, go on to the next question.
    • If the answer is yes, these individuals are automatically deemed to be a part of your food stamp household.
3. Do you customarily purchase and prepare food together?
    • If the answer is no, the person does not belong to your food stamp household (except if the person is your child and is younger than age 22).
    • If the answer is yes, the person belongs to your food stamp household. There is one exception to this rule. If you are age 60 or older and disabled and cannot independently purchase and prepare food, you can apply as a separate household from the people who live with you, even if they prepare your meals.[27]

What if you rent a room in a private house?

If you pay to live in a private house and share meals with the people living there, the food stamp program considers you to be a "boarder." As a boarder, you cannot apply for food stamps separately from the rest of the people in the house, and the person giving you meals cannot get food stamps separately from you.[28] If you pay to live in a private house but do not share meals, you can apply for food stamps individually.

Can persons who are not citizens get food stamps?

Maybe. The 1996 welfare act disqualified most immigrants from the food stamp program. Before the 1996 law, any lawful permanent resident (that is, a "green card" holder) could qualify for food stamps. Now, however, even long-term legal immigrants are barred from the program unless they fit into one of the new law's narrow categories. President Clinton, who signed the 1996 welfare act on August 22, 1996, announced the next day that he planned to seek new legislation to restore eligibility for legal immigrants, so the law described below may have changed by the time you read this book.[29]

As of September 1996, eligibility for food stamps is limited to the following individuals:

- United States citizens;
- Lawful permanent residents who have worked in the United States for the equivalent of forty qualifying quarters in the Social Security system or can otherwise be credited with forty quarters. Quarters of work creditable to an immigrant's parents while the immigrant was a minor and quarters creditable to the immigrant's spouse during their marriage count toward the forty required quarters.[30] (Appendix C to this book explains in greater detail how the forty quarters rule works.)
- Noncitizens lawfully residing in the United States who are active-duty members of the United States armed forces or honorably discharged veterans, or the spouses or unmarried dependent children of such individuals;[31] and
- Immigrants granted refugee, asylee, or "withholding of deportation" status (under sections 207, 208, or 243(h), respectively, of the Immigration and Nationality Act, but eligibility lasts only for five years from the date that the immigrant gained the status.[32]

Immigrants who were receiving food stamps on August 22, 1996 (the date the welfare bill became law) are eligible to continue receiving benefits at least until April 1, 1997. Between April 1, 1997, and August 22, 1997, states must redetermine the eligibility of any immigrant receiving food stamps and decide whether the immigrant continues to qualify for benefits under the new law.[33]

If you are an alien and apply for food stamps, the food stamp office will give your name to the Immigration and Naturalization Service to verify your immigration status. In addition, some of the income and resources of your sponsor and the sponsor's spouse will count when your eligibility is determined.[34]

Can students get food stamps?

It depends. You cannot get food stamps if you are enrolled at least half-time in a college or university, unless you also:

- Work twenty hours or more per week; or
- Get federal work-study money or assistance under the Job Training Partnership Act; or
   - Are under age 17 or over age 60; or
   - Are physically or mentally disabled; or
   - Receive AFDC; or
   - Take care of a small child.[35]

Even if you are an ineligible student, the people with whom you live may be eligible to participate.[36]

Do you need a fixed address to get food stamps?

No. If you are eligible for food stamps, you cannot be denied assistance simply because you do not have a fixed mailing address or lack access to a kitchen or a place to store food.[37] Also if you do not have a fixed address you can arrange to pick up your food stamps at a food stamp office.[38]

Can you get food stamps if you live in a shelter, group home, institution, or similar living arrangement?

It depends. You cannot get food stamps if you live in a boarding school, a jail, or other institutions that serve you more than half your meals.[39] Certain congregate settings, however, are not considered institutions, and residents may receive food stamps.[40] You are allowed to receive food stamp benefits if:

- You are elderly and live in federally subsidized public housing;[41]
- You live in a drug or alcohol treatment center;[42]
- You are disabled or receive Supplemental Security Income and live in a licensed group-living arrangement;[43]
- You live in a shelter for battered women or children;[44] or
- You live in a public or private nonprofit center for the homeless.[45]

Can workers on strike get food stamps?

You cannot get food stamps if you are on strike unless you were eligible for food stamps before you went on strike, but your food stamps will not increase to compensate for reduced income during the strike.[46] The anti-striker rule does not apply if you are locked out; if you are out of work because of someone else's strike; if you are in a different bargaining unit from the striking workers and you are afraid to cross a picket line; if you have been permanently replaced; or if you are exempt from food stamp work registration requirements, unless the reason you are exempt is that you are working.[47]

Are welfare recipients automatically eligible for food stamps?

It depends on the rules that your state has established. AFDC recipients were previously automatically eligible for food stamps. The 1996 welfare act, which repealed the AFDC program, authorizes states to establish a "Simplified Food Stamp Program" that would accord automatic eligibility to households receiving benefits under the Temporary Assistance for Needy Families block grant. It is therefore important to check with your state agency or with a legal services or legal aid office to find out whether automatic eligibility rules apply where you live.[48]

How much income can a household have and still qualify for food stamps?

The food stamp program has net and gross income tests.[49] To receive food stamps, a household that does not include an elderly or disabled member must meet a gross income test. Gross income is your income before any deductions for expenses, and includes your salary before taxes and union dues. All households, including those with elderly or disabled members, must also meet a net income test. Net income is your income after you have subtracted deductions for particular expenses. If your household does not include an elderly or disabled person, and your income gross or net is more than the limits set forth in Table 2-1, you cannot get food stamps.[50] Use Table 2-2 if a member of your household is elderly or disabled.[51]

What counts as gross income?

Gross income includes all money received by any member of your household, with certain exceptions. Those exceptions are

1. Benefits that you do not receive in cash, such as free housing, public housing, child care, WIC benefits, or food;[52]
2. Money that a third party who is not a member of your household (such as a Public Housing Authority or an ex-spouse) pays directly to someone to whom you owe money (such as your landlord, a utility company, or a doctor) for expenses like rent, gas, or medical bills;[53]
3. Money earned by a child under age 18 who is at least a half-time student;[54]

TABLE 2–1
1996–97 Food Stamp Income Limits

Number of People in Household	Monthly Gross Income Limit	Monthly Net Income Limit
1	$ 839	$ 645
2	$1,123	$ 864
3	$1,407	$1,082
4	$1,690	$1,300
5	$1,974	$1,519
6	$2,258	$1,737
7	$2,542	$1,955
8	$2,826	$2,174
Each additional person	$ 284	$ 219

Source: United States Department of Agriculture, Program Development Division (Sept. 10, 1996).
Note: Income limits are higher in Alaska and Hawaii.

TABLE 2-2
**1996–97 Food Stamp Gross Income Limits,
Elderly or Disabled Household**

Number of People in Household	Monthly Gross Income Limit
1	$1,065
2	$1,425
3	$1,785
4	$2,145
5	$2,506
6	$2,866
7	$3,226
8	$3,586
Each additional person	$ 361

Source: United States Department of Agriculture, Program Development Division (Sept. 10, 1996).
Note: Gross income limits are higher in Alaska and Hawaii.

4. Income that you do not receive on a regular basis (from, for example, babysitting or odd jobs) that is not more than thirty dollars in any three months;[55]

5. Money that you receive from private charities that does not exceed three hundred dollars in any three months;[56]

6. Certain loans;[57]

7. Pell Grants, work-study grants, Guaranteed Student Loans, Perkins Loans, and any other student assistance that goes for school expenses;[58]

8. Reimbursement for work or training expenses (such as the cost of special work clothes, travel to and from a training program, or the cost of using your car for work, but not reimbursement for normal living expenses);[59]

9. Money that you get for someone who is not in your household that you spend to help that person (for example, if your elderly uncle lives across town and has his pension check mailed to you for safe keeping, and you use the pension check to pay your uncle's living expenses, his pension does not count as income to you);[60]

10. Payments that you receive only once, such as an income tax refund, insurance settlement, security deposit refund, and retroactive AFDC, SSI, and Social Security benefits;[61]

11. Federal payments to help you pay your fuel or energy bills, such as money from the Low-Income Home Energy Assistance Program and public housing utility rebates, as well as one time federal or state payments or allowances for the costs of weatherization, emergency repairs, or replacement of inoperative heating or cooling devices such as a furnace (state energy assistance payments, however, count as income);[62]

12. On-the-job payments under the Job Training Partnership Act to children under age 19;[63]

13. Self-employment income used to defray work expenses, such as the cost of things you sell or costs for delivering goods[64] (farmers can deduct money that they lose from farming from any other income they earn);[65]

14. Payments received for community service projects if you are over age 55;[66]

15. Payments from ACTION programs, such as RSVP, SCORE, ACE, and Foster Grandparents (VISTA money counts unless you received food stamps or public assistance when you joined);[67]

16. Federal benefits that are excluded from food stamp income under other federal laws (such as certain payments to members of Indian tribes);[68]

17. Money withheld from federal benefits to offset a prior overpayment, unless you violated the other program's rules on purpose;[69] and

18. Any Earned Income Tax Credit that you receive under state or federal law.[70]

It is important to note that under the 1996 welfare act, vendor payments for transitional housing count as income for food stamp purposes.[71]

What is net income?

Net income is equal to your gross income less deductions for certain household expenses. Food stamp rules allow a household to take up to six different kinds of deductions:

- A standard deduction of $134 for each household.[72]
- A deduction for work expenses, taxes, and other mandatory deductions from salary equal to 20 percent of all income that you receive from a job or self-employment, except if the income is from compliance with a public assistance work requirement, such as a work supplementation or support program, or is otherwise excluded from income.[73]
- A deduction for dependent care, up to a maximum of $200 per month for each dependent child under age 2 and $175 per month for each other dependent, for the actual cost of payments necessary for such care if it allows a household member to accept or continue a job, or to do training or education that is preparatory to work.[74]
- A deduction for child support paid by a member of your household to a child outside the household, if the payor is legally obligated to make the payments.[75]
- A standard "homeless" shelter allowance at state option of a maximum of $143 per month for expenses "as may reasonably be expected to be incurred by households in which all members are homeless individuals but are not receiving free shelter throughout the month."[76]
- A medical deduction for nonreimbursed health care expenses that exceed thirty-five dollars a month for households that are elderly or disabled.[77]
- A deduction for housing costs—including mortgage, gas, oil, electricity, telephone, water, property taxes, and fire insurance payments—

TABLE 2-3
Monthly Excess Shelter Deductions

	8/22/96– 12/31/96	1/1/97– 9/30/98	FY 1999 & 2000	FY 2001
48 Contiguous States & District of Columbia	$247	$250	$275	$300
Alaska	$429	$434	$478	$521
Hawaii	$353	$357	$393	$429
Guam	$300	$304	$334	$364
Virgin Islands	$182	$184	$203	$221

Source: Personal Responsibility and Work Opportunity Reconciliation Act, Pub. L. No. 104–193, 110 Stat. 2105, § 804(a) (Aug. 22, 1996).

that are more than half of your remaining income after all deductions for which you qualify have been subtracted (in calculating utility costs, certain households can elect to use a standard utility allowance, even if it exceeds actual expenses).[78] The schedule of excess shelter deductions until the year 2001 is set forth in table 2-3.[79]

Can a poor person own any assets and still get food stamps?

Yes, but subject to strict resource limits. The resource limit is currently $2,000 per household and $3,000 if the household includes an elderly person.

What counts as a resource?

A "resource" is money or property that you own.[80] Resources include cash that you have in hand or in the bank, stocks and bonds, money from insurance settlements, most tax refunds, rebates, awards, prizes, and inheritances. Things like boats, camping trailers, snowmobiles, and some land that you own but do not live on also count as resources.[81]

Certain assets do not count as resources for food stamp purposes:

• Your residence, including land or a vacant lot where you plan to build a house;[82]
• Personal and household goods, such as clothes, tables, chairs, beds, and appliances;[83]
• Burial plots;[84]
• The cash or face value of a life insurance policy or pension fund;[85]

• Property that you use to earn income, such as a house you rent out for a fair rent, land that you farm, or tools, equipment, livestock, and buildings;[86]

• Property that you cannot sell or use for your own needs, such as money in a trust fund or the security deposit on your apartment;[87]

• Property that belongs to someone with whom you live but who is not a member of your food stamp household, unless that person is no longer a member of your household because he or she was disqualified from the food stamp program;[88]

• Vehicles used to produce earned income; that are necessary for the transportation of a physically disabled household member; or that the household depends on to carry fuel for heating or water for home use and that provides the primary source of fuel or water for the household; or the first $4,650 of value of any car that otherwise counts as a resource;[89]

• That portion of property subject to a lien;[90]

• Government assistance to help you repair your home after a disaster if you are legally required to use the money on your home;[91]

• Any Earned Income Tax Credit received under federal or state law for one year after its receipt.[92]

How many food stamps does an eligible household receive?

The amount of your food stamp allotment depends on the size of your household, your household's income, and whether any household members are elderly or disabled. Worksheets in appendix D at the end of this book detail how to calculate your income in order to determine your household's food stamp benefits. Once you have calculated your household income, you can use table 2-4 to find out the maximum monthly food stamp allotment that your household is entitled to receive, effective October 1996 through September 30, 1997.[93] Use table 2-5 to find out the maximum monthly food stamp allotment that an elderly or disabled separate household can receive at different income levels.[94]

How do you apply for food stamps?

You apply for food stamps by completing and submitting an application form. You can get an application at a food stamp or welfare office.[95] Applications are also often available at local legal services and legal aid offices, community action agencies, welfare rights organizations, soup kitchens, and shelters. Many states also have a toll-free hot line, a telephone number

TABLE 2-4
1996–97 Food Stamp Benefit Levels

Number of People in Household	Monthly Gross Income Limit	Monthly Net Income Limit	Maximum Monthly Food Stamps
1	$ 810	$ 623	$120
2	$1,087	$ 836	$220
3	$1,364	$1,050	$315
4	$1,642	$1,263	$400
5	$1,919	$1,476	$475
6	$2,196	$1,690	$570
7	$2,474	$1,903	$630
8	$2,751	$2,116	$720
Each additional person	$ 278	$ 214	$ 90

Source: United States Department of Agriculture, Program Development Division (Sept. 10, 1996).
Note: Allotment levels are higher in Alaska, Hawaii, Guam, and the Virgin Islands.

TABLE 2-5
**1996–97 Food Stamp Benefit Levels,
Elderly or Disabled Household**

Number of People in Household	Monthly Gross Income Limit	Maximum Monthly Food Stamps
1	$1,065	$120
2	$1,425	$220
3	$1,785	$315
4	$2,145	$400
5	$2,506	$475
6	$2,866	$570
7	$3,226	$630
8	$3,586	$720
Each additional person	$ 361	$ 90

Source: United States Department of Agriculture, Program Development Division (Sept. 10, 1996).
Note: Allotment levels are higher in Alaska, Hawaii, Guam, and the Virgin Islands.

you can call without charge to get information about food stamps and to request that an application be mailed to you.

It is important to submit your form as quickly as possible, because assistance will start, if you are eligible, from the date of your application. You can submit an incomplete form and, at least initially, you do not have to see a case worker. You do, however, have to sign the form and fill in your name and address and the date. The food stamp office must accept your application the same day you ask to apply and cannot make you wait a day to hand in your form.[96]

What is an authorized representative?

An authorized representative is a person who has your permission to apply for food stamps on your behalf. She or he can attend interviews for you, pick up your food stamps, and even purchase groceries for you. An authorized representative can be a friend, a relative, or a government worker. If you want someone to be your authorized representative, you should write to the food stamp office to request this service or to give permission to someone you have chosen as your representative.[97]

What is an interview?

An interview is a meeting between you and a food stamp worker that takes place after you submit your application and before your eligibility is determined.[98] At the interview, the worker will ask you questions about who lives with you, what your household's income and resources are, and whether you are exempt from work requirements. You will also have to provide the Social Security number of every member of your household.[99]

You can have your interview as early as the day you submit your application, but the food stamp office can ask you to come back another day. If you miss your first interview, the food stamp office must try to set up another appointment.[100] But if you miss two interviews, the office can deny your application, and you will have to reapply if you want assistance.[101]

Are interviews always held at the food stamp office?

Yes. The 1996 welfare act leaves it to the states to decide whether to require all applicants to come into the local office in person to have an interview.[102] These amendments thus eliminated the right of elderly and disabled applicants to have interviews at home or by telephone. The amendments do not, however, affect an applicant's right to designate an authorized representative on his or her behalf.

What documents should an applicant for food stamps bring to an interview?

The food stamp office will tell you what documents are relevant to your application.[103] You should bring them to the interview because the food stamp worker is going to look at them to verify your eligibility for assistance. Documents include such things as pay stubs, utility bills, a driver's license, and medical bills.[104]

Generally, you will need documents or some other proof of the following items:

- Identity;
- Income;
- The citizenship or immigration status of household members;
- Utility expenses;
- Social Security numbers of household members;
- Medical expenses;
- Where you live;
- The head of the household; and
- Disability benefits.

Will the food stamp worker inspect a poor person's home as part of the application process?

It depends. Food stamp regulations allow "visits" to an applicant's home if the worker cannot otherwise verify eligibility through documents or conversations with third parties.[105] Your worker must tell you in advance when the visit will take place.[106] Some states use private investigators to conduct these visits.

How long does it take to get food stamps?

The food stamp office must grant or deny an application within thirty days of the date of application.[107] Under certain circumstances, an applicant may be entitled to get food stamps within seven days (this is known as "expedited service").[108] When you apply, the food stamp worker will determine whether you are eligible for expedited service.[109]

The food stamp office must give you benefits within seven days if

- Your household has a gross monthly income of less than $150 and liquid resources of less than $100 (liquid resources are cash in hand, checking or savings accounts, savings certificates, and lump sum payments such as income tax refunds or retroactive Social Security, Supplemental Security Income, or AFDC);[110] or

• Your household's total monthly shelter cost (which includes rent, mortgage payments, utilities, and heat) is more than your household's gross income plus liquid resources.[111]

If your household qualifies for expedited service, you must provide identification to get your first month of food stamps.[112] If you apply after the fifteenth day of the month, the food stamp office may give you two months of benefits.[113] Under the 1996 welfare act, homeless households are no longer automatically eligible for expedited food stamp service.

Do all food stamp recipients have to register to work?

Yes, subject to limited exemptions. Generally speaking, all "physically and mentally fit" individuals who are over age 15 and under age 60 must register for employment at the time they apply for food stamps and every twelve months afterwards in order to be eligible for assistance.[114] "Registering" means signing up to be told about any jobs that are open.

After you register for work, the food stamp office or the state employment agency may send you a letter telling you to come for an interview. You can ask to change the date of the interview, but you must attend a rescheduled interview if you want to continue to receive assistance. At your interview, the food stamp office can refer you to a job or assign you to an employment and training program.

Can a state sanction a recipient who fails to meet work registration requirements?

Yes. The 1996 welfare act sets minimum disqualification periods for recipients who violate the food stamp program's work registration requirements. They are one month for the first violation; three months for the second violation; and six months for the third violation (or permanent disqualification at state option).[115]

Do food stamp recipients have to meet work requirements?

Yes. Under the 1996 welfare act, all able-bodied childless persons between the ages of 18 and 50 cannot get food stamps for more than three months in a 36-month period unless they work or participate in a federal or state employment program at least 20 hours or more per week, averaged monthly.[116] Job search or job-training programs do not apply. Qualifying work programs include programs under the Job Training Partnership Act or the Trade Adjustment Assistance Act; state or local programs approved by the governor, including food stamp employment and training programs; and workfare. A recipient who has already received three months of benefits and begins working but is then laid off may get one additional 3-month period of benefits.[117] States may apply for waivers from these requirements if they have an unemployment rate that is more than 10 percent. It is important to find out if your state has gotten a waiver from the work requirements that a recipient must otherwise meet in your state.[118]

Exemptions from the work requirements are available in limited circumstances and are of special importance to households with children. Generally, a pregnant woman or the full-time caretaker of a dependent child under age six is exempt from the work requirements. But under the 1996 welfare act, states have the option of requiring caretakers of children who are as young as age one to work if child care is available (only those states that requested a waiver for this purpose and had the waiver denied as of August 1, 1996 may impose this requirement).[119]

Does a food stamp recipient have to accept any job that the agency finds?

Yes, unless you have "good cause" for refusing to accept a job. For example, good cause exists if the job pays less than the minimum wage (except if it is a piece-work job, and then other rules apply). Good cause may exist in other circumstances as well.

Can a food stamp recipient quit a job and still get food stamps?

Only if you have good cause for quitting. Good cause means that you are not at fault and includes a range of facts and circumstances.[120] For example, you can show good cause if the employer discriminated against you because of your age, race, color, national origin, sex, handicap, religion, or political beliefs,[121] or if working conditions become unreasonable (for example, the employer consistently does not pay you on time).[122]

A worker is deemed to have quit without good cause if he or she is dismissed for participating in a strike against the government.[123] Also, if a worker voluntarily and without good cause reduces his or her work effort to less than thirty hours per week, he or she will not be eligible for food stamps.[124]

What if a food stamp recipient is fired?

If you are fired, you will continue to receive food stamps but must continue to meet work registration requirements.

What happens if the food stamp office terminates or reduces a household's benefits?

Generally, the food stamp office cannot terminate or reduce your benefits without first giving you written notice of the proposed action. The agency must send you the notice ten days before it stops or reduces your benefits, and the ten-day period starts when the notice is mailed.[125] The food stamp office can give you less than ten days notice only if you have provided written information that makes it clear that your food stamps should be reduced.[126] In this case, the food stamp office must give you notice no later than the day your food stamps would normally come.

The notice must be in writing and must tell you what the food stamp office plans to do, why the office is doing it, and when the office will do it.[127] The notice must also give you a telephone number to call for more information and the name of a legal aid or legal services office in your neighborhood that provides free representation. In addition, the notice must tell you about your right to a fair hearing and to receive food stamps while you wait for a hearing.[128]

What is a fair hearing?

A fair hearing is a meeting where you have the opportunity to challenge decisions that deny, terminate, or reduce your food stamps.[129] A hearing officer presides at the fair hearing. He or she is required to be impartial and cannot have participated in the decision that you are contesting.[130]

You can ask for a hearing whenever the food stamp office notifies you of a decision that you think is unfair. The notice will tell you the address and telephone number of the office to contact. You can request a hearing in writing, in person, or by telephone,[131] but it is best to make a written request and to keep a copy of your letter. In any case, your request should explain why you want a hearing.

You must ask for a hearing within ninety days of the decision you want to challenge.[132] If the decision proposes to cut or reduce your benefits and you ask for a hearing within ten days of the notice, you will continue to receive food stamps at the full amount until your challenge is decided.[133] If you lose your hearing, you will be responsible for paying back the extra amount of food stamps that you received while your case was in dispute.[134] If your certification period for food stamps ends while you are waiting for your fair hearing to be decided, you should reapply for benefits. If you do not reapply, you will not get food stamps beyond the end of your certification period, even if you win the hearing.

What rights does a poor person have at a food stamp fair hearing?

Federal law affords you many procedural rights at a food stamp fair hearing.[135] These procedures are designed to let you tell your side of the story at the hearing and to allow the hearing officer to reach an accurate and fair decision. Before the hearing, you can ask to see your case file and can request a free copy of any documents that you will need to prepare your case. The food stamp office must let you look at your file sufficiently in advance of your hearing to give you time to prepare.[136] You can attend your fair hearing alone, accompanied by friends or relatives, or represented by a lawyer, a paralegal, or another person of your choice. The agency must tell you of the availability of legal services or legal aid attorneys who can provide you with representation at no charge. At the hearing, you can present witnesses to support your case and cross-examine witnesses put forward by the food stamp office.[137] You also have a right to testify, to talk freely to the hearing official, and to reply to any statements that food stamp staff may present.[138] No one at the hearing can interrupt your testimony or yell at you while you are speaking. In addition, you can give the hearing officer any documents that you believe are relevant to your case.[139]

After the hearing, you are entitled to a decision by the hearing officer based on the testimony and documents submitted at the hearing.[140] If you disagree with the hearing officer's decision, you can take an appeal and challenge the action in court. If you decide to go forward, you should contact a legal services or legal aid lawyer for advice and possible representation.

WIC:
SPECIAL SUPPLEMENTAL NUTRITION PROGRAM FOR WOMEN, INFANTS AND CHILDREN

What is WIC?

WIC refers to the Special Supplemental Nutrition Program for Women, Infants and Children, a federal program designed for pregnant women, new mothers, infants, and young children who are at medical and nutritional risk.[141]

The federal government developed WIC in the late 1960s in response to research showing the adverse impact of hunger and malnutrition on the health of pregnant women and the development of newborn children.[142] The program began on an experimental basis in 1968, providing free food to pregnant women, new mothers, and children under age six who were poor and at risk of malnutrition. In 1972, following successful findings about the pilot program, Congress enacted WIC on a permanent basis to provide eligible families with food, nutrition education, and improved access to health care. By establishing WIC, the federal government intended to reduce and prevent nutrition-related health problems during pregnancy, infancy, and early childhood.[143]

For over twenty-five years, WIC has been a major success story, saving lives and improving the health status of indigent women and children. Indigent children are three to four times more at risk of having low-iron levels in their blood, a common cause of anemia that impairs cognitive development, and WIC has proved effective in reducing the incidence of such anemia among participating children.[144] It also has helped to reduce the incidence of premature birth, low birthweight, and fetal death among newborns and infants who participate.[145]

Studies by the federal government and others confirm that WIC is also a cost-effective program. For example, for every dollar spent by WIC for prenatal services, the Medicaid program saves between $1.92 and $4.21. Indeed, the United States General Accounting Office estimated that an investment of $296 million in WIC funding in 1990 would produce savings in health and education-related expenditures of $1.036 billion over the next eighteen years.[146]

What does WIC provide?

WIC provides eligible families with monthly vouchers that can be redeemed for foods that meet the nutritional needs of infants, children, and pregnant, postpartum, and breastfeeding women. The WIC food basket is intended to provide recipients with high levels of protein, iron, calcium, and vitamins A and C, nutrients that are typically missing from the diets of low-income women and children. In addition to food, WIC provides participants with nutrition education classes and access to medical care.

What foods can a participating household buy with WIC vouchers?

You can use WIC vouchers to purchase authorized food items. The foods are iron-fortified infant formula, infant cereal, milk, eggs, cheese, iron-fortified breakfast cereal, vitamin C-rich juice, beans, and peanut butter.[147]

WIC also offers a food package designed especially for lactating mothers, containing more juice, cheese, and legumes (beans, peas, or peanut butter), as well as carrots and canned tuna.

Where can you use WIC vouchers?

You can use WIC vouchers at your neighborhood grocery store if it participates in the program. In a few states, you can get WIC foods at warehouses or have them delivered to your home. You should also check with your local WIC clinic to find out where you can use your vouchers.

What kind of nutrition education does WIC offer?

Participants in the WIC program can attend two classes in nutrition education during each certification period. Classes discuss the specific nutritional needs of mothers, infants, and children, and stress the importance of regular medical care, the dangers of using alcohol or drugs during pregnancy, and the advantages of breastfeeding during infancy. They also offer homemaking tips, such as how to shop for nutritious foods and how to prepare economical, well-balanced meals. By attending these classes, you can gain a better understanding of how eating WIC foods can improve your health and that of your child.

What kind of medical care does WIC provide?

WIC makes it easier for you to get medical care. WIC centers are generally located at or near clinics that provide prenatal services, allowing you to coordinate your WIC session with other medical appointments. For example, you may be scheduled to pick up your WIC vouchers and have your child immunized on the same trip. In addition, WIC sometimes maintains joint medical records with health clinics, allowing WIC nutritionists and health professionals to share information and coordinate services. WIC also provides an active referral network that puts you in touch with doctors and other health providers.

Who is eligible for WIC?

Participation in the WIC program is limited to low-income pregnant and nursing women, new mothers, and children up to age five. To be eligible for WIC, you must meet four requirements:

- You must be a pregnant or breastfeeding woman, a new mother, an infant, or a child under age five;[148]
- A health professional must certify that you are at nutritional risk, which can include problems such as abnormal weight gain during pregnancy, a history of high-risk pregnancy such as a low-birthweight baby, or a child's iron-deficiency anemia or an inadequate diet;[149]
- You must reside in the state in which you want to participate (except if you are a migrant worker);[150] and
- Your household income must not exceed WIC program guidelines, which in most states is set at 185 percent of the poverty level.[151] If you receive AFDC, Medicaid, or food stamps, you automatically meet the WIC income requirements.[152]

Can a household own any assets and still be eligible for WIC?

Yes. Unlike the food stamp program, WIC does not limit the resources you can own.

Does a household automatically get WIC if it is eligible?

No. Unlike the food stamp program, WIC is not an entitlement and eligible WIC recipients do not automatically get WIC vouchers. Because of inadequate funding, WIC is not able to provide benefits to all the families that are eligible for assistance. Instead, the WIC program ranks applicants according to nutritional and other criteria and provides assistance to those who are considered most in need.

In order to assess an applicant's need, the WIC program has established a priority system. You are more likely to be accepted into a WIC program if you are in a top-ranked priority.[153] In order of preference, the priorities are as follows:

Preference one. Pregnant women, breastfeeding mothers, and infants who are at nutritional risk based on medical tests;

Preference two. Infants younger than age six months who are at nutritional risk;

Preference three. Children younger than age five;

Preference four. Pregnant women, breastfeeding mothers, and infants who are at nutritional risk because of poor diet;

Preference five. Children who are at nutritional risk because of poor diet;

Preference six. New mothers at nutritional risk;

Preference seven. Former WIC participants who may have nutritional problems if they cannot continue receiving WIC foods.

Even if you are not in a top-ranked priority group, you should nevertheless apply to the WIC program if you are pregnant or have very young children. Different clinics have different levels of funding and can service different numbers of participants. If your local WIC clinic cannot help you right away, ask them to put you on a waiting list and ask when the clinic thinks you will be accepted to participate.

How do you apply for WIC?

You can apply for WIC at the nearest WIC clinic, which you can locate by calling the city, county, or state health department. Call the WIC clinic to find out what information is required. All clinics will ask you questions about your income, residence, and nutritional risk, and some may ask you to bring a blood test (to document anemia). If a blood test is required, you should ask the clinic if it will do the test for you free of charge.

When you come to the clinic to apply, it is important that you bring relevant documents. Documents that you should bring include

1. Proof of income for all adults in your household (for example, pay stubs, income tax returns, or welfare notices);

2. Proof of residence (for example, a letter addressed to you in the state in which you are applying to participate);

3. Proof of identification for all applicants in your household;

4. If you are pregnant, proof of pregnancy (you must always bring the baby with you to the clinic after the child is born);

5. The Social Security number of each adult in your household, if they have one.

What is recertification?

Every six months you have to be recertified to participate in the WIC program. At recertification, you will be asked questions about your income, residence, and nutritional risk. It is important that you bring relevant documents to your recertification interview.

Can a person who is not a United States citizen receive WIC benefits?

Yes. You do not have to be a citizen to receive WIC. Under the 1996 welfare act, qualified aliens can participate in the program. A "qualified alien" is an immigrant who

1. is a lawful permanent resident ("green card" holder);
2. has obtained political asylum;
3. has been granted refugee status;
4. has been granted "withholding of deportation";
5. has been "paroled" into the United States for a period of at least one year; or
6. is a "Cuban-Haitian conditional entrant."

In addition, noncitizens who are or have been victims of domestic violence may qualify for WIC. Federal law provides that a noncitizen who has been "battered or subjected to extreme cruelty" in the United States by a spouse or parent, or by someone living in the spouse or parent's household, may qualify for benefits if

1. the individual has applied for or received lawful permanent resident status or suspension of deportation status based on the relationship with the abusive spouse or parent;
2. the person responsible for the battering or cruelty no longer lives with the individual; and
3. the attorney general determines that "there is a substantial connection between such battery or cruelty and the need for the benefits."

The parent of a battered or abused child may also qualify for benefits if the criteria above are met and the parent did not "actively participate in [the] battery or cruelty."

As this book goes to press, the Attorney General has yet to issue regulations describing how the government will decide whether battered or abused immigrants qualify for particular federal benefits such as WIC.[154]

The act further provides that it does not require or prohibit states to provide benefits under the Child Nutrition Act to persons who are not citizens or qualified aliens (the WIC program is codified under the Child Nutrition Act).[155]

NATIONAL SCHOOL LUNCH PROGRAM

What is the National School Lunch Program?

The National School Lunch Program began in 1946 as a way to provide wholesome meals to school-age children and to help dispose of surplus food.[156] The United States Department of Agriculture administers the program, and national guidelines have been in effect since 1970.

Research shows that children who are hungry or malnourished are often unable to concentrate in school, suffer an increased risk of illness, and are more anxious and less socially responsive.[157] As one researcher comments, "Nutrition is one of the most pervasive factors influencing growth, development and health. It is, in fact, central to child development." Another researcher concludes, "Health and nutrition are powerful determinants of educational competence."[158] Children who participate in the National School Lunch Program must be served lunches that on average over the week provide at least one-third of the daily recommended dietary allowances established by the Food and Nutrition Board of the National Research Council of the National Academy of Sciences.[159] By giving children healthful and nutritious foods, the National School Lunch Program has played a significant role in motivating children and helping them to learn.

What does the National School Lunch Program provide?

The National School Lunch Program gives participating students a nutritious midday meal. Meals are either free or sold at a reduced price, depending on the child's family income. A student's lunch must be healthful and filling and must be consistent with dietary guidelines. Unfortunately, the 1996 welfare act reduced the federal reimbursement rate for school lunches, which may reduce the program's effectiveness.[160]

How do you apply to the National School Lunch Program?

If you want your child to participate in his or her school's lunch program, you have to submit an application on the child's behalf. At the beginning of the school year, your school will tell you if it has a school lunch program and give you an application form.[161] The same application covers lunch and breakfast.[162] You can submit your application at any time during the school year.

The application will ask information about your family income, family composition, and Social Security numbers. Other questions about your family's personal life are not permitted and should not be on the application.[163] An adult member of the household must sign the application. Children in households that receive AFDC or food stamps are automatically eligible and you do not have to complete the entire application. If you move to another school within the same school district, you do not have to reapply.[164]

Who can participate in the National School Lunch Program?

All eligible children can receive lunch if their school participates in the program. Children in households that receive AFDC or food stamps are automatically eligible and do not have to complete the entire application.[165] A child is also automatically eligible if another child in her or his family already participates. All other applicants have to meet an income test. Your child can receive free meals if your family income is no more than 130 percent of the federal poverty level and reduced-price meals if your family income is no more than 185 percent of the poverty level. Table 2-6 sets forth the 1996–1997 income guidelines for the National School Lunch Program.[166]

Can noncitizens participate in the National School Lunch Program?

Yes. Under the 1996 welfare act, any person who is eligible to receive free public education benefits under state or local law "shall not be ineligible" for the school lunch program.[167] A few states, and most notably California, have been trying to exclude undocumented immigrant children from their public schools. Their efforts should be invalidated as a violation of equal protection under the federal Constitution.[168] State constitutional rights to a free public education may also be violated by these anti-immigrant measures.

Do all schools participate in the National School Lunch Program?

No, although many schools do. During the 1995–1996 school year, 92,000 schools and child care institutions offered school lunch and about 14 million low-income children ate a school lunch.[169] Any school district can participate in the National School Lunch Program if it requests permission from the state education agency.[170] Once the local school district asks to participate in the program, necessary funding must be provided to allow all eligible children to receive free or reduced-price meals. The state cannot

TABLE 2-6
**1996–97 Income Guidelines for the
National School Lunch Program, Forty-Eight Contiguous States**

Household Size	Free Lunch (130% of Poverty)			Reduced-Price Lunch (185% of Poverty)		
	Year	*Month*	*Week*	*Year*	*Month*	*Week*
1	$10,062	$ 839	$194	$14,319	$1,194	$276
2	$13,468	$1,123	$259	$19,166	$1,598	$369
3	$16,874	$1,407	$325	$24,013	$2,002	$462
4	$20,280	$1,690	$390	$28,860	$2,405	$555
5	$23,686	$1,974	$456	$33,707	$2,809	$649
6	$27,092	$2,258	$521	$38,554	$3,213	$742
7	$30,498	$2,542	$587	$43,401	$3,617	$835
8	$33,904	$2,826	$652	$48,248	$4,021	$928

Source: 61 Fed. Reg. 10720 (March 15, 1996).
Note: Income levels are higher in Alaska and Hawaii.

limit the number of participating schools or the number of children a school can serve.

Can a school discriminate against a child because she or he receives free or reduced-price lunch?

No. A school cannot discriminate against a child because she or he receives free or reduced-price lunch. Participating children cannot be sent to separate food lines, be given meals different from those of paying students, be asked to carry different-colored meal tickets, or be relegated to separate cafeteria entrances. Meals under the school lunch program must be served in the same dining area that paying children use and at the same time.[171] A school cannot force children who receive free or reduced-price meals to work or to perform chores as a condition of participation[172] and cannot punish a child by withholding a meal.[173]

Can a child get school lunch if his or her parent is suddenly unemployed?

Yes. If you become suddenly unemployed and your income falls within the eligibility guidelines, your child is immediately eligible for free or reduced-price meals if you apply to the program.[174]

What happens if a school refuses to give lunch to a child who applies?

You can appeal the school's action if you think it has unfairly refused to let your child participate in the lunch program.[175] If the school believes that your child should be removed from the program and you request a hearing, the school must continue to give your child lunch until the dispute is resolved.[176]

SCHOOL BREAKFAST PROGRAM

What is the School Breakfast Program?

The School Breakfast Program began in 1966 and provides breakfast to students at participating schools throughout the country.[177] As originally enacted, the program was designed to provide breakfast to children who lived in poor areas or had to travel a great distance to school. Congress has since permanently authorized School Breakfast as a program for eligible children attending schools in participating states. Depending on your family's income level, breakfast is provided either at no charge or at a reduced price.

The School Breakfast Program is an extremely important tool in the struggle against childhood hunger. Research shows that a child who starts his or her day hungry experiences serious learning difficulties in the classroom. Undernutrition has a negative effect on a child's cognitive ability; undernourished children are less physically active, less attentive, and less independent. The School Breakfast Program is important because it gives children the food and nutrition they need to learn. Low-income students who are able to eat school breakfast show significant increases in their standardized test scores and are less often absent or late to class.[178]

During the 1995–1996 school year, almost 65,000 schools and child care institutions offered school breakfast and about 5.6 million children participated in the program daily. More than seven of ten of the 92,000 schools that offered school lunch also offered school breakfast. And of the more than 14 million low-income children who participated in the School Lunch Program, 39.6 percent also participated in the School Breakfast Program.[179] Advocates are concerned, however, that the 1996 welfare act, which reduced federal reimbursement for school breakfast, will adversely affect the program and reduce the number of schools that choose to participate.[180]

Who is eligible for the School Breakfast Program?

Every student can receive breakfast if her or his school participates in the program. Breakfast is either free, reduced price, or fully paid. You are eligible for free breakfast if your household income is no more than 130 percent of the federal poverty level, and a reduced price if your household income is no more than 185 percent. If your family receives AFDC or food stamps, your child is automatically eligible for free breakfast. Table 2-7 sets forth the 1996–1997 income guidelines for the School Breakfast Program.[181]

How do you apply to the School Breakfast Program?

A parent applies for the School Breakfast Program on behalf of her or his child. You submit your application to the school, and the same application covers both lunch and breakfast. At the beginning of the school year, your child's school must tell you if it has a School Breakfast Program and how to apply. It must also give you the forms that you need to apply.[182] The application will ask you questions about your income, family composition, and Social Security numbers, and an adult must sign the application. Any other questions about your personal life should not be on the application.[183] Children in households that receive AFDC or food stamps are automatically eligible and do not have to complete the entire application.[184] In addition, if your child is eligible, and you move to another school within the same school district, you do not have to reapply.[185]

Can noncitizens participate in the School Breakfast Program?

Yes. Under the 1996 welfare act, any person who is eligible to receive free public education benefits under state or local law "shall not be ineligible" for the school breakfast program.[186] A few states, and most notably California, have been trying to exclude undocumented immigrant children from their public schools. Their efforts should be invalidated as a violation of equal protection under the federal Constitution.[187] State constitutional rights to a free public education may also be violated by these anti-immigrant measures.

Do all schools participate in the School Breakfast Program?

No. All public and private nonprofit schools, as well as child care institutions, can participate in the School Breakfast Program, but many do not. The 1996 welfare act, which reduced the federal reimbursement rate for the program, is likely to have a deleterious effect on school participation.[188]

TABLE 2-7
1996–97 Income Guidelines for the
School Breakfast Program, Fory-Eight Contiguous States

Household Size	Free Breakfast (130% of Poverty)			Reduced-Price Breakfast (185% of Poverty)		
	Year	Month	Week	Year	Month	Week
1	$10,062	$ 839	$194	$14,319	$1,194	$276
2	$13,468	$1,123	$259	$19,166	$1,598	$369
3	$16,874	$1,407	$325	$24,013	$2,002	$462
4	$20,280	$1,690	$390	$28,860	$2,405	$555
5	$23,686	$1,974	$456	$33,707	$2,809	$649
6	$27,092	$2,258	$521	$38,554	$3,213	$742
7	$30,498	$2,542	$587	$43,401	$3,617	$835
8	$33,904	$2,826	$652	$48,248	$4,021	$928

Source: 61 Fed. Reg. 10720 (March 15, 1996).
Note: Income levels are higher in Alaska and Hawaii.

Once a local school district asks to participate in the program, all schools within the district must be given funding for the program. The state government cannot limit the number of participating schools or the number of children a school can serve.

What foods are served for breakfast?

If your child participates in the School Breakfast Program, she or he will receive a morning meal that on average over the week provides at least one-fourth of the daily recommended dietary allowances.[189]

Can a school discriminate against a child who receives free or reduced-price breakfast?

No. A school cannot discriminate against a child who receives free or reduced-price breakfast. As with the National School Lunch Program, a school cannot relegate your child to a separate line or different cafeteria entrance, serve different meals, or use different-colored meal tickets. The school must serve free and reduced-price breakfast at the same time as paying children and in the same dining room.[190] Your child cannot be forced to work or perform chores to receive a free or reduced-price breakfast,[191] and she or he cannot be denied a meal as punishment.[192]

SUMMER FOOD SERVICE PROGRAM FOR CHILDREN

What is the Summer Food Service Program for Children?

The Summer Food Service Program, which began in 1968, is a federal entitlement program that provides meals during vacation and summer periods when school is not in session to school-age children in "areas where poor economic conditions exist."[193] The program is intended to meet the nutritional needs of indigent children who rely on free and reduced-price meals during the school year. Although more than 13 million children received free or reduced-price lunch in 1991, only 1.8 million received summer meals.[194]

Do all schools participate in the Summer Food Service Program?

No. A school can participate in the Summer Food Service Program if it meets either geographic or enrollment criteria.

- A school is geographically eligible if it is located in a school district or census tract in which 50 percent of the children qualify for a free or reduced-price meal.
- A school is enrollment-eligible if 50 percent of the children who are enrolled can be documented to qualify for a free or reduced-price meal.

Can groups other than schools participate in the Summer Food Service Program?

Yes. Many groups other than schools can participate in the Summer Food Service Program. These groups include public or nonprofit summer camps; National Youth Sports Program camps; local parks and recreation departments; and private nonprofit organizations, such as community action centers. About 26,000 schools, camps, and other groups currently provide summer meals.

Who can participate in the Summer Food Service Program?

All children up to age 18 who attend a program site participating in the program can receive a free meal, regardless of income.[195] You do not have to complete any application form.

SENIOR NUTRITION PROGRAMS

Are there any federal food programs for elder Americans?

Yes. In 1965, the federal government established two food assistance programs for elder Americans: Congregate Meals and Home-Delivered Meals.[196] The programs are designed to give elder Americans access to inexpensive, nutritious meals; to nutrition education; and to opportunities for socializing. The programs fill an important nutritional gap for elder Americans, of whom 12.9 percent were poor in 1992.[197] The American Public Health Association reports that 40 percent of persons admitted to nursing homes are malnourished,[198] and 25 percent of persons age 65 and older suffer from some form of malnutrition.[199]

What is the Congregate Meals Program?

The Congregate Meals Program provides meals to elders once a day, Monday through Friday, at a community center or neighborhood church or synagogue. The program is intended to provide seniors with food and fellowship, offering a hot meal, together with a chance to talk to other people. Many of the locations serving congregate meals provide transportation to and from the site; information and referral for health and welfare counseling; nutrition education; and help with shopping and recreation.

Who is eligible for the Congregate Meals Program?

Anyone age 60 or older can participate in the Congregate Meals Program. Participants' spouses can also participate no matter how old they are.

Are meals free?

Yes. No one is required to pay for congregate meals, although those who can afford to are encouraged to pay. Low-income seniors can use food stamps to pay for meals, but many advocates urge meal providers not to take food stamps for this purpose (for the 73 percent of elderly persons who live alone, the average monthly food stamp benefit is only thirty-five dollars).

What is the Home-Delivered Meals Program?

The Home-Delivered Meals Program, known as "meals-on-wheels," delivers a nutritious meal, Monday through Friday, to the homes of elder Americans who are permanently homebound or recovering from illness, injury, or surgery. Some programs also provide two additional frozen meals in the Friday delivery for use on the weekend.

Who is eligible for the Home-Delivered Meals Program?

Participants must be older than age 60, live in the program's service area, and be unable to prepare meals. As with Congregate Meals, meals are free.

What if a senior has special dietary needs?

Some programs are able to provide meals that meet special dietary needs, such as low-sodium or diabetic meals. Check with the program in your area.

How do you apply for a senior nutrition program?

To sign up for a senior food program, call your local Agency on the Aging. You can find its phone number in the government pages of the phone book.

Notes

The authors gratefully acknowledge the assistance of Carrie Lewis and Geri Henchy (together with Hunter S. Labovitz and Szerina Perot) of the Food Research and Action Center in the preparation of this chapter.

1. *See, e.g., Dandridge v. Williams*, 397 U.S. 471 (1970).

2. *See United States Dep't of Agriculture v. Moreno*, 413 U.S. 528 (1973) (invalidating provision of food stamp act that denied assistance to households made up of unrelated individuals, noting that "[a] bare congressional desire to harm a politically unpopular group cannot constitute a legitimate governmental interest such as will sustain a legislative classification against an equal protection challenge"); *United States Dep't of Agriculture v. Murry*, 413 U.S. 508 (1973) (invalidating provision of food stamp act that denied assistance to any household containing a person who had been claimed as a dependent by a taxpayer who was ineligible for food stamps); *but see Lyng v. International Union, UAW*, 485 U.S. 360 (1988) (upholding provision of food stamp act that excluded households with a member on strike).

3. State constitutional provisions that deal explicitly with poverty are collected in Burt Neuborne, *Foreword: State Constitutions and the Evolution of Positive Rights*, 20 Rutgers L.J. 881, 893–95 & nn. 60–82 (1989). The Constitution of the Commonwealth of Puerto Rico explicitly recognizes a right to food: "The right of every person to [a] standard of living adequate for the health and well-being of himself and his family, and *especially to food*, clothing, housing and medical care and necessary social services." Puerto Rico Const. art. II, § 20 (emphasis added). This section was excepted from the approval of the Puerto Rico Constitution by a Joint Resolution of Congress of July 3, 1952, c. 567, 66 Stat. 327.

4. The information in this chapter is drawn largely from Food Research and Action Center, *FRAC's Guide to the Food Stamp Program* (9th ed. 1994). The governing statute for the program is codified at 7 U.S.C.A. §§ 2011–2028 (West 1996), and implementing regulations of the Department of Agriculture are located in Title 7 of the Code of Federal Regulations.

5. *See* Pub. L. No. 104-193, 110 Stat. 2105 (1996). Title VII of the 1996 welfare act makes important changes to the food stamp program and amends 7 U.S.C.A. §§ 2011–2028.

6. *See* Robert Greene, *Welfare Overhaul Keeps Food Stamps, Curbs Spending*, 1996 WL 4432671 (7/23/96 ASSOCPR No Page).

7. Staff of House Comm. on Ways and Means, 103d Cong., 2d Sess., *Overview of Entitlement Programs: 1994 Green Book, Background Material and Data on Programs within the Jurisdiction of the Committee on Ways and Means* 776 (Comm. Print 1994) (hereinafter, *1994 Green Book*).

8. *See* U.S. Dep't of Agriculture, Economic Research Service, *The Nutrition, Health, and Economic Consequences of Block Grants for Federal Food Assistance Programs*, Executive Summary ii (1995).

9. *See* Thomas M. Fraker, *The Effects of Food Stamps on Food Consumption: A Review of the Literature* (U.S. Dep't of Agriculture, 1990).

10. 7 U.S.C.A. § 2016(i) (West 1996), as amended by Pub. L. No. 104-193, 110 Stat. 2105 (1996).

11. *Id.* at § 2017(b) (West 1996).

12. *Id.* at § 2012(g) (West 1996), as amended by Pub. L. No. 104-193, 110 Stat. 2105 (1996).

13. *Id.*; 7 C.F.R. § 271.2 (1996) (definition of "eligible foods").

14. 7 C.F.R. § 271.2 (1996).

15. *Id.* and at §§ 273.11(e), 274.10(f)(2) (1996).

16. *Id.* at §§ 271.2, 273.11(f)–(g), 274.10(f)(3) (1996).

17. *Id.* at §§ 271.2, 278.1(d) (1996).

18. *Id.* at § 278.2(k) (1996).

19. *Id.* at §§ 273.11(h), 274.10(g), 278.1(r), 278.2(b) (1996).

20. 7 U.S.C.A. § 2012(g)(9) (West 1996), as amended by Pub. L. No. 104-193, 110 Stat. 2105 (1996).

21. 7 C.F.R. § 278.2(b) (1996).

22. *Id.*

23. *Id.* at §§ 274.10(j), 278.2(d) (1996).

24. *Id.* at §§ 273.2(g)(1)(i)(3), 274.1(a) (1996).

25. *Id.* at § 273.1(a)(1)(i)–(iii) (1996).

26. *Id.* at §273.1 (a)(2)(i)(A)–(D)(1996); *see also* Pub. L. No. 104-193, 110 Stat. 2105, § 803 (1996) (amending 7 U.S.C.A. § 2012(i)(2) (West 1996)).

27. 7 C.F.R. § 273.1(a)(2)(ii) (1996).

28. *Id.* at § 273.1(c)(1)–(2) (1996).

29. Pub. L. No. 104-193, 110 Stat. 2105, § 803 (1996) (amending 7 U.S.C.A. § 2012(i)(2) (West 1996)).

30. Pub. L. No. 104-193, 110 Stat. 2105, § 402(a)(2)(B) (1996).

31. *Id.* at § 402(a)(2)(C) (1996).

32. *Id.* at § 402(a)(2)(A) (1996).

33. 8 U.S.C.A. § 1612(a)(2)(D)(ii)(West 1996).

34. 7 C.F.R. § 273.11(j) (1996).

35. *Id.* at § 273.5(a), (b)(1) (1996).

36. *Id.* at §§ 273.1(e)(1)(iv), 273.11(d) (1996).

37. *Id.* at § 273.3 (1996).

38. *Id.* at §§ 273.3, 273.1(a)(1) (1996).

39. *Id.* at § 273.1(e)(1)(i) (1995).

40. *Id.* at § 273.1(e)(1) (1996).

41. *Id.* at § 273.1(e)(1)(i) (1996).

42. *Id.* at § 273.1(e)(1)(ii) (1996); *see also* Pub. L. No. 104-193, 110 Stat. 2105, § 830 (1996) (amending 7 U.S.C.A. § 2017(f) (West 1996)).

43. 7 C.F.R. § 273.1(e)(2)(iii) (1996).

44. *Id.* at § 273.1(e)(1)(iv) (1996).

45. *Id.* at § 273.1(3)(1)(v) (1996); *see also Van Dusen v. Commonwealth, Dep't of Public Welfare,* 79 Pa. Commw. 60, 468 A.2d 540 (Pa. Commw. Ct. 1983).

46. The United States Supreme Court rejected a challenge to the antistriker provision in *Lyng v. International Union, UAW,* 485 U.S. 360 (1988).

47. 7 C.F.R. § 273.1(g) (1996).

48. Pub. L. No. 104-193, 110 Stat. 2105, § 854 (1996).

49. 7 C.F.R. §§ 273.9(a)(2), 273.10(e)(1)(i)(A) (1996).

50. U.S. Dep't of Agriculture, Program Development Division (Sept. 10, 1996). Income limits are higher in Alaska and Hawaii.

51. *Id.* Gross income limits are higher in Alaska and Hawaii.

52. 7 C.F.R. § 273.9(c)(1) (1996).

53. Pub. L. No. 104-193, 110 Stat. 2105, § 808 (1996)(amending 7 U.S.C.A. § 2014 (d)(7) (West 1996)).

54. 7 C.F.R. § 273.9(c)(7) (1996).

55. *Id.* at § 273.9(c)(2) (1996).

56. *Id.* at § 273.9(c)(13) (1996)

57. *Id.* at § 273.9(c)(4) (1996).

58. *Id.* at § 273.9(c)(3) (1996).

59. *Id.* at § 273.9(c)(15) (1996).

60. *Id.* at § 273.9(c)(6) (1996).

61. *Id.* at § 273.9(c)(8) (1996).

62. Pub. L. No. 104-193, 110 Stat. 2105, § 808 (b)(2) (1996)(amending 7 U.S.C.A. § 2014(k)(1)(b) (West 1996)); 7 C.F.R. § 273.9(c)(11) (1996).

63. 7 C.F.R. § 273.9(b)(1)(v) (1996).

64. *Id.* at § 273.9(c)(9) (1996).

65. *Id.* at § 273.11(a)(2)(iii) (1996).

66. 42 U.S.C.A. § 3056g (West 1996); 7 C.F.R. § 273.9(c)(10)(iii) (1996).

67. 7 C.F.R. § 273.9(c)(10)(iii) (1996).

68. *Id.* at § 273.9(c)(10) (1996).

69. *Id.* at § 273.9(b)(5)(i) (1996).

70. 7 U.S.C.A. § 2014(g)(3) (West 1996).

71. Pub. L. No. 104-193, 110 Stat. 2105, § 811 (1996)(amending 7 U.S.C.A. § 2014(k)(2)(F) & (G) (West 1996)).

72. *Id.* at § 809(a) (1996)(amending 7 U.S.C.A. § 2014 (West 1996)). The standard deduction for households in Alaska, Hawaii, Guam, and the Virgin Islands is $229, $189, $269, and $118, respectively.

73. *Id.* at § 809 (1996) amending 7 U.S.C.A. § 2014 (E)(2)(A)(i)(ii) (West 1996)). The 1996 welfare act requires the Secretary of Agriculture to establish procedures by which states may use reasonable estimates of the cost of producing self-employment income instead of actual costs for purposes of this deduction. *Id.*

74. *Id.* at § 809(a) (1996)(amending 7 U.S.C.A. § 2014(e)(3) (West 1996)).

75. *Id.* at § 809(a) (1996)(amending 7 U.S.C.A. § 2014(e)(4)(A) (West 1996)). Title VII of the 1996 welfare act authorizes the Secretary of Agriculture to "prescribe by regulation the methods, including the calculation on a retrospective basis, that a state agency shall use to determine the amount of the deduction." *Id.* at § 809(a) (1996) (amending 7 U.S.C.A. § 2014(e)(4)(B) (West 1996)).

76. *Id.* § 809(a) (1996)(amending 7 U.S.C.A. § 2014(E)(5) (West 1996)). A person who is "temporarily living in the home of another" may be considered homeless for only three months. *See id.* at § 805 (amending 7 U.S.C.A. § 2012(s)(2)(C) (West 1996)).

77. *Id.* at § 809(e)(6) (1996). In addition, the state agency is required to establish a method for claiming this deduction that is "designed to minimize the burden for the eligible elderly or disabled household choosing to deduct recurrent medical expenses." *Id.* at § 809(e)(6)(B)(ii) (1996).

78. 7 C.F.R. § 273.9(d)(6) (1996). Under the 1996 welfare act, a food stamp household that does not incur a heating or cooling expense may not use a standard utility allowance in calculating the excess shelter deduction. In addition, the allowance may not be used by a household that does include expenses but lives in a public housing unit that has central utility meters and charges households only for their excess utility costs. Also, households that live with individuals who do not receive food stamps or with another food stamp household can use the allowance but only a pro rata portion.

79. Pub. L. No. 104-193, 110 Stat. 2105, § 804(a) (1996). The 1996 welfare act amended the food stamp program, 7 U.S.C.A. § 2014(k)(7)(B) (West 1996), by repealing the Leland bill provisions that would have removed the cap on the food stamp shelter deduction. The shelter deduction for elderly and disabled households is not subject to a cap.

80. 7 C.F.R. § 273.8(a)–(b) (1996)

81. *Id.* at § 273.8(c) (1996)

82. *Id.*

83. *Id.* at § 273.8(e)(1) (1996).

84. *Id.* at § 273.8(e)(2) (1996).

85. *Id.*

86. *Id.*; Pub. L. No. 104-193, 110 Stat. 2105, § 810 (1996)(amending 7 U.S.C.A. § 2014(g)(2) (West 1996)).

87. 7 C.F.R. § 273.8(e)(4)–(5)(1996).

88. *Id.* at § 273.8(e)(8) (1996)

89. Pub. L. No. 104-193, 110 Stat. 2105, § 810 (1996)(amending 7 U.S.C.A. § 2014(e)(3) (West 1996)); 7 C.F.R. § 273.11 (c)–(d) (1996).

90. 7 C.F.R. § 273.8(e)(15) (1996).

91. *Id.* at § 273.8(e)(7) (1996).

92. 7 U.S.C.A. § 2014(g)(3) (West 1996).

93. U.S. Dep't of Agriculture, Program Development Division (Sept. 10, 1996). Allotment levels are higher in Alaska, Hawaii, Guam, and the Virgin Islands.

94. *Id.* Allotment levels are higher in Alaska, Hawaii, Guam, and the Virgin Islands.

95. 7 C.F.R. § 273.2(c)(1) (1996).

96. Pub. L. No. 104-193, 110 Stat. 2105, § 835 (1996)(amending 7 U.S.C.A. § 2020 (West 1996)).

97. 7 C.F.R. § 273.1(f)(1)(ii) (1996).

98. *Id.* at § 273.2(e)(1) (1996).

99. *Id.* at § 273.2(a) (1996).

100. *Id.* at §§ 273.2(e)(3), (h)(1)(i)(D) (1996).

101. *Id.* at §273.2(e)(3)(1996)

102. Pub. L. No. 104-193, 110 Stat. 2105, § 835(1)(A) (1996)(amending 7 U.S.C.A. § 2020(e)(2) (West 1996))(eliminating the right of elderly, disabled, and individuals subject to hardship to apply for food stamps by mail or phone).

103. 7 U.S.C.A. § 2020(e)(3)(A) (West 1996).

104. 7 C.F.R. § 273.2(f)(4)(i) (1996).

105. *Id.* at §§ 273.2(f)(4)(iii), (5)(ii) (1996).

106. *Id.* at § 273.2(f)(4)(iii) (1996).

107. *Id.* at § 273.2(g)(1) (1996).

108. *Id.* at § 273.2(i)(3)(i) (1996). The 1996 welfare act enlarged the waiting period for expedited service from five to seven days.

109. *Id.* at § 273.2(i)(2) (1996).

110. *Id.* at § 273.2(i)(1)(i) (1996).

111. *Id.* at § 273.2(i)(1)(iv) (1996).

112. *Id.* at § 273.2(i)(4)(i)(A) (1996).

113. *Id.* at § 273.2(i)(4)(iii) (1996). Until the 1996 welfare act, states were required to give the household two months of benefits.

114. Pub. L. No. 104-193, 110 Stat. 2105, § 815(a) (1996)(amending 7 U.S.C.A. § 2015(d)(1)(A)(I) (West 1996)).

115. *Id.* at § 815(a) (1996)(amending 7 U.S.C.A. § 2015(d)(1)(C) (West 1996)).

116. *Id.* at § 824(a) (1996) (creating 7 U.S.C.A. § 2015(o)(2) (West 1996)).

117. *Id.* (creating 7 U.S.C.A. § 2015(o)(5) (West 1996)).

118. *Id.* at § 824 (creating 7 U.S.C.A. § 2015(o)(4) (West 1996)).

119. *Id.* at § 816 (1996)(amending 7 U.S.C.A. § 2015(d)(2) (West 1996)).

120. 7 C.F.R. § 273.7(n) (1996).

121. *Id.* at § 273.7(n)(3)(i) (1996).

122. *Id.* at § 273.7(n)(3)(ii) (1996).

123. Pub. L. No. 104-193, 110 Stat. 2105, § 815 (1996) (amending 7 U.S.C.A. § 2015(d) (West 1996).

124. *Id.*

125. 7 C.F.R. § 273.13(a)(1) (1996).

126. *Id.* at §§ 273.13(a)(3)(i)–(iii), 273.21(j)(2)(ii) (1996).

127. *Id.* at § 273.12(a)(2), 273.13(a)(1) (1996).

128. *Id.* at §§ 273.12(a)2, 273.13(a)(3)(iv)–(v) (1996).

129. *Id.* at § 273.15(a) (1996).

130. *Id.* at § 273.15(m) (1996).

131. *Id.* at § 273.15(h) (1996).

132. *Id.* at § 273.15(g) (1996).

133. *Id.* at § 273.15(k)(1)–(2) (1996).

134. *Id.* at § 273.15(k)(1) (1996).

135. *Id.* at § 273.15 (1996).

136. *Id.* at §§ 273.15(h), (i)(1), (l)(3)–(4), (p)(1), 272.1(c)(3) (1996).

137. *Id.* at § 273.15(p)(3) (1996).

138. *Id.* at § 273.15(p)(2), (4), (5) (1996).

139. *Id.* at § 273.15(p)(6) (1996).

140. *Id.* at § 273.15(q)(1) (1996).

141. 42 U.S.C.A. § 1786 (West 1996), as amended by Pub. L. No. 104-193, 110 Stat. 2105 (1996).

142. *See* Jonathan Kotch & Jo Shackelford, *The Nutritional Status of Low-Income Preschool Children in the United States: A Review of the Literature* (1989).

143. *See* American Civil Liberties Union & Food Research and Action Center, *Introduction to the WIC and CSFP Programs*, 24 Clearinghouse Rev. 820 (1990); Food Research and Action Center, *Feeding the Other Half: Mothers and Children Left Out of WIC* (1989).

144. *See* Children's Defense Fund, *The Odds Against Poor Children*, 15 Children's Def. Fund Rep. 6 (1994).

145. *See* Food Research and Action Center, *WIC: A Success Story* (3d ed. 1991); Children's Defense Fund, *A Children's Defense Budget, FY 1988: An Analysis of Our Nation's Investment in Children* 127 (1987).

146. See Food Research and Action Center, *The Special Supplemental Food Program for Women, Infants and Children (WIC)* 2 (1992).

147. 7 C.F.R. § 246.10(c) (1996).

148. *Id.* at § 246.7(b) (1996).

149. *Id.* at § 246.7(b)(3), (d) (1996).

150. *Id.* at § 246.7(b)(1) (1996).

151. *Id.* at § 246.7(b)(2), (c)–(d) (1996).

152. *Id.* at § 246.7(d)(2)(vi) (1996).

153. *Id.* at § 246.7(e)(4) (1996).

154. 8 U.S.C.A. § 1641(c) & (c)(2) (West 1996).

155. Pub. L. No. 104-193, 110 Stat. 2105, §§ 401, 403(c), 431 (1996); *id.* at § 742. Certain provisions of the Immigration and Nationality Act should also be consulted, *see* Im-

migration and Nationality Act §§ 207; 208; 243(u); 212(d)(5); and 203 (a)(7), as in effect prior to April 1, 1980.

156. 42 U.S.C.A. §§ 1751–69(e) (West 1996), as amended by Pub. L. No. 104-193, 110 Stat. 2105 (1996).

157. National Education Association, *The Relationship between Nutrition and Learning: A School Employee's Guide to Information and Action* 8 (1989).

158. Merrill S. Read, *Malnutrition and Behavior* (1982), quoted in *id.* at 5, Sonia Nazario, *Hunger: Schools See Marked Rise in Malnutrition*, L.A. Times, Nov. 20, 1994, A37 (quoting Ernesto Pollitt, Professor of Human Development at the University of California-Davis, whose 1993 study found that children who are iron deficient or anemic fall 25 percent behind in mental development).

159. Pub. L. No. 104-193, 110 Stat. 2105, § 702 (1996) (amending 42 U.S.C.A. § 1758(f) (West 1996)).

160. Pub. L. No. 104-193, 110 Stat. 2105, § 706(b)(l)(B) (1996)(reducing school lunch reimbursement rates to $1.97 per meal per child).

161. 7 C.F.R. § 245.5(a)(1) (1996).

162. *Id.* at § 245.6(a), (c) (1996).

163. *Id.*

164. *Id.* at § 245.3(c) (1996).

165. *Id.* at § 245.2(a)(4) (1996)(definition of "documentation").

166. 61 Fed. Reg. 10720 (March 15, 1996). Income levels are higher in Alaska and Hawaii.

167. Pub. L. No. 104-193, 110 Stat. 2105, § 742 (1996).

168. *See Plyler v. Doe*, 457 U.S. 202 (1982).

169. Food Research and Action Center, School Breakfast Scorecard (Oct. 1996).

170. 7 C.F.R. § 245.10(a) (1996).

171. *Id.* at § 245.8(b), (d) (1996).

172. *Id.* at § 245.8(c) (1996).

173. U.S. Dep't of Agriculture, Food and Nutrition Service, FNS Instruction 791-1 (July 12, 1988).

174. 7 C.F.R. § 245.3, 245.6 (1996).

175. *Id.* at § 245.7(a) (1996).

176. *Id.* at § 245.6(b)(2), 245.7(b) (1996).

177. 42 U.S.C.A. § 1773 (West 1996), as amended by Pub. L. No. 104-193, 110 Stat. 2105 (1996).

178. *See* Michele Tingling-Clemmons, *BREAKFAST: Don't Start School Without It!* (Food Research and Action Center, undated); Food Research and Action Center, *Fuel for Excellence: FRAC's Guide to School Breakfast Expansion* 12–15 (1987).

179. *See* Sonia Nazario, *Going to School Hungry*, L.A. Times, Nov. 20, 1994, A1; Food Research and Action Center, *School Breakfast Scorecard* (Oct. 1996).

180. Pub. L. No. 104-193, 110 Stat. 2105, § 706(b)(1)(B) (1996); *see Breakfast Funds Cut Has Schools Scrambling*, Star Tribune, Oct. 8, 1996, 3A (1996 W L 6931684).

181. 61 Fed. Reg. 10720 (March 15, 1996). Income levels are higher in Alaska and Hawaii.

182. 7 C.F.R. § 245.5(a)(1) (1996).

183. *Id.* at § 245.6(a) (1996).

184. *Id.* at § 245.2(a-4) (1996)(definition of "documentation").

185. *Id.*

186. Pub. L. No. 104-193, 110 Stat. 2105, § 742 (1996).

187. *See Plyler v. Doe,* 457 U.S. 202 (1982).

188. Pub. L. No. 104-193, 110 Stat. 2105, § 706(b)(1)(B) (1996).

189. *Id.* at § 702(c) (1996)(amending 42 U.S.C.A. § 1758 (West 1996)).

190. 7 C.F.R. § 245.8(b), (d) (1996).

191. *Id.* at § 245.8(c) (1996).

192. U.S. Dep't of Agriculture, Food and Nutrition Service, FNS Instruction 791-1 (July 12, 1988).

193. 42 U.S.C.A. §§ 1751–1769(e) (West 1996), as amended by Pub. L. No. 104-193, 110 Stat. 2105 (1996).

194. Campaign to End Childhood Hunger, *Summer Food Service Program for Children* (Aug. 1992).

195. 7 C.F.R. § 225.6(e)(3) (1996).

196. 42 U.S.C.A. §§ 3021–3032 (West 1996).

197. *1994 Green Book, supra* note 7, table A-6 at 859.

198. Testimony of Mary Ellen Natale, Esq., Food Research and Action Center, before the Select Comm. on Aging, U.S. House of Representatives, *Old, Poor, and Forgotten: Elderly Americans Living in Poverty* (June 24, 1992).

199. *Malnutrition Hits Many Elderly,* N.Y. Times, July 3, 1995, B28.

III

Health Services

Is there a federal constitutional right to health care?

No. The United States Supreme Court has never found a right to health care under the federal Constitution. While recognizing medical care to be " 'a basic necessity of life',"[1] the Court has declined to impose on government an affirmative obligation to provide or subsidize health services,[2] except in the narrow case where an individual is in the custody of the state.[3]

Within this constitutional regime, health care delivery in the United States is truly unique. In contrast to most other countries, the United States uses a pay-as-you-go health care system, and that system is the most expensive in the world. Yet our infant mortality rates exceed, and childhood immunization rates lag behind, those of many other countries. The ability to pay for care, either directly or through insurance, is the crucial factor to receiving necessary and appropriate services. Sadly, one of the cruel ironies of today's health care system is that the very groups most in need of care are those least able to get it. This chapter discusses the major federal and state programs designed to help poor people receive the medical care they need.

Is there a state constitutional right to health care?

The answer to this question is still emerging. As in other areas affecting social and economic life, state constitutions are a separate and independent source of rights from the federal Constitution. A number of state constitutions contain provisions dealing with matters of public health, such as the maintenance of public hospitals, treatment of the mentally ill, and provision of medical assistance.[4] Whether a particular clause will be read to establish an affirmative right to health care (or to a specific health service) depends on the language of the text, its history and purpose, and the general principles of interpretation that guide a state court in its decisionmaking.[5]

MEDICAID

What is Medicaid?

The Medicaid program was created by the federal government in 1965 to provide health care and services to people who cannot afford them.[6] Medicaid is the largest public health insurance program for the poor. Every state has a Medicaid program.

What is the difference between Medicaid and Medicare?

Medicaid is not the same as Medicare. Medicare, which is described later in this chapter, is health insurance for people age 65 or older and some people with disabilities. That program is run by the Social Security Administration and is solely a federal program. Whether or not a person receives Medicare is not determined by his or her income.

Medicaid, on the other hand, is a program only for low-income people. It is run by a cooperative effort of the federal, state, and local governments. The state usually administers the program through its health and welfare department. Locally, county departments of social services administer the program. The Health Care Financing Administration (HCFA) of the United States Department of Health and Human Services is in charge of Medicaid at the federal level.

The cost of the Medicaid program is shared by federal, state, and local governments. The federal government pays 50 to 83 percent of the cost (depending on how many poor people live in the state), and the state is responsible for the rest.

If you are poor and are also aged or disabled, you should be able to get *both* Medicare and Medicaid as a Qualified Medicare Beneficiary (QMB). If you qualify, Medicaid will pay for some important medical services that Medicare does not cover, such as drugs, and will also pay for Medicare expenses, such as deductibles.

Medicaid is not charity. It is a right to which you are entitled by law—like the right of a child to attend public school. Medicaid differs from state to state in terms of who is eligible, what services are covered, and how services are paid. So you need to discuss your state's coverage rules with your welfare department or local legal services office. However, *all* states must follow some specific federal rules in administering their programs. Some of these basic rules are discussed below.

Who can get Medicaid?

Anyone has the right to apply for Medicaid, but not everyone can get it. First of all, the person must have limited income and limited resources (things such as savings accounts, property, and jewelry). Next, the person has to fall into a group that is covered by Medicaid. Some groups *must* be covered by a state. The groups the state must cover are listed below.

Families and Children

1. Medicaid must cover families that currently meet the AFDC eligibility rules that existed in their state on July 16, 1996, even if the family does not receive AFDC (the Personal Responsibility and Work Opportunity Reconciliation Act of 1996—the welfare act that Congress passed and the President signed in August 1996—abolished the AFDC program effective July 1997). Medicaid must cover such people whether or not they currently receive any public assistance.[7]

2. Medicaid must cover pregnant women and children under age 6 if the family income is less than 133 percent of the federal poverty level (the federal poverty level is approximately $15,600 for a family of four in 1996).[8]

3. Medicaid must cover any child under age 14, if family income is less than the federal poverty level. Eligibility increases from age 14 to age 15 in October 1997 and will continue to expand each year until 2001, when all poor children below age 19 will be covered.[9]

4. Women who applied for and received Medicaid while they were pregnant remain eligible for Medicaid for all pregnancy and postpartum services during the sixty-day period beginning on the last day of the pregnancy.[10]

5. Infants born to women who are eligible for and receiving Medicaid on the date of the child's birth are automatically eligible for Medicaid for one year from birth, as long as the mother remains eligible. This means that the mother does not have to fill out a new application to qualify the child for Medicaid.[11]

As discussed above, the 1996 welfare act abolishes the AFDC program, but requires states to provide Medicaid to families that currently meet the AFDC eligibility rules in effect July 16, 1996. Families that qualified for

Medicaid in this way, but no longer meet the old AFDC eligibility rules, are entitled to continued Medicaid coverage in the following situations:

1. A family that no longer meets the AFDC eligibility rules because a family member takes a job may still qualify for Medicaid.[12] This is sometimes called "transitional Medicaid."

2. A family that no longer meets the AFDC eligibility rules because of increased child or spousal support may still qualify for Medicaid for the four months following the loss of AFDC eligibility.[13]

3. A family qualifies for Medicaid if it lost AFDC eligibility solely because the AFDC payment would be less than ten dollars.[14]

4. Families that participate in a work supplementation program and would be eligible for AFDC if there were no such work program are automatically eligible for Medicaid.[15]

5. Minor children cannot be cut off Medicaid because of their parent's failure to participate in work programs that may be required if the family receives cash assistance under a state program funded by the Temporary Assistance for Needy Families block grant.[16] Nor may a minor child be cut off for the parent's failure to cooperate in establishing paternity.[17]

6. Children who receive federal adoption assistance or foster care maintenance payments must be covered by Medicaid.[18]

Clearly, Medicaid has taken particular steps to make sure that needy, pregnant women and needy children are covered through the program. As a result, a woman who is pregnant for the first time can now qualify for Medicaid even if she has no other dependent children in the house. And a child may qualify for Medicaid even if the parent does not. *It is important that you exercise your child's right to receive Medicaid even if you are not eligible yourself. And, due to the recent welfare reform changes, it is essential that you file an application for Medicaid for you and/or your children.*

Aged, Blind, or Disabled

1. In most states, all aged, blind, or disabled poor people who get SSI also get Medicaid.[19] In a few states, such persons are not automatically eligible. They must meet a "spend down" before Medicaid can begin.[20] Spend down is explained below. As of January 1996, the states

where SSI recipients do not automatically get Medicaid are Connecti-cut, Hawaii, Illinois, Indiana, Minnesota, Missouri, New Hampshire, North Dakota, Ohio, Oklahoma, and Virginia.

2. Medicaid must cover persons receiving mandatory state supple-ments.[21]

3. Medicaid covers the working disabled.[22]

4. Medicaid must cover certain disabled adult children[23] and dis-abled widows or widowers.[24]

5. Medicaid must also cover "Pickle people" (named after an elected official named Pickle). While eligibility for this program may, at first, seem complicated, it is really quite straight forward. The "Pickle program" maintains the Medicaid eligibility of persons who lose SSI be-cause they have received an Old Age, Survivors and Disability Insurance (OASDI or "social security") cost-of-living increase. A Pickle person is one who (a) was receiving both OASDI and SSI at the same time in some month after April 1977, (b) is currently receiving OASDI, (c) is ineligi-ble for SSI because of excess income, and (d) would be eligible for SSI if the OASDI cost-of-living increases received since the individual was last eligible for both OASDI and SSI were deducted from his or her in-come.[25]

6. Medicaid covers Medicare Part A and Part B premiums, deduct-ibles, and coinsurance for elderly and disabled Qualified Medicare Beneficiaries (QMBs).[26] QMBs are elderly and disabled persons who are entitled to Medicare Part A (hospital insurance) benefits and have in-comes at or are below the federal poverty level and resources that do not exceed twice the SSI resource eligibility standards. Unfortunately, states have not done a good job of informing people about the QMB program, and many who are eligible are not receiving the benefit.

States can decide to give Medicaid to other groups.[27] For example, states can decide to cover

1. Persons who could get SSI but have not applied for it.

2. Children under state adoption assistance programs (foster chil-dren). Most states cover these children.

3. Pregnant women and infants with incomes up to 185 percent of the federal poverty level.[28] The state gets to determine the exact percent-age of poverty it will cover.

4. Persons who are age 65 or older or disabled with incomes up to the federal poverty level.[29] The state gets to determine the exact percentage of poverty it will cover. Only a few states have chosen to cover this group of the aged and disabled.

Check with your local Medicaid office to find out which additional groups your state has chosen to cover.

Who are the medically needy?

The medically needy are people who would qualify for Medicaid, except that their incomes or resources are too high.[30] In other words, they are families with dependent children, or aged, blind, or disabled persons and have income and/or resources exceeding AFDC or SSI eligibility cutoffs. The medically needy are presumed to be able to meet the costs of daily living—food, clothing, and shelter. But if they have chronic, on-going medical needs or if a medical crisis occurs, they will not be able to afford the care they need.

Eligibility workers often do not explain the medically needy program to applicants. Basically, the program works as follows: States set a medically needy income level based on family size. The medically needy income level historically has been fixed at an amount somewhat higher than the AFDC income eligibility level. All persons with incomes below the medically needy income level automatically qualify for Medicaid.

Persons with incomes above the medically needy income level do not automatically get Medicaid. They must first meet a "spend down," also called a "share of cost" in some states. The spend down is the amount by which the applicant's income exceeds the medically needy income level. Applicants must spend all of this excess income on medical expenses at some time during the "spend down period." The state can set the spend down period to last anywhere from one to six months. Once the spend down is met, Medicaid coverage begins. The spend down acts like an insurance deductible that must be met before coverage begins.

Here is an example of how the medically needy program's spend down works: Suppose the state's medically needy income level is $500 per month and the spend down period is one month. If Ms. Jones's income is $700, then she will have to incur a total of $200 in medical bills during the one month spend down period before Medicaid coverage will begin.

States do not have to offer Medicaid to the medically needy. This means that in a state like Colorado, which has no program for the medically needy, a person who has income just one dollar over the public assistance level will

TABLE 3-1
States with Medically Needy Programs

California	Kansas	Nebraska	Rhode Island
Connecticut	Kentucky	New Hampshire	Texas
District of	Louisiana	New Jersey	Utah
Columbia	Maine	New York	Vermont
Florida	Maryland	North Carolina	Virginia
Georgia	Massachusetts	North Dakota	Washington
Hawaii	Michigan	Oklahoma	West Virginia
Illinois	Minnesota	Oregon	Wisconsin
Iowa	Montana	Pennsylvania	

not be able to get Medicaid no matter how much she spends on medical bills.

Luckily, most states do have medically needy programs. Table 3-1 lists the states that have medically needy programs as of 1996. States choosing to cover the medically needy must, at least, cover pregnant and postpartum women and children under age 18.

What bills count toward the medically needy spend down?

You can count almost any bill for "medical or remedial care" toward your spend down.[31] The amount need not have been actually paid—only incurred. Medical expenses for all your family members can be counted. Old bills that you incurred before you applied can also be counted.

You can count bills for health insurance and for a variety of medical services, such as doctor bills, physical therapy, home health care, prescriptions, dentures, eyeglasses, and mental health bills. You can also count bills for over-the-counter drugs or purchases like cold medications, laxatives, bandages, needles, eyeglasses, and hearing aids.

You must be able to show that you have actually incurred the medical expense. It is important that you keep good records, including all the receipts that you get for the services you receive. Check with your doctor and home health agency to see whether they will be submitting their bills directly to Medicaid or whether you need to submit copies of the bills.

What income can you have and still be eligible for Medicaid?

The eligibility worker will always look at the applicant's income to decide whether or not she or he qualifies for Medicaid.[32] Income consists of earnings from wages, pension benefits, tax refunds, and the like. Income may also include in-kind income, which is the value of food or shelter acquired by an applicant living in someone else's house.

The eligibility worker will exempt or disregard certain types of income. Applicants are entitled to the same income exemptions that apply to the public assistance group to which they are most closely linked (AFDC or SSI). For example, AFDC exempts certain amounts of income spent on child care and disregards a portion of the applicant's earned income.[33] Therefore, Medicaid will do the same for applicants who are women and dependent children.

What resources can you have and still be eligible for Medicaid?

In most instances, the eligibility worker will also look at the applicant's resources or assets to decide whether or not he or she qualifies for Medicaid.[34] Resources are cash or other property that the person can liquidate or convert into cash. Savings accounts, certificates of deposit, real property, automobiles, stocks, and life insurance policies are examples of resources.

Once again, applicants are entitled to the same resource exemptions that apply to the public assistance group to which they are most closely linked (AFDC or SSI). For example, SSI exempts such things as the home, household goods, personal effects and jewelry, burial spaces and funds, and automobile and life insurance policies up to a certain value.[35] Therefore, Medicaid will do the same for applicants who are aged, blind, or disabled.

Can you transfer assets to someone else in order to qualify for Medicaid?

If you transfer assets in order to qualify for Medicaid, a transfer-of-assets penalty may apply. In addition, a 1996 law makes it a crime, punishable by up to one year in jail and $10,000 in fines, to knowingly dispose of assets in order to obtain Medicaid benefits unlawfully.[36]

The transfer-of-assets penalty only affects Medicaid eligibility for long-term care services. These include nursing facility services, as well as services provided through a home or community care program. Other services, such as doctor visits, drugs, and preventive care, are not affected by the penalty.

If you transfer assets for less than fair market value within thirty-six months of the date you need nursing level services, Medicaid will not cover your long-term care for a period of time. The period of disqualification is the number of months that results from dividing the uncompensated value of the transfer by the private pay cost of a nursing home for one month.

For example, assume that Mr. Jones gives a $10,000 certificate of deposit to a friend within thirty-six months of the day he enters a nursing home and that the private pay nursing home rate in his state is $1,000 a month. Medicaid will not cover his nursing facility services for ten months. During those months Mr. Jones will have to pay the nursing home out of his own funds.

Some transfers are not penalized. A transfer of your home is not penalized if the home is transferred to your spouse, your child who is under age 21 or disabled, a sibling who has an equity interest in the home and was residing there for at least one year prior to your need for long-term care, or a child of any age who was residing in the home at least two years prior to the need for care and who provided care that permitted you to reside at home rather than in an institution.

Transfers of other assets will not be penalized if made to your spouse or to a blind or disabled child. Finally, the penalty will not apply if you can show the Medicaid agency that the transfer was made exclusively for reasons other than to qualify for Medicaid.

Can you transfer assets into a trust fund in order to qualify for Medicaid?

Yes. There are several types of trusts that may be used to help you qualify for Medicaid.

Individual Trusts for Persons with Disabilities under Age 65

If you are under age 65 and disabled, you may transfer assets into an individual trust established solely for your benefit. This kind of trust is commonly known as a "supplemental needs trust" and is usually designed to pay for goods and services not covered by government benefits. The trust must be established by your parent, grandparent, legal guardian, or by court order. Assets placed into a supplemental needs trust do not count as a resource for purposes of Medicaid eligibility, and you may transfer assets into a properly structured trust without suffering any transfer-of-assets penalty.[37] This is a valuable feature if you receive long-term care services or may require such services within thirty-six months of the transfer.

There are several other advantages to transferring your excess assets into a trust. If the money is placed in a supplemental needs trust, it must be used to purchase goods and services that benefit you directly and improve your

quality of life. In addition, transferring excess assets into a properly structured trust not only will allow you to qualify for Medicaid, but also will allow
you to qualify for Supplemental Security Income if you are otherwise eligible.[38]

There are a few disadvantages to transferring resources into a supplemental needs trust. First, a trust document must be drafted, which usually
requires the assistance of a legal professional. Second, a trustee is needed to
manage the trust property. (Ordinarily the trustee should not give you substantial amounts of cash from the trust, because cash distributions count as
income for purposes of Medicaid eligibility and, if you are receiving Supplemental Security Income benefits, may reduce the amount of your SSI grant.
Instead, the trustee should use trust funds to purchase the goods and services that you need.) Finally, any amount remaining in the trust at your
death will be used first to repay the Medicaid program for medical assistance received during your lifetime.

Pooled Trusts for Disabled Individuals

If you are disabled, you may transfer resources into a "pooled trust,"
regardless of your age. A pooled trust is established by a not-for-profit organization and supplements your government benefits in the same way as an
individual supplemental needs trust. Pooled trusts have separate accounts
for each individual beneficiary. Assets in a qualifying pooled trust do not
count as resources for purposes of Medicaid eligibility.[39]

One advantage of the pooled trust is that you can set up an individual
account in the trust yourself; there is no requirement that the account be
established by a parent, grandparent, legal guardian, or court, as is the case
with an individual trust. Another advantage of a pooled trust is that you
may choose to have the funds remaining at your death stay in the trust and
be used for the benefit of other people with disabilities, as opposed to being
used to repay the state for Medicaid you received.

A disadvantage is that, under the Health Care Financing Administration's current interpretation of the law, transfers of assets into a pooled trust
by an individual age 65 or over are subject to the transfer-of-asset penalties
described in the preceding question and so may result in a period of ineligibility.[40] Some advocates believe that the government's interpretation is in-
correct and should be challenged.

Individual Irrevocable Trusts

Any person, regardless of age, and whether or not disabled, may transfer
assets into an individual irrevocable trust. This is an "income-only" trust,

which means that the trustee can use the income generated by the trust (e.g., interest payments, dividends, etc.) to provide for your needs, but the assets you place into the trust cannot be withdrawn during your lifetime. Assets placed into an individual irrevocable trust do not count as resources for purposes of Medicaid eligibility.[41]

The major advantage of an individual irrevocable trust is that you control who gets the trust assets at your death; the state payback provisions do not apply. The disadvantages are that you do not have access to the principal of the trust, and transfers into the trust are subject to the transfer-of-assets penalty and so may result in a period of Medicaid ineligibility.

Can relatives be legally required to pay for a poor person's medical care?

Eligibility for Medicaid is determined only by the income and resources that a person or family actually has. Support from relatives living away from home can only be counted if it is actually available to meet your current needs on a regular basis.

In some cases, the law automatically treats certain members of a family as being responsible for others. However, there are fewer legally responsible relatives under Medicaid than under other public assistance programs. In Medicaid, spouses are liable for the support of each other, and parents are liable for the support of their children who are under age 21 or disabled. For example, the parents' income is automatically considered available to the child when Medicaid eligibility of the child is being determined. However, in determining Medicaid eligibility, the state cannot make children responsible for their parents or siblings responsible for each other.[42]

Can the state Medicaid agency take a recipient's home or property to recoup amounts it has paid for care?

State Medicaid programs can use two devices to recoup Medicaid benefits they have paid on behalf of a recipient: liens and estate recovery.

The state may, but is not required to, use liens to recoup Medicaid benefits. A lien is a claim the state files on your property that gives it the right to get back amounts it has paid for Medicaid benefits. States can use liens in very limited circumstances. A state can place a lien on a recipient's property if a court has found that Medicaid benefits were incorrectly paid for that individual.[43] A state can also place a lien on a recipient's real property for correctly paid benefits if the recipient is in a nursing home and is not reasonably expected to return home.[44] There must be a notice and opportunity for a hearing to determine if the person will be able to return home. And if the recipient does return home, then the lien must be canceled.

Liens cannot be imposed on the recipient's home if any of the following persons live there: the spouse, a blind or disabled child or child under age 21, or a sibling with an equity interest in the home.

States are required to engage in estate recovery. Estate recovery allows the state to be reimbursed for Medicaid payments from the property and assets (called the "estate") left by a deceased recipient. As with liens, the state's ability to recover is limited. Recovery applies to the estates of deceased recipients who were age 55 or older when Medicaid was received. Recovery applies to amounts spent for nursing facility services, home and community services, and related hospital and prescription drug services received at age 55 or older. States have the option to seek recovery for other services covered by Medicaid.

The estate includes all real and personal property owned by the recipient at the time of death. Thus, the state can seek to recover the amounts it paid out from this property. The state can even seek recovery against property held in joint tenancy, tenancy in common, and life estates.

Estate recovery can occur only after the death of the individual's surviving spouse and only at a time when he or she has no surviving child who is disabled or under age 21.

What happens to a family's savings if a spouse has to go into a nursing home?

Federal laws have been passed to make sure that the costs of nursing home care do not cause the at-home spouse to live without adequate income or resources.[45] These "spousal impoverishment" protections extend to couples where one spouse is likely to remain in a hospital or nursing facility for more than thirty days.

The income protections entitle the institutionalized spouse to keep certain income. The state decides which spouse is the recipient of the income by looking at the "name on the check." This means that whoever's name is on the check is considered to have sole rights to that income. Obviously, the name-on-the-check rule could cause the at-home spouse to be left with nothing. To avoid this, federal law entitles the institutionalized spouse to certain income deductions, which include an allowance for the at-home spouse. The income deductions for the institutionalized spouse are made in the following order:

1. A personal needs allowance of thirty dollars per month (for extra food, magazines, clothing);

2. A minimum monthly needs allowance for the at-home spouse of $1,245 in 1996 (adjusted annually based on cost-of-living increases) if the spouse's own income is below this amount;

3. An allowance for each family member;

4. Deductions for medical or remedial care not covered by Medicaid.

The monthly needs allowance for the at-home spouse can be increased by a fair hearing before the Medicaid agency if it can be demonstrated that "exceptional circumstances" require higher deductions or by a court order that the at-home spouse receive increased support.[46]

There are also protections for a couple's resources, such as savings accounts, property, and jewelry. When an institutionalized person applies for Medicaid, the eligibility worker will include all countable (or nonexempt) resources owned by the institutionalized spouse, the at-home spouse, or both, at the beginning of the period of institutionalization. Exempt resources include the home, household goods, an automobile, and a burial fund. From the total available resources, the at-home spouse is allowed to retain a minimum of $15,348 or one-half of the total resources, whichever is greater, up to a maximum of $76,740. These are the 1996 amounts, and they are adjusted annually based on cost-of-living increases. The resource allowance can be increased by a fair hearing if it can be demonstrated that "exceptional circumstances" require higher deductions, or by a court order that the at-home spouse receive increased support.[47]

What does Medicaid pay for?

State Medicaid programs *must* pay for

- Inpatient hospital services (other than services in an institution for mental disease);
- Outpatient hospital services;
- Physician services;
- Rural health clinic services;
- Federally qualified health center services (community and migrant health clinics);
- Laboratory and x-ray services;

- Preventive care and treatment for children (described below);
- Nursing facilities services for persons age 21 or older;
- Family planning services and supplies;
- Services furnished by a licensed nurse-midwife;
- Home health services for persons entitled to receive nursing services; and
- Services furnished by a certified pediatric nurse practitioner or certified family nurse practitioner.[48]

State Medicaid programs *may* pay for the following services for adults (as discussed below, the law requires these services to be covered for children):

- Medical care or other types of remedial care recognized under state law and furnished by licensed practitioners (e.g., psychology services);
- Private duty nursing services;
- Dental services;
- Physical therapy;
- Prescription drugs (all states cover);
- Dentures;
- Eyeglasses;
- Prosthetic devices;
- Intermediate care facility services;
- Hospice care;
- Services provided by a certified pediatric nurse practitioner or family nurse practitioner;
- Case management services;
- Community-supported independent living arrangement services;
- Respiratory care services;
- TB-related services;
- Personal care services; and
- Other diagnostic, screening, preventive, and rehabilitative services.[49]

Check with your local social services or legal services office to find out which of these services your state covers.

All services must be covered in sufficient amount, duration, and scope.

This means, for example, that a state cannot limit its coverage of eyeglasses to persons who are nearsighted.[50] In addition, states cannot arbitrarily deny or reduce services because of the diagnosis, type of illness, or condition.[51] For instance, a state that covers prescription drugs (all do) cannot issue a blanket refusal to cover AZT for people with AIDS.[52]

The state can, however, place reasonable limits on the amount of a service it will cover for adults.[53] But, as discussed immediately below, the EPSDT program for children prohibits states from placing such limits on children's services. For example, the state may cover only twelve inpatient hospital days per year for adults, but it cannot apply this automatic cut off to Medicaid-eligible children who are in the hospital. The state can also make a service subject to prior authorization, preadmission screening, or second opinion.[54] These types of "utilization controls" mean that the provider will have to get the state's agreement that the service is medically necessary before Medicaid will cover the service.

Will Medicaid cover preventive care and treatment needed by a child?

Yes. Early and Periodic Screening, Diagnosis, and Treatment (EPSDT) is a free, mandatory Medicaid service for *all* children and adolescents under age 21 who are eligible for Medicaid.[55] EPSDT is a preventive care program that offers poor children and adolescents checkups when they are feeling well—not just when they are sick or injured, getting ready to enter school, or preparing to play organized sports. Early and periodic care is crucial because children and youth are not little adults. Their health care needs and development differ from those of adults. Children experience numerous developmental milestones that must be assessed on time. If abnormal development is not diagnosed promptly, the benefits of treatment can be lost forever. Moreover, during childhood, health habits are learned (or not learned).

Your state may call its EPSDT program by another name, such as Health Track, Health Check, or Child Health and Disability Prevention. Regardless of its name, however, the program must offer certain services.

EPSDT must include medical, vision, hearing, and dental screens at preset intervals. For example, babies are entitled to at least six medical checkups before age one and at least four medical checkups between twelve and twenty-four months.[56] And at each medical checkup, the screen must include a comprehensive physical and mental health assessment, unclothed physical exam, laboratory tests (including lead blood tests), appropriate immunizations, and health education (for the child and caretaker).

EPSDT also covers a broad range of treatment services. According to the law, Medicaid must cover care that is "necessary . . . to correct or ameliorate defects and physical and mental illnesses or conditions" diagnosed during a screen.[57] Thus, if your child needs a service, it should be covered by Medicaid even though the program does not cover the service for adults. And the service should be covered even if it is to treat a problem that existed prior to Medicaid eligibility (known as a "preexisting condition"). This means that your child is entitled to such treatments as case management, prescription drugs, eyeglasses, physical therapy, private duty nursing, and, in fact, any of the other Medicaid services listed earlier in this chapter.

States are supposed to engage in aggressive outreach and information programs to make sure that families and children know about the benefits of preventive care and EPSDT.[58] This includes providing outreach and information in languages other than English, but states do not always do this. You should be informed about EPSDT orally. You should also be given written information, such as a brochure or pamphlet, that describes the program in easy-to-understand language. In addition, states are required to provide you with transportation and appointment-scheduling assistance for all EPSDT visits.

If you do not enroll in Medicaid for yourself, you can still enroll in Medicaid on behalf of your child. If you are not familiar with EPSDT, contact your Medicaid office and get complete information about the program. EPSDT will assure that your child gets regular medical checkups, needed immunizations, and early treatment of any medical problems that may be discovered.

What are case management services?

Medicaid broadly defines "case management" as services that will assist individuals "in gaining access to needed medical, social, education, and other services."[59] Case management involves a wide range of activities, including providing transportation and appointment-scheduling assistance for medical visits, prior authorization of medical services, referrals to needed special education programs, management of complex treatment plans, and counseling. Trained professionals, such as social workers and Medicaid eligibility workers, provide case management services.

Case management services are optional Medicaid services for adults.[60] However, under the EPSDT program, case management is mandatory for children under age 21 if medically necessary. Case management is particularly important for children with chronic or multiple physical or mental problems and children who are at a high risk of developing such problems.

Must a provider accept a Medicaid card?

Provider participation in Medicaid is, for the most part, voluntary. This means that you will need to find a hospital, doctor, or pharmacist who has agreed to participate in the program. This can be difficult because, in some areas, few providers accept Medicaid. Providers complain that Medicaid rates are too low, and in many states payment is indeed inadequate. Although federal law makes it illegal for a state to pay providers inadequate amounts,[61] states have not often been forced to comply with the law.[62]

Medicaid is a vendor payment program. This means that the state Medicaid agency will pay the provider directly. Medicaid recipients do not receive cash or vouchers that they can use to purchase care.

Will Medicaid pay a recipient's full health care bill?

The law allows states to place "nominal" copayments on Medicaid services.[63] Most states now use copayments for one or more Medicaid service. In these states, the recipient is responsible for paying the copayment directly to the provider. Copayments usually range from fifty cents to five dollars; however, they can be greater than this. It is illegal to charge copayments for children under age 18 (and at state option 19, 20, or 21), nursing facility residents, services related to pregnancy, emergency services, family planning services, services furnished to individuals enrolled in an HMO, and hospice services. In addition, some states, such as New York, allow copayments to be waived in cases of hardship. And in general, the provider may simply agree not to pursue collection of the copayment amount.

States can also impose cost sharing on disabled working individuals, persons receiving extended Medicaid work transition benefits, and on infants under age one and pregnant women with incomes above 150 percent of the federal poverty level.[64]

Aside from these limited circumstances, *Medicaid payment is payment in full.* Once a patient is accepted as a Medicaid patient, the provider must accept Medicaid as payment in full—whatever the amount Medicaid pays. The provider cannot bill you for any additional amounts. You cannot be charged a deposit, nor can the doctor pick and choose the services for which he or she will accept Medicaid. In addition, if the provider fails to follow a Medicaid payment rule, she or he cannot then seek payment from you. For example, if the doctor fails to submit the bill to Medicaid on time, he or she cannot bill you for the service.

The state makes Medicaid payments directly to the provider. And Medicaid is always the last to pay. This means that Medicaid will cover only what other insurance and Medicare does not cover.

What happens if a Medicaid cardholder cannot afford a trip to the doctor?

Every state must provide some method of transportation to and from hospitals, clinics, and doctors' offices for people on Medicaid. For example, the state may provide ambulance or medi-van services, public transport tokens/money, or money to allow people to use a taxi or a private car. Your local Medicaid office should be prepared to offer a full description of the Medicaid transportation service.

What happens if a poor person needs medical care before applying for Medicaid?

In some circumstances, Medicaid will allow retroactive coverage. This coverage extends to medical services covered by the state's Medicaid program and provided to an individual in or after the third month before the month in which he or she made the application *if* the individual would have been eligible for Medicaid had he or she applied for coverage at the time the services were received.[65] Retroactive coverage is available even if the person has become ineligible for Medicaid on the date of the application. Retroactive coverage is also available regardless of whether the recipient is alive when the application for Medicaid is submitted.

What is Medicaid managed care?

You have probably been getting health care from the doctor you choose. Each time you go to the doctor, Medicaid pays for the services you use. Increasingly, Medicaid beneficiaries are being asked to enroll in a managed care program by "choosing a health plan." These health plans may go by different names—health maintenance or HMOs, managed care organizations or MCOs. No matter what they are called, they will change the way you get health care.

The vast majority of states already require some or all Medicaid recipients to choose a health plan. The states that do not are planning to. So far, families and children have been most affected. However, an increasing number of states are extending managed care to the disabled and to those needing behavioral and mental health care. In addition the federal government is looking for ways to increase managed care for aged and disabled Medicare beneficiaries.

Once you enroll in a managed care plan, you can use only the doctors and hospitals *in that plan.* These doctors and hospitals have agreed to take care of you for a set amount of money each month—no matter how much care you need or use. If you need health care, you must first get permission from your primary care provider. If you want to see a doctor who is not in your plan, you may have to pay for the visit yourself. If you go to the emergency room for care that is not an emergency, you may be billed for the care.

Some people have criticized managed care saying that it causes doctors to provide too little care to needy people. Others say that managed care is good because it saves money and increases access for poor people who have had trouble finding doctors to accept their Medicaid cards.[66]

What can you do to make sure that you choose the right managed care plan?

There may be many health plans to choose from, so it is important to pick the best one for you and your family. Before you sign up for a plan, use this checklist. The more "yes" answers you have, the better the plan may be for you:

- Are my family's doctors, clinics, and hospital part of the health plan?
- Is there a drugstore near me that is part of the plan?
- Do I get a list of doctors, hospitals, and drugstores in the plan and a member booklet that explains how the plan works?
- Does that plan have doctors, nurses, and other staff who speak my language and are friendly to me?
- Can I use the doctors' offices even if I am in a wheelchair or have a vision or hearing problem?
- Can I choose my doctor and change doctors in the plan if I am unhappy? Can I change plans?
- Does the plan ask me to get a checkup within sixty days after I have signed up?
- Is there a twenty-four-hour phone line so that I can reach my doctor during and after office hours?

• Will I get to see a doctor right away if there is an emergency; within two weeks for a checkup or for special care?

• *Think about what your family needs.* Does the plan cover all these health care needs—for example, does it cover the drugs my child needs, mental health services, pregnancy and well-baby care, home care, and physical therapy? Does the plan put any limits on these services—for example, only ten mental health visits? If someone in my family has special health care needs, will the plan give us all the doctors, services, and medicines that we need?

• Will my doctor discuss the most up-to-date treatments with me, even if my plan does not include them?

• Can I get another doctor's opinion if my doctor or the plan says that I don't need care that I think I need?

• If I do not agree with the plan's or the doctor's decision about my care or if I am unhappy in the plan, will the plan handle my problem fast—right away if my life is in danger and within twenty-four hours if I feel very sick?

• Does the plan tell me what to do if I have a question or problem? Is there an 800 number I can call?

• Can I get the services I need without having to travel far?

• Does the plan give me transportation to get to the doctor or hospital even if my life is not in danger?

• Will someone at the health plan help me learn how to use the plan?

• Does the plan limit the amount of money I will have to pay out of my own pocket for health care?

• Has the plan agreed not to place a limit on what it will cover if someone in my family becomes disabled?

Answer as many of these questions as you can. Talk to your doctors, your boss, Medicaid, or Medicare. Talk to your neighbors, coworkers, and friends. Talk to people who work at the health plans you might choose. The National Committee for Quality Assurance reviews health plans and can tell you if it has found a problem with a plan you might choose. Call 202-955-3515.

What do I do if things go wrong?

Regardless of the health plan, you have legal rights. You have the right to get truthful information; to get the services that are listed by your health plan *as you need them*; to get emergency care immediately from the emergency room that is closest to you; to be free from discrimination based on your disability or race or the country you are from; to obtain copies of your medical records; to keep your health care needs private; to have your right to file a complaint explained to you clearly; to file a complaint; and to request a state hearing.

If you have problems, you can file a complaint with the health plan's membership services office listed in your member booklet, the state Medicaid agency, and the state Department of Managed Care at 410-786-1357. You can ask a lawyer to help you. You may be able to get free legal help from your legal aid office, listed in the yellow pages of your phone book.

How do you apply for Medicaid?

Applicants for Medicaid ordinarily apply through the state or local welfare agency. You must be given the opportunity to apply for Medicaid without delay. If you are concerned that you will not understand the application process, you can bring someone with you to help you.

States must accept and process Medicaid applications for pregnant women and children at locations other than welfare offices. These locations must include public hospitals, community and migrant health clinics, and other facilities serving large numbers of poor pregnant women and children.

At the time of application, it is wise to take documents such as birth certificates, wage stubs, Social Security cards, and letters showing the amount of Social Security, SSI, VA, and retirement benefits. Bank books, insurance policies, and tax valuation of real estate could also prove helpful. These documents may be needed to verify the information you give on the application.

All applicants have the right to apply for Medicaid on the day assistance is sought. The state has forty-five days to make its decision, except that it has ninety days to process applications based on disability. If you are eligible, you will receive a card that shows your name and Medicaid number. If you are enrolled in a managed care plan, this will also be indicated on your card. You should take your card with you when you go to the doctor and are away from home.

Does Medicaid have any special residence requirement?

Yes. States can limit Medicaid benefits to persons who are residents. However, federal law defines the state of residence broadly. For example, for an adult who is not in an institution, the state of residence is the state in which the person is living with the intention of remaining permanently or indefinitely, or where the person is living, having entered with a job commitment or seeking employment.[67] Moreover, states cannot exclude an otherwise eligible person because he or she does not have a permanent dwelling or a fixed mailing address. Rather, states are required to have a process for making eligibility cards available to such people. This procedure is designed to help homeless people get Medicaid.

Is Medicaid limited to citizens?

Undocumented aliens have long been barred from receiving Medicaid for other than emergency purposes. The 1996 welfare act includes a number of provisions that severely limit Medicaid coverage of many legal immigrants.[68]

Legal immigrants who arrive in the United States after August 22, 1996 are automatically barred from Medicaid coverage for nonemergency Medicaid services for five years, though states may provide medical assistance to such immigrants under a state-funded Medicaid program. Moreover, as of January 1, 1997, states have the option to terminate Medicaid coverage of nonemergency services to legal immigrants until they become citizens. After the five-year ban and until they become citizens, states will count the immigrant sponsor's and his/her spouse's income for purposes of determining the immigrant's Medicaid eligibility.

Some groups of legal immigrants are excluded from these bans and thus will be eligible for full Medicaid coverage: veterans or active duty military (and their dependents), refugees and persons who have been granted asylum, persons who have held refugee or withholding-of-deportation status within the last five years, and those who, together with a spouse or parent, have forty quarters of creditable work covered by the Social Security system. (Appendix C explains in greater detail how the forty qualifying quarters rule works.) In addition, the Attorney General has discretion to require that certain immigrants who have been "battered or subjected to extreme cruelty" in the United States be permitted to receive Medicaid.

Notably, states must continue to cover emergency medical treatment for legal immigrants and undocumented aliens who are otherwise eligible for Medicaid—that is, if they fall into one of the categories described earlier in this chapter and are of low income. An emergency is "a medical condition (including severe pain) such that the absence of immediate medical attention could reasonably be expected to result in (A) placing the patient's health in serious jeopardy, (B) serious impairment of bodily function, or (C) serious dysfunction of any bodily organ or part."[69] Those persons who do not apply for Medicaid coverage of emergency services do not have to furnish a Social Security number to the provider of the Medicaid agency.

What do you do if Medicaid is denied or terminated or the state refuses to cover a service that you need?

If your Medicaid is denied, terminated, or reduced, you have a right to a fair hearing before a state agency hearing officer. The state, directly or through the managed care plan, must inform you in writing of the action and how to appeal. Generally, you will have sixty days from the date on the letter to appeal and request a hearing. It is important to note, however, that you have only ten days to request that benefits be continued pending the hearing. After the ten days, benefits will be discontinued unless you prevail on your claim, which could take some time. If you get Medicaid pending the hearing and the decision is ultimately against you, you could be required to reimburse the state for amounts paid.

Before the hearing, you must be given an opportunity to review your Medicaid file and any documents the Medicaid agency will use at the hearing. At the hearing, you can present witnesses, cross-examine the state's witnesses, and present arguments. You may choose to have someone else, such as a legal services attorney, act as your legal representative at the hearing.

By law, the Medicaid agency must make its decision within ninety days from the date of your request for a hearing. If you are still dissatisfied, you can appeal to court. You may also be able to go to court to force your state to implement Medicaid the way the federal law requires. You should contact your local legal aid or legal services office for assistance in your appeal to the state agency or the court.

If you are enrolled in a Medicaid managed care plan, your health plan must also allow you to complain to the plan. The plan must explain its complaint process to you. The plan should reach its decision promptly, and its activities cannot interfere with your right to appeal to the state Medicaid agency as described above.

VACCINES FOR CHILDREN

What can a family do if it cannot afford to pay for child immunizations?

The Vaccines For Children (VFC) program provides free vaccines for children. The federal government began this program on October 1, 1994 in an effort to immunize fully all children before age two. The program covers four groups: (1) any child who receives Medicaid; (2) any child who is uninsured; (3) any child whose private insurance does not cover vaccines; and (4) Native American children.[70]

The program pays for the following shots: diphtheria, pertussis (whooping cough), tetanus, mumps, measles, rubella, polio, hepatitis B, and Hemophilus influenza B. To be fully immunized, a child needs eleven shots (and at least five visits to the doctor).

Public health clinics and private physicians participate in the program. These providers will not charge you for the vaccine, but they can charge you a fee for administering the shot. For VFC information, call 1-800-232-2522.

Medicare

What is Medicare?

Medicare is a federal health insurance program that pays some of the costs of hospital, doctor, skilled nursing, home health, and outpatient care for people age 65 and older and some disabled persons. Eligibility is not based on financial need, so you do not need to be poor to get Medicare. Medicare is run by the Health Care Financing Administration (HCFA), an agency of the Social Security Administration.

Medicare has two parts: hospital insurance (Part A) and medical insurance (Part B). Your Medicare card will show which parts of Medicare you have. Part A of Medicare is paid for through Social Security payroll tax deductions. Part B of Medicare is a voluntary program that is paid for through federal contributions and premiums paid by the people who enroll in it.

How do you apply for Medicare?

Applications for the program are taken at district offices of the Social Security Administration. You may call 1-800-772-1213 to begin the application process. There are no time limits within which decisions on applications must be made.

When you qualify for Medicare, you will get a Medicare card. Among other things, the card will show your name and your Medicare claim number. The claim number has nine digits and a letter. Make sure to use your full name and Medicare claim number on all Medicare claims and letters. Do not use your spouse's card or claim number. You should carry your Medicare card with you when you are away from home.

Medicare Part A Hospital Insurance

Who is eligible for Medicare Part A?

Medicare Part A is automatic and free to most people over age 65. Three groups are automatically eligible for Part A hospital insurance:

- Anyone age 65 or older who has worked long enough in Social Security covered employment, the Railroad Retirement system, or a federal, state, or local government to be insured for Medicare;
- Anyone under age 65 who has been receiving Social Security disability benefits for 24 months;
- Any worker, spouse, or dependent of any age with kidney failure requiring dialysis or a kidney transplant.

Other persons over age 65 can enroll in Medicare upon payment of a monthly premium ($289 in 1996). Such persons must be citizens or legal residents.[71] The premium is adjusted upward annually to account for inflation.

What are the Part A benefits?

Medicare Part A helps pay for four health services: inpatient hospital services, skilled nursing services, home health services, and hospice care. A doctor must certify that you need these services.

Inpatient hospital services. Medicare helps pay for inpatient hospital care at hospitals that have joined the Medicare program. Most hospitals have joined.

Medicare's inpatient hospital coverage is based on the "benefit period," sometimes called a "spell of illness." The benefit period is a way of measuring Medicare beneficiaries' use of hospital services covered by Medicare Part A. A benefit period begins on the first day the beneficiary is hospitalized and ends after the patient has been out of the hospital for sixty days in a row. If the beneficiary is hospitalized again after sixty days have elapsed, a new benefit period begins.

In each new benefit period, the Medicare beneficiary is responsible for paying a Part A deductible ($736 in 1996). In addition, the patient is responsible for coinsurance for hospital care received from the sixty-first through the ninetieth day of each benefit period ($184 per day in 1996). There is no limit to the number of benefit periods a person can have. If the hospitalization lasts more than ninety days, the patient can choose to use one or more of his or her sixty "lifetime reserve days." There is a daily coinsurance charge for each reserve day that equals one-half of the Part A deductible ($368 per day in 1996). The average length of Medicare hospital stay is about nine days, so it is unusual for a Medicare patient to exhaust the ninety days of inpatient coverage available during each benefit period.

Here is an example of how the benefit period works. Suppose Mr. Jones was admitted to the hospital on January 1 and two weeks later he was discharged, only to be readmitted on February 20. Since sixty days have not passed between the discharge and readmission dates, Mr. Jones is still in the same benefit period and does not have to pay the deductible again. Additionally, he is in the fifteenth day of covered hospital care for the benefit period. However, if instead of being readmitted on February 20, Mr. Jones was readmitted May 3, more than sixty days would have passed since his previous discharge from the hospital, and he would be in a new benefit period. In that case, he would again have to pay the Part A deductible, but his coverage would start from day one instead of day fifteen.

During the inpatient hospital stay, Medicare will pay for a semiprivate room, meals (including special diets), regular nursing services, and intensive care. Medicare also covers drugs, blood, laboratory tests (including x-rays and radiology), medical supplies and equipment, operating and recovery room costs, and rehabilitation services (such as physical therapy).

Medicare will not pay for private duty nurses, luxury items (for example, TV or radio) and hospital stays that Medicare determines are not medically necessary. Medicare will pay the hospital directly and then send you a statement. You should never have to pay a deposit before you are admitted into the hospital.

What is a DRG?

Medicare pays for inpatient hospital care using "diagnosis related groupings" (DRGs). This means that the hospital gets paid a fixed amount of money based on the doctor's diagnosis of the patient's medical problem. If the patient's care costs more than the amount of money received, the hospital loses money on that patient. If the care costs less than the amount received, the hospital makes money. Some patient advocates are concerned that DRGs cause hospitals to discharge patients too early, discharge them without adequate post-hospital care, or otherwise limit the care they provide.

What sort of discharge planning accompanies Medicare inpatient hospital services?

DRGs should not cause your care to be adversely affected. To make sure that you are protected, federal law provides that you have a right to a discharge plan and to discharge planning services if the hospital has determined that you would suffer adverse health consequences upon discharge if a discharge plan and planning services are not provided.[72] The hospital must identify such patients at an early stage of hospitalization. Other Medicare patients have the right to request discharge planning which, if requested, must be provided by the hospital. This means that you should ask your doctors, nurses, social workers, and other health care providers about the care and services you will need after you are discharged from the hospital. Also, make sure that your discharge planner arranges services through providers who accept Medicare assignment (discussed below); this will save you money.

Medicare beneficiaries must be given a notice that explains these rights. The discharge plan must be discussed with the patient and made a part of the patient's medical record.

Also, when a hospital plans to discharge a patient, it should provide a notice called "An Important Message from Medicare" that explains post-hospital services, including discharge planning and appeal rights regarding the denial of Medicare-covered services. The notice should be given to the patient or to the patient's next of kin if the patient is expected to be unable to comprehend the notice.

If you feel you are being discharged from the hospital too soon or your discharge plan is inadequate, contact the local peer review organization (discussed below) and file a complaint. Your local legal aid or legal services office or your local Older Americans Act-funded legal assistance program can help you file this complaint.

Will Medicare cover nursing care?

Nursing home benefits under Medicare Part A are very limited. Medicare will cover only care received at Medicare-certified skilled nursing facilities. These nursing facilities have the staff and equipment qualified to provide skilled nursing care and a full range of rehabilitation therapies. Custodial care is not covered by Medicare.

Skilled nursing facility coverage is also based on benefit periods. Part A of Medicare will cover up to one hundred days of medically necessary skilled nursing care per benefit period. The care must be preceded by a hospital stay of at least three days. The first twenty days of skilled care are covered in full, but the patient has to pay coinsurance for care received from the twenty-first through the one-hundredth day in each benefit period ($92 per day in 1996).

Medicare will cover a semiprivate room, meals (including special diets), nursing services, rehabilitation services, drugs, and medical equipment and supplies used during the skilled nursing facility stay. Private duty nurses, luxury items, and services determined not to be medically necessary are not covered.

Will Medicare pay for home health care services?

Medicare Part A will pay for home health visits if the patient needs intermittent, skilled nursing care. The patient must be at least temporarily confined to the home, and the patient's doctor has to prescribe a home health treatment plan. The home health agency must be Medicare certified. Medicare will pay the full cost of medically necessary home health, which includes skilled nursing services, physical therapy, speech therapy, and home health aids. Medicare will not pay for custodial or around-the-clock home care.

Will Medicare cover hospice care?

A hospice is an agency that provides support services, pain relief, and counseling to terminally ill patients and their families. Medicare Part A will pay for hospice care. To get the coverage, a doctor and the hospice medical director must certify that the patient is terminally ill. The patient must choose hospice care, and the care must be provided by a Medicare-certified hospice. Medicare coverage is limited to a maximum of 210 days. Medicare will cover nursing and physician services, drugs, therapy, home health aides and homemaker services, medical supplies, and counseling.

Medicare Part B Medical Insurance

Who is eligible for Part B?

To get Part B, you must enroll and pay a premium ($42.50 per month in 1996).[73] Everyone automatically eligible for Part A is "deemed" to want Part

B, and premiums are automatically deducted from the Social Security check.

Other persons age 65 and older can enroll in Part B three months before or after their 65th birthday and at the beginning of each calendar year. Your monthly Part B premium could be 10 percent higher than the basic premium for each year you could have been enrolled but were not.

What are the Part B benefits?

The Medicare Part B medical insurance program covers doctors' services, outpatient hospital care, ambulance services, and medical equipment and prosthetic devices.

- *Doctors' services.* Medically necessary doctors' services are covered by Medicare. The services can be furnished in the doctor's office, a clinic, a hospital, a skilled nursing facility, or at home. The doctors' services that are covered by Medicare include medically necessary visits to a doctor (not routine checkups), hospital visits and consults, surgery, anesthesia, diagnostic tests, drugs, and medical supplies.
- *Outpatient services.* Medicare Part B covers services received as an outpatient of a hospital. These services include medical and surgical services in an emergency room or outpatient clinic, lab tests, medical supplies, and drugs. Part B also covers outpatient physical therapy, occupational therapy, and speech therapy.
- *Ambulance services.* Medicare will pay for ambulance services if the ambulance, equipment, and personnel meet Medicare requirements, and transportation by other means would endanger the patient's health. Medicare will pay for transport to or from a hospital or skilled nursing facility. Medicare will not pay for ambulance transportation from your home to a doctor's office.
- *Medical equipment.* Medicare will pay for medically necessary "durable medical equipment" such as wheelchairs, walkers, oxygen services, beds, and other equipment the doctor prescribes for use in your home. You can either rent or buy this equipment. Before making your decision, ask the doctor how long the equipment will be needed and ask the equipment supplier for information about the purchase price versus the rental payment for that period of time. Then, you can choose to rent or buy, depending on what is most economical in your situation. Medicare will also cover prostheses such as artificial limbs, cardiac pacemakers, colostomy supplies, and breast prostheses following mastectomy.

What services does Medicare Part B refuse to cover?

Unfortunately, Medicare will not pay for many of the services that older and disabled people especially need. Medicare will not pay for routine physical checkups, eyeglasses or eye exams (except after cataract surgery), hearing aids or hearing exams, routine dental care, long-term nursing home care, immunizations (except flu and hepatitis B vaccines), custodial care, full-time nursing care in the home, naturopathy, acupuncture, and drugs and medications taken at home.

How does Part B pay for care?

Medicare Part B also uses deductibles and coinsurance. Some people purchase supplemental "Medigap" insurance to cover these amounts. If you are thinking about buying a Medigap policy, you should shop carefully and make sure you obtain only the coverage you need at the most economical price. Your state department of insurance or department on aging can direct you to free counseling regarding the purchase of Medigap insurance. And you can obtain a helpful pamphlet, *Guide to Health Insurance for People with Medicare*, free from the Social Security office.

The Medicare Part B deductible does not change; it is presently fixed at $100. Once you have received covered services that cost more than $100, Part B will pay 80 percent of the "approved amounts" for additional covered services for the rest of the year. You are responsible for the "coinsurance"— the remaining 20 percent.

What is the Medicare-approved amount?

Medicare Part B payments are made by "carriers," insurance companies such as Blue Shield, that have agreements with Medicare to handle Part B payments. The Part B payments are based on a "fee schedule" which lists a payment amount for each service. This amount is often less than what the doctor or supplier has charged you for the service. When a Part B claim is submitted, the carrier compares the actual charge on the claim with the fee schedule amount for that service. The Medicare-approved amount is the lower of the actual charge or the fee schedule amount. Part B pays 80 percent of the Medicare-approved amount.

What does it mean for a doctor to accept assignment?

When a doctor accepts assignment, it means that he or she has agreed to accept the Medicare-approved amount as payment in full. The doctor will submit the claim directly to the carrier, and the carrier will pay the doctor 80 percent of the approved amount. The doctor can then bill you no more than the remaining 20 percent of the approved amount—regardless of the actual charge. Here is an example of a claim where the doctor accepts assignment (assuming that the $100 deductible has been met):

Doctor's actual charge:	$600
Medicare-approved amount:	$500
Medicare pays the doctor:	$400
(80 percent of approved amount)	
You pay the doctor:	$100
(20 percent of approved amount)	

Doctors can agree in advance to accept assignment on all Medicare claims. If they do this, they are called "Medicare-participating doctors." The names and addresses of Medicare-participating doctors (and suppliers) are listed in the *Medicare-Participating Physician/Supplier Directory*, which can be obtained free from your Medicare Part B carrier.

If the doctor has refused to accept assignment, then Medicare will pay 80 percent of the approved amount. The doctor can bill you for the 20 percent coinsurance *and* up to 15 percent above the Medicare-approved amount. This is called the "limited charge rule." Here is an example of a claim where the doctor does not accept assignment (assuming that the $100 deductible has been met):

Doctor's actual charge:	$600
Medicare-approved amount:	$500
Medicare pays:	$400
(80 percent of approved amount)	
You pay:	$175
(20 percent coinsurance + 15 percent of approved amount)	

If the doctor charges more than allowed under the 15 percent limited charge rule, this is illegal. You should consult an attorney who can go to court to obtain a refund for you. You may also consider reporting the doctor for Medicare fraud and abuse. Contact your Medicare carrier or call 1-800-638-6833.

What if you cannot afford the Medicare cost sharing or a Medigap policy?

Your state Medicaid program must pay the Medicare premiums, deductibles, and coinsurance costs for qualified Medicare beneficiaries (QMBs)—low-income, elderly, and disabled individuals. Apply for the program at your local social services office. A similar program serves qualified disabled and working individuals.

What happens if a Medicare beneficiary disagrees with a decision regarding a Medicare claim?

If you do not agree with a decision by Medicare regarding coverage of Part A or Part B services or how much Medicare will pay for these services, you have the right to appeal the decision.[74] When you are admitted to the hospital, you should be given a copy of "An Important Message from Medicare." This notice describes your appeal rights.

You may first learn of a coverage decision when you receive a notice from your provider that tells you why it thinks Medicare will not cover the service and what it plans to do. You do not have a right to appeal this decision because it is not yet a decision by Medicare. If you disagree with the decision, you can ask the provider to file a claim on your behalf to Medicare, and the provider must do this. Medicare will then issue a decision, which you can appeal.

Whenever a claim is decided by Medicare, you will receive a notice from Medicare that explains the coverage decision and tells you what to do if you want to appeal. If you don't understand this notice, call the Social Security office, the peer review organization in your state (discussed below), or your local legal aid or legal services office. Normally, you have sixty days from the date of the notice to appeal.

Appealing PRO hospital care decisions. The peer review organization (PRO) is a group of doctors in your state that is paid by Medicare to make decisions about the need for inpatient hospital care and to assure quality care for Medicare patients. The name and phone number of the PRO for your state is listed in "An Important Message from Medicare."

You can seek reconsideration of a decision by a PRO to deny coverage. Reconsideration decisions have to be made within certain timeframes. For example, if you appeal a decision to discharge you from the hospital while you are still in the hospital, the PRO has only three days to make its decision. If you disagree with the PRO reconsideration decision and the amount involved is $200 or more, you can request a hearing by an administrative law judge. If you do not accept the administrative decision, cases involving more than $2,000 can be appealed to federal court.

Appealing other hospital insurance decisions. Unless you are enrolled in a Medicare HMO, all other decisions about your Medicare hospital insurance (skilled care, home care) are initially handled by Medicare "intermediaries." Intermediaries are insurance companies that have contracts with the federal government to make coverage and payment decisions on Part A services in hospitals, skilled nursing facilities, home health agencies, and hospices. If you disagree with an intermediary's decision, you can request reconsideration. You can submit this request either to the intermediary or to your Social Security office. If you disagree with the decision on reconsideration and the amount involved is $100 or more, you can request a hearing by an administrative law judge. If you do not accept the administrative decision, cases involving more than $1,000 can be appealed to federal court.

Appealing decisions by HMOs. If you are enrolled in a Medicare-certified HMO, the appeal process is similar to that provided under traditional Medicare. The HMO must give you a full, written explanation of appeal rights at the time of enrollment and at least annually after that.

Appealing decisions on medical insurance claims. Medicare issues its decisions on Part B claims on a form called "An Explanation of Medicare Benefits" (EOMB). The form will also explain how you can appeal if you disagree with a decision.

If you disagree with the EOMB and the amount involved is more than $100, you can request a hearing by the Part B carrier. If you disagree with the carrier's decision and the amount involved is more than $500, you can request a hearing before an administrative law judge. If you do not accept the administrative decision, cases involving $1,000 or more can be appealed to federal court.

Where can you get additional information about the Medicare program?

The Medicare program is obviously complicated. If you are applying for or receiving Medicare, you should get a copy of *The Medicare Handbook* from your local Social Security office. This handbook contains an extensive discussion of Medicare's rules, important telephone numbers and addresses, and an explanation of your appeal rights if you disagree with a decision regarding your Medicare-covered care. The *Medicare Managed Care Resource*

Information Directory gives information on choosing a managed care plan. For your free copy, contact the Office of Managed Care, HCFA, 7500 Security Blvd., Rm. 3-02-1, Baltimore, MD 21244-1850. The names and addresses of Medicare participating doctors and suppliers are listed in the *Medicare-Participating Physician/Supplier Directory*, which you can obtain free from your Medicare Part B carrier. A tollfree hotline provides direct text telephone (TTY/TDD) services to people with hearing and speech impairments. The hotline will provide information about Medicare and also will accept reports of Medicare waste, fraud, and abuse. The telephone number for the hotline is 1-800-820-1202 and will require text telephone capability. Persons without hearing or special disabilities can obtain the free information by calling 1-800-638-6833. You can obtain additional information about Medicare, free of charge, by writing to the Consumer Information Center, Dept. 59, Pueblo, CO 81009.

STATE AND LOCAL PROGRAMS

What health services are available to poor people who do not qualify for Medicaid or Medicare?

Millions of poor people are not poor enough to qualify for Medicaid or old or disabled enough to qualify for Medicare, but they cannot afford America's expensive health care. Most of these people work; however, their employers do not provide health insurance coverage through the workplace. Or, they may have insurance but it will not cover a preexisting condition—a problem, such as heart trouble, that the person already had before he or she applied for insurance.

There are state and local programs in some states that may reimburse hospitals and doctors for providing health care to persons who are uninsured. Check with your local social services office to see whether these programs exist in your state.

County-funded public hospitals. These hospitals and their clinics often make adjustments in fees on the basis of ability to pay, or give free care to poor people who do not qualify for Medicaid. However, the public hospitals can be overcrowded, and it may take time to get in even if you cannot afford to go anywhere else.

General assistance. A number of states have general assistance programs that provide free or low cost care. Usually, the services covered under these programs are more limited than Medicaid and Medicare. In recent years, state and local efforts to cut government spending have caused these programs to become even more limited or to be dropped altogether.

High risk insurance. A few states have established programs to provide insurance to persons who cannot get private insurance because they have preexisting conditions.[75] Unfortunately, these plans are usually beyond the financial reach of the poor because of high premium and other cost-sharing requirements.

Experimental state programs. An increasing number of states are seeking federal permission to conduct experiments to expand their Medicaid programs to the uninsured poor and working poor individuals and families.[76] To qualify for these programs, individuals and families typically need to have incomes below a preset percentage of the federal poverty level (about $15,600 for a family of four in 1996). Most states use prepaid managed care plans, such as HMOs, as providers. So far, Arizona, Delaware, Hawaii, Massachusetts, Minnesota, Oregon, Rhode Island, Tennessee, and Vermont are using these special programs to operate programs that expand Medicaid to the uninsured poor. About one-third of the remaining states are seeking or considering similar programs.

PUBLIC HEALTH SERVICE ACT PROGRAMS

There are a number of programs funded through the Public Health Services Act that make free or reduced-cost health care service available to the poor.[77] The programs also provide important social and support services to needy populations. Usually, these programs are operated through clinics or health centers. Your county social services agency or the local health department will be able to give you information about the location of the participating clinics in your area.

Community Health Clinics. The United States Department of Health and Human Services makes grants to public and nonprofit community health centers that agree to provide services to populations that do not currently have adequate health care or adequate numbers of health care providers.[78] To get these grants, the community health center must agree to provide primary health care to needy populations. It must also agree to provide services that will help these populations get care. For example, community health clinics must provide outreach to non-English speaking people to make sure that needy people get care. These clinics also provide a range of other social and support services. Community health centers are supposed to make every effort to participate in Medicare and Medicaid and to bill these programs whenever possible. However, as a vital link between health care and the uninsured, the centers are also required to prepare a schedule of fees for service and fee discounts for services based on the patient's ability to pay.

Migrant Health Clinics. The United States Department of Health and Human Services also makes grants to public and nonprofit health clinics that agree to provide services to migrant agricultural workers, seasonal agricultural workers, and their families.[79] The required services and obligations are almost identical to those of community health clinics except that migrant health clinic funds can only be used to serve migrants. Because of inadequate funding, this program is able to serve only about 15 percent of the estimated farmworker population in need.

Rural Health Clinics. The United States Department of Health and Human Services' Health Care Financing Administration designates certain clinics in rural areas to receive grant assistance. Services at these clinics include physician, nurse practitioner, and physician assistance services.[80] Many of the services and payment rules that apply to community health clinics also apply to rural clinics.

HILL-BURTON

What is the Hill-Burton Act?

The Hill-Burton Act is a federal law that provided thousands of hospitals and nursing homes with money for construction and renovation.[81] In return, the facilities accepted two distinct obligations: the uncompensated care obligation and the community service obligation.[82]

What is the uncompensated care obligation?

Hospitals and nursing homes accepting Hill-Burton funds agreed to provide a "reasonable volume of services to persons unable to pay."[83] Federal laws say that these facilities must provide an annual amount of free care to people who cannot pay in an amount equal to 10 percent of all grants received or three percent of annual operating costs.[84] The obligation lasts for twenty years from the date of the grant. Persons who tell the hospital or nursing home they cannot afford to pay for their care are supposed to be offered free care through the Hill-Burton program if the annual free care obligation has not already been used up. This important source of free hospital care is rapidly coming to an end as hospitals' twenty-year obligations come to term.

What is the community service obligation?

Facilities accepting Hill-Burton funds also agreed to a community service obligation. This obligation is significant because it never ends.

The community service obligation prevents discrimination on any ground unrelated to an individual's need for services or the availability of the needed services in the facility.[85] This means that the facility cannot turn you away because of your race, ethnicity, source of payment, or inability to pay an up-front deposit. The community service obligation also requires Hill-Burton facilities to accept all persons able to pay for their care, either directly or through insurance coverage. Insurance coverage specifically includes Medicaid, Medicare, and state or local governmental programs that pay for services. Further, the facility has the duty to take reasonable steps to ensure that admission to and services of the facility are available to beneficiaries of public assistance programs, such as Medicaid and Medicare. For example, a Hill-Burton hospital should have obstetricians on staff who will deliver babies for pregnant women on Medicaid. In addition, Hill-Burton facilities must take reasonable steps to assist patients by notifying them of any governmental programs for which they might be eligible. Finally, the community service obligation requires the hospital to *open its emergency room for everyone* in its service area, even those unable to pay.

How can you find out if a hospital or nursing home has a Hill-Burton obligation?

Many hospitals ignore their Hill-Burton obligations. Community members should investigate the situation in their area before they need care and insist that facilities live up to their obligations. If the facility refuses to adhere to its community service or uncompensated care obligations, a complaint can be filed with the Department of Health and Human Services Office for Civil Rights. An individual can also file a court action. A person who cannot afford legal representation may be able to find assistance with a complaint from a local legal aid or legal services attorney.

You should be able to determine quickly the extent of a local facility's uncompensated care obligations because all Hill-Burton facilities are required by law to post notices about the program in admitting and other areas. These notices must be easy to see and to read and must be printed in languages other than English if a significant part of the community has limited English proficiency.

Facilities are also supposed to submit annual compliance reports to the state Hill-Burton agency (which is usually the department of health and welfare). This state agency has a list of Hill-Burton facilities. The Department of Health and Human Services Bureau of Health Facilities lists Hill-Burton facilities in the *Facilities Obligated to Provide Uncompensated Services and Community Service*. You can also obtain information about the Hill-Burton facilities in your area by contacting the National Health Law Program in Los Angeles, California, 310-204-6010.

EMERGENCY CARE

It is against the law for a hospital with an emergency room to turn you away for lack of money if you are very sick or badly hurt and would get worse if the hospital did not treat you. The hospital cannot turn you away until a medical person has examined you. It is also against the law for a hospital to turn you away if you are going to have a baby and are in active labor.

This does not necessarily mean that your care will be free. It does mean that you cannot be turned away just because you cannot pay.

There are a number of laws that make denial of emergency care and "patient dumping" illegal.

What is patient dumping?

Transferring or refusing to treat emergency patients because they are poor, uninsured, or otherwise considered undesirable is known as "patient dumping." Hospitals have engaged in the practice for years, but during the mid-1980s, reported incidents of patient dumping jumped dramatically. Some public hospitals have reported a 1,000 percent increase in patient dumping.

The most common type of dumping is the transfer of a patient from one hospital emergency room to another due to lack of insurance and the inability to pay. Dumping also results when a hospital refuses to accept people who are on Medicaid or who have certain conditions, such as drug overdose symptoms or AIDS. Dumping can also result from requiring payments or deposits prior to receiving emergency treatment.

Dumping can be accomplished by rerouting ambulances with needy patients to other hospitals, refusing to provide treatment, or delaying treatment for so long that persons seeking treatment simply leave. Testimony presented to the United States Congress indicates that African Americans, Hispanics, and Native Americans are more likely to be the victims of patient dumping.

The delay or denial of emergency treatment can cause serious physical harm and even death. Turning away women in labor has been associated with infant and maternal death and birth defects. Young men with gun shot wounds to the head have been refused emergency treatment even though the wounds were affecting the major artery to the brain.[86]

What is the Emergency Medical Treatment and Active Labor Act?

The increase in patient dumping has resulted in an important federal law that establishes rigorous criteria for the safe transfer between hospitals of critically ill or injured patients and women in active labor.[87] This law, the Emergency Medical Treatment and Active Labor Act, applies to every hospital that is certified to participate in the Medicare program (virtually all hospitals) and that has an emergency room. This law is sometimes called simply the "antidumping law."

What does the federal antidumping law require?

Under the federal law, a hospital must

1. Provide a medical screening examination without delay to the individual to determine if an emergency medical condition exists.

2. Provide stabilizing treatment to any individual with an emergency medical condition prior to any transfer.

3. Authorize the transfer to another hospital only if the responsible physician certifies in writing that the benefit of the transfer outweighs the risk, the receiving hospital has space and personnel to treat the patient and has accepted the transfer, the transferring hospital sends medical records along with the patient, and the transfer is made in appropriate transportation equipment with life support if needed.

4. Be terminated or suspended from participation in the Medicare program if a hospital knowingly or negligently violates any of the requirements above.

5. Pay a civil money penalty of up to $50,000 if a physician or the hospital knowingly violates the law. This penalty can be imposed on each or either of them for the violation of the law.

The law defines an emergency medical condition as one with symptoms of sufficient severity, including severe pain, such that the absence of immediate medical attention could reasonably be expected to result in placing the health of the individual (and in the case of a pregnant woman, the health of the woman or her unborn child) in serious jeopardy, at risk of impairment to any bodily function, or at risk of dysfunction of any bodily organ or part. Also with respect to pregnant women having contractions, an emergency exists if there is inadequate time for a safe transfer before delivery or if the transfer could pose a threat to the health of the mother or child.

How is the antidumping law enforced?

The United States Department of Heath and Human Services Health Care Financing Administration (HCFA) is supposed to enforce the antidumping law. Violations of the law should be reported to HCFA. Also, many states place a division of the department of health and welfare in charge of securing appropriate implementation of all emergency medical services legislation. Violations of the law can be reported to this state agency.

Unfortunately, federal and state enforcement of the antidumping law has not been aggressive. For the most part, enforcement has been pursued by individuals in court. Individuals who have been harmed by patient dumping can go to court and seek damages from the hospital but will probably need an attorney to do this.

What other laws make it illegal for hospitals to refuse to provide emergency care?

State antidumping laws. Most states have laws that require hospitals to provide emergency care to anyone who needs it. These laws also say that once the hospital has started to provide the care, it cannot stop helping the patient until the emergency has ended. Thus, the hospital must either continue to treat the patient or transfer him or her safely to another hospital.

Some states, such as California, Louisiana, Maryland, Massachusetts, New York, Tennessee, and Virginia, have enacted antidumping statutes similar to the federal antidumping statute.[88] A few of these laws contain very strong language to protect indigent patients who need emergency care and services from being transferred to another hospital for nonmedical reasons. The California statute, for example, provides: "No person needing emergency services and care may be transferred from a hospital to another hospital for any nonmedical reason (such as the person's inability to pay for any emergency service or care)" unless it is determined "that the transfer or delay . . . will not create a medical hazard to the person."[89]

Hill-Burton. As discussed above, Hill-Burton hospitals have a community service obligation to allow anyone in their service area to obtain emergency care from the emergency room.[90]

Nonprofit hospitals. If a hospital is a nonprofit, tax exempt hospital, it is subject to Internal Revenue Service or state tax commission investigation and loss of its tax exempt status if it fails to provide care to anyone who comes into its emergency room seeking treatment, even if the patient cannot pay a deposit or other fees.[91] Some state courts have required hospitals to provide an open emergency room to all, regardless of ability to pay as a condition of state tax exemption.[92]

Notes

Jane Perkins of the National Health Law Program authored this chapter.

1. *Memorial Hosp. v. Maricopa County*, 415 U.S. 250, 259 (1974).

2. *E.g., Harris v. McRae*, 448 U.S. 297 (1980) (no constitutional duty to fund abortions for indigent women).

3. *E.g., Youngberg v. Romeo*, 457 U.S. 307 (1982) (institutions for the mentally retarded); *Estelle v. Gamble*, 429 U.S. 97 (1976) (prisons); *see LaShawn v. Dixon*, 762 F. Supp. 959 (D.D.C. 1991), *aff'd in part and remanded in part*, 990 F.2d 1319 (D.C. Cir. 1994), *cert. denied*, 114 S. Ct. 691 (1994) (foster care).

4. *E.g.,* Ala. Const. amend. 72 (special tax for hospital and public health purposes in counties except Mobile, Montgomery, and Jefferson); Alaska Const. art. VII, § 4 ("The legislature shall provide for the promotion and protection of public health."); Hawaii Const. art. IX, § 1 ("The State shall provide for the protection and promotion of the public health.") and § 3 ("The State shall have the power to provide . . . medical assistance . . . for persons who are found to be in need"); Kansas Const. art. VII ("The respective counties of the State shall provide, as may be prescribed by law, for those inhabitants who, by reason of . . . infirmity . . . , may have claims upon the aid of society."); La. Const. art. XII, § 8 ("The legislature may establish a system of . . . public health."); N.Y. Const. art. XVII, § 3 ("The protection and promotion of the health of the inhabitants of the state are matters of public concern and provision therefor shall be made by the state and by such of its subdivisions and in such manner, and by such means as the legislature shall from time to time determine."); N.C. Const. art. XI, § 4 ("Beneficent provision for the . . . unfortunate . . . is one of the first duties of a civilized and a Christian state.").

5. *See, e.g., Hope v. Perales*, 634 N.E.2d 183 (N.Y. 1994) (declining under the New

York Constitution to order abortion funding for women with family income between 100 and 185 percent of the poverty level); *Moe v. Secretary of Admin. & Fin.*, 417 N.E.2d 387 (Mass. 1981) (holding that restrictions on Medicaid funding for abortion violate Massachusetts Constitution); *Right to Choose v. Byrne*, 450 A.2d 925 (N.J. 1982) (holding that certain restrictions on Medicaid funding for abortion violate New Jersey Constitution).

6. 42 U.S.C.A. §§ 1396a *et seq.* (West 1996).

7. *Id.* at § 1396a(a)(10)(A) (West 1996). For the 1996 welfare act provisions, *see* Pub. L. No. 104-193, 110 Stat. 2105, § 114 (1996) (creating new § 1391(a) of the Social Security Act (1996)).

8. 42 U.S.C.A. §§ 1396a(a)(10)(A) and 1396a(l) (West 1996).

9. *Id.*

10. *Id.* at § 1396a(e)(5) (West 1996).

11. *Id.* at § 1396a(e)(4) (West 1996).

12. 42 U.S.C.A. § 1396a(a)(10)(A) (West 1996).

13. *Id.*

14. *Id.*

15. *Id. See* Pub. L. No. 104-193, 110 Stat. 2105, § 114 (1996) (creating new § 1931 of Social Security Act).

16. 42 U.S.C.A. § 1396k(a)(1)(B) (West 1996). *See* Pub. L. No. 104-193, 110 Stat. 2105, § 114 (1996).

17. 42 U.S.C.A. § 1396a(a)(10)(A) (West 1996). This includes children in child care institutions.

18. *Id.* at § 1396r-6 (West 1996). For the 1996 welfare act provisions, *see* Pub. L. No. 104-193, 110 Stat. 2105, § 114 (1996) (creating new § 1391 of the Social Security Act (1996)).

19. *Id.*

20. *Id.* at § 1396a(f) (West 1996).

21. *Id.* at § 1396a (West 1996) (note). Mandatory state supplements are cash payments states are required to make to persons who are aged, blind, or disabled in order to provide them with the same amount of cash assistance they were receiving under the old Aid to the Permanently and Totally Disabled, Old Age Assistance, Aid to the Blind, or Aid to the Aged, Blind, and Disabled programs.

22. *Id.* at §§ 1396a(a)(10)(A), 1396d(q), 1396d(s) (West 1996).

23. *Id.* at §§ 1396a(a)(10)(A), 1383c(c) (West 1996).

24. *Id.* at §§ 1396a(a)(10)(A), 1383c(b) (West 1996).

25. *Id.* at § 1396a (West 1996) (note). The program is named after Congressman Pickle, who introduced the legislation. *See also Lynch v. Rank*, 74 F.2d 528 (9th Cir. 1984).

26. 42 U.S.C.A. § 1396d(p) (West 1996). These terms are discussed later in this chapter.

27. These groups are listed at 42 U.S.C.A. § 1396a(a)(10)(C) (West 1996).

28. *Id.* at §§ 1396a(a)(10)(A), 1396a(l)(2)(A)(i) (West 1996).

29. *Id.* at §§ 1396a(a)(10)(A), 1396a(m)(1)(A) (West 1996).

30. *Id.* at § 1396a(a)(10)(C) (West 1996). As in other programs, resources are possessions like savings accounts, property, and jewelry.

31. *Id.* at § 1396a(a)(17)(D) (West 1996).

32. *Id.* at § 1396a(a)(17) (West 1996).

33. *Id.* at § 602(a)(8) (West 1996); 45 C.F.R. §§ 233 *et seq.* (1995). The 1996 welfare act, Pub. L. No. 104-193, 110 Stat. 2105 (1996), does not affect this. The act requires states to use the AFDC rules in effect as of July 19, 1996. SSI income disregards are found at 42 U.S.C.A. § 1382a(b) (West 1996) and 20 C.F.R. § 416, subpt. K (1994).

34. 42 U.S.C.A. § 1396a(a)(17) (West 1996). Notably, states can drop resource tests for pregnant women and children who are applying for Medicaid because their income is below a percentage of the federal poverty level, and a number of states have chosen this option.

35. 42 U.S.C.A. § 1382b(a), (d) (West 1996). Medicaid must apply the AFDC resource exclusions used by the state AFDC program as of July 19, 1996. *See* Pub. L. No. 104-193, 110 Stat. 2105, § 114 (1996) (creating new § 1931 of the Social Security Act).

36. 42 U.S.C.A. § 1396p (West 1996). The criminal penalties were included in the Health Insurance Portability and Accountability Act of 1996, Pub. L. No. 104-191, 110 Stat. 1936, § 217 (1996).

37. *Id.* at §§ 1396p(c)(2)(b)(iv), 1396p(d)(4)(A) (West 1996).

38. Unfortunately, trusts are treated somewhat differently under the SSI and Medicaid programs, depending on the structure of the trust and how it is treated under the relevant state law. *Compare* Program Operations Manual System (POMS) § SI 01120.200 (1996) (SSI) *with* 42 U.S.C.A. § 1396p(d)(4)(A) & (C) (West 1996) (Medicaid). The use of supplemental needs trusts to qualify for SSI is discussed in the SSI section of chapter 1 of this book.

39. 42 U.S.C.A. § 1396p(d)(4)(C) (West 1996).

40. *See* HCFA Transmittal 64 (November 1996), revising *State Medicaid Manual*, Part 3—Eligibility §§ 3258.10 & 3259.7 (HCFA Pub. 45–3).

41. *See* 42 U.S.C.A. § 1396p(d)(3)(B) (West 1996).

42. *Id.* at § 1396a(a)(17)(D) (West 1996).

43. *Id.* at § 1396p (West 1996).

44. *Id.*

45. *Id.* at § 1396r-5 (West 1996).

46. *Id.* at § 1396r-5(d)(5) (West 1996).

47. *Id.* at §§ 1396r-5(e)(2), 1396r-5(f)(3) (West 1996).

48. *Id.* at § 1396d(a) (West 1996).

49. *Id.*

50. *See generally White v. Beal*, 555 F.2d 1146 (3d Cir. 1977).

51. 42 C.F.R. § 440.230(c) (1996).

52. *See Weaver v. Reagan*, 886 F.2d 194 (8th Cir. 1989).

53. *E.g., Charleston Memorial Hosp. v. Conrad*, 693 F.2d 324 (4th Cir. 1982); *see generally Alexander v. Choate*, 469 U.S. 287 (1985).

54. 42 U.S.C.A. § 1396a(a)(30) (West 1996).

55. *Id.* at §§ 1396a(a)(43), 1396d(a)(4)(B), 1396d(r) (West 1996).

56. American Academy of Pediatrics, *Recommendations for Preventive Pediatric Health Care* (Sept. 1987).

57. 42 U.S.C.A. § 1396d(r)(5) (West 1996).

58. *Id.* at § 1396a(a)(43) (West 1996).

59. *Id.* at § 1396n(g)(2) (West 1996).

60. *Id.* at § 1396d(a)(19) (West 1996).

61. *Id.* at § 1396a(a)(30)(A) (West 1996).

62. For an example of a recent challenge, *see Clark v. Kizer,* 758 F. Supp. 572 (E.D. Cal. 1990), *aff'd and remanded sub nom. Clark v. Coye,* 967 F.2d 585 (9th Cir. 1992) (requiring Medicaid agency to pay sufficient rates and assure availability for dental care providers).

63. 42 U.S.C.A. § 1396o (West 1996).

64. *Id.*; 42 U.S.C.A. § 1396r-6 (1992).

65. 42 U.S.C.A. § 1396a(a)(34) (West 1996).

66. A recent study of managed care, published in the Journal of the American Medical Association, concluded: "Patients who were elderly and poor were more than twice as likely to decline in health in an H.M.O. as in a fee-for-services plan." *See* Robert Pear, *Elderly and Poor Do Worse Under H.M.O. Plans' Care,* N.Y. Times, Oct. 2, 1996, A10.

67. 42 C.F.R. § 435.403 (1995).

68. Pub. L. No. 104-193, 110 Stat. 2105, § 401 *et seq.* (1996).

69. 42 U.S.C.A. § 1396(v)(3) (West 1996). Organ transplants are excluded from the definition. *Id.* at § 1396(v)(2)(C).

70. *Id.* at § 1396s (West 1996).

71. *See Mathews v. Diaz,* 426 U.S. 67 (1976).

72. 42 U.S.C.A. § 1395x(ee) (West 1996); 42 C.F.R. §§ 482 *et seq.* (1995).

73. As discussed, Medicaid will pay the premiums for low-income qualified medicare beneficiaries.

74. 42 C.F.R. §§ 473 *et seq.* (1996).

75. These states include Connecticut, Florida, Indiana, Minnesota, Maryland, Vermont, Nebraska, North Dakota, and Rhode Island.

76. 42 U.S.C.A. § 1315 (West 1996) (allows Secretary of U. S. Dep't of Health and Human Servs. to waive Medicaid rules for experimental health programs).

77. *Id.* at § 213 (West 1996).

78. *Id.* at § 254c *et seq.* (West 1996).

79. *Id.* at § 254b (West 1996).

80. *Id.* at § 1395x(aa) (West 1996).

81. The Hospital Survey and Construction (Hill-Burton) Act, Pub. L. No. 79-725 (1946).

82. *See generally* Michael A. Dowell, *Hill-Burton: The Unfulfilled Promise,* 12 J. Health Politics, Pol'y and Law 153 (1987); James E. Rohrer, *The Political Development of the Hill-Burton Program: A Case Study in Distributive Policy,* 12 J. Health Politics, Pol'y and Law 137 (1987).

83. 42 U.S.C.A. § 291c(e) (West 1996).

84. 42 C.F.R. § 53.111(d)(i) (1995). *See Newsom v. Vanderbilt Univ.,* 453 F. Supp. 301 (M.D. Tenn. 1978), *mod.,* 653 F.2d 1100 (8th Cir. 1981).

85. 42 C.F.R. § 124.603 (1995).

86. For a discussion of patient dumping, *see* Maria O'Brien Hylton, *The Economics and*

Politics of Emergency Health Care for the Poor: The Patient Dumping Dilemma, 1992 B.Y.U. L. Rev. 971.

87. 42 U.S.C.A. § 1395dd (West 1996).

88. Cal. Health & Safety Code § 1317.2 (West 1996). California law further requires as a condition of licensure that each hospital "adopt a policy prohibiting discrimination in the provision of emergency services and care based on . . . insurance status, economic status or ability to pay for medical services. . . . " *Id.* at § 1317.3 (West 1996). For similar statutes in other states, *see* La. Rev. Stat. Ann. § 40:2113.6 (1995); Md. Code Ann., Health-Gen. § 19-308.2 (1996); Mass. Ann. Laws ch. 111, § 70E(n) (1996); N.Y. Pub. Health Law § 2805-b (McKinney's 1996); Tenn. Code Ann. §§ 68-11-701 to 705 (1996); Va. Code Ann. § 32.1-138.1 (1996).

89. Cal. Health & Safety Code § 1317 (1995).

90. 42 C.F.R. § 124.603(b) (1995).

91. IRC Rev. Ruling 69-545 (1969).

92. *E.g., Cook v. Rose,* 299 S.E.2d 3 (W. Va. l982). *See Utah County v. Intermountain Health Care,* 709 P.2d 265 (Utah l985) (requiring affirmative demonstration of the provision of free care as a condition of tax exemption).

IV

Housing

Is there a right to housing under the federal Constitution?

No. The United States Supreme Court has never found a right to housing under the federal Constitution. In 1972 in a case called *Lindsey v. Normet*,[1] the Court seemed to reject the proposition that the federal Constitution creates a right to housing. The Court acknowledged "the importance of decent, safe, and sanitary housing" but nevertheless found that the Constitution contains no "guarantee of access to dwellings of a particular quality."[2] Although some commentators believe that *Lindsey v. Normet* does not foreclose a federal constitutional right to housing,[3] it is unlikely that the Court as presently constituted will declare such a right.

Is there a state constitutional right to housing?

It depends. Unlike the federal Constitution, some state constitutions contain language that explicitly requires the provision of assistance to low-income persons.[4] Whether a state court will interpret a particular state constitution to create a right to housing depends on the language of the document, its history, the purposes it is meant to serve, and the general principles that guide the court in its decisionmaking. An example of a state constitutional provision that has been read to create a right to housing (or at least to emergency shelter for the homeless) is Article XVII of the New York Constitution which mandates that "the aid, care and support of the needy are public concerns, and shall be provided by the state . . . , and in such a manner and by such means, as the legislature may from time to time determine."[5]

Has Congress recognized the need to provide affordable housing to indigent Americans?

Yes. Sixty years ago, Congress passed the Housing Act of 1937, committing the United States "to remedy . . . unsafe and unsanitary housing conditions" and to meet the "acute shortage of decent, safe and sanitary dwellings for families of lower income."[6] Congress subsequently reaffirmed this national commitment in 1949, calling for "the realization as soon as feasible of the goal of a decent home and a suitable living environment for every American family."[7] In 1968, as part of the War on Poverty, Congress further directed that the nation accord "the highest priority . . . to meeting the housing needs of those families for which the national goal has not become a reality."[8]

Congress has never explicitly abandoned the policy of providing affordable housing to all needy Americans. But the most recent housing appropriations bill slashed federal spending for new subsidized housing units to zero. As this book goes to press, Congress is considering proposals that would erode still further the national commitment to decent and affordable housing. The "Contract with America," for example, would bar unmarried teen mothers from public housing. The Office of Management and Budget wants to reduce its inventory of project-based subsidized housing. And the Department of Housing and Urban Development plans to eliminate all subsidized housing programs and substitute instead block grant funding. As one commentator puts it, this is "a time of reckoning for national housing policy."[9]

Does Congress currently provide affordable housing to all needy Americans?

No. Despite the important federal policy of providing affordable housing to all needy Americans, Congress has never authorized sufficient funding to meet this goal. At a time when more than 30 million Americans are poor, and 15 million households qualify for federal housing assistance,[10] the federal government subsidizes only 4.5 million low-income housing units, at an annual cost of $18.3 billion.[11] By contrast, the federal government spends $66 billion a year for mortgage-interest and property tax deductions, and more than two-thirds of this subsidy goes to families with incomes higher than $75,000 a year.[12] Five million households, without any federal housing assistance at all, have to pay more than half of their income for rent.

For thousands of other economically marginal households, decent, afford-able housing remains out of reach, and they are instead relegated to live in temporary shelters, doubled or tripled up with relatives, on the streets, or in other substandard conditions.[13] A conservative estimate of the number of homeless Americans at any given time is 600,000.[14] The United States De-partment of Housing and Urban Development estimates that as many as seven million Americans are homeless over any five-year period.[15] And ad-vocates place the annual number of homeless persons as high as three mil-lion.[16]

What is HUD?

The United States Department of Housing and Urban Development, known as HUD, is the federal agency that administers many of the most important federal housing programs for indigent Americans. HUD has a national office that is located in Washington, D.C. The address is 451 Seventh St. S.W., Washington, DC 20410. HUD also has ten regional offices located around the country, and there are branch, division, and area offices within each region.

What are the different HUD-administered housing programs for low-income persons?

HUD administers a number of different low-income housing pro-grams.[17] The structure of these programs is very complex, and there are significant differences among the programs. One of the most important dif-ferences is the role of the private sector. The oldest of the HUD housing programs, public housing, is owned by the government and managed by a local governmental entity known as a "public housing authority" (PHA). More recent programs, referred to in this chapter as "federally subsidized" housing, rely on private ownership and typically provide a rent subsidy that is tied to the apartment unit in which the tenant lives. In addition, the Sec-tion 8 Certificate and Voucher programs provide portable subsidies that travel with the tenant and are used to subsidize the tenant's rent.

The major HUD programs that are available for low-income tenants in-clude the following:

Conventional public housing. The oldest form of government housing for low-income persons is the conventional public housing program, enacted as part of the Housing Act of 1937.[18] The program has created more than 1.3 million housing units. Conventional public housing is owned and operated by a local PHA, which is created by state-enabling legislation and governed by a locally appointed board of commissioners. No person may be banned from serving on a PHA board because of his or her tenancy in public housing.[19]

Section 8 Existing Housing Certificate and Voucher programs. Congress established the Section 8 housing program as part of the Housing and Community Development Act of 1974.[20] Under the Section 8 Existing Housing Certificate program, a family applies for participation with the PHA, which determines eligibility and issues a Certificate of Family Participation, generally after the family has had a long wait on the waiting list. The family is responsible for finding a landlord willing to enter into a Section 8 lease. Once the family finds a willing landlord, it then signs a lease with the landlord after the PHA has inspected and approved the unit. The PHA simultaneously signs a housing assistance payments contract with the owner, under which it agrees to subsidize the tenant's rent.[21]

The landlord may charge a rent that is no more than the "fair market rent" that HUD establishes and publishes every fall in the Federal Register.[22] The landlord receives from the PHA payment of the difference between the contract rent (not to exceed the fair market rent) and the tenant's share of the rent payment. The PHA regulates the relationship between the owner and Section 8 Existing Certificate tenant in a number of important respects. The PHA must approve the lease between the owner and tenant;[23] ensure through an initial and annual inspection that the apartment unit meets housing quality standards;[24] and annually reexamine the tenant's family income.[25]

Congress established the Section 8 Voucher program in 1983.[26] The Section 8 Voucher program resembles the Section 8 Existing Housing Certificate program in many respects. Under the Voucher program, HUD contracts with PHAs to run the program, and applicants apply to the PHA for vouchers. Once an applicant receives a voucher, she or he is responsible for locating an apartment unit on the private market that meets housing quality standards. The PHA enters into a contract with the owner for assistance payments and must approve the lease between the voucher tenant and the private owner.

Rents are generally higher for Section 8 tenants with vouchers than those with certificates. Unlike owners leasing to tenants under the Section 8 Existing Housing program, owners under the Section 8 Voucher program can charge rent that exceeds the fair market rent established by HUD. The

owner receives an assistance payment that is capped at the difference between the "payment standard" of the unit and 30 percent of the tenant's
adjusted income. The tenant is responsible for paying the rest of the rent.
Although HUD must annually adjust fair market rents under the Section 8
Existing Housing program, PHAs are not required to adjust the payment
standard under the Voucher program. As a result, voucher tenants may pay
more than 30 percent of their adjusted incomes for rent, which would be
highly unusual for a Section 8 Certificate tenant.

   Federally subsidized housing. Unlike Section 8 Existing Housing, federally subsidized housing complexes were constructed under various federal
housing laws designed to increase the housing stock available to low-income
tenants. Although the programs differ in detail, the common thread is that
a private landlord in most cases enters into a contract with HUD under
which the tenant's rent is subsidized. Although new units are no longer being constructed under these programs, there are many existing units under
which tenant rents are currently subsidized.

   1. *Section 221(d)(3) Below Market Interest Rate program.* Congress
enacted the Section 221(d)(3) program as part of the Housing Act of
1961.[27] The program was designed to assist private developers to con-
struct rental and cooperative housing for low- and moderate-income
families by providing below market interest rate mortgages insured by
the Federal Housing Administration. The mortgage interest rate was initially linked to the government borrowing rate but became fixed at 3
percent late in the 1960s. Developers were required to pass the reduced
interest rates on to tenants through decreased rents, typically about 75
to 80 percent of rents in comparable unsubsidized projects. Section
221(d)(3) projects have not been built since 1968, when the Section 236
program was enacted. Most owners of Section 221(d)(3) complexes
have entered into contracts with HUD for Section 8 subsidies through
the Section 8 Set Aside program, under which the tenant's share of the
rent is limited to 30 percent of monthly income. Early case law found
sufficient involvement in the program by federal and state government
to trigger protection by the Fifth and Fourteenth Amendments.[28]

   2. *Section 236 program.* Congress enacted the Section 236 program
in 1968 as part of the Housing and Urban Development Act of 1968.[29]
Under the Section 236 program, private developers received FHA-in-
sured market rate mortgages but were obligated to make loan payments
to the lending institution as though the loan bore only a 1 percent inter-

est rate. The remainder of the payment was made by HUD directly to the lender. The tenant's rent in Section 236 housing is equal to 30 percent of adjusted tenant income but cannot exceed the "market rent" that would be charged if there were no subsidy and must be no less than the "basic rent" that would be charged if the mortgage interest rate was in fact 1 percent. In other words, regardless of income a tenant must pay *at least* the basic rent unless he or she receives a Section 8 subsidy on the unit. Rents collected in excess of the basic rent are returned to HUD. At many Section 236 apartment complexes, the owner also contracts with HUD for Section 8 subsidies for all or some of the apartments. The courts have divided on whether there is sufficient state or federal involvement in Section 236 projects to trigger constitutional protection.[30]

3. *Section 8 New Construction and Section 8 Substantial Rehabilitation programs.* Congress established the Section 8 New Construction and Substantial Rehabilitation programs in 1974.[31] Under these programs, HUD contracted with private owners and PHAs to pay rental assistance equal to the difference between the contract rent and the tenant's share of rent (the assistance contracts are not less than twenty years and not more than thirty years). The owner is responsible for all management and maintenance functions, including financing the construction or rehabilitation of units and selection of tenants. One federal appeals court has held that the eviction of a tenant from a Section 8 new construction apartment does not involve sufficient state or federal action to trigger constitutional protection.[32]

4. *Section 8 Moderate Rehabilitation program.* Congress established the Section 8 Moderate Rehabilitation program as part of the Housing and Community Development Act of 1978 to encourage the upgrading of lower-income housing.[33] Under the program, a PHA applies to HUD and receives program funds under an annual contributions contract. The PHA selects proposals for specific projects and enters into housing assistance contracts with owners. Owners finance and carry out rehabilitation of at least one thousand dollars per unit, and the PHA provides a Section 8 rental subsidy.

5. *Section 8 Set-Aside program.* Section 8 Set-Aside is a rental assistance program for existing multifamily projects with HUD-insured or HUD-held mortgages,[34] such as Section 221(d)(3), Section 236, and Section 202 complexes. Tenant rents are determined in the same manner as under the other Section 8 programs.[35]

6. *Section 202 for the Elderly and Handicapped program.* Congress

established the Section 202 program as part of the Housing Act of 1959.[36] Under the Section 202 program, HUD provides direct loans at below market rates to consumer cooperatives, limited profit sponsors, private nonprofit developers, and public agencies that agree to provide housing and related facilities to elderly or handicapped families. Since 1975, approved Section 202 loan applications must be for projects that will receive rent subsidies under Section 8. Congress restructured the Section 202 program in 1990, creating one program for elderly and one for handicapped people, both of which have their own rental assistance authorization.[37] As a result, Section 8 will no longer be used in conjunction with new Section 202 projects.

7. *Other federally assisted housing programs.* Other programs include the Rent Supplement program enacted in 1965 and now almost entirely replaced by the Section 8 program;[38] Section 8 through state housing agencies, a rental assistance program that is administered through state agencies;[39] Section 8 for the disposition of previously HUD-owned projects, a rental assistance program in connection with the sale of HUD-owned housing;[40] Section 8 Project-Based Certificate Assistance, which authorizes a PHA to tie up to 15 percent of its Section 8 Existing Housing Assistance "to structures," in exchange for which the owner agrees to do rehabilitation work of a minimum of one thousand dollars for each project-based unit;[41] and the Section 8 Set-Aside for the Farmers Home Administration Section 515 program.[42]

Are there federal home-ownership programs for low-income people?

Yes. One of the more recent federal home-ownership programs for low-income people is HOPE—Homeownership and Opportunity for People Everywhere—which involves the sale of existing public housing to eligible families.[43] Under the HOPE program, HUD makes planning and implementation grants available to eligible applicants to assist in developing and carrying out home-ownership programs for low-income people. The grantees act as intermediaries between the PHA and the homeowners. Current tenants may not be evicted during the conversion to home-ownership. Other low-income home-ownership programs include the Public Housing Home-ownership Demonstration program of 1984,[44] the Section 5(h) program,[45] and the program authorized by Section 123 of the Housing and Community Development Act of 1987.[46] These programs have not been widely used. For more information, you should contact your local HUD office or a legal services attorney.

In addition, the Personal Responsibility and Work Authorization Reconciliation Act of 1996—the "welfare reform" act—allows states to use their Temporary Assistance for Needy Families block grants to help eligible families with children to purchase a first home. Specifically, the act authorizes states to establish Individual Development Accounts for eligible participants. The account is organized as a trust and is funded through contributions of earned income that are then matched by qualifying entities. Moneys collected in the account are disregarded for purposes of determining eligibility or assistance levels under other federal programs. Federal law specifically provides that the account may be used to purchase a first residence. For more information on how to set up an Individual Development Account, contact a local welfare office or a legal services attorney.[47]

What is the Family Self-Sufficiency Program?

The Family Self-Sufficiency Program is a recent federal initiative aimed at achieving "upward mobility" for indigent Americans. The program links subsidized housing with social services, education and training, and employment opportunities.[48] Congress established the program in 1990 as part of the Cranston-Gonzalez National Affordable Housing Act.[49] The program is open to tenants in public housing or Section 8. Participation is not a condition of tenancy, and if a tenant decides not to participate, his or her housing assistance may not be delayed.[50] Also, not all PHAs offer the program.[51]

Participation in the program brings certain benefits and obligations. Participating families are eligible to receive a broad range of services, including child care, service-related transportation, education and job training, substance abuse treatment, homemaking advice, and counseling. The family may also receive financial incentives (for example, any increase in family income because of program participation will be set aside in an escrow account that the family can use for education, to buy a house, and for other purposes).[52] The head of a participating household is required to seek "suitable" employment.

Is there a statutory entitlement to affordable housing?

No. A poor person does not have a statutory entitlement to affordable housing under any of HUD's programs. Even if an applicant meets HUD's eligibility guidelines, many years may pass before a subsidized apartment becomes available because the number of applicants for each federal housing program far exceeds the number of available units. Only one eligible applicant in three ever receives federal housing assistance. The rest of this chapter is designed to explain how to apply for HUD housing and to set out some of the rights and obligations that subsidized tenants have.

How do you apply for federal housing?

There are a variety of federal housing programs. A family that wants housing has to file a separate application for each program and for each development in which it wants to live. The family should begin by getting from the local PHA or local HUD office a list of federal low-income developments in its community. Local community action agencies, fair housing groups, and legal services and legal aid offices may also have information. If a family wants to relocate to a different community or to an adjoining suburb, it should contact a local legal services or legal aid office for advice on how to get information about developments.

When a family requests an application, it should also ask for a copy of the admission policies that apply to the development. Many PHAs, Section 8 landlords, and subsidized developments will refuse to mail an application, and will only give them to applicants who request them in person. Even if the waiting list is very long for a particular program, the manager must accept an application unless the average wait for the size apartment that a family needs is excessive (for example, more than one year), and the owner has closed the waiting list. If the waiting list is closed, the owner must nevertheless place the family on the waiting list if the owner is using federal preferences in selecting tenants and the family is claiming a federal preference, unless there is an adequate pool of other applicants likely to qualify for a federal preference and it is unlikely that the family would qualify for admission before other applicants on the waiting list.[53] ("Federal preferences" are explained later in this chapter.)

The application will ask questions about income and assets, the people who live with the applicant, the names of previous landlords, and credit and criminal history. An applicant must provide the Social Security or employer identification number of each member of the household, but no person can be denied participation if she or he does not have a Social Security number.[54]

After handing in an application, the applicant will be asked to verify its contents through written proof such as paycheck stubs, income tax returns, birth certificates, and law enforcement criminal history reports. Home visits may also be a part of the application process (to check, among other things, the tenant's housekeeping), and management may want to talk to former landlords.[55] HUD has authority to verify wages through computer matches with the State Wage Information Collection Agency, but can do so only with the applicant's written consent.[56] Landlords cannot charge a fee for processing an application, for credit history reports, for criminal history reports, or for the cost of a home visit.

The application will be reviewed under three different factors: eligibility standards, any preferences used by the PHA or owner, and tenant-selection criteria. Eligibility standards vary from program to program, but generally speaking the individual or family must meet income limits. Preferences and the date of the application then determine the order in which eligible applicants are considered for admission. The PHA or landlord then chooses tenants from among eligible applicants.

What are the income limits for federal housing?

Income limits for federal housing vary from program to program. Every year, HUD publishes estimated median family income limits, using the fair market rent definitions in the Section 8 program. These estimates are then subject to individual program guidelines.[57] To obtain a copy of the income limits for a particular federal housing program, call HUD USER, 1-800-245-2691. For fiscal year 1996, the median income limit for a family of four ranged from a high of $57,400 in New Jersey to a low of $30,200 in Montana.[58]

What counts as income in determining tenant eligibility for federal housing?

HUD has developed a uniform definition of income to determine tenant eligibility under the public housing, Section 8, and federally subsidized housing programs. Income in this context refers to annual income and is the expected total income from all sources (other than payments that HUD has specifically excluded from the definition of income) received by the head of the household, by his or her spouse, and by each additional family member.[59] The kinds of payments that are counted as annual income include welfare assistance, disability payments, unemployment compensation, Social Security payments, child support payments, wages and tips, payments in place of earnings, and net income from the operation of a business.[60] It is important to include with an application any available information concerning situations and events that might affect how much anticipated income the family will actually receive during the coming year. For example, if a custodial parent has a right to child support payments, but the noncustodial parent has missed payments in the past, then there may be a good reason for excluding some of these payments from the tenant's anticipated annual income in the coming year.[61]

Does a lump sum payment of Supplemental Security Income count as annual income?

No. In 1992, Congress amended the definition of income for Public Housing and Section 8 Existing Certificate and Voucher programs to exclude all retroactive payments received from the Social Security Administration. These payments include Social Security and SSI.[62] In addition, HUD specifically states in its handbook for federally subsidized housing that lump sum Social Security and Supplemental Security Income awards are excluded in determining annual income.[63]

Are any other payments excluded from annual income?

Yes. Federal law excludes certain kinds of specific payments from annual income. These exclusions include the value of food stamps, Earned Income Tax Credits, payments under the federal Low-Income Housing Energy Assistance Program, payments under the Job Training Partnership Act, and lump sum additions to family assets. HUD periodically publishes a notice in the *Federal Register* listing the federal benefits that are excluded from annual income.[64]

In addition, HUD excludes the following cash and goods from annual income:

1. Employment income of children younger than age 18 and employment income in excess of $480 for each full-time student over age 18, except the head of the household and spouse;

2. Income of people living in the rental unit who are not regular household members, such as live-in attendants or foster children;

3. Student loans;

4. Full amount of student financial assistance, such as Pell Grants, Supplemental Opportunity Grants, State Student Incentive Grants, college work-study, and Byrd scholarships;

5. Resident service stipends of less than $200 each month;

6. Adoption assistance payments in excess of $480 per adopted child;

7. Adult foster care payments;

8. Temporary, nonrecurring, or sporadic income, such as gifts;

9. Annual rent credits or rebates paid to elder Americans by government agencies and state tax rent credits and rebates for property taxes paid on a dwelling;

10. Hazardous duty pay to members of the military;

11. Meals provided under the Home Delivery Meal program;

12. Payments received under HUD training programs or state or local employment training programs;

13. Payments received by a person with disabilities under a plan to attain self-sufficiency, specifically for an auxiliary apparatus, medical care, or expenses for attendant care;

14. Payments received for out-of-pocket expenses from another publicly assisted program;

15. Reimbursement for the cost of medical expenses;

16. Homecare payments for amounts paid by a state agency to families that have developmentally disabled children or adult family members living at home; and

17. Holocaust reparation payments.[65]

Can you own any assets and still live in federal housing?

Yes. There is no asset limit for federally assisted tenants, although the income from assets or (where the combined total assets are worth more than five thousand dollars) the greater of actual income or the imputed income is included in annual income.[66] Assets include individual retirement accounts, cash held in savings and trust accounts, and equity in real property but not necessary personal property such as clothing, furniture, cars, or life insurance payments or assets that are not effectively owned by the family or are not accessible (because, for example, the tenant is only a beneficiary and not a coowner). Lump sum additions to family assets from sources such as inheritances, insurance payments, worker's compensation, capital gains, one-time lottery winnings, and settlement for property loss or personal injury are also assets, not income, and do not affect eligibility.[67]

What is a "family" for purposes of federal housing?

Federal housing law defines family in a broad, all-encompassing way. A family includes

1. Any family with children, even if the children are temporarily absent or placed in foster care;

2. A family whose head or spouse or sole member is over age 50 or disabled;

3. Two or more individuals living together who are over age 50 or disabled;

4. A displaced individual;

5. A disabled individual;

6. An individual who is the remaining member of a tenant family that is already in residence; and

7. Any other single person who lives alone and does not qualify as an elderly family, a displaced person, or as the remaining member of a tenant family.[68]

The federal definition of family does not require that the people residing together be joined by blood relation, marriage, or the operation of law.[69]

Within this definition, HUD affords an owner or PHA considerable latitude in the selection of tenants. Management sometimes tries to exclude an applicant because of his or her nontraditional living arrangements. Families that may face difficulty include homosexual couples, unmarried heterosexual couples, unmarried pregnant women, and elderly people caring for grandchildren. In the past, courts have largely invalidated these restrictions.[70] Contact a legal aid or legal services lawyer if management has a policy of denying housing to nontraditional families.

Can single individuals live in federal housing?

Yes. Federal housing is not only for families with children. Single individuals, including those who are neither elderly nor disabled, are eligible for Public Housing, Section 236, Section 221(d)(3), Rent Supplement, and all Section 8 programs. Of course, at Section 202 apartments, single persons and families qualify only if elderly or handicapped.[71]

Does a family for purposes of federal housing include children who are temporarily in foster care?

Yes, for the public housing and all Section 8 programs. Congress has specifically provided that the temporary absence of a child due to placement in foster care shall not be considered in determining his or her family's composition and size.[72]

Are noncitizens eligible to receive federal housing assistance?

It depends. In 1996 Congress took steps in the Personal Responsibility and Work Opportunity Reconciliation Act—the 1996 welfare act—to bar noncitizens, even legal immigrants, from receiving most forms of public assistance. But the new law specifically protects noncitizens who were residing in subsidized housing under Title V of the Housing Act as of August 22, 1996 (the new law's enactment date).[73] Even before the 1996 welfare act, however, Congress had severely restricted the eligibility of noncitizens to housing assistance,[74] and these prohibitions are enforced by HUD regulations.[75]

These prohibitions generally withhold federal housing assistance from most noncitizens, with the following *exceptions*:

1. Aliens lawfully admitted for permanent residence (i.e., immigrants who have "green cards");

2. Political asylees;

3. Aliens who entered the country after 1972, have continuously maintained residence in the United States since then, and have been "registered" by the attorney general as lawfully admitted for permanent residence;

4. Refugees;

5. Aliens who are lawfully present as a result of the attorney general's withholding of deportation; and

6. Aliens lawfully admitted for temporary or permanent residence under the immigrant "amnesty" program.[76]

Under federal law, any family applying for housing assistance after June 19, 1995, has to establish whether each family member is eligible.[77] If any family members are not eligible, the housing assistance the family would otherwise receive will be adjusted so that the ineligible family members do not receive the benefit of a subsidized rent but the eligible family members do receive the benefit of a subsidized rent.[78] A family will be denied assistance only if no member of the household is eligible.[79]

Families living in HUD-assisted housing on June 19, 1995, must also establish eligibility.[80] A family in which no member has eligible immigration status will have its rent subsidy terminated, unless it shows it needs additional time to relocate to other affordable housing. The family may receive extensions on termination of assistance for up to eighteen months (longer extensions may be granted if a family member is seeking political asylum or refugee status).[81]

Families living in HUD-assisted housing on June 19, 1995 with eligible members may either continue receiving assistance indefinitely or qualify for prorated assistance or extensions on termination of assistance.[82] The exact result depends upon which family members are eligible.

What is a preference?

Under federal housing law, having a "preference" means that an applicant should be housed before other families who need the same size apartment but who do not have a preference.

For example: Ms. Smith is near-elderly (i.e., over age 50) and the caretaker of her four grandchildren. She currently pays more than half of her income for rent and utilities. Ms. Jones lives with Mr. Jones and their three children. Mr. and Ms. Jones pay 20 percent of their income for rent and utilities. Each family applies for subsidized housing. Ms. Smith has a preference for "rent overburden." Ms. Jones has no preference. Therefore, the Smith family will get priority on the waiting list over the Jones family.

A PHA or federally subsidized owner must grant all elderly, disabled, and displaced applicants preference over all other single applicants, regardless of the single applicant's federal preference status.[83]

How does an applicant receive a preference for federal housing?

Generally speaking, federal law gives a preference to three kinds of applicants for federally subsidized housing programs, other than Section 221(d)(3) and Section 236 apartment complexes that do not receive additional subsidies.[84] Congress, however, eliminated for fiscal year 1996 the three federal preferences.[85] HUD issued notices instructing owners that they may eliminate federal preferences for fiscal year 1996, but they are not required to do so.[86] Thus, many PHAs and owners continue to use preferences in selecting tenants.

People who are involuntarily displaced. This means a person who has vacated or will have to vacate housing because of a disaster, such as a fire, that makes the unit uninhabitable or because of government code enforcement or certain landlord actions.[87] A preference on this basis is also available for applicants subject to domestic violence, whether threatened or actual, by a spouse or other member of the household.[88] HUD recently expanded this preference to include cases where the family is in danger of reprisal for providing information on criminal activity to law enforcement; where the family is a victim of a hate crime; where the applicant has a mobility impairment and is no longer able to use the existing unit; and where the family is being displaced by disposition of a HUD multifamily development.[89]

People who live in substandard housing, including homeless people. Substandard housing includes housing that is dilapidated (which means, among other things, housing that is not safe or requires considerable repair; that is without operable indoor plumbing, such as housing without a usable flush toilet or a bathtub inside the unit for the household's exclusive use; that is without electricity or with inadequate or unsafe electrical service; that is without a safe or adequate source of heat; that should but does not have a kitchen; or that has been declared uninhabitable by the government). A preference for substandard housing is also given to people who are homeless and have no place to live other than a shelter or transitional housing.[90]

Families that pay more than 50 percent of family income for rent. An applicant can get a preference for rent overburden if he or she has been paying more than 50 percent of family income (as defined by federal law) for rent and tenant-purchased utilities for more than ninety days.

PHAs and landlords using the federal preferences have discretion in applying these federal preferences. As a result, in one complex, a landlord may choose to give priority to a family that has been displaced, while a landlord in another complex might give priority to a family with rent overburden. Other landlords elsewhere may choose to treat all applicants with any preference in chronological order. Despite this broad discretion, no landlord can exclude or otherwise penalize a request for Section 8 Certificate or Voucher assistance solely because the applicant lives in public housing.[91] Nor may a public housing tenant be denied a preference for a Section 8 Certificate or Voucher, or delayed or otherwise treated unfavorably because of her or his current tenancy.[92] In addition, HUD has generally taken the position that applicants with special needs because of disability or age should be given priority for units built for that purpose.[93]

In addition to these federal preferences, local preferences may also apply to some developments. In July 1994, HUD published regulations allowing PHAs to allow up to 50 percent of new public housing tenants to be nonfederal preference; to allow up to 30 percent of new tenants in federally subsidized Section 8 to be nonfederal preference; and to allow up to 10 percent of new tenants in Section 8 Existing Certificate and Voucher programs to be nonfederal preference.[94] Local preferences may be developed after public hearings to solicit public comment on local needs. The landlord can provide a copy of the local preferences that apply. Some localities grant preferences to veterans. Others give preferences to community residents. Some kinds of preferences (such as a preference for residents) may make it difficult for low-income families to move into a new community. Such policies may violate various federal laws prohibiting discrimination. If management's use of a preference unfairly discriminates against an applicant on the basis of race, ethnicity, gender, or disability, talk with a legal services or legal aid lawyer about legal options.

What happens if an applicant is denied a federal preference?

An applicant who is denied a federal preference has a right to prompt notice of the decision.[95] The notice must state the reasons for the denial and inform the applicant that she or he may meet with the PHA or designee to review the determination.

What size apartment does a family get?

Even if an applicant has a preference, an apartment of appropriate size must be available before the family can be selected for housing. Whether an apartment is appropriate depends on the particular program and the family's size. Typically, children of the same sex will be expected to share a bedroom, and two people will generally be required to share a bedroom, unless they are not related or are of the opposite sex.

To determine the number of tenants in a family, include the following individuals

- Individuals who live with the applicant full time;
- Children who are away at school, but live with the applicant at recess;
- Children under joint custody who live with the applicant at least half time;
- Foster children;
- If the applicant is pregnant, the fetus;
- Medically necessary live-in attendants;[96] and
- Children temporarily away from home because of placement in foster care.[97]

TABLE 4-1
Public Housing Apartment Size Guidelines

	Number of Persons	
Number of Bedrooms	*Minimum*	*Maximum*
0	1	1
1	1	2
2	2	4
3	3	6
4	5	8
5	7	10

Source: United States Department of Housing and Urban Development, Occupancy Requirements for Subsidized Multifamily Programs, ¶ 2–18, CHG (Jan. 1993).

Project owners and PHAs have flexibility in assigning families to units of a particular size. HUD previously suggested the guidelines in table 4-1 for PHAs, and project owners followed similar guidelines.[98] A PHA is currently allowed to establish its own policies on the appropriate number of bedrooms for a family.[99] Apartment size guidelines are different for the Section 8 Voucher and Certificate programs.

How does an applicant know if he or she is selected as a tenant?

Applicants for HUD-assisted housing are entitled to notice of acceptance or rejection. If an application is accepted, and a unit of the right size is available, the applicant will be housed or placed on a waiting list if there is a wait; if a unit is not available, the applicant will be placed on the waiting list. If the application is rejected, the applicant is entitled to know the specific reasons for the denial.[100] If the application is for public housing, the denial can be challenged at an "informal hearing."[101] If the application is for Section 8 Certificate or Voucher assistance, the applicant can ask to provide additional written information or request an "informal review" of the decision.[102]

What if an applicant is discriminated against during the admission process?

Landlords and PHAs must obey all federal, state, and local laws that prohibit discrimination. Federal laws forbid discrimination on the basis of race, color, religion, sex, national origin, handicap, or children in the family.[103] Laws in some states expand the categories of protected status. Judicial or other remedies may be available if an applicant has been discriminated against during the admission process. For more information, contact the local Human Rights Commission or regional HUD Office of Fair Housing and Equal Opportunity.

What is a lease?

When a person becomes a tenant, he or she is asked to sign a lease. A lease is a contract that defines the legal relationship between the tenant and the landlord, setting out their respective rights and responsibilities and dealing with such matters as rent, extra charges, pets, security deposits, rent redeterminations, evictions, and inspections. Although some provisions of the lease are required under federal or state law, others must be negotiated directly with the landlord or PHA. A tenant must know what the lease says, because he or she can be evicted for not complying with material terms of the agreement.

The lease must provide basic information about the tenancy. This includes:

- The name of the landlord and the name of the tenant;
- The landlord's repair obligations;
- The length of the lease;
- The amount of rent;
- Household members;
- Which services require tenant payment in addition to rent;
- Any policy regarding entry of the unit by the landlord during the tenancy and notice requirements;
- Regulations about late payment;
- Eviction procedures; and
- Procedures for recertification and reporting requirements.[104]

Ask management to attach to the lease any house rules that tenants are also required to follow. House rules can span a variety of issues but must be reasonable.[105] Examples include prohibitions on having bicycles on balconies and restrictions on walking on the grass.

Are there any provisions that federal housing leases cannot contain?

Yes. Federal regulations prohibit the following provisions in leases for federally assisted housing:

- *Confession of judgment.* The lease cannot require the tenant to consent to a judgment in favor of the landlord.
- *Exculpatory clauses.* The lease cannot require the tenant to agree to limit the landlord's liability for personal or property damage.
- *Waiver of legal notice.* The lease cannot authorize the landlord to take important legal steps (like raising the rent, evicting the tenant, or changing the terms of the lease) without giving the tenant prior written notice.
- *Waiver of jury trial.* The lease cannot require the tenant to give up the right to a jury if the landlord brings an eviction action.
- *Waiver of legal proceedings.* The lease cannot require the tenant to give up the right to a day in court before being evicted or having property removed.
- *Waiver of appeal rights.* The lease cannot require the tenant to give up the right to go to court to appeal a judgment in favor of the landlord.
- *Distraint for rent.* The lease cannot authorize the landlord to take the tenant's possessions or lock the tenant out of the apartment to satisfy an alleged claim of unpaid rent.
- *Attorney's fees and costs.* The lease cannot obligate the tenant to pay the landlord's legal costs if he or she loses a lawsuit involving the tenancy.[106]

In addition, lease terms must be reasonable, and the tenant can challenge them in court if they are not.[107]

How much rent does a tenant in federal housing pay?

The amount of rent a tenant pays depends on the kind of federal housing and the family's income. Under the public housing and Section 8 programs, rent can generally not exceed 30 percent of the family's monthly adjusted income.[108] However, in January 1996, Congress enacted the Balanced Budget Downpayment Act, I, which requires tenants to pay, for fiscal year 1996, a minimum rent of $25 per month.[109] Congress amended this law on April 26, 1996 to allow for a three-month waiver for hardship cases.[110]

HUD has interpreted this law and has mandated that the $25 minimum rent be waived for all existing tenants living in project-based Section 8 apartments for the months of July, August, and September 1996.[111]

A tenant in a Section 236 apartment without a Section 8 subsidy must pay at least the "basic rent" or 30 percent of monthly adjusted income, whichever is greater. The lease will state the amount of rent that the tenant must pay. Check with a local legal aid or legal services office to answer any questions about the amount of rent that must be paid.

What is adjusted income for purposes of calculating rent?

A tenant's adjusted income is equal to annual income less various allowances that are set out in federal statute and regulation. These allowances include:

A standard deduction of $480 for each dependent. A dependent means any member of the tenant's household, other than a spouse or partner, who is younger than age 18; a person with disabilities; or a full-time student. A fetus does not count as a dependent.

A standard deduction of $400 for any elderly family. A family is elderly if the head of the household or his or her spouse is age 62, disabled, or handicapped.[112]

A deduction for medical expenses for an elderly, disabled, or handicapped family. An elderly, disabled, or handicapped family that has no handicapped assistance expenses may take a deduction for medical expenses equal to the amount by which those expenses exceed 3 percent of annual income. An elderly, disabled, or handicapped family that has handicapped assistance expenses that are less than 3 percent of annual income may take a deduction for combined handicapped assistance expenses and medical expenses that is equal to the amount by which the sum of these expenses exceeds 3 percent of annual income. And an elderly, disabled, or handicapped family that has handicapped assistance expenses that exceed 3 percent of annual income may take a deduction equal to the amount by which such expenses exceed 3 percent of annual income (but not more than the combined employment income of family members who are age 18 or older who are able to work as a result of such handicapped assistance expenses), plus a deduction for medical expenses that is equal to the family's medical expenses.

A deduction for child care expenses. A tenant can take this deduction for money spent for the care of children under age 13 when such care is needed to allow the tenant or a family member to be employed or to continue education. The amount of the deduction cannot be more than the amount of employment income received, and expenses paid to a family member residing in the unit cannot be deducted.[113]

Can a family's rent change during its tenancy?

Yes. A family's rent may change if its income or family composition changes, and the tenant has an absolute right to a rent reduction if income decreases, or if family size increases, but income does not. A tenant in public housing or federally subsidized housing is required to report changes, such as changes in income or family composition, whenever they occur. The kind of changes the tenant must report include the birth of a child, an increase in welfare, or a new job. Tenants with a Section 8 Voucher or Certificate may also be required by their PHA to report interim changes in income. Check with the PHA to see what must be reported. The lease will also say what the tenant has to report.[114]

In addition, all public housing, Section 8, and federally subsidized tenants have to go through an annual process known as recertification.[115] During the recertification process, a tenant will be asked to provide proof of family income. Rent can increase or decrease depending on what has happened to income and family composition during the year. Public housing tenants must also report changes in family composition. Again, the lease will describe the procedures governing recertification.

Finally, rent can change in Section 236 or Section 221(d)(3) complexes without a Section 8 subsidy if the landlord convinces the federal government to approve a building-wide rent increase (unless rent is subsidized under the Section 8 program).[116] Landlords can ask for rent increases whenever they believe that they need additional income to cover the building's operating expenses or to keep the building well maintained. Some landlords, however, might try to get a rent increase simply to make a bigger profit. The landlord is required to inform the tenants in writing of any proposed building-wide rent increase. A tenant can challenge the rent increase but has only thirty days from the date of receiving the landlord's written notice to file a protest. Tenants might want to contact a local legal services or legal aid office for advice.

Does a tenant have to pay for utilities in addition to rent?

It depends on where the tenant lives and how the apartment is metered. But when a tenant pays for utilities, the PHA or owner must offset a utility allowance against the tenant's share of the rent.[117] The lease will say whether the tenant has to pay for utilities. The term "utilities" includes electricity, gas, heating fuel, water and sewerage services, and trash and garbage collection services.

Utilities can be metered in one of three ways.

Retail metered. An apartment is retail metered if it has its own utility meter and the tenant pays for utilities directly to the utility company. The landlord or PHA will reduce the rent the tenant would otherwise pay (if the landlord paid all utilities) by an allowance for reasonable utility service.

Check metered. An apartment is check metered if it has its own utility meter but the landlord pays for utilities directly to the utility company. An allowance for reasonable utility service will be included in the rent, and the landlord or PHA may impose a surcharge for excess consumption.

Master metered. An apartment is master metered if the building has a single utility meter and the landlord pays for utilities directly to the utility company. Under a master-meter system, the tenant is not charged for utility use except for utility consumption attributed to tenant-owned major appliances and optional use of PHA-furnished equipment such as air conditioning, over and above the cost estimated for reasonable use of such equipment. For example, the landlord may charge for utility use according to a fixed schedule for tenant-owned major appliances, such as an air conditioner or electric clothes dryer.[118]

Can the landlord charge a tenant extra rent for services other than utilities?

No. The landlord cannot charge extra rent for services that are a necessary incident of the tenancy, such as use of a stove or insect control. On the other hand, the lease can set extra fees for optional services, such as cable television or parking.[119] If the tenant fails to pay an extra charge, he or she cannot be evicted for nonpayment of rent, and the landlord can seek eviction only if the nonpayment is a material violation of the lease,[120] except that subsidized landlords cannot evict for nonpayment of late charges.[121]

Does a tenant have to pay a security deposit?

Generally, yes. Most leases in federal housing provide for a security deposit. A security deposit is a payment by the tenant that the landlord may use to remedy actions that breach the lease agreement, such as tenant-caused damage to the apartment that exceeds so-called normal wear and tear. The amount of the security deposit depends on the kind of subsidized housing in which the tenant lives and how much rent is paid. In public housing, HUD regulations provide that a security deposit cannot be more than one month's rent or a reasonable amount fixed by the PHA.[122] In Section 236 or Section 221(d)(3) housing without a rental subsidy, the security deposit cannot exceed rent.[123] A tenant with a Section 8 Certificate or Voucher can be charged whatever security deposit the market will bear as long as the amount does not exceed the amount charged to unassisted tenants.[124] Subsidized owners must comply with state laws regarding investment of security deposits and distribution of any earned interest.[125]

Can tenants have pets and still live in federal housing?

Yes, but with important limitations. Federal law allows tenants in federal housing for the elderly or disabled to have pets.[126] A landlord can charge a tenant who wants a pet a refundable deposit for repairs, fumigation, and other reasonable expenses related to the pet.[127]

There is otherwise no general federal right to have a pet in assisted housing, and the tenant can have a pet only with the landlord's consent. Tenants who want a pet must be sure that the lease specifically says that pets are allowed and whether extra fees will be charged. Tenants who need a pet for assistance because of a disability can challenge a landlord's refusal to rent as a violation of 1988 amendments to the Fair Housing Act,[128] the Rehabilitation Act of 1973, and the Americans with Disabilities Act,[129] which ban discrimination on the basis of disability.[130]

Does the landlord have to maintain the building in good repair?

Yes. Federal housing laws are designed to remedy "unsafe and unsanitary housing conditions," and landlords must maintain subsidized buildings in good repair.[131] In addition, state and local law obligates all landlords to maintain buildings in good repair, and the lease also sets out this duty. Although the landlord's specific responsibilities vary depending on the kind of housing in which a tenant lives, in general a subsidized landlord is responsible for the following:

- Regular cleaning of all common areas;
- Maintaining common areas in safe condition;
- Arranging for trash and garbage removal;
- Keeping all equipment and appliances in working order;

- Making necessary repairs with reasonable promptness;
- Maintaining exterior lighting in good working order;
- Providing for extermination services; and,
- Maintaining grounds and shrubs.[132]

The tenant should check the lease to find out the landlord's specific responsibilities.

Can a tenant sue his or her landlord if the building is not maintained in good repair?

Yes, but there are other steps that a tenant might first consider short of litigation that could result in better maintenance of a building. For example, a tenant can try to organize a tenants' association to influence the landlord to make needed repairs. Or a tenant might take photographs of unsafe and unsanitary conditions and send them to the local public health department. A tenant can ask the local Bureau of Building Inspectors to inspect the premises. Or a tenant can become involved in the management of the building. In public housing, a tenant can also file a grievance (described later in this chapter) and use the grievance procedure to remedy maintenance problems in the project.[133]

If you decide to go to court, it is important to contact a legal services or legal aid attorney to discuss how to file a lawsuit and to learn about any expenses that might result. The lawyer can also explain the different remedies that are available. In addition to getting repairs, some tenants have won substantial damage awards for faulty maintenance, especially where the landlord failed to provide tenants with adequate security against crime.[134]

Can tenants help manage their building?

Yes. HUD encourages tenants to participate in the management of public housing and other assisted units. The most extensive opportunities for tenant management are in public housing, where HUD has enacted a comprehensive program allowing a PHA to contract for resident management with qualifying tenant associations (called "resident management corporations").[135]

There are also other, more limited, opportunities for tenants to participate in how their complexes are run. For example, tenants are permitted to participate in the development of lease and grievance procedures,[136] the selection of hearing panels and officers,[137] the review of proposed rent increases,[138] and the decision to convert from master metered utility service to check-metered or retail-metered units.[139]

What is an eviction?

An eviction is a legal proceeding through which a landlord or PHA terminates a lease and repossesses the tenant's apartment. The possibility of eviction is a very serious event. Eviction means that the tenant will not be able to live in his or her current apartment, and will lose the federal subsidy, unless it is a Section 8 Certificate or Voucher. The tenant will also face other legal consequences that can delay or even prevent future government rental subsidies.[140] It is important to recognize, however, that a landlord or PHA cannot evict a tenant unless it goes to court and gets an order of eviction from a judge. A tenant who is threatened with eviction should seek advice from a legal services or legal aid lawyer.

When can a tenant be evicted?

Special rules apply when a tenant is being evicted from federal housing, although the procedures vary from program to program. In general, tenants in federal housing can be evicted only for serious or repeated violations of material terms of their lease or for "good cause." In all but the Section 8 Certificate and Voucher programs, good cause is limited to tenant misbehavior, lease violation, or violation of program regulations.

Under all HUD-assisted housing programs, the regulatory and lease language defining the good cause standard is very general, and ultimately a court must decide if good cause is met. In applying the standard, courts have emphasized the following principles:

- Eviction cannot be based on arbitrary grounds;[141]
- Eviction has serious consequences for the health and welfare of the tenant;[142]
- Eviction based on the tenant's misconduct should occur only after serious wrongdoing that threatens or harms the well-being of the program, other tenants, or PHA employees;[143] and,
- Eviction can occur only if the tenant was aware of and able to control the conduct that forms the basis of the violation.[144]

A number of different situations can lead to eviction from subsidized housing.

First, the landlord or PHA can threaten eviction whenever a tenant or a household member or a guest or individual under the tenant's control engages in "criminal activity that threatens the health, safety, or right to peaceful enjoyment of the premises by other tenants or any drug-related criminal activity."[145]

Second, a tenant can be evicted if he or she is in material or serious noncompliance with the terms of the lease. This means that the tenant has repeatedly violated important provisions of the lease. It is well settled, for example, that a tenant's failure to pay rent is good cause for eviction.[146] On the other hand, the landlord does not have good cause to evict if the tenant did not pay the full rent because he or she had reported a reduction in income but the rent had not been properly reduced. Good cause to evict is also generally found where the tenant does not comply with obligations imposed by federal regulations that govern the development in which the tenant lives. For example, management may try to evict a tenant who refuses to disclose his or her Social Security number (if the tenant has one) or if the tenant uses the apartment for business purposes other than those that are considered incidental (such as typing or babysitting).

Third, a tenant can be evicted for violating state landlord and tenant laws.

Finally, a tenant can be evicted for "other good cause" that the landlord puts forward. In subsidized housing, the landlord can evict for "other good cause" only at the end of the lease term and only if he or she has warned the tenant that the conduct constitutes "other good cause" for which the tenant may be evicted if the conduct continues.[147]

Can a tenant be evicted for having guests in the apartment?

No, if the person is a guest and not an unauthorized resident. Public housing leases specifically grant tenants the right to reasonable accommodation of guests. Although some landlords require tenants to register overnight guests, courts have generally invalidated these restrictions as a violation of the tenant's right to privacy.[148] But if the guest stays in the apartment for an extended period, the tenant may have to report this to the landlord as a change in household composition and have the individual added to the lease.[149] The change in family composition could affect whether the apartment is still of an appropriate size for the household. In defending against evictions based on guests in the apartment, the tenant's right to privacy and associational autonomy should be considered paramount.[150]

Can a tenant be evicted for refusing to let management inspect his or her apartment?

Yes, although the tenant should check the lease to find out the scope of his or her obligation. Leases in federal housing typically require the tenant to allow the landlord access to the apartment upon reasonable notice and during business hours. The landlord can enter the apartment to inspect, to make repairs, or to show the apartment to prospective tenants. Forty-eight hours notice is considered reasonable notice in public housing; twenty-four hours notice is usually sufficient in other subsidized units. The landlord generally does not need the tenant's permission to enter the premises if an emergency exists.[151]

Can a tenant be evicted because the lease has expired?

No. A landlord cannot evict a tenant who lives in public or federal subsidized housing simply because the lease has expired. The landlord must have good cause to refuse to renew the tenant's lease and terminate the tenancy.[152] Although HUD regulations require that owners leasing to Section 8 Certificate or Voucher tenants must have good cause to evict at the end of the lease term,[153] Congress suspended this requirement for fiscal year 1996.[154] However, owners with leases requiring good cause to evict at the end of the lease term must still have good cause, since Congress cannot impair existing contracts.

Can a tenant in federal housing be evicted for joining a tenants' association?

No. A tenant in federal housing cannot be evicted for organizing or joining a tenants' association, for talking to the press about conditions at the apartment complex, or for complaining to neighbors or to government agencies about the landlord. A PHA is considered a government representative and is obliged to respect the First Amendment, which includes the right to speak, to associate with others, and to protest.[155] As Justice William O. Douglas, Jr. explained in *Thorpe v. Housing Authority* (a decision of the United States Supreme Court), "The recipient of a government benefit . . . [such as] a home in a public housing project, cannot be made to forfeit the benefit because he exercises a constitutional right."[156] Subsidized owners under Section 236, Section 202, and Section 221(d)(3) are barred by federal regulation from impeding the reasonable efforts of tenants to organize.[157]

The same principle of protection against retaliatory eviction should extend to Section 8 Certificate and Voucher tenants.[158]

Can a tenant be evicted if the head of the household dies or moves?

It depends. A remaining household member in public housing is eligible for continued occupancy[159] and has a right to a grievance hearing to determine whether he or she can stay in the apartment.[160] Under all Section 8 programs, a remaining member of a tenant family is eligible for assistance.[161] Questions may arise, however, whether as a remaining household member the tenant succeeds to rights under the lease of the head of the household. A remaining household member should consult a local legal aid or legal services attorney for advice.[162]

Can management ever evict a tenant without good cause relating to the conduct of the tenant, other household members, or guests?

Only if the tenant lives in housing under the Section 8 Certificate or Voucher programs. In this kind of housing, the landlord may evict a tenant for a valid business reason unrelated to tenant misbehavior but may do so only after the first year of the tenant's lease. Valid business reasons include a desire to collect more rent than the PHA will authorize or to use the apartment for personal reasons.[163]

What happens if a landlord or PHA tries to evict a tenant?

Under federal and state law, the landlord must give the tenant notice of the proposed eviction and an opportunity to challenge management's action. If the tenant opposes the eviction, the landlord will have to prove good cause, as well as compliance with federal, state, and local law. A tenant cannot be evicted unless the court issues an order.[164]

What kind of notice must management give a tenant before going to court to evict?

Tenants in federal housing cannot be evicted without prior notice of the landlord's proposed action. The kind of notice depends on the specific housing in which the tenant lives. A tenant who faces eviction should talk to a legal services or legal aid lawyer about the notice procedures that apply to his or her circumstances. If the landlord does not comply with these procedures, the tenant may be able to stop the eviction from happening.

In all cases, management must give the tenant written notice of the reasons for the proposed eviction. The notice is not sufficient if it says merely that a provision of the lease has been violated. It must instead state the specific factual circumstances that form the basis of the violation. Public housing tenants must also be told they have a right to examine PHA documents relevant to the eviction and a right to ask for a grievance hearing (in certain cases, public housing tenants have an absolute right to a grievance hearing if they make a timely request).[165] In Section 8 federally subsidized housing, tenants must be told that they have a right to meet with the landlord within ten days to discuss the matter, that they have the right to defend against the eviction in court, and that the landlord may evict only through the judicial process.[166] In Section 8 Certificate housing, the landlord must send the tenant a notice (with a copy to the PHA) stating the reasons for the eviction.[167]

How long is the notice period prior to eviction?

The notice period varies with the housing program and the grounds for eviction. In public housing, if the eviction is for nonpayment of rent, the PHA must give the tenant fourteen days notice. If the eviction is for conduct that threatens the health and safety of other tenants, then the PHA must give reasonable notice of not more than thirty days.[168] In any other case, the PHA must give thirty days notice.[169] In Section 8 federally subsidized housing, the landlord must give at least ten days notice since the tenant has ten days within which to discuss the proposed eviction with the landlord.[170] If the eviction is for material noncompliance, the landlord must give ten days notice and any notice required under state law.[171] If the eviction is for good cause, the landlord can give the notice only at the end of the lease term, and it must afford the tenant at least thirty days.[172] In the Section 8 Certificate and Voucher programs, the landlord has to give notice that complies with state or local law requirements, but no minimum time period is prescribed.[173]

Does the landlord have to deliver the notice of eviction in a particular way?

Yes. The way in which the landlord delivers the notice of eviction is called "service." The rules regarding service vary depending on the program that applies to the complex in which the tenant lives. In public housing, the notice of termination may be delivered to any adult member of the tenant's household or sent by prepaid first-class mail.[174] It is not sufficient for the landlord to place an eviction notice in the tenant's mail slot. Under the federally subsidized housing programs (Section 236, Section 221(d)(3), Section 202), the landlord must serve two copies of the eviction notice, one by prepaid first-class mail and the other by personal delivery on an adult at the apartment.[175] Federal law does not specify how landlords in the Section 8 Certificate and Voucher programs have to serve eviction notices. At a minimum, the landlord must satisfy the requirements of state law to terminate a tenancy and must also furnish a copy of the notice to the PHA.[176]

What is the grievance process?

The grievance process is a procedure that allows a tenant to voice complaints about unfair treatment by the landlord or PHA. The primary purpose of the grievance process is to protect tenants against arbitrary or illegal management practices. The grievance process is much more extensive for public housing than for other HUD-assisted tenants.

The PHA cannot take an unfavorable action against a public housing tenant—including most evictions—without first doing the following as part of the grievance process:

- Giving the tenant written notice of the specific grounds of the proposed adverse action;
- Giving the tenant a chance, upon timely request, to present his or her views in person before an impartial hearing officer;
- Giving the tenant an opportunity to examine documents, records, or regulations related to the proposed action;
- Allowing the tenant to bring a friend, attorney, or other representative to the hearing;
- Allowing the tenant a chance to question witnesses at the hearing and to have others make statements on his or her behalf; and,
- Giving the tenant a written decision on the proposed action.[177]

These procedural rights must be incorporated into the public housing lease. The specific details of the grievance process differ from PHA to PHA. Ask management for a copy of the procedures that apply in a particular project.

Tenants in federally subsidized housing have more limited opportunities to challenge unfavorable decisions by their landlords. The grievance process in these programs guarantees only notice of the adverse action and a chance to comment. A tenant does not have a right to a fair hearing or to present witnesses.[178]

Tenants participating in the Section 8 Existing Certificate or Voucher program have available a grievance process they can use to dispute most PHA actions or failures to act.[179] Section 8 participants have a right to

- Receive written notice of the specific grounds of a proposed adverse action;
- Review before the hearing and to copy any PHA documents that are directly relevant;
- Be represented by a lawyer or other representative at the hearing;
- Have a hearing officer who is someone other than a person who made the decision, or a subordinate of this person;
- Question witnesses; and
- Receive a written decision stating the reasons for the decision.[180]

What kinds of disputes can be resolved through the grievance process?

The grievance process can be used to resolve complaints by an individual tenant against the PHA for failure to act or for acts taken under the lease or federal regulation that relate to the rights, duties, welfare, or status of a tenant. For example, if the building has not been maintained in good repair, a tenant can use the grievance process to bring a claim for monetary damages against the PHA to seek a rent abatement for substandard conditions.[181]

A tenant cannot use the grievance process to bring a complaint directly against another tenant. A complaint about another tenant should be given to the PHA. Preferably the complaint should be in writing and describe the problem and the individuals involved. Management then has a duty to take corrective action to resolve the complaint. If the PHA fails to take action, and the problem continues, then the tenant can use the grievance process to complain about management's failure to take reasonable steps.

Does the public housing grievance process cover evictions?

Yes, but with important exceptions. A PHA can offer public housing tenants an expedited grievance process or exclude entirely from the grievance process any eviction that involves drug-related criminal activity on or near the premises or involves any other criminal activity that threatens the health, safety, or right to peaceful enjoyment of the premises by other tenants or PHA employees. Congress also recently mandated that HUD revise its regulations to allow PHAs to exclude from the grievance procedure evictions (1) premised on conduct that threatens health, safety, or right to peaceful enjoyment (in other words, the conduct that forms the basis of the eviction no longer has to be "criminal") and (2) premised on drug-related conduct "on or off" the PHA premises.[182] Such exclusions are proper if HUD has determined that the tenant's right to due process will be otherwise protected through the state eviction procedure.[183] If a PHA has excluded certain kinds of evictions from the apartment's grievance process, it is important to check with a legal services or legal aid attorney to make sure that the procedures in place in fact meet due process. In addition, the eviction notice must explain why the grievance process is being skipped and describe the state court procedures that are available.[184]

How does a public housing tenant initiate a grievance?

A public housing tenant can initiate a grievance by filing a grievance complaint. The complaint must be "personally presented" to the PHA or apartment office and can be done orally or in writing.[185] As a practical matter, it is sensible to have a record of having filed a grievance, so it is best to file a complaint by certified mail or to hand deliver it. The complaint should describe the facts supporting the grievance. The complaint should also specify the kind of relief the tenant wants the PHA to give.

At some PHAs, grievance complaints have to be filed within a very short time after the unfavorable event has occurred. For example, some local grievance procedures require complaints to be filed within five days of the grievable action, although at least one federal court has held that a public housing tenant must have at least one year within which to file a grievance (at least in a situation that did not involve eviction).[186] If the complaint is late, the PHA has grounds to refuse to hear the grievance. A tenant does not, however, have to go through the grievance process before filing a court action or defending against an eviction proceeding.[187]

What happens after a public housing tenant files a grievance complaint?

After a public housing tenant files the grievance complaint, the first step in the process is an informal conference with management. The tenant can bring a friend, lawyer, or other person to the discussion as a representative. After the conference, the PHA must give the tenant a written summary, including the names of the participants, the date of the meeting, the proposed decision, and the reasons for the decision. The summary must also explain that the tenant has a right to request a formal hearing if he or she is not satisfied with the proposed resolution and the steps that must be taken to obtain a formal hearing. At least some courts have dismissed eviction actions where the PHA failed to inform the tenant of the procedures for obtaining a formal hearing.

How does a public housing tenant request a formal hearing?

A public housing tenant can request a formal hearing by submitting to the PHA or management office a written statement of the reasons for the grievance and the relief requested. The tenant can file the request even before receiving the informal-conference summary and must file it within "a reasonable time" after receipt.

If the complaint relates to proposed termination of the lease, and the eviction is based on nonpayment of rent, the PHA can demand payment of the undisputed portion of the rent into an escrow account as a condition of holding a formal hearing. The PHA cannot ask the tenant to pay disputed charges that are not rent, such as meal charges. The PHA can waive the escrow requirement if it chooses to do so.[188]

The hearing officer is required to schedule the hearing promptly and at a time and place reasonably convenient to both the tenant and management. At this point in the process, the tenant should receive a written notice saying when and where the hearing will take place and describing the procedures that govern the hearing.

What rights does a public housing tenant have at a formal hearing?

Federal law guarantees public housing tenants a number of procedural protections during the formal hearing process. Although the procedures governing formal hearings differ from PHA to PHA, at a minimum a tenant has the following rights:

• A right to a hearing officer who is impartial and disinterested. This means that the hearing officer cannot have participated in the decision under challenge. In addition, a lower-level employee of the PHA cannot be asked to review decisions made by a superior.[189]

• A right to examine and copy (at the tenant's expense) all relevant PHA documents.[190]

• A right to have the hearing held in private, rather than in public.[191]

• A right to present evidence and argument in favor of the complaint.[192]

- A right to challenge evidence presented by the PHA and to cross-examine witnesses. It is a denial of due process for the PHA to rely on written statements of witnesses without making the individual available for cross-examination at the hearing.[193]

- A right to have the hearing recorded and transcribed at personal expense.[194]

- A right to a decision based on the facts that are developed at the hearing. The decision must be in writing and must set forth the reasons for the determination.[195]

What happens if a public housing tenant loses the formal hearing?

If a public housing tenant loses the formal hearing, he or she still has a right to go to court to challenge the unfavorable decision. Indeed, even if the tenant does not follow the grievance process, he or she has a right to go to court. Although the regulations do not provide for any further administrative appeal, the tenant may always ask to appear before the PHA's executive director or board of commissioners and ask for review of the hearing officer's decision. This should be done within a "reasonable time," which generally means within a few weeks of the unfavorable decision. The executive director or board has the authority to overrule the hearing officer's decision, if it chooses to do so.

Notes

The authors gratefully acknowledge the assistance of Fred Fuchs of Legal Aid of Central Texas in the preparation of this chapter. We also thank David B. Bryson of the National Housing Law Project for permission to draw extensively from *HUD Housing Programs: Tenant's Rights* (2d ed. 1994).

1. 405 U.S. 56 (1972).

2. *Id.* at 74.

3. *See* Florence Wagman Roisman, *Establishing a Right to Housing: A General Guide*, 25 Clearinghouse Rev. 203, 209 (1991).

4. State constitutional provisions protecting the poor are collected in Burt Neuborne, *Foreword: State Constitutions and the Evolution of Positive Rights*, 20 Rutgers L.J. 881, 893–94 & nn. 60–82 (1989).

5. *See McCain v. Koch*, 117 A.D.2d 198, 502 N.Y.S.2d 720 (N.Y. App. Div. 1986)

(denial of injunctive relief), *rev'd on other grounds,* 70 N.Y.2d 109, 511 N.E.2d 62, 517 N.Y.S.2d 918 (1987). The state constitutional issue was not before the highest court.

6. The Housing Act of 1937, Pub. L. No. 412, 50 Stat. 888 (Sept. 1, 1937), *formerly codified at* 42 U.S.C.A. §§ 1401–30. The 1937 Act was revised and readopted in 1974 and codified at 42 U.S.C.A. § 1437 (West 1994 & West Supp. 1996).

7. Former 42 U.S.C.A. § 1401, *revised and now codified at* 12 U.S.C.A. § 1701t (West 1989).

8. *Id.*

9. *To Be or Not to Be: A Time of Reckoning for National Housing Policy,* 25 Housing L. Bull. 1 (1995); *see also* Jason DeParle, *Slamming the Door,* The New York Times Magazine, Oct. 20, 1996, 53; Barbara Weiner, *Will Six Decades of National Housing Policy Succumb to the Congressional Wrecking Ball?,* 1996 Legal Services J. 1 (1996).

10. *See* Staff of House Comm. on Ways and Means, 103d Cong., 2d Sess., *Overview of Entitlement Programs: 1994 Green Book, Background Material and Data on Programs Within the Jurisdiction of the Committee on Ways and Means* 1153 (Comm. Print 1994) (hereinafter, *1994 Green Book*).

11. *See* Edward Lazere, *A Place to Call Home* (1991).

12. DeParle, *supra* note 9, at 53. In 1994, the federal government spent $49 billion for homeowner tax breaks, and 99 percent of these tax expenditures went to households with income of $20,000 or more. Twenty thousand dollars is one and a half times the federal poverty level. *See* Michael Wines, *Taxpayers Are Angry. They're Expensive, Too,* N.Y. Times, Nov. 20, 1994, § 4, at 5.

13. *See* The U.S. Conference of Mayors, *A Status Report on Hunger and Homelessness in America's Cities, 1990: A 30-City Survey* 2 (1990) (discussing survey results that lack of affordable housing by poor persons is "the main cause of homelessness").

14. Statistics cited in Robin Wright, *Gimme Shelter: The Plight of the Homeless in Lands of Plenty,* L.A. Times, Oct. 4, 1994, C1.

15. *Id.*

16. Statistics cited in Robert C. Coates, *The Legal Rights of Homeless Americans,* 24 U.S.F. L. Rev. 297, 298 (1990). *See* William R. Breakey & Pamela J. Fischer, *Homelessness: The Extent of the Problem,* 4 J. Social Issues 31 (1990) (discussing difficulty of counting the number of homeless people).

17. The information in the rest of this chapter is drawn largely from National Housing Law Project, *HUD Housing Programs: Tenants' Rights* (2d ed. 1994) (hereinafter, *HUD Housing Programs*). Another helpful resource is Erica Silverberg & Gina Cherry, *Tenants' Rights: A Manual for Tenants Who Live in Privately Owned, Federally Subsidized Housing* (1992).

18. 42 U.S.C.A. § 1437 (West 1994); 24 C.F.R. pts. 5, 913, 941, 960, 963, 964, 965, 966, 968, 969, 970, and 990 (1996).

19. 42 U.S.C.A. § 1437 (West 1994).

20. 42 U.S.C.A. § 1437f (West 1994). Implementing regulations are located at 24 C.F.R. pts. 5, 813, 982 (1996).

21. 42 U.S.C.A. § 1437f(d)(1)(A) (West 1994).

22. *Id.* at § 1437f(c)(1) (West 1994).

23. 24 C.F.R. § 982.308(b) (1996).

24. *Id.* at § 982.405(a) (1996). The housing quality standards are set forth at *id.* at § 982.401 (1996).

25. *Id.* at § 982.153(b)(15) (1996).

26. 42 U.S.C.A. § 1437f(o) (West 1994). Implementing regulations are located at 24 C.F.R. pt. 982 (1996) and 24 C.F.R. pt. 5 (1996). HUD merged the regulations for the Section 8 Certificate program and Voucher program in Part 982 with regulations published in 1994 and 1995. *See* 59 Fed. Reg. 36682 (July 18, 1994); 60 Fed. Reg. 34660 (July 3, 1995).

27. 12 U.S.C.A. § 1715*l*(d)(3) (1994). Implementing regulations are located at 24 C.F.R. §§ 219, 221.501–.795, 245, 246, 247–48, 290 (1996). The regulations at 24 C.F.R. pt. 5 (1996) apply to § 221(d)(3) apartments receiving Section 8 rent subsidies. Relevant HUD handbooks are U.S. Dep't of Housing and Urban Dev., *Occupancy Requirements for Subsidized Multifamily Programs* 4350.3, through CHG-27 (Nov. 1981–Sept. 1995) (hereinafter *Subsidized Multifamily Programs*); U.S. Dep't of Housing and Urban Dev., *Section 8 Additional Assistance* 4350.2 (June 1992).

28. *See, e.g., Joy v. Daniels,* 479 F.2d 1236 (4th Cir. 1973); *McQueen v. Druker,* 317 F. Supp. 1122 (D. Mass. 1970), *aff'd,* 438 F.2d 781 (1st Cir. 1971); *Hahn v. Gottlieb,* 430 F.2d 1243 (1st Cir. 1970); *McKinney v. Washington,* 442 F.2d 726 (D.C. Cir. 1970); *but see Falzarano v. United States,* 607 F.2d 506 (1st Cir. 1979).

29. 12 U.S.C.A. § 1715z-1 (West 1989 & West Supp. 1996). Implementing regulations are located at 24 C.F.R. pts. 219, 236.1–.1001, 245–48, 290. The regulations at 24 C.F.R. pt. 5 (1996) also apply to Section 236 apartments receiving Section 8 rental subsidies. *Subsidized Multifamily Programs, supra* note 27.

30. *Compare Lopez v. Henry Phipps Plaza South,* 498 F.2d 937 (2d Cir. 1974) *with Weigand v. Afton View Apartments,* 473 F.2d 545 (8th Cir. 1973).

31. Pub. L. No. 93-383, 88 Stat. 662, § 201(a) (1974), *formerly codified at* 42 U.S.C.A. § 1437f(b)(2) (West 1994), *repealed for future projects by* Pub. L. No. 98-181, 97 Stat. 1153, 1183, § 209 (1983). Implementing regulations are located at 24 C.F.R. pts. 880–81 and 5 (1996). *Subsidized Multifamily Programs, supra* note 27; U.S. Dep't of Housing and Urban Dev., *New Construction Processing* (1981 with changes through 1983); U.S. Dep't of Housing and Urban Dev., *Substantial Rehabilitation Processing,* 7420.1, through CHG-1 (Feb. 1981–Dec. 1983).

32. *See Miller v. Hartwood Apartments,* 689 F.2d 1239 (5th Cir. 1982).

33. 42 U.S.C.A. § 1437f(e)(2) (West 1994). Implementing regulations are located at 24 C.F.R. §§ 882.401 *et seq.* (1994). The regulations at 24 C.F.R. pt. 5 (1996) also apply. The relevant HUD handbook is U.S. Dep't of Housing and Urban Dev., *Existing Housing and Moderate Rehabilitation Processing* 7420.3, through CHG-18 (June 1978–Feb. 1993).

34. 42 U.S.C.A. § 1437f (West 1994). Implementing regulations are set forth at 24 C.F.R. pts. 886 and 5 (1996). The relevant HUD handbook is *Subsidized Multifamily Programs, supra* note 27.

35. 24 C.F.R. § 813.107 (1996).

36. 12 U.S.C.A. § 1701(q) (West Supp. 1996). Implementing regulations are located at 24 C.F.R. pts. 245–47 and 891 (1996). The regulations at 24 C.F.R. Part 5 (1996) also apply to Section 202 apartments receiving Section 8 subsidies. The relevant HUD hand-

books include *Subsidized Multifamily Programs, supra* note 27; U.S. Dep't of Housing and Urban Dev., *Section 202 Supportive Housing for the Elderly* 4571.3 (June 1991–Apr. 1993); U.S. Dep't of Housing and Urban Dev., *Supportive Housing for Persons with Disabilities* 4571.2 (June 1991).

37. 12 U.S.C.A. § 1701q (West Supp. 1996); 42 U.S.C.A. § 8013 (West 1995).

38. 12 U.S.C.A. § 1701s (West 1989); 24 C.F.R. pts. 219, 245–47 (1996).

39. 42 U.S.C.A. § 1437f (West 1994); 24 C.F.R. pts. 883, 5 (1996).

40. 42 U.S.C.A. § 1437f(e)(2) (West 1994); 12 U.S.C.A. § 1701z-11 (West 1995); 24 C.F.R. § 886.301–.338 (1996).

41. 42 U.S.C.A. § 1437f(d)(2) (West 1994); 24 C.F.R. pt. 983 (1996).

42. 42 U.S.C.A. § 1485 (West 1994); 24 C.F.R. pt. 884 (1996). This is a Section 8 subsidy program for rental housing financed by the Farmers Home Administration. For more information, see the revised edition of National Housing Law Project, *FMHA Housing Programs: Tenants' and Purchasers' Rights.*

43. 42 U.S.C.A. § 1437aaa (West 1994).

44. 49 Fed. Reg. 43,028 (Oct. 25, 1984) (Notice of Funding Availability setting forth demonstration requirements).

45. 42 U.S.C.A. § 1437c(h) (West 1994).

46. *Id.* at § 1437s(a) (West 1994).

47. *See* Pub. L. No. 104-193, 110 Stat. 2105, § 404(h) (1996); Center for Law and Social Policy, Mark Greenberg & Steve Savner, *A Detailed Summary of Key Provisions of the Temporary Assistance for Needy Families Block Grant of H.R. 3734, The Personal Responsibility and Work Opportunity Reconciliation Act of 1996* 23–24 (Aug. 13, 1996).

48. For background, *see* U.S. Dep't of Housing and Urban Dev., Div. of Policy Studies, Office of Policy Dev. and Research, *Project Self-Sufficiency: An Interim Report on Progress and Performance* (1987)(discussion of HUD's Project Self-Sufficiency demonstration program).

49. 42 U.S.C.A. § 1437u (West 1994).

50. *Id.* at § 1437u(b)(4) (West 1994); *see also* 24 C.F.R. Part 984 (Family Self-Sufficiency Program for Public Housing and Section 8) (1996).

51. 42 U.S.C.A. § 1437u(b)(2) (West 1994).

52. *See* National Housing Law Project, *Housing Assistance Programs as an Anti-Poverty Strategy,* 24 Housing L. Bull. 51, at 51–52 (1994).

53. *Subsidized Multifamily Programs* 4350.3, *supra* note 27, ¶ 2-29e, CHG-24.

54. 42 U.S.C.A. § 3543 (West 1994); *see* 24 C.F.R. § 5.216(d)(1)(ii) (1996).

55. *Subsidized Multifamily Programs, supra* note 27, ¶ 2-25, CHG-24 (Jan. 1993).

56. 42 U.S.C.A. § 3544 (West 1994); *see* 24 C.F.R. §§ 5.210 *et seq.* (1996).

57. *See* U.S. Dep't of Housing and Urban Dev., Office of Policy Dev. and Research, *Estimated Median Family Incomes for Fiscal Year 1996* (1996).

58. *Id.*

59. 24 C.F.R. §§ 813.106(b)(Section 8); 913.106(b)(public housing) (1996).

60. *Id.*

61. For an analogy to the food stamp program, *see Johnson v. United States Dep't of Agriculture,* 734 F.2d 774 (11th Cir. 1984).

62. 42 U.S.C.A. § 1437(b)(4) (West 1994), as amended by Pub. L. No. 102-550, 106 Stat. 3672, § 103(a)(1) (1992).

63. *Subsidized Multifamily Programs, supra* note 27, at ¶ 3-20, CHG-27 (Sept. 29, 1995).

64. *See, e.g.,* 60 Fed. Reg. 17388 (April 5, 1995)(interim rule adding nine exclusions to definition of annual income; 24 C.F.R. §§ 813.106(c)(16) (Section 8), 913.106(c)(12) (public housing) (1996).

65. 24 C.F.R. §§ 813.106(c)(Section 8), 913.106(c)(public housing) (1996).

66. *Id.* at §§ 813.106(b)(3)(Section 8), 913.106(b)(3)(public housing) (1996).

67. *Id.* at §§ 813.106(c)(3)(Section 8), 913.106(c)(3)(public housing) (1996).

68. *See* 42 U.S.C.A. § 1437a(b)(3) (West 1994)(public housing and Section 8); 12 U.S.C.A. § 1715z-1(j)(2) (West 1989)(Section 236 defines family by reference to Section 221 program (12 U.S.C.A. § 1715*l* (West Supp. 1996) and elderly or handicapped family by reference to Section 202 (12 U.S.C.A. § 1701q) (West Supp. 1996)); 12 U.S.C.A. § 1715*l*(f) (West Supp. 1996) (Section 221 defines family to include singles, as well as elderly); 24 C.F.R. § 5.403 (1996)(definition of "family" for public housing and all Section 8 programs).

69. *Id.*

70. *See, e.g., Hann v. Housing Auth.,* 709 F. Supp. 605 (E.D. Pa. 1989) (invalidating eligibility requirement limiting Section 8 housing to married heterosexual parents with children); *Thomas v. Housing Auth.,* 282 F. Supp. 575 (E.D. Ark. 1967) (public housing cannot exclude unwed mothers).

71. *See* 42 U.S.C.A. § 1437a(b)(3)(A) (West 1994) (definition of single person); *see also* 24 C.F.R. § 5.403 (1996).

72. 42 U.S.C.A. § 1437a(b)(3)(C) (1994).

73. *See* Pub. L. No. 104-193, 110 Stat. 2105, § 401(b)(1)(E) (1996).

74. *See* 42 U.S.C. § 1436a(a) (1996).

75. *See* 24 C.F.R. § 5.506 (1996).

76. *See* 8 U.S.C.A. § 1255(a) (West 1996).

77. *See* 24 C.F.R. § 5.508 (1996).

78. *See id.* at § 5.506(b)(2) (1996); 42 U.S.C.A. § 1436a(b), as amended by the Illegal Immigration Reform and Immigrant Responsibility Act of 1996, § 572.

79. 24 C.F.R. § 5.06(b)(1) (1996).

80. *See id.* at § 5.516(c) (1996).

81. 42 U.S.C.A. § 1436a(c)(1), as amended by the Illegal Immigration Reform and Immigrant Responsibility Act of 1996, § 573.

82. 24 C.F.R. § 5.518 (1996).

83. *Subsidized Multifamily Programs, supra* note 27, ¶ 2-28, CHG-24 (Jan. 1993); 24 C.F.R. §§ 5.410–5.430 (1996)(selection preference regulations for public housing and all Section 8 programs).

84. *See* 24 C.F.R. § 5.420 (1996).

85. *See* Balanced Budget Downpayment Act I, Pub. L. No. 104-99, 110 Stat. 26, § 402 (1996).

86. *See* HUD Notices PIH 96-6 (HA) (issued Feb. 13, 1996; expires Sept. 30, 1996); H 96-7 (HUD) (issued Mar. 15, 1996; expires Mar. 31, 1997).

87. 24 C.F.R. § 5.420(b)(4) (1996).

88. *See id.* at § 5.420(b)(5)–(8) (1996).

89. *See id.* at § 5.425 (1996).

90. Housing and Community Development Act of 1987, § 146, 42 U.S.C.A. § 1437f(s) (West 1994).

91. *See* 24 C.F.R. §§ 982.205(c, 982.210(c)(4) (1996).

92. *See id.* (1996).

93. 59 Fed. Reg. 65842 (Dec. 21, 1994) (final rule allowing certain subsidized owners to give elderly applicants preferences); *Subsidized Multifamily Programs, supra* note 27, at ¶ 2-49, CHG-24 (Jan. 1993).

94. *See* 42 U.S.C.A. §§ 1437f(d)(1)(A)(i) (certificate), 1437f(o)(3)(B) (voucher) (West 1994); 24 C.F.R. § 5.410(d)(2)(iv) (1996).

95. 24 C.F.R. § 5.410(g) (1996).

96. *See, e.g.,* 42 U.S.C.A. § 1437a(b)(3)(B) (West 1994).

97. *Id.* at § 1437a(b)(3)(C) (West 1994).

98. *See Subsidized Multifamily Programs, supra* note 27, at ¶ 2-18, CHG-24 (Jan. 1993).

99. *See* 24 C.F.R. §§ 982.4 (1996)(definition of "family unit size"), 982.402 (requirements PHA must apply in determining unit size) (1996).

100. 42 U.S.C.A. § 1437d(c)(3) (West 1994); 24 C.F.R. §§ 960.207(a) (public housing), 982.554(a) (Section 8 certificate and voucher) (1996).

101. 42 U.S.C.A. § 1437d(c)(3) (West 1994); 24 C.F.R. § 960.207(a) (1996).

102. 24 C.F.R. § 982.554(b) (Section 8 certificate and voucher) (1996).

103. *See* Title VI of the Civil Rights Act of 1964, *codified at* 42 U.S.C.A. § 2000d (West 1996); Title VIII of the Civil Rights Act of 1968, *codified at* 42 U.S.C.A. §§ 3601 *et seq.* (West 1996); the Civil Rights Act of 1870, *codified at* 42 U.S.C.A. § 1981 (West 1996); the Civil Rights Act of 1866, *codified at* 42 U.S.C.A. § 1982 (West 1996); Section 504 of Rehabilitation Act of 1973, *codified at* 29 U.S.C.A. § 794 (West 1996); 24 C.F.R. pt. 100 (1996) (regulations implementing Fair Housing Act); 24 C.F.R. Part 8 (1996) (regulations implementing Section 504).

104. 24 C.F.R. § 966.4 (public housing) (1994); *Subsidized Multifamily Programs, supra* note 27, at Apps. 19a, 19b, and 20 (Nov. 1981) and CHG-22 at 4-2 (federally subsidized housing); 24 C.F.R. § 982.308 (1996) (Section 8 certificate and voucher lease requirements).

105. *See* 24 C.F.R. § 966.4(f)(4) (1996) (public housing); *Subsidized Multifamily Programs, supra* note 27 at ¶ 4-4, CHG-22 (federally subsidized housing).

106. 24 C.F.R. §§ 966.6 (1996) (public housing), 982.308(d) (1996) (Section 8 certificate and voucher).

107. 42 U.S.C.A. § 1437d(*l*)(1) (1994); *see, e.g., Richmond Tenants v. Richmond Development & Housing Authority,* 751 F. Supp. 1204 (E.D. Va. 1990).

108. 42 U.S.C.A. § 1437a(a) (West 1994).

109. Pub. L. No. 104-99, 110 Stat. 26, § 402 (1996)(to be codified at 42 U.S.C.A. § 1437a).

110. The Omnibus Consolidated Rescissions and Appropriations Act of 1996, Pub. L. No. 104-134, 110 Stat. 1321, § 230 (1996).

111. *See* HUD Notice H-96-51 (HUD) (issued June 12, 1996; expires June 30, 1997).

112. *See* 24 C.F.R. §§ 813.102 (Section 8), 913.102 (public housing).

113. *Id.*

114. *See, e.g., id.* at §§ 880.603(c), 982.551(h), 966.4(c)(2) (1996) (duty to report changes in family composition that affect unit size).

115. *Id.* at §§ 813.109 (Section 8), 913.109 and 960.209 (public housing) (1992); 42 U.S.C.A. §§ 1437d(c)(2) (public housing), 1437f(c)(3)(A) (Section 8) (West 1994); 12 U.S.C.A. §§ 1715z-1a (Section 236), 1701s(e)(2) (rent supplement) (West 1989).

116. *See* 24 C.F.R. § 245.305–.330 (1994) (regulations on rent increase procedure).

117. *See id.* at §§ 813.102, 913.102 (1996)(definition of "tenant rent" for all Section 8 programs and public housing).

118. *Id.* at §§ 965.476(a)(retail and check metered), 965.477(b) (master metered) (1994).

119. *See HUD Housing Programs, supra* note 17, at ch. 5.

120. *See, e.g.,* 24 C.F.R. §§ 247.3(c)(4), 880.607(b)(3), 966.4(*l*)(2), 982.310(a) (1996).

121. *See Subsidized Multifamily Programs, supra* note 27, at ¶ 4-15, CHG-22 (June 1992) and App. 19a, ¶ 5 (Nov. 1981).

122. 24 C.F.R. § 966.4(b)(5) (1996).

123. *Subsidized Multifamily Programs, supra* note 27, at ¶ 4-8(b)(3), CHG-22 (June 1992).

124. 24 C.F.R. § 982.313(b) (1996).

125. *See Subsidized Multifamily Programs, supra* note 27, at ¶ 4-10, CHG-22 (June 1992) (interest on security deposits); *see also* 24 C.F.R. § 982.313(c) (1996).

126. 12 U.S.C.A. § 1701r-1(a) (West 1989); 24 C.F.R. § 5.300 (1996).

127. 24 C.F.R. §§ 5.315, 5.318 (1996).

128. *See* 24 C.F.R. pt. 100 (1996).

129. 29 U.S.C.A. § 794 (West Pamph. Supp. 1996); 42 U.S.C.A. § 12132 (West 1995).

130. *See, e.g., Majors v. Dekalb Co. Hous. Auth.,* 652 F.2d 454 (5th Cir. 1981)(PHA's failure to allow a disabled tenant a pet could violate the Rehabilitation Act of 1973).

131. 42 U.S.C.A. § 1437 (West 1994).

132. *Id.* at § 1437d(*l*)(2) (West 1994); *see* 24 C.F.R. § 966.4(e) (1996) (PHA's maintenance obligations in public housing).

133. *See* 24 C.F.R. § 966.53(a) (1996) (definition of grievance).

134. *See, e.g., Kline v. 1500 Massachusetts Ave. Apt. Corp.,* 439 F.2d 477, 478 (D.C. Cir. 1970).

135. *See* 24 C.F.R. pt. 964 (1996).

136. *Id.* at §§ 966.3, 966.5 (1996).

137. *Id.* at § 966.55(b)(2) (1996).

138. *Id.* at § 966.4(c) (1996).

139. *Id.* at § 965.407(c) (1996).

140. *See, e.g.*, 42 U.S.C.A. § 1437f(d)(1)(A)(iii) (West 1994) (Section 8 certificate applicant may be denied preference for admissions for three years if evicted for drug-related activity); 24 C.F.R. § 982.552(b)(2) (1996) (PHA may deny Section 8 certificate or voucher if any member of the family has ever been evicted from public housing).

141. *See, e.g.*, *McQueen v. Druker*, 317 F. Supp. 1122 (D. Mass. 1970), *aff'd*, 438 F.2d 781 (1st Cir. 1981).

142. *See, e.g.*, *Caramico v. Sect'y of the Dep't of HUD*, 509 F.2d 694 (2d Cir. 1974).

143. *See, e.g.*, *Thorpe v. Housing Auth.*, 386 U.S. 670, 679–80 (1967) (Douglas, J., concurring).

144. *Compare Charlotte Housing Auth. v. Patterson*, 464 S.E.2d 68 (Ct. App. N.C. 1995) and *Diversified Realty Group Inc. v. Davis*, 628 N.E.2d 1081 (Ill. App. 1993) (both courts refusing to evict tenant for illegal conduct of household member or guest committed without tenant's knowledge) *with Housing Auth. of New Orleans v. Green*, 657 So. 2d 552 (Ct. App. La. 1995), *writ of cert. denied*, 661 So. 2d 1355 (La. 1995)(with two judges dissenting from refusal to grant writ) and *City of San Francisco Housing Auth. v. Guillory*, 49 Cal. Rptr. 2d (367) (Cal. Super. 1995)(both courts applying strict liability standard in upholding eviction of tenant for illegal conduct of guest or household member).

145. 42 U.S.C.A. §§ 1437d(*l*)(5) (public housing), 1437f(d)(1)(B)(iii) (West 1994) (Section 8 certificate). Congress recently enacted a law requiring PHAs to provide in their leases for eviction for drug-related criminal activity "on or off" PHA property. *See* Housing Opportunity Program Extension Act of 1996, Pub. L. No. 104-120, 110 Stat. 834, § 9(a) (1996).

146. *See, e.g.*, 24 C.F.R. §§ 247.3(c)(4), 880.607(b)(3), 966.4(*l*)(2) (1996).

147. *See* 24 C.F.R. §§ 247.4(c)(good cause termination shall be effective at end of a term), 247.3(b) (notice of good cause) (1996).

148. *See, e.g.*, *McKenna v. Peekskill Hous. Auth.*, 647 F.2d 332 (2d Cir. 1981); *Messiah Baptist Hous. Dev. Fund Co. v. Rosser*, 92 Misc. 2d 383, 400 N.Y.S.2d 306 (1977).

149. Public housing lease regulations require a tenant to secure permission from the PHA before adding a new member to the household. *See* 24 C.F.R. § 966.4(d)(1) and (f)(3) (1996).

150. *See HUD Housing Programs, supra* note 17, at § 14.2.6.3.

151. *See* 24 C.F.R. § 966.4(j) (1996) (public housing lease regulations).

152. *Id.* at §§ 966.4(*1*)(2) (public housing), 247.2(a), 247.3(a) (federally subsidized housing).

153. *See* 24 C.F.R. §§ 982.309–.310 (1996).

154. *See* Omnibus Consolidated Rescissions and Appropriations Act of 1996, Pub. L. No. 104-134, 110 Stat, 1321, § 203 (1996).

155. *See Thomas v. Chicago Housing Auth.*, 919 F. Supp. 1159, 1167 (N.D. Ill. 1996) (finding that tenant stated cause of action on First Amendment claim); *Herring v. Chicago*

Hous. Auth., 850 F. Supp. 694 (N.D. Ill. 1994) (PHA violated tenant's First Amendment right of association); *Crowder v. Hous. Auth.*, 990 F.2d 586 (11th Cir. 1993) (PHA's complete ban on tenant's Bible studies violated First Amendment).

156. *Thorpe v. Housing Auth.*, 386 U.S. at 670, 678–79 (1967); *see also Davis v. Village Park II Realty Co.*, 578 F.2d 461 (2d Cir. 1978); *McQueen v. Druker*, 438 F.2d 781 (1st Cir. 1971); *Rudder v. United States*, 226 F.2d 51 (D.C. Cir. 1955).

157. 24 C.F.R. § 245.105 (1996).

158. *See HUD Housing Programs, supra* note 17, at § 14.2.9.1; *Edwards v. Habib*, 397 F.2d 687, 700 (D.C. Cir. 1968), *cert. denied*, 393 U.S. 1016 (1969) (barring private retaliatory eviction as violation of "a strong and pervasive congressional concern to secure for the city's slum dwellers decent, or at least safe and sanitary, places to live").

159. 42 U.S.C.A. § 1437a(b)(3)(C) (West 1994).

160. *See id.* at § 1437d(k); 24 C.F.R. § 966.51 (1996).

161. *See* 24 C.F.R. § 5.403(b) (1996) (definition of family); *NSA North Flatbush Associates v. Mackie*, 632 N.Y.S.2d 388 (N.Y. Co. Civ. Ct. 1995)(discussing eligibility of remaining family member to remain in occupancy).

162. *See HUD Housing Programs, supra* note 17, at § 14.2.6.4.

163. 24 C.F.R. § 982.310(d) (1996).

164. *See, e.g., id.* at § 247.6(a), (c) (1996); *Leake v. Ellicott Redev. Phase II*, 470 F. Supp. 600 (W.D.N.Y. 1979).

165. 24 C.F.R. §§ 966.4(*l*)(3), (n), 966.54 (1996).

166. *See id.* at §§ 880.607(c)(1), 881.607(c)(1), 883.708(c)(1) (1996); *Subsidized Multifamily Programs, supra* note 27, at App. 19a, ¶ 23(c), CHG-22 (June 1992).

167. 24 C.F.R. § 982.310(e) (1996).

168. 42 U.S.C.A. § 1437d(*l*)(3) (West 1994); 24 C.F.R. § 966.4(*l*)(3)(i) (1996).

169. *Id.*

170. *Subsidized Multifamily Programs, supra* note 27, at App. 19a, ¶ 23(c), CHG-22 (June 1992).

171. *See* 24 C.F.R. § 247.4(c) (1996).

172. *Id.* at § 247.4(c) (1994).

173. *Id.* at § 982.310(e) (1996).

174. *Id.* at § 966.4(k) (1996).

175. *Id.* at § 247.4(b) (1996).

176. *Id.* at § 982.310(e) (1996).

177. *See id.* at § 982.555 (1996)(informal hearing requirements).

178. *Id.* at § 982.555 (c), (e) (1996).

179. *Id.* at § 966.56 (1996).

180. *See, e.g., id.* at § 880.607(c)(1) (1996); *Subsidized Multifamily Programs, supra* note 27, at ¶ 4-21, CHG-22.

181. *See Samuels v. District of Columbia*, 770 F.2d 184 (D.C. Cir. 1986), *on remand*, 650 F. Supp. 482 (D.D.C. 1986).

182. *See* Housing Opportunity Program Extension Act, Pub. L. No. 104-120, 110 Stat. 834, § 9(a) (1996).

183. 42 U.S.C.A. § 1437d(k) (West 1994), *as amended by* Pub. L. No. 101-625, 104 Stat. 4079, § 503 (1990); 24 C.F.R. §§ 966.51(a)(2), 966.55(g) (1996).

184. 24 C.F.R. § 966.4(*l*)(3)(v) (1996); *see Housing Auth. of City of Newark v. Raindrop*, 670 A.2d 1087 (N.J. Super. D. Ct. App. Div. 1996) (holding in favor of tenant because PHA eviction notice did not comply with regulations).

185. 24 C.F.R. § 966.54 (1994); *see, e.g., Housing Auth. of New Iberia v. Austin*, 478 So. 2d 1012 (La. Ct. App. 1985), *writ denied*, 481 So. 2d 1334 (La. 1986)(tenant's failure either to write or to call PHA to request a conference within five-day period specified in notice of termination constitutes waiver of right to continued occupancy).

186. *Samuels v. District of Columbia*, 669 F. Supp. 1133 (D.D.C. 1987).

187. 24 C.F.R. § 966.55(c) (1996).

188. *Id.* at § 966.55(e)(1996).

189. *See, e.g., Escalera v. New York City Hous. Auth.*, 425 F.2d 853 (2d Cir. 1970), *cert. denied*, 400 U.S. 853 (1970).

190. 42 U.S.C.A. § 1437d(k)(3) (1995); 24 C.F.R. § 966.56(b)(1) (1996).

191. 24 C.F.R. § 966.56(b)(3) (1996).

192. *Id.* at § 966.56(b)(4) (1996).

193. *See, e.g., Escalera*, 425 F.2d at 862–63.

194. 24 C.F.R. § 966.56(g) (1996).

195. *Id.* at § 966.57 (1996).

V

Education

Does the federal Constitution guarantee a right to education?

No. The United States Supreme Court has not yet found a right to education under the federal Constitution. In the landmark decision of *San Antonio Independent School District v. Rodriguez*,[1] the Court held that education "is not among the rights afforded explicit protection under our federal Constitution" and refused to "find any basis for saying it is implicitly so protected."[2] Although the Court recognized "the vital role of education in a free society,"[3] it nevertheless found that the supervision of public schools is more properly a duty of local school boards than of federal courts. Thirteen years later, in *Papasan v. Allain*,[4] the Court stated that the *Rodriguez* decision had not "definitively settled the question whether a minimally adequate education is a fundamental right."[5] But later in *Kadrmas v. Dickinson School District*,[6] the Court again declined to recognize such a right.

The absence of an explicit federal constitutional right to education stands in marked contrast to international human rights norms.[7] For example, Article 26 of the Universal Declaration of Human Rights declares: "[E]veryone has the right to education. Education shall be free, at least in the elementary and fundamental stages. . . . Education shall be directed to the full development of the human personality and to the full strengthening of respect for human rights and fundamental freedoms."[8] Many commentators believe that education deserves federal constitutional protection because it is a foundational aspect of the right to vote, of the right to petition government, and of the right to free speech. Certainly an educated citizenry is essential to democratic life.[9] It nevertheless seems unlikely that the Court as presently constituted will recognize a right to an adequate education under the federal Constitution.

Do state constitutions guarantee a right to education?

Yes. All fifty states have constitutions providing for the establishment of free public schools.[10] Although state constitutional language varies from state to state, broad similarities can be found in education clauses across the country. The Alabama Constitution, for example, requires the state to "establish, organize and maintain a liberal system of public schools."[11] The Montana Constitution declares, "It is the goal of the people to establish a system of education which will develop the full educational potential of each person."[12] And the New Hampshire Constitution recognizes "knowledge and learning, generally diffused through a community, to be essential to the preservation of a free government."[13]

Although education is a constitutional duty of the state, funding for public schools typically relies on local property taxes. The quality of education that a child receives thus often depends on the wealth of the community in which she or he lives. Because property wealth is unevenly distributed throughout a state, school districts vary considerably in the revenue they can raise to support local education. Poor and minority children, frequently living in low-wealth communities, too often are relegated to schools that lack sufficient funding for even the basics of a minimally adequate education.[14]

In many communities, parents have gone to court to enforce their children's state constitutional right to an adequate education. In some of these lawsuits, parents claim that the state has a duty to create a public school system that distributes educational opportunities equitably, without regard to local wealth, and that educational resources must also be adequate to afford all students a chance to achieve high standards.

In response to these lawsuits, courts in about one-third of the states have struck down school funding methods and in some states have even found entire public school systems to be unconstitutional. These court victories have precipitated legislative efforts to provide increased funding for education and, in some states, to restructure public schools in ways that are important for poor children.[15]

If you are concerned about the quality of your child's education, as a first step you should speak with his or her teacher or principal. You should also contact other parents to exchange information and ideas about how to improve the quality of your school and to obtain resources that may be lacking. You might also consider participating in educational decisions that affect your child's school life. If you believe that your school system needs systemwide change, you should consult with a legal services or legal aid lawyer about ways to use the courts to enforce rights you may already have.[16]

The rest of this chapter describes the right to a free, quality education as it exists under state and federal law. Some educational programs are targeted to low-income children, while others provide services to children with special educational needs regardless of income. Almost all of these programs allow parents to participate in decisionmaking about their child's schooling. In addition, this chapter discusses tracking, suspension, and expulsion and how they affect the educational opportunities of low-income children. Finally, the chapter includes information about federal programs that help low-income students obtain an education beyond high school.

Is a child required to attend school?

Yes. Every state, as well as the District of Columbia, Puerto Rico, and the Virgin Islands, has enacted a compulsory school attendance law requiring parents and guardians to send children of prescribed ages to school. The term "school age" refers to the entry-level age generally set within states by school districts. If state law requires all public school districts in a state to provide kindergarten for eligible children, then the school district will determine the entry age for kindergarten. For example, a school district may decide that a child must be age 5 by August 1 of the year she or he wishes to attend kindergarten. You should contact your neighborhood school to find out the entry age for your child.

A parent or guardian can choose to send a child to public school or to private school.[17] A family that chooses to send a child to private school is generally responsible for the payment of tuition, fees, and expenses, although some states have established voucher programs to subsidize a part of these costs for poor children.[18] In addition, some states permit parents and guardians to educate their children at home, as long as the "home schooling" program meets state requirements.[19] In all states, it is a crime not to provide a child with some form of schooling.[20]

Must a child attend school for his or her family to receive welfare?

It depends. Under the AFDC program, some states reduced or terminated a household's welfare if a dependent child did not regularly attend school. Wisconsin was the first state to impose this requirement, which is referred to as "Learnfare."[21] Studies of Learnfare in Wisconsin failed to establish any improvement in teenage school attendance patterns.[22] Under the

1996 welfare act, states have the option of withholding "temporary assistance" benefits if a participating household's dependent children do not regularly attend school.[23] In addition, federal law requires states to withhold temporary assistance payments from teen parents whose children are older than twelve months unless the teen parent successfully completes high school or its equivalent, or works toward a high school diploma or its equivalent, or participates in an alternative education or training program.[24] States will begin implementing these provisions as they put their new temporary assistance block grant programs into effect (implementation must begin no later than July 1997).[25]

If your welfare benefits are reduced or terminated because your child is considered truant, you should speak with a school guidance counselor about how to encourage regular attendance. You should also talk to a legal services or legal aid lawyer about how to restore your welfare payments.

Does a child have to reside in a state to attend its public schools for free?

It depends on the state in which you want your child to attend school. The United States Supreme Court has held that states can limit tuition-free education to residents, but only if the residence requirement is "bona fide," "appropriately defined," and "uniformly applied" to further "a substantial state interest."[26] In approving good faith residence requirements, the Court recognized their importance to "the proper planning and operation" of a state's school system.[27]

A majority of states have enacted residence requirements.[28] These laws generally allow a child to establish residence separate from his or her parents, but only if the child is not in the school district solely to attend its public schools.[29] Some states require the parent or guardian to provide written documentation of the child's living arrangements.[30] Residence requirements may not be used to exclude otherwise eligible homeless children from a community's public schools.[31]

Can public schools charge fees for tuition, instructional materials, and school-related activities?

Generally no, if the fee is for an educational service or activity that relates to a core curricular function. Even if the service or activity is not considered central, courts have typically required schools to establish waiver procedures for children whose families are indigent.

Under this standard, state courts have almost universally interpreted state constitutional guarantees of a free public school education to bar states from charging tuition to students.[32] Because public education must be tuition-free, schools may also not charge students for textbooks or other materials that are required as part of daily instructional activities.[33]

In some states, however, courts have upheld school fees, even for essential services like instructional material and transportation, where the state has a procedure to waive charges for indigent students.[34] If your school charges a fee for a particular service or activity, you should ask the principal or administrator whether a waiver is available, and you can request that your inquiry be treated in confidence.[35] Some states have specific school-fee waiver statutes and regulations, and local policy cannot be more restrictive than state law.[36] Eligibility for fee waivers is generally based on family income, and the school should presumptively waive its fee if your household income is less than 200 percent of the federal poverty index, if your child is eligible for free or reduced-price school meals or food stamps, or if your family receives welfare.

Courts have allowed states to charge fees, even without a waiver for indigence, for services and activities that are considered extra or incidental. Indeed, despite the importance of extracurricular activities, some courts have upheld fees for activities like summer school[37] and nonacademic courses (for example, behind-the-wheel sessions of driver-education courses).[38] If a school fee prevents your child from participating in an extracurricular activity that is "educational in nature," you should speak to a legal services lawyer about requesting a fee waiver.[39]

Can a public school punish a student who cannot pay a fee for books or other services?

No. If a student cannot pay a fee for books or other school services, the school cannot suspend the child, lower his or her grade, or otherwise treat the student unfavorably. Apart from the question of whether a particular fee is unlawful or must be waived, constitutional rights may be violated if a school punishes a child for parental indigence or for family actions that the student cannot control.[40]

Can a public school exclude children because of race, gender, or condition?

No. Forty years ago, in the historic decision of *Brown v. Board of Education*,[41] the United States Supreme Court declared it a violation of equal protection of law for public schools to exclude or segregate children because of their race or color. As the Court explained:

Today, education is perhaps the most important function of state and local governments. Compulsory school attendance laws and the great expenditures for education both demonstrate our recognition of the importance of education to our democratic society. It is required in the performance of our most basic public responsibilities, even service in the armed forces. It is the very foundation of good citizenship. Today it is a principal instrument in awakening the child to cultural values, in preparing him for later professional training, and in helping him to adjust normally to his environment. In these days, it is doubtful that any child may reasonably be expected to succeed in life if he is denied the opportunity of an education. Such an opportunity, where the state has undertaken to provide it, is a right which must be made available to all on equal terms.[42]

The principle of *Brown* has been extended and reaffirmed to guarantee access to equal educational opportunity for all children, regardless of race, color, or national origin.[43]

Since *Brown*, numerous federal statutes, regulations, and judicial decisions have barred states from excluding specific categories of eligible school-age children from the public schools or from refusing to allow these children to participate fully in academic and extracurricular activities: children with disabilities; children whose immigration status is not documented; children who have only limited proficiency in the English language; children who are pregnant or parenting; and children who are homeless. Federal civil rights laws also prohibit educational programs that receive federal funds from discriminating on the basis of race, ethnicity, gender, and color.[44]

Can a public school exclude a child with disabilities?

No. Federal law prohibits public schools from excluding children with disabilities, regardless of the severity of the disability.[45] When Congress enacted the Education for All Handicapped Children Act in 1975, one million of the nation's eight million children with disabilities were excluded from the public schools and three million were not receiving an appropriate education.[46] Federal law now requires that all public schools provide a free appropriate public education, together with necessary support services, to children with disabilities from age 3 through 21.[47] Moreover, to the maximum extent possible, the public school must include the disabled child in a regular classroom setting with nondisabled peers.[48] A free, appropriate public education must also be provided to children with disabilities who are in hospitals, mental health institutions, and correctional institutions.

Can a public school exclude a child whose immigration status is not documented?

No. In 1982 in the case of *Plyler v. Doe*,[49] the United States Supreme Court held that the Fourteenth Amendment to the federal Constitution prohibits states from denying undocumented school-age children the same education they provide to children who are citizens or lawfully admitted aliens. Any other result, the Court explained, would mark the excluded immigrant children with "[t]he stigma of illiteracy" and create a permanent "underclass." The Court further stated: "[E]ducation has a fundamental role in maintaining the fabric of our society. We cannot ignore the significant social costs borne by our nation when select groups are denied the means to absorb the values and skills upon which our social order rests."[50]

Despite *Plyler v. Doe*, the State of California recently amended its state constitution to deny education services to children whose immigration status is undocumented. Advocates have challenged this action as a violation of the federal Constitution, and a state court issued a temporary restraining order to maintain educational services for the children while the case is being litigated.[51]

Can a public school exclude a child who does not speak English?

No. Public schools cannot exclude children who do not speak English or who have only limited proficiency in English.[52] Exclusion of language-minority children is considered discrimination on the basis of ethnicity and a violation of Title VI of the Civil Rights Act of 1964.[53]

Can a public school exclude a student who is pregnant or a parent?

No. Federal civil rights law prevents public schools from excluding school-age children who are pregnant or parenting, or from otherwise penalizing such students because of their condition or family status.[54] A student who is pregnant or a parent cannot be barred because of this condition or status from required school-related programs or from programs equivalent to a school-run activity.[55] These include work study, cooperative employment, student teaching, vocational internship, and foreign studies.

Can adults who have not completed high school return to school and receive a free education?

Yes. A number of federally funded programs are available to allow adults who have not completed high school to return to school. Some programs are offered at no cost; others require the payment of tuition.

In addition, under the 1996 welfare act, some adults who have not completed high school will be required to earn a high school diploma or its equivalent as a condition of receiving benefits under state programs established under the "Temporary Assistance for Needy Families" block grant. The new law, which was enacted in August 1996, allows states to sanction families that receive TANF benefits unless any adult household member who is older than age 20 and younger than age 51 has a high school diploma or is working to attain one.[56]

Federal law provides low-income adults with a number of opportunities to continue their education. The Carl D. Perkins Vocational and Applied Technology Education Act allows adults who are single parents, displaced homemakers, or single pregnant women to attend public high school, a post-secondary technical school, or a community college.[57] Similarly, under the federal Even Start Family Literacy Program, low-income adults who are parents of children from birth to age 7 may be eligible to attend school at no cost.[58] Even Start participants can receive an educational assessment, developmental and support services, child care, transportation, high-quality instructional programs, and home-based programs on a year-round basis.[59] Not all school districts operate these programs. But if you are interested in participating, you should contact your local high school or community college for additional information.

PRESCHOOL PROGRAMS

Are there federal education programs for indigent preschool children?

Yes. The federal government provides free educational services to indigent infants, toddlers, and preschool children through two programs: Early Intervention Services and Head Start. Both programs are designed to help low-income children become ready for school as a first step toward learning and academic achievement.

What are Early Intervention Services?

Early Intervention is a federally funded program for children who are delayed in development (including those who are disabled) and in some states for children who are "at risk" of slow development. Congress adopted the Early Intervention Act in 1986 as Part H of the Individuals with Disabilities Education Act.[60] Recognizing the critical link between a child's ability to learn and his or her early childhood development, the act authorizes federal funds for states to provide education and other services to children, from birth to age 3. Children with disabilities are eligible for the program, and in a handful of states, children who are at risk of developmental delay are also eligible. Arkansas, California, Colorado, Guam, Hawaii, Indiana, Massachusetts, Michigan, New Hampshire, New Mexico, and North Carolina are states that currently have Early Intervention Services programs serving at-risk children, although each state's definition of developmental delay differs.

How do you enroll a child in an Early Intervention Services program?

Each state keeps a directory, updated each year, of all its Early Intervention Services programs. Different agencies run the program in each state, but the most common departments are education, health, mental health, human services, and welfare or public assistance. One of those departments should be able to identify the appropriate agency in your state and help you to obtain the directory of available programs.

A child can be referred to the program by several different sources. By law, however, a parent or guardian can also directly refer a child for evaluation by contacting one of the programs.

Each state has its own eligibility criteria. If a child qualifies, the entire family will be entitled to free services[61] (but participation is voluntary). The kinds of services that are provided include physical therapy, speech therapy, nursing and health services, early education services, nutritional planning, family training and counseling, and transportation.

What is Head Start?

Head Start is a federally funded program designed to provide enrichment opportunities and support services to disadvantaged infants, toddlers, and preschoolers.[62] Head Start services are free.[63] Although Head Start enrolls more than forty thousand children each year,[64] it is not an entitlement program, which means that there are not enough places for all eligible children who want to participate. Federal regulations require that at least 90 percent of the enrolled children be from low-income families,[65] and generally 10 percent of the participants must also be children with disabilities or children who are experiencing developmental delays.[66] If a child has not yet entered kindergarten or first grade, she or he may be eligible to participate in Head Start.[67]

How do you enroll a child in Head Start?

You can apply to enroll your child at any time during the program year.[68] Enrollment decisions are made at the site where the program takes place. You can obtain a list of Head Start programs in your community by contacting the regional office of the Administration for Children and Families, which is part of the United States Department of Health and Human Services.

When you apply, you will be asked to give the Head Start agency various information, including your name, address, the name of your child, the child's birthday, and your family income. You will have to verify the income information that you submit through such documents as an income tax return, pay stubs, written statements from an employer, or documentation of your status as a welfare recipient. If the program in your neighborhood cannot accept any more children, you should ask to have your child's name placed on a waiting list so you can be contacted if a vacancy occurs.[69] You can also apply to more than one center at a time.

Once your child is enrolled in Head Start, the presumption is that she or he can continue to participate until a local kindergarten or first-grade program is available.[70] Income eligibility for a child lasts through the next enrollment year.[71] If your child repeatedly does not attend class, the program should not consider her or his slot vacant but rather should discuss with you the reasons for the absenteeism and provide family support services if appropriate.[72]

What services does Head Start provide?

Head Start programs provide a half-day preschool setting to enrolled children. The programs are intended to encourage a child's social, intellectual, physical, and emotional development through a variety of learning environments. They also provide the child with nutritious foods, as well as access to comprehensive health services, including preventive, medical, dental, mental health, and nutrition services.[73]

Head Start contains a number of guarantees to ensure high-quality service. Every local program must meet personnel standards regarding class size and training. Every classroom must have at least one teacher, one teacher's aide, and preferably a volunteer as well.[74] The teachers must be appropriately educated[75] and the volunteers appropriately trained.[76] Class size cannot exceed twenty for 4- and 5-year-olds and must be even smaller for younger children.[77] Classes meet four or five days a week (over 120 days per year) for at least three and one-half hours per day.[78] In home-based programs, the child must receive at least one visit per week (with make-ups) and two group activities per month. Each home visitor is allowed to serve a maximum of twelve families.[79]

In addition, each Head Start program must develop a plan for implementing performance standards in the areas of education, health, and social services.[80] If the program serves children with disabilities, the plan must also specifically address the needs of such children.[81] Finally, every three years, Head Start is required to conduct a community-needs assessment.[82]

Can a parent participate in a community's Head Start program?
Yes. Head Start is built on the premise that parents are the "prime educators of their children,"[83] and the program provides parents with many opportunities to become involved.[84] Parent participation is entirely voluntary,[85] but if you choose, you can participate in decisions affecting your child's program; work in the program as a volunteer, observer, or paid employee; interact with other program parents; or work with your child in program activities.[86] Parents are the sole members of the Head Start Center Committee, which is responsible for working with the program in its day-to-day operation, including the development of curriculum. Parents also make up 50 percent of the members of the Head Start Policy Council, which is responsible for personnel decisions, setting eligibility criteria, and approving local centers.[87] If you want to participate in your child's Head Start program, contact the local director for additional information.

Goals 2000

What is Goals 2000?
Goals 2000 is a major federal initiative to improve the quality of America's public schools and to ensure that all children, including poor children, are encouraged to meet high academic standards.[88] Goals 2000 is built on the principle that all children can learn at high levels, and policy-makers are optimistic that the program will improve the quality of education provided to indigent children.[89] Under Goals 2000, participating states receive fed-

eral funds that can be used in local education-reform efforts, including additional resources for overall school improvement, teacher training, professional development, and parent and community involvement.[90] States are also encouraged to use Goals 2000 funds to develop new content standards (what will be taught), performance standards (what schools expect students to do), and assessment measures (how schools find out if students are achieving at levels that meet the performance standards).

Can indigent parents participate in the Goals 2000 program?

Yes. The Goals 2000 program provides important opportunities to indigent parents to participate in school decisionmaking. The act calls for the establishment of parent-information and resource centers to provide training, information, and support to parents.[91] In order to receive federal funding, a center must demonstrate that it will meet the needs of parents of "minority, low-income, and other individuals and groups that have an interest in compensatory education and family literacy."[92]

Parents should also be able to participate in education-improvement panels that every state must establish after the first year of Goals 2000 funding. The law says that these panels must be "broad-based."[93] School districts that receive Goals 2000 funds must establish their own "broad-based" improvement panels.[94] These panels develop state and school district improvement plans.[95] Once plans are developed, the state and school district must consult closely with parents to implement and monitor them.[96] By participating in a state's Goals 2000 program, an individual can help shape a local educational system and make it more responsive to the needs of low-income children.

TITLE I

What is Title I?

Title I of the Improving America's Schools Act of 1994, also known as Chapter 1, is the federal government's major response to the educational needs of poor children.[97] It is the largest federal elementary and secondary education program in the country, serving more than five million children in approximately 50 percent of all public schools.[98] Title I funds are allocated to local educational agencies to enable them to provide extra educational services to students who are failing or who are most at risk of failing to meet state performance standards.[99] The amount of such funding is based on the number of low-income families in the school district.[100]

Title I began in 1965 as part of the nation's War on Poverty in the belief that improved educational opportunities would provide indigent children with a road out of poverty and would also enhance the economic health of the country. During its first twenty years, Title I focused essentially on remedial education and the development of basic skills, relying on "pullout" programs that separated participating children from the regular classroom. Reports indicate that Title I contributed to higher achievement among poor children who participated in the program, although it did not "close the gap with 'non-needy' students."[101] Moreover, some educators objected that by relying on pullout programs to teach basic reading and math, Title I caused participating students to miss entire subjects such as social studies and science and prevented them from developing higher-order skills.

Congress responded to these criticisms in 1988, amending the law to ensure that schools receiving Title I funds help eligible children to attain grade level, to succeed in the regular classroom, and to achieve the basic and more advanced skills expected of all children.[102] In 1994, Congress reinforced the requirements of the 1988 law and sought to improve Title I still further by including it under the umbrella of the Goals 2000: Educate America Act.[103] If your state has developed or adopted challenging content and performance standards that all children are expected to meet, those same high standards now apply to children receiving extra educational services through Title I.[104] Title I is thus critical to education reform for low-income, low-achieving students.

Are there different types of Title I programs?

Yes. Public schools can qualify for one of two types of Title I programs: schoolwide or targeted assistance.[105] In a schoolwide program, at least 60 percent of the school's students come from low-income families.[106] A schoolwide program can use its Title I funds in combination with other federal, state, and local funds to improve the school's entire educational program, thereby serving all children in the school.[107] By contrast, a targeted assistance school can use its Title I funds only for students who are failing or who are most at risk of failing to meet the state's student performance standards.[108] Generally, in a targeted assistance school the number of children from low-income families does not meet the requirements of a schoolwide program.[109]

How can schools use Title I funds?

Title I funds are meant to supplement, not supplant, state or local educational funds[110] and therefore must be used to provide extra educational services to eligible students[111] to assist them to meet challenging state standards (or until these standards are in place, to achieve the basic and more advanced skills expected of all children). Schools can do this in many ways.[112] Schools may hire teachers, aides, and tutors to work with children; they may provide family literacy programs; they may conduct training of all school personnel; and they may purchase materials and equipment. Schools may use their Title I funds for before- and after-school, weekend, or summer school programs.[113] In schoolwide programs, Title I funds may be used to assist all students, including such strategies as reducing class size and increasing staffing to two teachers per classroom.

Schools must use effective instructional practices that minimize "pull out" programs during regular school hours[114] and that assist participating children in meeting state performance standards.[115] Most important, schools must provide qualified teachers[116] who will coordinate and support the regular education program.[117]

Can a parent participate in a child's Title I program?

Yes. The 1994 amendments to Title I strengthened its parental participation requirements. Indeed, although the law authorizes schools to seek waivers of many requirements, the parental involvement sections of Title I may not be waived.[118] Moreover, schools must set aside 1 percent of the total amount of Title I funds they receive to support parental involvement activities.[119] A parent of a child participating in Title I has the right to be involved in deciding how the 1 percent is allocated.[120]

Title I requires participating schools and school districts to work with parents in an organized, ongoing, and timely way on all aspects of the Title I program.[121] For example, school staff from your child's school, as well as from the district, should assist and encourage you to participate in your child's education,[122] to write your school's parental involvement policy[123] and school-parent compact,[124] to implement parental involvement activities,[125] to identify children most in need of services,[126] to develop a Title I school plan,[127] and to develop or revise the school improvement plan.[128] Parents can obtain training and materials to accomplish these goals.[129]

Also, every year your child's school must convene a meeting with parents of participating children to inform you about Title I and to explain your parental involvement rights.[130] The school should schedule as many meetings as necessary to reach parents, and these meetings should be at a variety of times, i.e., morning, afternoon, and evening, to accommodate different parent schedules.[131] The school may provide transportation, child care, home visits, and other services to improve parental involvement and enable parents to attend meetings about Title I.[132] Schools must make every effort to accommodate parents with disabilities and parents who are learning English as a second language, including providing information and school profiles in languages and forms that can be understood.[133]

What is a parental involvement policy?

The "parental involvement policy" is a written document that describes Title I parental involvement activities.[134] Your child's school and the school district must jointly develop the written policy with you.[135] Parents must agree with the policy and the school must distribute it to all parents of children receiving Title I services.[136] If your child's school already has a parental involvement policy that applies to all parents, the school, together with parents of children receiving Title I services, may revise the existing policy to incorporate the requirements of Title I.[137] You are entitled to meaningful consultation on the drafting, planning, and implementation of the policy.[138]

What is a School-Parent Compact?

The School-Parent Compact is an important part of the school-level parental involvement policy. Your child's school must develop the compact jointly with you and other parents of students receiving Title I services. The compact describes how parents, school staff, and students will share responsibility for ensuring improved student achievement[139] and student success at meeting state performance standards.[140] Among its specific requirements, the compact must describe the school's responsibility to provide high quality curriculum and instruction in a supportive and effective learning environment.[141] In addition, the compact should list the parent's responsibility with respect to such activities as the child's attendance, homework, and television viewing habits.[142]

Through the compact, parents and school staff should also address the importance of ongoing communication.[143] At least once a year, parents of elementary school students and their teachers should meet to discuss the children's achievement and how the compact is working toward ensuring progress.[144] Further, schools, at a minimum, should provide frequent reports on your child's progress, as well as reasonable access to school staff, including opportunities to visit, participate, observe, and volunteer in your child's classroom.[145]

If you want to be part of drafting the School-Parent Compact, let the principal of your child's school know. This is a new requirement and some school personnel may not know about it or may be unsure about how to go about developing the compact. Sometimes schools merely repeat the legal requirements listed above without spelling out how those requirements will be met. Such a compact is inadequate. To make the compact represent a meaningful partnership, parents and school personnel must prepare for its drafting. You will need time to think about what role you can play in your child's education, to work with other parents and school staff to identify the needs of students, and to decide jointly how to meet those needs through specifically described responsibilities.

What can a parent do if the school's Title I program does not improve his or her child's academic achievement?

Schools must give you the opportunity to be involved in decisions relating to your child's education and provide you with timely responses to your suggestions or concerns.[146] To ensure that you are able to participate fully, the school must describe and explain the school's curriculum, the proficiency levels expected of your child, and the forms of assessments used to evaluate her or his progress.[147] You are also entitled to your child's assessment results (including scores and interpretation of the scores in light of the student performance standards) and the school profiles that describe the results of the annual assessment of all students served by Title I.[148]

Schools are accountable under the law to ensure that all participating children receive the assistance they need to meet the proficient and advanced levels of the state performance standards.[149] Any school that does not make adequate yearly progress toward that goal for two consecutive years must initiate a school improvement plan.[150] The school must consult with parents to develop or revise an improvement plan with the greatest likelihood of improving the performance of participating children.[151]

The district must assist schools in their improvement efforts.[152] While the district may initiate corrective measures against the school at any time, if the school continues to fail to make adequate yearly progress after two years in the improvement process, the district must take corrective action.[153] Some examples of corrective actions are withholding funds, developing agreements among public agencies to provide services needed to remove barriers to student progress, revoking schoolwide project status, decreasing decisionmaking at the school level, making personnel changes, and authorizing student transfers, including transportation costs, to other public schools in the district.[154]

The state educational agency has the responsibility to ensure that the district's schools are making adequate yearly progress.[155] It, too, is authorized to take corrective action at any time against school districts with schools that fail to make adequate yearly progress, and it must do so during the fourth year of an improvement plan if the school continues not to make adequate yearly progress.[156]

Are there other ways to challenge the way a school runs its Title I program?

The United States Department of Education is developing an administrative complaint procedure for challenges to the way a school runs its Title I program.[157] In addition, if your child's school is seeking waivers of certain requirements of Title I that you do not agree with or that you are unsure about, contact a legal services program or other advocacy group for advice.

VOCATIONAL EDUCATION

What is the Perkins Vocational Education Act?

The Carl D. Perkins Vocational and Applied Technology Education Act, or the Perkins Act, is the federal government's major effort to improve the quality of vocational education programs. Its provisions apply to high schools, area vocational schools, and community colleges that receive funding under the act.[158] Many indigent students rely on vocational education programs to acquire the skills and experience that are needed to find meaningful employment after high school. Critics of vocational education often claim, however, that it relegates indigent students to a second-class education without preparing them for the jobs of the twenty-first century.

In 1990, Congress responded to some of these criticisms and amended the Perkins Act to improve the quality of vocational education. A key provision of the act now requires schools to integrate vocational and academic education and to prepare students in all aspects of the industry that they intend to enter.[159] Students must be given opportunities to study and to have experience in the areas of planning, management, finance, technical and production skills, principles, technology, labor, community, health, safety, and environmental concerns. In addition, students must be taught to develop problem-solving skills, as well as basic and advanced academic skills, in the areas of math, reading, writing, science, and social studies.

The Perkins Act requires schools to give special attention to so-called special populations: students who are low income or low achieving; disabled; of limited proficiency in English; participants in programs designed to eliminate sex bias; or incarcerated in correctional institutions.[160] Members of these special populations are protected under law against discrimination and are guaranteed equal access to programs. They may also be able to receive special assistance such as education assessments, supplemental services, guidance, counseling, career development services, and other instructional services to help in the transition from school to work.[161] Support services such as transportation and child care may also be available.[162]

Can parents participate in a school's Perkins Act program?

Yes. The Perkins Act requires each state Board of Vocational Education to establish procedures enabling parents, as well as students, to participate in decisionmaking about vocational and technical programs. The state must ensure that parents have access to information about their participation rights and must provide parents with technical assistance if requested.[163]

In addition, parents are entitled to information in a language and form they can understand about vocational education opportunities, such as eligibility and enrollment requirements, courses and special services, employment opportunities, and placement.[164] Schools must provide this information at least one year before a student enters a vocational program (or is of an age for the grade level in which vocational educational programs are available) but no later than the beginning of the ninth grade.[165]

Complaints may be filed against schools that fail to provide information about vocational educational opportunities. The complaints are filed through an expedited administrative appeals process that states are supposed to establish.[166] Other than this expedited appeals process, the Perkins Act does not otherwise establish a general complaint procedure. A person with concerns about vocational education should talk to a school principal and, if necessary, to a legal services or legal aid attorney.

What is the School-to-Work Opportunities Act?

The School-to-Work Opportunities Act of 1994 governs certain programs that teach academic and vocational skills.[167] Students in such programs divide their time between school and a workplace where they have the opportunity to apply what they are learning in school.[168] School-to-work programs must provide all students with the opportunity to complete a career major, which typically includes two years of high school and one or two years of college.[169]

The standards for school-to-work programs are in some ways similar to Perkins Act programs. Programs must teach all aspects of the industry that students are preparing to enter and must integrate academic and vocational education.[170] The school-based learning component must be designed to meet the same academic standards set by the state for all students to prepare students for post-secondary education and to earn skills certificates.[171]

School-to-work programs must prepare students not just for their first jobs, but also for longer-term work in a broad occupational cluster.[172] Programs must provide students with equal access to the full range of program components and related activities, including career awareness, exploration, and counseling to begin no later than seventh grade.[173] Students also should receive regularly scheduled evaluations to identify academic strengths and weaknesses, academic progress, workplace knowledge, goals, and the need for assistance to master core academic and vocational skills.[174]

THE MCKINNEY ACT AND HOMELESS CHILDREN

Does federal law guarantee equal educational opportunity to homeless children?

Yes. Homeless children are guaranteed equal educational opportunity under the federal Stewart B. McKinney Homeless Assistance Act.[175] The McKinney Act requires participating states to adopt plans ensuring the provision of public school services to school-age and preschool children who are homeless.[176] The education services must meet state standards, and each state must have a coordinator to develop and carry out the plan.[177]

A school cannot segregate a homeless child from the regular classroom or school environment or otherwise isolate or stigmatize him or her.[178] In addition, the McKinney Act requires state and local school districts to identify barriers that might prevent a homeless child from attending school and to take steps to remove them.[179] Examples of barriers that the school must help a homeless family to overcome include lack of transportation; lack of immunization that might delay a child's enrollment; inability to prove residence; lack of documentation, such as a birth certificate or school records; and guardianship issues.[180]

Where do homeless children attend school?

If a family becomes homeless during the school year, it has the right to request that a dependent child stay in the school she or he currently attends (known as the "school of origin").[181] If the family becomes homeless during the summer when school is not in session, it can ask to keep the child in his or her school of origin for the following school year.[182] Alternatively, the family can request that the child attend school in the area in which the family currently resides.[183] A parent must be given an opportunity to choose his or her child's school even if they are not currently living together.[184]

Every school district that receives McKinney funds must designate a homelessness liaison to assist homeless families and children obtain education and social services.[185] The liaison will want to know where you want your child to attend school. The school will try to determine what is in the best interest of the child[186] and is required to respect, "to the extent feasible," your choice as a parent.[187] If you disagree with the school's decision, you should contact your state coordinator for assistance. You can find out the name of your state coordinator by asking the school principal or district liaison.

What can be done if a school refuses to admit a homeless child or does not help the parent obtain necessary services?

If a school refuses to admit your child you should contact the district liaison or state coordinator responsible for homeless children. Each state must have written procedures for resolving disputes about school selection, and you can obtain a copy of these procedures from the state coordinator.[188]

The liaison can also help you get necessary services. The liaison's job is to make sure you and your family receive all educational services for which you are eligible, such as special education, Head Start, Even Start, Title I, or public preschool.[189] The liaison must also refer you and your family to health care, dental care, mental health services, and other necessary services.[190]

In addition, the state coordinator must make sure that your school district complies with the McKinney Act.[191] If efforts through the liaison or coordinator do not succeed, you should consider trying to enforce your rights under the McKinney Act through a lawsuit.[192] Contact your local legal services or legal aid program for advice and assistance.

LANGUAGE-MINORITY PROGRAMS

Does federal law guarantee equal educational opportunity to poor children whose primary language is not English?

Yes. Two federal antidiscrimination laws require public school systems to meet the education needs of all language-minority students. These laws are Title VI of the Civil Rights Act of 1964[193] and the Equal Educational Opportunities Act of 1974.[194] The United States Supreme Court, in the case of *Lau v. Nichols,* held that Title VI regulations and program guidelines require schools to take "affirmative steps to rectify the language deficienc[ies]" of students who are otherwise "effectively foreclosed from any meaningful education."[195] In response to the *Lau* decision, Congress enacted the Equal Educational Opportunities Act, which requires all states and school systems (whether or not they receive federal funds) "to take appropriate action to overcome language barriers that impede equal participation by students in their instructional programs."[196]

Are public schools required to provide specific services to students who are learning English?

No. The federal laws that protect students who are learning English do not mandate particular educational services, nor do they prescribe procedures that schools must follow in developing programs. In particular states, state law imposes specific programmatic requirements, but many states do not have their own language-minority legislation.[197] Guidance on what a program should provide can be gleaned, however, from judicial opinions.

First, the school system must adopt a comprehensive educational approach, one that experts believe to be sound or promising as a new strategy. Such an approach typically includes a strategy for identifying language-minority students, including children who are not currently in school; ways to assess a student's ability to read, write, and comprehend English; and the development of an adequate curriculum, texts, and materials.[198] Children must be taught reading and writing in English and must also receive academic instruction in a language they understand.[199] Schools must assess students in their primary language to ensure that they are meeting academic standards and to provide compensatory services as needed.[200]

Second, the school system must provide adequate resources for language-minority programs. Staff must be trained, and teachers in bilingual programs must be qualified not only to speak, read, and write in two languages, but also to teach the academic subjects.[201] Students must have access to all facets of the school's educational program, including Title I services, vocational education, and special education services when necessary.

Finally, the school system must ensure that the approach it uses is effective in reaching educational goals.[202] Federal law may be violated if a school retains an approach that does not allow language-minority students to learn.[203] The school must have "exit criteria" to determine when students can read, write, and comprehend English well enough to learn successfully in an English-only program. Exit criteria that simply test a student's oral skills are inadequate,[204] and the school should continue to monitor a student's progress even after she or he enters the regular classroom. A school's exit criteria would seem to be insufficient if students terminated from language-minority programs need simplified English materials or have higher grade retention or dropout rates than their English-speaking peers.[205]

What can a parent do if a child's school fails to provide appropriate educational services to language-minority students?

If you believe your child is not receiving an education that allows him or her to acquire English-language skills, to learn academic subjects, and to meet the same high educational standards expected of his or her English-speaking peers, you should speak with your child's teachers or principal. If you are not satisfied with their responses, you may want to consult a legal services or legal aid lawyer about ways to compel the school to provide your child with necessary educational services that are on a par with those provided to English-speaking peers. An individual or organization believing that a school system is violating its obligations under Title VI of the Civil Rights Act of 1964 may file an administrative complaint with the United States Department of Education, Office for Civil Rights, in the appropriate regional office.[206] You can obtain the address of the regional office by calling the Department of Education in Washington, D.C. Title VI and the Equal Educational Opportunities Act also have private rights of action that allow aggrieved individuals to file a lawsuit in federal court.[207]

EDUCATION OF CHILDREN WITH DISABILITIES

Does federal law guarantee equal educational opportunity to indigent children with disabilities?

Yes. Under federal law, any child with disabilities is entitled to a free appropriate public education. Three different statutes protect this right: the Individuals with Disabilities Education Act (known as IDEA);[208] Section 504 of the Rehabilitation Act of 1973 (known as Section 504);[209] and Title II of the Americans with Disabilities Act (known as the ADA).[210]

IDEA is a detailed statute addressing the educational needs of children with disabilities. Section 504 and the ADA are broad civil rights statutes on behalf of persons with disabilities. Section 504 prohibits discrimination on the basis of disability by programs that receive federal funds. The ADA bans such discrimination in services provided by state or local government.

Who is protected under these statutes?

IDEA applies to a child if she or he has one of the disabilities specifically listed in the statute and as a result needs special education.[211] These disabilities are mental retardation; hearing impairments including deafness; speech or language impairments; visual impairments including blindness; serious emotional disturbance; orthopedic impairments; autism; traumatic brain injury; other health impairments; or specific learning disabilities.[212] Section 504 and the ADA are broader, and protect your child if she or he has (or is treated as having or has a record of) *any* physical or mental impairment that substantially limits a major life activity. If your child has a disability, she or he is entitled to the same quality of education that her or his nondisabled peers receive.[213]

What is a free appropriate public education?

A free appropriate public education is one that meets the unique needs of a child with disabilities, including special or regular education and related services that are provided by the school in the "least restrictive environment" possible.[214] In *Board of Education of the Hendrick Hudson Central School District v. Rowley*, the United States Supreme Court held that in order to be "appropriate" under the Individuals with Disabilities Act, educational services must be "reasonably calculated to enable the child to receive educational benefits."[215] Under IDEA, as well as Section 504 of the Rehabilitation Act of 1973, the education provided must also meet challenging state standards and be designed to enable the child to master the skills and knowledge required of all students.[216] The educational needs of children with disabilities must be met at least as well as the needs of their nondisabled peers.[217]

"Special education" is not a place but means only "specialized instruction."[218] A school may provide special education in a variety of settings, including a regular education classroom, as long as the setting is the least restrictive environment in which the child can learn. A school district violates its obligation to provide an appropriate education if it automatically places a child with a particular disability in a separate class designated for that group.[219] A child's school cannot remove her or him from the regular education classroom unless it demonstrates that the child's educational needs cannot be met there even with specialized instruction and services.[220]

Depending on a child's needs, a child with disabilities may also be entitled to educational services beyond the length of the regular school day, or during the summer,[221] or at a residential placement.[222] A very small number of children with disabilities have such severe cognitive impairments that they cannot master the knowledge and skills all children are expected to learn, even with appropriate special education and related services. Individually tailored education programs for these few students must be as effective as programs for other students in meeting their educational, developmental, and learning needs and in preparing them for adult life.[223] Like all other children with disabilities, these students are entitled to the educational programming necessary to allow them to succeed in post-school activities, including vocational training, employment (including supported employment), independent living, and community participation.[224]

What is an Individualized Education Program?

An Individualized Education Program (IEP) is a written document that a child's school must develop at least once a year for a child with disabilities to describe his or her educational needs, to set educational goals, and to specify the special education and related services that are to be provided.[225] The IEP must also describe the extent to which the child will participate in regular education classes.[226] In developing IEPs, schools are required to keep themselves informed of promising new strategies for meeting the educational needs of children with disabilities, and to use these strategies in designing educational programs. As one federal appeals court has explained, "educational methods . . . are not static, but are constantly evolving and improving. It is the school district's responsibility to avail itself of these new approaches in providing an education program geared to each child's individual needs."[227]

The IEP can be thought of as a contract between the school and a family,[228] and in developing the IEP, the school is required to seek the family's active participation and to obtain information about the child's needs.[229] The school is likely to ask a number of questions: How well does the child currently perform? What are the child's education goals? What services does she or he need to help achieve these goals? To what extend can the child participate in the regular education program? When should the school evaluate her or him to make sure that goals are being reached? What criteria should the school use in making decisions about the child?[230] A school's failure to consult the family in developing a child's IEP can constitute a violation of the right to a free appropriate public education.[231]

What related services may a child with disabilities receive?

Under IDEA, "related services" mean supportive services that a child needs in order to benefit from special education.[232] A child is entitled to needed related services under Section 504 even if he or she does *not* need special education.[233] Related services can include: transportation, school health services, psychological services, counseling, parent counseling and training, physical and occupational therapy, speech pathology and audiology, recreation (including therapeutic recreation), social work services, and rehabilitation counseling.[234] These are merely *examples* of related services; if a child needs a particular service in order to benefit from special education, the school must provide it even if it is not listed.[235]

For example, if a child needs the help of a part-time or full-time aide, such assistance would be a required related service.[236] The same principle applies if a child needs equipment or assistive technology, such as a computer or tape recorder;[237] health-related assistance during the school day, such as catheterization;[238] or alcohol-abuse treatment.[239]

Does a family have to pay for special education and related services?

No. If a child needs special education or related services, the school district must provide it free of charge and at public expense, from preschool to high school, age 3 through 21. A school district cannot charge for any evaluation, special education, or related services that a child might need.[240] This includes computers and other assistive technology devices. A school also cannot ask a family to use the child's Social Security or SSI to pay for services that are required under IDEA or Section 504,[241] nor may they require use of private insurance if doing so would entail any financial loss.[242]

What if the school district does not have the services a child needs?

Children with disabilities are entitled to all necessary services, not just those that the school district already has in place. If the school district cannot provide necessary services, it must place the child who needs such services in a private program at public expense and free of charge to the family.[243]

How do you know if a child has a disability or needs special education or related services?

A parent who believes that his or her child has a disability or may need special education can ask the school to provide a comprehensive educational evaluation.[244] Any student suspected of having a disability must receive an evaluation before special education services can begin, and the evaluation and resulting placement cannot be done without parent consent.[245] In addition, some state laws require schools to try various strategies to resolve learning, behavior, and other problems that a student might have in the classroom before the school initiates an evaluation. These are commonly called prereferral interventions.[246]

In evaluating the child, the school cannot use methods that are racially or culturally discriminatory, and must make the assessment using the child's primary language (unless clearly not feasible).[247] Properly trained persons must administer all tests and assessments used for special education evaluation,[248] and school systems may not rely on a single test or evaluative tool (such as an IQ test) for determining that a child has a disability.[249] The school must make sure that every such test has been approved for the *specific use* the school is making of it.[250] It must also ensure that tests of children with impaired hearing or vision or manual or speaking skills actually reflect the child's aptitude.[251]

Once a parent agrees to have his or her child evaluated, the school will examine all areas related to the suspected disability, including health, vision, hearing, social and emotional status, general intelligence, academic performance, ability to communicate, and motor abilities.[252] In reaching its assessment, the school must take into account a variety of information, including social or cultural background and adaptive behavior.[253] ("Adaptive behavior" refers to how effectively a child meets standards of personal independence and social responsibility that are expected of his or her age and cultural group.)[254] If the school decides that a child needs special education, it must prepare an IEP within thirty days of the comprehensive evaluation.[255] Some states require schools to complete the IEP in a shorter time.

A parent who disagrees with the school's evaluation has the right to obtain an independent evaluation at public expense.[256] The school must pay for the evaluation, unless it requests an administrative hearing and demonstrates that its own evaluation was appropriate.[257] State law may provide for additional rights should disputes arise.

What are the rights of children with disabilities who do not speak English?

Children with disabilities whose primary language is not English are entitled to all of the educational services that children with limited English proficiency are otherwise entitled to, as well as special education and related services.[258]

What information does the school have to give a parent about his or her child's education?

Federal law entitles a parent to a great deal of information about his or her child's education. As a first step, the school is required to give the parent written notice of his or her rights *as a parent* whenever it proposes to take action regarding the child (for example, doing an evaluation or changing his or her services). These rights include the parent's right to review records, to request an independent evaluation, to request a hearing, to seek an administrative appeal, and to file a lawsuit in either state or federal court.[259] In addition, the school must give prior written notice of any changes or proposed changes in the child's placement, eligibility, or evaluation, and of the school's refusal to introduce any changes in the IEP that a parent requests.[260] The notice must explain the reasons for the school's decision or proposal.[261] All notices must be translated into the parent's primary language or, if needed, delivered orally or in sign.[262]

What can a parent do if he or she disagrees with a school's placement decisions?

IDEA gives a parent the right to challenge decisions affecting his or her child's education. This includes whether the child is eligible for special education and related services, placement options, evaluations, and the amount, type, and quality of the special education and related services.[263] As an initial matter, a parent who has concerns about a child's placement should ask to meet with the child's teacher, the special education supervisor, or members of her or his evaluation team. The parent might also consider talking to the child's doctor or therapist for guidance, or contacting a local group of parents of other children with disabilities. It is useful to have a copy of the child's records, and the parent should be sure to keep copies of all notices received from school.

What is an administrative due process hearing?

Sometimes informal discussion can help resolve concerns about a special education placement. But if concerns remains, IDEA allows a parent to request an administrative due process hearing.[264] The hearing provides a formal opportunity to challenge decisions made by the school about a child in special education.[265] Under IDEA, you must go through this administrative process before you can go to court and file a lawsuit.[266] This is called the "exhaustion of administrative remedies" requirement.

A parent who wants to request a hearing should check with the state education regulations to learn how it is conducted in his or her community. You also may want to contact a legal services program or other advocacy organization for advice and possible representation. If you do not know how to locate free or low-cost legal assistance or other advocacy services, you have the right to request that information from the school.[267]

After a due process hearing is requested, the hearing office has forty-five days to complete the hearing and send the parent a written decision.[268] A hearing officer presides at the hearing and is required to be impartial. The officer cannot be a school employee.[269] All parties have the right to present evidence, to cross-examine witnesses, and to get a written or taped transcript of the hearing.[270] You have the right to be represented by an attorney and to receive assistance throughout the hearing from a special education advocate.[271]

After the hearing, the hearing officer will prepare a written decision to resolve the complaint. The decision will set forth the facts of the case and the hearing officer's legal conclusions.[272] The decision can award appropriate relief, such as changing the child's IEP; ordering the school to implement an IEP; placing your child in a particular public or private school; or ordering the provision of related services.[273] The hearing officer can also order the school to provide the child with compensatory or supplemental education to remedy any services that were wrongfully denied.[274]

If you lose your administrative due process hearing (or in states with a "two-tier system," if you lose your appeal to the state educational agency after the due process hearing),[275] you have the right to appeal the decision to a state or federal district court.[276] You should check your state special education laws to determine what kind of administrative process is required before bringing a civil action in court.

Throughout the administrative process and any appeals, the child is entitled to remain in his or her present educational placement, unless you and the school agree to a different setting (this is known as the "stay put" or "status quo" provision).[277] If you win your dispute, you may be entitled to payment of your attorney's fees, expert witness fees, and other reasonable fees and costs.[278] Fees may also be available for work done in settling a case before a hearing, as well as for prevailing at a hearing or in court.[279]

What is the state complaint process?

The state complaint process is another available option if a parent feels that the school is violating his or her child's right to a free appropriate public education.[280] A complaint can be filed by writing a letter to the designated state educational agency and should set forth how the parent thinks the school has violated IDEA.[281] The state educational agency will investigate these concerns and issue a written decision within sixty days.[282] Filing a complaint is not the same as requesting a due process hearing and does not satisfy the administrative exhaustion requirement that must be met before bringing your case to court.

Do guardians have a right to challenge school decisions affecting their child's special education placement?

Yes. IDEA defines parent to include guardians, other persons acting as parents, and surrogate parents.[283] The state assigns a surrogate parent to a child when the parents are unavailable or unknown or when the child is in the custody of the state.[284] Surrogate parents are entitled to all of the same rights afforded parents and guardians.

Certain individuals cannot serve as surrogate parents.[285] These include employees of the school that will be making decisions about the child and employees of the agency that has custody of the child.[286] For example, a social worker or a case manager from a social service agency that has legal custody of a child may not be assigned to serve as the child's surrogate parent. Nor may a teacher, administrator, support staff, or other school personnel of a child's school system.

If you do not have custody of your child but want to remain involved in decisions affecting her or his education, you can serve as a surrogate parent if there is no conflict of interest between you and the child and you have the skills and knowledge needed to represent the child adequately. Relatives, friends, and community volunteers can also serve as surrogate parents if they meet these requirements.[287]

Are there any other ways to challenge decisions affecting a child's special education placement?

Yes. In addition to the procedural rights provided under IDEA, Section 504 of the Rehabilitation Act of 1973 also affords procedural protection. Under Section 504, the school is required to give a parent notice, to allow inspection of the child's records, and to provide an impartial hearing should disputes arise on issues concerning the identification, evaluation, or placement of the child.[288] School systems must also establish procedures to allow parents to appeal from unfavorable decisions.[289]

Section 504 requirements apply to all public schools that receive federal funds, and its protections extend to guardians as well as to parents. Under Section 504, a school may be found liable for discrimination if its practices have a discriminatory impact on students with disabilities, or impair or defeat their ability to meet educational goals.[290] Such practices can include a school's failure to coordinate pullout programs (such as resource rooms) with the regular curriculum; a school's provision of a diluted special education curriculum in a separate program; and a school's failure to structure its programs to allow children with disabilities to be integrated into the regular classroom.

In many states, the same state agency responsible for IDEA hearings also conducts Section 504 hearings.[291] As a result, a parent who has claims under both IDEA and Section 504 may want to combine them into one complaint and present them at one hearing. You should contact the state education department for a copy of the procedures that govern Section 504 hearings.

In addition, a parent who believes that a school is discriminating against his or her child because of disability has the right to file a written complaint with the United States Department of Education, Office for Civil Rights (OCR), which oversees state compliance with Section 504 requirements.[292] A complaint to OCR is filed with the OCR office responsible for the region in which the child's school district is located (the Department of Education in Washington, D.C., will provide the address). The complaint must be filed within 180 days of the actions that are said to violate Section 504.[293] Once the complaint is filed, OCR is required to investigate, and if it finds that a violation has occurred, OCR will attempt to resolve the complaint informally by obtaining voluntary compliance from the child's school district.[294] If OCR cannot obtain voluntary compliance, it may terminate the district's federal funding and take other legal action.[295]

A Section 504 hearing or OCR complaint does not satisfy the exhaustion of administrative remedies requirement under IDEA.

Can a public school expel a student with disabilities?

No. Expulsion of a student for conduct that results from a disability is discrimination under Section 504 and the ADA.[296] Under IDEA, a child is entitled to a free appropriate public education, and cannot be expelled whether or not the misconduct is related to the disability.[297] A school may transfer the student to a different educational placement, but in that case the school is required to give the parent notice, an opportunity to meet with the child's IEP team, and a hearing to resolve disputes. Any suspension that lasts more than ten days constitutes a change of placement, triggering IDEA's due process protections.[298] Once a complaint is filed, the child has the right to remain in her or his current placement until administrative proceedings and any judicial appeals are completed.[299] A school may then exclude the student only by obtaining a court injunction on a showing that the status quo is likely to result in injury to the student or to others. Even then, the child has a right in the interim to alternative educational services meeting the definition of a free appropriate public education.[300] The sole exception to the requirement of a judicial order applies to children with disabilities who bring firearms to school if the child's conduct is unrelated to his or her disability. Under this limited circumstance, the child's IEP team may place him or her in a temporary alternative educational placement, in accordance with state law, for up to forty-five days, even if a parent objects.[301] This exception, added to the law in 1994, was scheduled to expire upon later enactment of legislation reauthorizing IDEA.[302] Such legislation was pending before Congress as of September 1, 1996, but had not yet been passed at the time this book went to press. This proposed legislation would give schools new power to exclude more children from their current school placements for behavior reasons.

PREGNANT AND PARENTING STUDENTS

Does federal law guarantee equal educational opportunity to pregnant and parenting students?

Yes. Title IX of the Education Amendments of 1972 prohibits schools that receive federal funds from discriminating against students who are pregnant or parenting in matters involving classes, programs, and extracurricular activities.[303] Title IX provides important protection to the more than one million teenagers who become pregnant every year. Half of all teenage mothers do not complete school, and most of these students cite pregnancy as the reason for their decision.[304] As one commentator explains: "[T]he educational consequences of teenage pregnancy and parenting are twofold: young mothers, and to some extent young fathers, do not gain the educational skills necessary to be self-supporting, economically productive citizens, and their children often enter the educational system with economic and developmental disadvantages."[305] Title IX affords extremely important protection to students who might otherwise face barriers to completing their education.

Can pregnant and parenting students be asked to attend special schools?

Yes, but only on a voluntary basis. Some school systems have designed special schools for pregnant and parenting students that provide flexible schedules and comprehensive assistance. In some of these programs, students receive instruction in parenting and homemaking activities in addition to academic instruction. A school can recommend that a student participate in such a special program but cannot compel him or her to do so.

HIGHER EDUCATION

Are there federal education programs for low-income students who want to attend college?

Yes. The federal government has a number of programs to encourage low-income students to attend college. If you are interested in attending college but cannot afford to do so, you should speak with your teacher or guidance counselor. Two important federal programs for indigent students who want to attend college are Upward Bound[306] and Talent Search.[307]

Upward Bound. Upward Bound was established during the War on Poverty in the 1960s and targets educational services to low-income students in grade nine through twelve. Colleges and universities that participate in Upward Bound become partners with local high schools in year-round educational programs. While the programs vary from school to school, students generally receive tutoring, homework assistance, enrichment classes, and SAT or ACT preparation.[308] During the summer, students participate in a full academic program, usually on a college campus.[309] Some Upward

Bound programs give students an opportunity to live on campus for the summer.[310] Participating students receive guidance in how to apply to college and to obtain scholarships and financial aid. A student who wants more information should talk to a school guidance counselor.

Talent Search. Talent Search is a federal program designed to assist low-income students to finish high school and receive post-secondary education.[311] Talent Search provides a range of services, including academic counseling, tutoring, and assistance in completing college and financial aid applications.[312] Talent Search is also open to individual who dropped out of school and want to reenter or to pursue an alternative educational opportunity.[313] To be eligible, students must have completed at least five years of elementary school and be between ages 11 and 27.[314] For more information about Talent Search, talk to a school guidance counselor or call the state education department.

Do low-income students have particular rights to attend college?

Under the Perkins Act, low-income students have the right to equal access to all vocational programs at any community college or technical institute that receives Perkins funds (which includes most of them). These schools cannot discriminate against a poor person on the basis of income, previous low grades, disability, limited English proficiency, or desire to be in a program that is not traditional to his or her sex. Moreover, they must provide a low-income student with information about their program and, if needed, help with application to the program. They may also be required to provide the student with special assistance.

Are there federal financial aid programs for low-income students who want to attend college?

Yes. The federal government sponsors a number of financial aid programs for low-income students who want to attend college. Some of these programs provide grants, which are funds that do not have to be repaid. The two most important grant programs are federal Pell grants and Federal Supplemental Educational Opportunity grants.[315] During the 1992–1993 school year, 18.5 million students were enrolled in post-secondary education, either full time or part time. Two out of every ten students received a federal grant, and one out of every three students received some kind of federal aid.[316]

What is a federal Pell grant?

A federal Pell grant is money that the federal government gives to needy students to help them pay for their education after high school. How much money an eligible student receives depends on the student's financial circumstances, tuition, and other costs and whether she or he attends school full time or part time and for the full academic year. For the 1993–1994 school year, the largest amount of money a Pell grant recipient could receive was $2,000.

What is a Federal Supplemental Educational Opportunity grant?

A Federal Supplemental Educational Opportunity (FSEO) grant is money that the federal government gives to undergraduates with *exceptional* financial need to help them pay for their education after high school. The program differs from the federal Pell grant program in two ways: (1) Instead of being run directly by the federal government, each school runs the program for its own students; and (2) not every eligible student receives a FSEO grant because each school receives a limited amount of FSEO money and when it has given out that money, no other students at the school can receive FSEO grants that year. Students who are interested in this program should therefore apply for it at their school as early as possible.

If a student receives an FSEO grant, the amount of the award is determined by financial need, the amount of other financial aid the student will receive, and the availability of funds at the student's school, subject to a cap that changes each year.

Does the federal government have loan programs to help low-income students attend college?

Yes. The federal government sponsors four financial aid loan programs to help low-income students attend college. The programs are: (1) Perkins Loans; (2) Stafford Loans; (3) PLUS Loans; and (4) at some schools, Direct Student Loans. If you are interested in any of these programs, you can contact the United States Department of Education at 800 4FED AID (800-433-3243). You might also talk to school administrators and others who know about financial aid programs, such as a high school guidance counselor or the financial aid administrators at the schools you want to attend. Other sources of information include the state higher education agency, the public library, and the local veterans' affairs office.

Does the federal government offer any other kinds of financial aid to needy students?

Yes. The federal government also offers the National Service Trust Program and federal work-study programs.

National Service Trust Program. The National Service Trust Program[317] provides a living allowance, salary, and health and child care benefits for students who undertake up to two years of community service in the fields of education, human services, the environment, or public safety. Participants must work 1,700 hours a year. This money can be used to pay tuition or financial-aid loans.

Federal work-study programs. Federal work-study programs provide jobs for undergraduate and graduate students who need financial aid.[318] Students are paid directly and are supposed to use the money they earn at these jobs to help pay their educational expenses. Each school runs its own work-study program for its own students, and not every eligible student can participate because of limited funding. Students who are interested in participating in federal work-study programs should apply at their school as early as possible.

If a student is accepted into a program, the total amount of money he or she will be able to earn at a work-study job is determined by financial need, the amount of other financial aid the student will receive, and the availability of funds at the student's school. Work-study jobs, which can be on campus or off campus, pay at least the current federal minimum wage.

Can states use their Temporary Assistance for Needy Families block grants to help low-income persons get a post-secondary education?

Yes. Federal law allows states to use their Temporary Assistance for Needy Families block grants to establish Individual Development Accounts for eligible families with children to allow a household member to attend college. An eligible individual contributes earned income to the account, and funds are disregarded for purposes of determining eligibility or amount of assistance under any provision of federal law (other than the Internal Revenue Code). Funds may be withdrawn from the account to pay post-secondary education expenses directly to an eligible educational institution. Further information about Individual Development Accounts should become available as states begin to implement their block grant programs. Implementation must begin no later than July 1997.[319]

Notes

The authors gratefully acknowledge the assistance of Maura Kelly, Eileen Ordover, Bernard Lee, and Kathleen Boundy (together with Lauren Jacobs and Margot Rogers) of the Center for Law and Education in the preparation of this chapter.

1. 411 U.S. 1 (1973).

2. *Id.* at 35.

3. *Id.* at 30.

4. 478 U.S. 265 (1986).

5. *Id.* at 285.

6. 487 U.S. 450 (1988).

7. *See* Comment, *Human Rights and Basic Needs: Using International Human Rights Norms to Inform Constitutional Interpretation*, 34 UCLA L. Rev. 1195 (1987).

8. Universal Declaration, G.A. Res. 217A, U.N. Doc. A/810 at 71 (1948), *quoted in* Connie de la Vega, *Using International Human Rights Law in Legal Services Cases*, 22 Clearinghouse Rev. 1242 (1989).

9. *See, e.g.,* Susan H. Bitensky, *Theoretical Foundations for a Right to Education under the U.S. Constitution: A Beginning to the End of the National Education Crisis*, 86 Nw. U.L. Rev. 550 (1992); Akhil Reed Amar, *Forty Acres and a Mule: A Republican Theory of Minimal Entitlements*, 13 Harv. J.L. & Pub. Pol'y 37 (1990); David A. J. Richards, *Equal Opportunity and School Financing: Towards a Moral Theory of Constitutional Adjudication*, 41 U. Chi. L. Rev. 32 (1973).

10. State constitutional provisions guaranteeing a right to education are collected in Allen W. Hubsch, *The Emerging Right to Education Under State Constitutional Law*, 65 Temple L. Rev. 1325, 1343–48 (1992).

11. Ala. Const. art. XIV, § 256.

12. Mont. Const. art. X, § 1.

13. N.H. Const. art. 83.

14. *See* K. Forbis Jordan & Teresa S. Lyons, *Financing Public Education in an Era of Change* (Phi Delta Kappa Educational Foundation, 1992).

15. The following cases have invalidated school finance systems on state constitutional grounds: *Roosevelt Elementary Sch. Dist. No. 66 v. Bishop*, 877 P.2d 806 (Ariz. 1994); *DeRolph v. Corrigan*, 67 Ohio St. 3d 1477 (Court of Common Pleas, Perry Co. July 1, 1994); *Committee for Educ. Equality v. Missouri*, 878 S.W.2d 446 (Mo. 1994); *McDuffy v. Sec'y of the Exec. Office of Educ.*, 615 N.E.2d 516 (Mass. 1993); *Tennessee Small Sch. Sys. v. McWherter*, 851 S.W.2d 139 (Tenn. 1993); *Harper v. Hunt*, Appendix to the Opinion of the Justices, 624 So. 2d 107 (Ala. 1993); *Abbott v. Burke*, 643 A.2d 575 (N.J. 1994); *Rose v. Council for Better Educ.*, 790 S.W.2d 186 (Ky. 1989); *Helena Elem. Sch. Dist. No. 1 v. Montana*, 769 P.2d 684 (Mont. 1989); *Edgewood Indep. Sch. Dist. v. Kirby*, 777 S.W.2d 391 (Tex. 1989); *Dupree v. Alma Sch. Dist.*, 651 S.W.2d 90 (Ark. 1983); *Washakie Co. Sch. Dist. v. Herschler*, 606 P.2d 310 (Wyo. 1980); *Pauley v. Kelley*, 255 S.E.2d 859 (W. Va. 1979); *Seattle Sch. Dist. v. Washington*, 585 P.2d 71 (Wash. 1978); *Horton v. Meskill*, 376 A.2d 359 (Conn. 1977); *Robinson v. Cahill*, 303 A.2d 273 (N.J.), *cert. denied sub nom.*, *Dickey v. Robinson*, 414 U.S. 976

(1973); *Serrano v. Priest,* 487 P.2d 1241 (Cal. 1971); *Claremont Sch. Dist. v. Governor,* 635 A.2d 1375 (N.H. 1993).

16. *See* Christopher Edley, Jr. & Jay P. Heubert, Project Directors, *School Reform: The Rules of Law, Lawyers and Legal Institutions: An Activist's Guide to Education Reform and the Law* (Harvard Graduate School of Educ., 1994).

17. *See Pierce v. Society of Sisters,* 268 U.S. 510 (1925).

18. For example, Wisconsin established a voucher program that allows low-income students to attend private school with the costs of tuition partially subsidized at state expense. *See Wis. Stat. Ann.* § 119.23 (1993–1994), as amended by Wis. Legis. Serv. 216 (West 1996). Private school voucher programs raise a number of constitutional concerns. *See generally* Note, The Limits of Choice: School Choice Reform and State Constitutional Guarantees of Educational Quality, 109 Harv. L. Rev. 2002 (1996). Moreover, at least some research studies question the effectiveness of voucher programs in improving achievement. *See* Bob Davis, Class Warfare: Dueling Professors Have Milwaukee Dazed Over School Vouchers, Studies on Private Education Result in a Public Spat About Varied Conclusions, Wall St. J., Oct. 11, 1996, A1.

19. *See, e.g.,* N.Y. Educ. §§ 3204, 3205 (McKinney's 1996); 8 N.Y.C.R.R. § 100.10 (1996).

20. *See, e.g.,* N.Y. Educ. §§ 3204, 3205, 3212, 3233 (McKinney's 1996).

21. *See* Lucy Williams, *The Ideology of Division: Behavior Modification Welfare Reform Proposals,* 102 Yale L.J. 719, 726 (1992).

22. *See* John Pawasarat, Lois Quinn & Frank Stetzer, *Evaluation of the Impact of Wisconsin's Learnfare Experiment on the School Attendance of Teenagers Receiving Aid to Families with Dependent Children* (Evaluation report submitted to the Wisconsin Dep't of Health and Social Services and the U.S. Dep't of Health and Human Services) (Univ. of Wisconsin-Milwaukee, 1992); John Pawasarat & Lois Quinn, *The Impact of Learnfare on Milwaukee County Social Service Clients* (Univ. of Wisconsin-Milwaukee, 1990).

23. *See* Pub. L. No. 104-193, 110 Stat. 2105, § 103 (1996). Section 103 creates a new section to Title IV of the Social Security Act, allowing states to "sanction welfare recipients for failing to ensure that minor dependent children attend school."

24. *See id.* at § 103 (1996)(creating 42 U.S.C.A. § 408(a)(5)(1996)(obligations of teen parents to attend school and obtain high school diploma or equivalent as condition of receiving temporary-assistance benefits).

25. The Temporary Assistance for Needy Families block grant is discussed in chapter 1 of this book.

26. *Martinez v. Bynum,* 461 U.S. 321, 328–30 (1983). *See also Horton v. Marshall Pub. Sch.,* 769 F.2d 1323 (8th Cir. 1985) (finding school district's application of Arkansas residence requirement to violate the due process and equal protection clauses of the U.S. Constitution).

27. *Martinez v. Bynum,* 461 U.S. at 339.

28. *See, e.g.,* Ariz. Rev. Stat. Ann. § 15-823(E) (West 1996); Colo. Rev. Stat. Ann. § 22-1-102 (West 1996); Mass. Gen. Laws Ann., c. 76, §§ 5-6 (West 1996); R.I. Gen. Laws § 16-64-1 (Michie 1995); Utah Code Ann. §§ 53A-2-201, 53A-2-202 (Michie 1996).

29. *See Major v. Nederland Indep. Sch. Dist.,* 772 F. Supp. 944 (E.D. Tex. 1991); *Nancy M. v. Scanlon,* 666 F. Supp. 723 (E.D. Pa. 1987).

30. *See In re Curry,* 318 N.W.2d 567 (Mich. App. 1982). For more information, *see* Glenn Renner, with revision and update by Julia Hyun, *Public School Residency Requirements for Students Living with Non-Parent, Non-Guardian Caretakers* (Center for Law and Education, 1994).

31. *See* Stewart B. McKinney Homeless Assistance Act, 42 U.S.C. §§ 11431-35 (West 1996). The Improving America's Schools Act of 1994 amended the McKinney Act.

32. *See, e.g., Concerned Parents v. Caruthersville Sch. Dist.,* 548 S.W.2d 554 (Mo. 1977); *Dowell v. Sch. Dist.,* 250 S.W.2d 127 (Ark. 1952); *Batty v. Board of Educ.,* 269 N.W. 49 (N.D. 1936); *Special Sch. Dist. v. Bangs,* 221 S.W. 1060 (Ark. 1920); *Board of Educ. v. Dick,* 78 P. 812 (Kan. 1904).

33. *See Union Free Sch. Dist. v. Jackson,* 403 N.Y.S.2d 621 (N.Y. Sup. Ct. 1978); *Granger v. Cascade Co. Sch. Dist.,* 499 P.2d 780 (Mont. 1972); *Paulson v. Minidoka Co. Sch. Dist.,* 463 P.2d 935 (Idaho 1970); *Bond v. Public Schools of Ann Arbor Sch. Dist.,* 178 N.W.2d 484 (Mich. 1970).

34. *See, e.g., Arcadia Unified Sch. Dist. v. State Dep't of Educ.,* 825 P.2d 438 (Cal. 1992) (transportation fees); *Crim v. McWhorter,* 252 S.E.2d 421 (Ga. 1979) (summer school tuition); *Gohn v. Akron Sch.,* 562 N.E.2d 1291 (Ind. Ct. App. 1990) (textbook fee); *Attorney Gen. v. East Jackson Public Sch.* 372 N.W.2d 638 (Mich. 1985) (interscholastic sports fee); *Vandevender v. Cassell,* 208 S.E.2d 436 (W. Va. 1974) (textbooks, workbooks, and required materials fee).

35. *See Attorney Gen. v. East Jackson Public Sch.,* 372 N.W.2d 638, 639 (Mich. 1985) (example of fee waiver provision with confidential process).

36. *See Lorenc v. Call,* 789 P.2d 46 (Utah 1990).

37. *Crim v. McWhorter,* 252 S.E.2d 421 (Ga. 1979).

38. *Parsippany-Troy Hills Educ. Ass'n v. Board of Educ.,* 457 A.2d 15 (N.J. Super. 1983). *But see Driving Sch. Ass'n of Cal. v. San Mateo Union High Sch. Dist.,* 11 Cal. App. 4th 1513 (Cal. 1st Dist. 1992)(finding that driver education is an integral part of high school education and thus prohibiting fees).

39. *Hartzell v. Connell,* 35 Cal.3d 899, 907–08, 911 (Cal. 1984).

40. *See Carder v. Michigan City Sch. Corp.,* 552 F. Supp. 869, 870 (N.D. Ind. 1982) ("suspension of a student from school for a parent's failure to pay textbook fees or sign waiver request form amounts to a denial of equal protection"); *Chandler v. South Bend Comm. Sch. Corp.,* 312 N.E.2d 915 (Ind. App. 1974) (enjoining school system from suspending students, withholding report cards, or taking other disciplinary action based on parents' nonpayment of school fees).

41. 347 U.S. 483 (1954).

42. *Id.* at 493.

43. *Freeman v. Pitts,* 503 U.S. 467 (1992) (race); *Keyes v. Sch. Dist. No. 1,* 413 U.S. 189 (1973) (national origin).

44. *See* Section 504 of the Rehabilitation Act of 1973, 29 U.S.C.A. § 794a (West 1996)(prohibiting discrimination based on disability by any program receiving federal

funds); Title 2 of the Americans with Disabilities Act, 42 U.S.C.A. § 12132 (West 1996)(prohibiting discrimination based on disability by any public entity); Title VI of the Civil Rights Act of 1964, 42 U.S.C.A. § 2000d (West 1996) (prohibiting discrimination based on race, color, or national origin, including language and ethnicity, by programs receiving federal funds); Title IX of the Education Amendments of 1972, 20 U.S.C.A. § 1681 (West 1996)(prohibiting discrimination on the basis of sex by any program receiving federal funds); Equal Educational Opportunities Act of 1974, 20 U.S.C.A. § 1703 (West 1996) (prohibiting denial of equal educational opportunities on the basis of race, color, sex, or national origin). Members of "special population" groups are also entitled to equal access to vocational education programs that receive funds under the Perkins Act. *See* Carl D. Perkins Vocational and Applied Technology Education Act, 20 U.S.C.A. §§ 2328–2471 (West 1996). Special populations include children with disabilities; low-income and low-achieving children (including foster children); children whose proficiency in English is limited; students who participate in programs designed to end sex bias; and children in correctional institutions. *Id.* at § 2471(31)(West 1996).

45. *See Timothy W. v. Rochester, New Hampshire, Sch. Dist.,* 875 F.2d 954 (1st Cir.), *cert. denied,* 493 U.S. 983 (1989); 20 U.S.C.A. §§ 1412(l), 1412(2)(C), 1414(a)(West 1996); 34 C.F.R. § 104.33(a)(1996).

46. *See* 20 U.S.C.A. § 1400(b)(West 1996).

47. 20 U.S.C.A. §§ 1401(18), 1412(2)(B), 1419 (West 1996).

48. 20 U.S.C.A. § 1412(5)(B)(West 1996); 34 C.F.R. § 104.34(a)(1996).

49. 457 U.S. 202 (1982).

50. *Id.* at 221.

51. *League of United Latin American Citizens v. Wilson,* 908 F. Supp. 755 (C.D. Cal. 1995); *see* B. Drummond Ayres, Jr., *Court Blocks New Rule on Immigration,* N.Y. Times, Nov. 17, 1994, at A16, col. 1; Lynn Schnaiberg, *Approval of Prop. 187 Spurs Suits, Protests,* 14 Educ. Week, Nov. 16, 1994, 1.

52. 42 U.S.C.A. § 2000d (West 1996); 20 U.S.C.A. § 1703 (West 1996).

53. 42 U.S.C.A. § 2000d (West 1996).

54. *See* Title IX of the Education Amendments of 1972, 20 U.S.C.A. § 1681 (West 1996); 34 C.F.R. § 106.40 (1996).

55. *See* 34 C.F.R. § 106.31(d) (1996).

56. Sanctions cannot be imposed if the adult is determined to lack "the requisite capacity" to complete a course of study. *See* Pub. L. No. 104-193, 110 Stat. 2105, § 103 (1996).

57. 20 U.S.C.A. §§ 2335, 2335a (West 1996).

58. *Id.* at §§ 6361–70 (West 1996). State and local educational agencies wishing to participate in the Even Start Family Literacy Program, and thus receive federal funds, must identify and recruit families that are most in need of services based on income, literacy, English proficiency, and other needs. *See id.* at §§ 6361–65 (West 1996).

59. *Id.* at § 6365(1)–(7) (West 1996).

60. *Id.* at §§ 1471–85 (West 1996); 34 C.F.R. pt. 303 (1996).

61. *See* 34 C.F.R. § 303.520(b)(3)(ii) (1996) (prohibiting denial of services based on family's ability to pay).

62. *See generally* Edward Zigler & S. J. Styfco, *Head Start and Beyond: A National Plan for Extended Childhood Intervention* (1993).

63. 45 C.F.R. § 1305.9 (1996).

64. Mary Kay Stein, Gaea Leinhardt & William Bickel, "Instructional Issues for Teaching Students At Risk," in *Effective Programs for Students At Risk* 150 (Robert E. Slavin, Nancy L. Karweit & Nancy A. Madden eds. 1989).

65. 45 C.F.R. § 1305.4(b) (1996).

66. 42 U.S.C.A. § 9835(d) (West 1996); 45 C.F.R. § 1305.6(c) (1996).

67. 42 U.S.C.A. § 9831 (West 1996); 45 C.F.R. §§ 1305.4, 1305.6–.7 (1996).

68. 45 C.F.R. § 1306 (1976), *as amended at* 57 Fed. Reg. 58092 (1992).

69. *Id.* at § 1305.6(d) (1996).

70. *Id.* at § 1305.7(a) (1996).

71. *Id.* at § 1305.7(c) (1996).

72. *Id.* at § 1305.8 (1996).

73. *See* Stein, Leinhardt, & Bickel, *supra* note 64, at 149.

74. 42 U.S.C.A. § 9832(7) (West 1996).

75. *Id.* at § 9843 (West 1996); 45 C.F.R. § 1306.21 (1996).

76. 45 C.F.R. § 1306.23 (1996).

77. *Id.* at § 1306.32(a) (1996).

78. *Id.* at § 1306.32(b) (1996).

79. *Id.* at § 1306.33(a) (1996).

80. *Id.* at § 1304.1–4 (1996). *See id.* at §§ 1304.2–1 to .5–5 (1996) for the standards in these areas. Under the Human Services Amendments of 1994, Pub. L. No. 103-252, 100 Stat. 631, § 100 (1994), regulations establishing new nationwide standards were to have been issued by May 18, 1995. *See* 42 U.S.C.A. § 9836a (West 1996). They had not yet been as of Aug. 2, 1996.

81. 45 C.F.R. §§ 1308.4–.21 (1996). Where a public school places a child with disabilities in a Head Start program, she or he must be given an Individualized Education Program, developed with full parent participation, consistent with the requirements of the Individuals with Disabilities Education Act. *See* 20 U.S.C.A. §§ 1401(a)(18), (20) & 1415 (West 1996); 34 C.F.R. §§ 300.340–.347, 300.500–.515, 300.534, 300.552 (1996).

82. 45 C.F.R. § 1305.3(b) (1996).

83. *Id.* at § 1304.5–1 (1996); *see id.* at § 1304.5-1 to .5-5 (1996) and app. B—Head Start Policy Manual: The Parents.

84. *See, e.g.,* 42 U.S.C.A. §§ 9833(a) (West 1996) (parent participation in Head Start programs required as condition of federal funding); 9836(d) (West 1996) (significant parent and community involvement required in selection of Head Start agencies); 9837(b) (West 1996) (mandating parental involvement in all aspects of Head Start programs, including decisionmaking and implementation.)

85. 45 C.F.R. § 1304.5-2(b) (1996).

86. *Id.* at § 1304.5-1(c) (1996).

87. *Id.* at § 1304, app. B (1996).

88. Goals 2000: Educate America Act of 1994, 20 U.S.C.A. §§ 5801-6084 (West

1996). Portions of the act have been repealed by the Improving America's Schools Act of 1994, Pub. L. No. 103-382 (Part C—Leadership in Educational Technology), *see* 20 U.S.C.A. §§ 5861–64, repealed, Oct. 20, 1994.

89. *See* "School Reform: Getting It Right," 18 *Am. Educator* 12 (1994).

90. 20 U.S.C.A. §§ 5885 (State Applications), 5886, 5888–89 (West 1996).

91. *Id.* at §§ 5911–18 (West 1996).

92. *Id.* at § 5912(a)(2)(B)(ii); *see generally id.* at § 5912 (West 1996).

93. *Id.* at § 5886(b)(1)(D) (West 1996).

94. *Id.* at § 5889(a)(3)(A) (West 1996).

95. *Id.* at §§ 5886(b)(1)(D), 5889(a)(3)(A) (West 1996).

96. *Id.* at §§ 5889 (a)(5), 5886 (b)(9) (West 1996).

97. The Improving America's Schools Act of 1994 amended Title I of the Elementary and Secondary Education Act of 1965, 20 U.S.C.A. §§ 2701–31 (West 1996). The amendments took effect July 1, 1995, and the Department of Education recently issued regulations implementing the new law. For up-to-date information about Title I, please contact the Title I and School Reform Project, Center for Law and Education, 1875 Connecticut Avenue, Suite 510, Washington, DC 20009, (202) 986-3000.

98. *See Making Schools Work for Children in Poverty* vii (Commission on Chapter 1, Dec. 1992) (quoting U.S. Dep't of Educ., *National Assessment of the Chapter 1 Program: Interim Report* (1992).

99. 20 U.S.C.A. §§ 6301(b), 6314(b), 6315(a)–(b) (West 1996).

100. *Id.* at § 6313 (West 1996).

101. *Quoted in* Robert E. Slavin, et al., *SUCCESS FOR ALL! A Relentless Approach to Prevention and Early Intervention in Elementary Schools* 82 (Educational Research Service, 1992).

102. 20 U.S.C.A. § 2701(b), *as amended and replaced by* Improving America's Schools Act of 1994, 20 U.S.C.A. §§ 6301-8962 (West 1996).

103. *Id.* at §§ 5801–6084 (West 1996).

104. *Id.* at §§ 6314(b)(1)(A)–(D), 6315(c)(1), (2)(A)–(B) (West 1996).

105. *See id.* at §§ 6314 (schoolwide programs), 6315 (West 1996)(targeted assistance schools). The school district may also serve eligible children in private schools. *Id.* at § 6321 (West 1996).

106. As of July 1, 1995. The percentage decreased to 50 percent as of July 1, 1996. 20 U.S.C.A. § 6314(a)(1)(A) and (B) (West 1996).

107. *Id.* at § 6314(a)(1) and (3) (West 1996).

108. *Id.* at § 6315(b) (West 1996).

109. *Id.* at § 6315(a) (West 1996). There are situations, however, in which a school meets the schoolwide program requirements but chooses to retain a targeted assistance program. *Id.* If a school qualifies as a schoolwide program, it must inform parents so that decisions about the type of Title I program are made jointly by school administrators, parents, and teachers. *See* 20 U.S.C.A. § 6312(c) (West 1996). *See also id.* at § 6319 (West 1996)(Parental Involvement).

110. *Id.* at § 6322(b) (West 1996).

111. *Id.* at § 6322(b)–(c) (West 1996).

112. *See, e.g., id.* at §§ 6314(b), 6315(c) (West 1996).

113. *Id.* at §§ 6314(b)(1)(B)(iii)(I), 6315(c)(1)(D)(i) (West 1996).

114. *Id.* at § 6315(c)(1)(D) (West 1996).

115. *Id.* at §§ 6314(b)(1)(B)(i), 6315(c)(1)(A) (West 1996).

116. *Id.* at §§ 6314(b)(1)(C), 6315(c)(1)(F) (West 1996).

117. *Id.* at § 6315(c)(1)(E) (West 1996)(in targeted assistance schools).

118. *Id.* at § 8881(c)(6) (West 1996). *See* 20 U.S.C.A. § 8881 (West 1996)(setting forth waiver provisions, including requirements that may not be waived).

119. *Id.* at § 6319(a)(3)(A) (West 1996). This does not apply if 1 percent of the school district's allocation is $5,000 or less. *Id.*

120. *Id.* at § 6319(a)(3)(B) (West 1996).

121. *Id.* at § 6319(c)(3) (West 1996).

122. *Id.* at § 6319(a)–(g) (West 1996).

123. *Id.* at § 6319(a)–(b) (West 1996).

124. *Id.* at § 6319(d) (West 1996).

125. *Id.*

126. *Id.* at § 6312(b)(6) (West 1996).

127. *Id.* at § 6312(d)(1) (West 1996).

128. *Id.* at § 6317(c)(2)(A) (West 1996).

129. *Id.* at § 6319(e)(2)(A)–(B) (West 1996).

130. *Id.* at § 6319(c)(1) (West 1996).

131. *Id.* at § 6319(c)(2) (West 1996).

132. *Id.*

133. *Id.* at § 6319(f) (West 1996).

134. *Id.* at § 6319(a)(2), (b)(1) (West 1996).

135. *Id.*

136. *Id.*

137. *Id.* at § 6319(b)(2) (West 1996).

138. *Id.* at § 6319(a)(1) (West 1996).

139. *Id.* at § 6319(d) (West 1996).

140. *Id.*

141. *Id.* at § 6319(d)(1) (West 1996).

142. *Id.*

143. *Id.* at § 6319(d)(2) (West 1996).

144. *Id.* at § 6319(d)(2)(A) (West 1996).

145. *Id.* at § 6319(d)(2)(B)–(C) (West 1996).

146. *Id.* at § 6319(c)(4)(D)–(E) (West 1996).

147. *Id.* at § 6319(c)(4)(c) (West 1996).

148. *Id.* at § 6319(c)(4)(B) (West 1996). *See also id.* at §§ 6317(a)(1)–(4) (West 1996).

149. *Id.* at §§ 6311(b)(2)(A)–(B), 6317(a) (West 1996).

150. *Id.* at § 6317(c)(1)(B) (West 1996).

151. *Id.* at § 6317(c)(2) (West 1996).

152. *Id.* at § 6317(c)(4) (West 1996).

153. *Id.* at § 6317(c)(5)(A) (West 1996).

154. *Id.* at § 6317(c)(5)(B) (West 1996).

155. *Id.* at § 6317(d)(1), (3), and (5) (West 1996).

156. *Id.* at § 6317(d)(6)(A) (West 1996). *See also id.* at § 6317(d)(6)(B) (West 1996)(listing possible corrective actions, including additional actions of appointing a trustee or receiver to govern the district and abolishing or restructuring the district).

157. As of August 1996, the procedure had not been finalized. *See also Valdez v. Grover,* 563 F. Supp. 129 (W.D. Wis. 1983); *Nicholson v. Pittenger,* 364 F. Supp. 669 (E.D. Pa. 1973)(regarding law suits to enforce Title I).

158. 20 U.S.C.A. § 2301 *et seq.* (West 1996). The Perkins Act provides specific opportunities for Native Americans and Hawaiian natives to obtain grants for vocational programs. 20 U.S.C.A. § 2313 (West 1996). As of September 1, 1996, two bills that would repeal the Perkins Act (the Workforce Development Act, S. 143, and the Careers Act, H.R. 1617) were pending before Congress, but were stalled in a House-Senate conference committee. Readers should check for any subsequent statutory developments.

159. 20 U.S.C.A. § 2323(a)(3)(B)(i)–(ii) (West 1996).

160. *Id.* at § 2471(31) (West 1996)(definitions).

161. *Id.* at § 2328(c) (West 1996).

162. *Id.* at §§ 2335(a)(4), 2343(12)(C) (West 1996).

163. *Id.* at § 2328(d)(1)–(2) (West 1996).

164. *Id.* at § 2328(b) (West 1996).

165. *Id.*

166. *Id.* at § 2328(d)(1) (West 1996).

167. School-To-Work Opportunities Act of 1994, 20 U.S.C.A. §§ 6101–6251 (West 1996). As of September 1, 1996, two bills that would repeal the School-to-Work Act (the Workforce Development Act, S. 143, and the Careers Act, H.R. 1617) were pending before Congress, but were stalled in a House-Senate conference committee. Readers should check for any subsequent statutory developments.

168. 20 U.S.C.A. § 6111 (West 1996).

169. *Id.* at §§ 6111(2), 6103(5)(c) (West 1996).

170. *Id.* at §§ 6111(1), (4); 6112(4) (West 1996).

171. *Id.* at § 6112(3) (West 1996).

172. *Id.* at § 6102 (West 1996)(purposes and congressional intent).

173. *See id.* at §§ 6112–14 (West 1996).

174. *Id.* at § 6112(5) (West 1996).

175. Subtitle B of Title VII of the Stewart B. McKinney Homeless Assistance Act, 42 U.S.C.A. § 11431(4) (West 1996). The Improving America's Schools Act of 1994, Pub. L. No. 103-382 (108 Stat. 3518), § 721 (1994), amended the McKinney Act.

176. *Id.* at §§ 11431(4), 11432(g)(1) (West 1996).

177. *Id.* at § 11432(d) (West 1996).

178. *Id.* at §§ 11431(3), 11433(b)(4) (West 1996).

179. *Id.* at §§ 11431(2), 11432(f)(2), 11432(g)(1)(E)–(G), 11433(a) (West 1996).

180. *Id.* at § 11432(g)(1)(F) (West 1996).

181. *Id.* at § 11432(g)(3)(A)(i)(I) (West 1996).

182. *Id.* at § 11432(g)(3)(A)(i)(II) (West 1996).

183. *Id.* at § 11432(g)(3)(A)(ii) (West 1996).

184. *Id.* at § 11432(g)(3)(D) (West 1996).

185. *Id.* at § 11432(g)(6)–(7) (West 1996).

186. *Id.* at § 11432(g)(3)(A)–(B) (West 1996).

187. *Id.* at § 11432(g)(3)(B) (West 1996).

188. *Id.* at § 11432(g)(1)(A) (West 1996).

189. *Id.* at § 11432(g)(7)(A)(ii) (West 1996).

190. *Id.*

191. *Id.* at § 11432(f)–(g) (West 1996).

192. *See Lampkin v. District of Columbia,* 27 F.3d 605 (D.C. Cir. 1994), *cert. denied,* 115 S. Ct. 578 (1994).

193. 42 U.S.C.A. § 2000d (West 1996); 34 C.F.R. pt. 106 (1996).

194. 20 U.S.C.A. § 1703 (West 1996).

195. 414 U.S. 563, 566–68 (1974).

196. 20 U.S.C.A. § 1703(f) (West 1996). The federal statute that provides funding to some state and local school systems for meeting the needs of students who are learning English stresses programs that help children develop proficiency in English and their native language and that also "meet the same challenging State content . . . and student performance standards expected for all children." Section 7111 of the Elementary and Secondary Education Act of 1965, 20 U.S.C.A. §§ 2701–3386 (West 1996).

197. Parents and advocates should investigate state laws, regulations, or policies that affect the education of limited English proficient students. *See, e.g.,* Ariz. Rev. Stat. Ann. § 15-751 (West 1996); Mass. Gen. L. A. ch. 71A, § 1 (West 1996).

198. For a detailed blueprint of one comprehensive approach to the educational needs of students with limited English proficiency, *see League of United Latin American Citizens v. Florida Board of Educ.,* C.A. No. 90-1913 (S.D. Fla. Aug. 14, 1990) (Final Order and Settlement Agreement). For additional information, please contact Multicultural Education Training and Advocacy (META), 524 Union Street, San Francisco, CA 94113.

199. *See Keyes v. School Dist. No. 1, Denver,* 576 F. Supp. 1503, 1518 (D. Colo. 1983), *cert. denied,* 498 U.S. 1082 (1991).

200. *See Castaneda v. Pickard,* 648 F.2d 989, 1014 (5th Cir. 1991).

201. *See Keyes,* 576 F. Supp. at 1516–17; *Castaneda,* 648 F.2d at 1013. *See also* Memorandum from Michael L. Williams, Assistant Secretary for Civil Rights to OCR Senior Staff Regarding Policy Update on School's Obligations toward National Origin Minority Students with Limited English Proficiency 5 (Sept. 27, 1991)(hereinafter "OCR Memorandum"). (A copy of the memorandum may be obtained from the U.S. Department of Education Office of Civil Rights in Washington, D.C. or from any OCR regional office.)

202. *See Keyes,* 576 F. Supp. at 1518; *see also* OCR Memorandum, *supra* note 201, at 9.

203. *See Castaneda,* 648 F.2d at 1010.

204. *See Keyes,* 576 F. Supp. at 1518 (noting importance of testing reading and writing as well as oral language skills); OCR Memorandum, *supra* note 201, at 7.

205. OCR Memorandum, *supra* note 201, at 6.

206. For the regulations governing the filing and investigation of OCR complaints, *see* 34 C.F.R. § 100.7–.11 (1996).

207. *See* 20 U.S.C.A. § 1706 (West 1996). The Attorney General has authority to institute a civil action on behalf of an individual whose rights under the Equal Educational Opportunities Act have been violated.

208. 20 U.S.C.A. §§ 1400–14910 (West 1996). IDEA was formerly known as both the Education for All Handicapped Children Act (EAHCA) and the Education of the Handicapped Act (EHA).

209. 29 U.S.C.A. § 794 (West 1996).

210. 42 U.S.C.A. §§ 12101–12213 (West 1996).

211. 20 U.S.C.A. § 1401(a)(1) (West 1996).

212. *Id.*; *see also* 34 C.F.R. § 300.7 (1996).

213. 29 U.S.C.A. § 706(8)(b) (West 1996); 34 C.F.R. §§ 104.3(j)(1), 104.4(b)(i), (iii), 104.33(b)(1) (1996); 42 U.S.C.A. § 12102(2) (West 1996); 28 C.F.R. § 35.130(b) (1996) & 61 Fed. Reg. 51348 (1996); 20 U.S.C.A. § 1401(a)(18)(B)–(C) (West 1996).

214. 20 U.S.C.A. §§ 1401(a)(18) (West 1996), 1412(5)(B) (West 1996); 34 C.F.R. §§ 104.33(b), 104.34(c) (1996); *see also* 34 C.F.R. § 300.17 (1996).

215. 458 U.S. 176, 207 (1982).

216. 20 U.S.C.A. § 1401(a)(18)(B)–(C) (West 1996); 34 C.F.R. §§ 104.33(b)(1)(i), 104.4(b)(1)(ii)–(iii) (1996) (U.S. Dep't of Educ. regulations implementing Section 504); 28 C.F.R. § 35.130(b) (1996) (U.S. Dep't of Justice regulations implementing Title II of ADA). Schools are prohibited from providing students with disabilities "an opportunity to participate in or benefit from . . . [an] aid, benefit or service that is not equal to that afforded others" or to provide an "aid, benefit or service" that is not as effective as that provided to others.

217. 34 C.F.R. § 104.33(b)(1)(i) (1996).

218. 20 U.S.C. § 1401(a)(16) (West 1996).

219. *See, e.g., Board of Educ. of the County of Cabell v. Dienelt,* 1986–87 EHLR 558:305, 558:308 (S.D. W. Va. 1987), *aff'd per curiam,* 843 F.2d 813 (4th Cir. 1988). In addition to violating IDEA, such conduct constitutes illegal discrimination under Section 504 regulations. *See* 34 C.F.R. § 104.4(b)(1)(iv) (1996) (prohibiting recipients of federal funds from providing different or separate services to any category of people with disabilities unless such treatment is necessary to provide them with services as effective as those provided to nondisabled people).

220. 20 U.S.C.A. § 1412(5)(B) (West 1996); 34 C.F.R. § 104.34(c) (1996); *see also* 28 C.F.R. § 35.130(d) (1996)(implementing ADA) ("a public entity shall administer services, programs and activities in the most integrated setting appropriate to the needs of qualified individuals with disabilities").

221. *See, e.g., Johnson v. Ind. Sch. Dist. No. 4,* 921 F.2d 1022 (10th Cir. 1990), *cert. denied,* 500 U.S. 905 (1991); *Cordrey v. Euckert,* 917 F.2d 1460 (6th Cir. 1990), *cert. denied,* 499 U.S. 938 (1991); *Alamo Heights Ind. Sch. Dist. v. State Board of Educ.,* 790 F.2d 1153 (5th Cir. 1986); *Georgia Assoc. of Retarded Citizens v. McDaniel,* 716 F.2d 1565 (11th Cir. 1983), *modified in part,* 740 F.2d 902 (1984), *cert. denied,* 469 U.S. 1228 (1985); *Battle v. Pennsylvania,* 629 F.2d 269 (3d Cir. 1980).

222. 34 C.F.R. § 300.302 (1996); *Chris D. v. Montgomery Board of Educ.,* 743 F. Supp. 1524 (M.D. Ala. 1990).

223. 34 C.F.R. §§ 104.4(b), 104.33(b) (1996); *see also Timothy W. v. Rochester, New Hampshire, Sch. Dist.,* 875 F.2d 954, 962 (1st Cir. 1989), *cert. denied,* 493 U.S. 893 (1989);

Polk v. Central Susquehanna Intermediate Unit 16, 853 F.2d 171, 176 & n.8, 181–83 (3d Cir. 1988); *Kruelle v. New Castle Co. School Dist.,* 642 F.2d 687, 693–94 (3d Cir. 1981); *Stacey G. v. Pasadena Ind. School Dist.,* 547 F. Supp. 61, 77 (S.D. Tex. 1982) ("an essential element of an appropriate education for a child as handicapped as Stacey is an opportunity to develop skills that would allow Stacey to be as self-sufficient as possible and to function outside of an institution").

224. *See* 20 U.S.C.A. § 1401(a)(19)–(20) (West 1996).

225. *Id.* at § 1401(a)(20) (West 1996).

226. *Id.*

227. *Timothy W. v. Rochester, New Hampshire, Sch. Dist.,* 875 F.2d 954, 973 (1st Cir.), *cert. denied,* 493 U.S. 983 (1989).

228. *See* 34 C.F.R. §§ 300.340, 300.342–.346 (1996).

229. *See* 20 U.S.C.A. §§ 1401(a)(20), 1415 (West 1996); 34 C.F.R. §§ 300.340–.347, 300.500–.515, 300.534, 300.552 (1996).

230. 20 U.S.C.A. §§ 1401(a)(19), 1414(a)(5) (West 1996); 34 C.F.R. § 300.345–.346 (1996).

231. *Board of Educ. of Hendrick Hudson Central Sch. Dist. v. Rowley,* 458 U.S. 179, 206 (1982).

232. 20 U.S.C.A. § 1401(a)(17) (West 1996).

233. 34 C.F.R. § 104.33(b) (1996).

234. 20 U.S.C.A. § 1401(a)(17) (West 1996); *see also* 34 C.F.R. § 300.16 (1996).

235. *See* Comment to 34 C.F.R. § 300.16 (1996).

236. *See, e.g., Thornock v. Boise Ind. Sch. Dist. #1,* 767 P.2d 1241 (Idaho 1988), *cert. denied,* 490 U.S. 1068 (1989).

237. 34 C.F.R. § 300.308 (1996).

238. *Irving Ind. Sch. Dist. v. Tatro,* 468 U.S. 883 (1984).

239. *See, e.g., Babb v. Knox Co. Sch. Syst.,* 965 F.2d 104 (6th Cir. 1992), *cert. denied,* 506 U.S. 941 (1992).

240. 20 U.S.C.A. §§ 1401(a)(16) (West 1996), 1401(a)(18) (West 1996), 1413(a)(4)(B)(i) (West 1996); 34 C.F.R. §§ 300.8(a), 300.14, 104.33(c) (1996).

241. *McLain v. Smith,* 16 EHLR 6 (E.D. Tenn. 1989). *See also Jenkins v. Florida,* 931 F.2d 1469 (11th Cir. 1991).

242. *Shook v. Gaston Co. Board of Educ.,* 882 F.2d (4th Cir. 1989), *cert. denied,* 493 U.S. 1093 (1990); *Seals v. Loftis,* 614 F. Supp. 302 (E. D. Tenn. 1985); *Inquiry of Simon,* 17 EHLR 225 (U.S. Dep't of Educ. Nov. 9, 1990); *Trans Allied Medical Services,* 16 EHLR 96 (U.S. Dep't of Educ. May 30, 1990).

243. 34 C.F.R. §§ 300.348, 300.401 (1996); 34 C.F.R. § 104.33(b)(3) (1996); 34 C.F.R. pt. 300, app. C, ¶ 44 (1996).

244. 20 U.S.C.A. § 1412(2)(C) (West 1996); 34 C.F.R. §§ 300.128(a)(1), 104.32 (1996).

245. 34 C.F.R. §§ 300.531 (comprehensive evaluation), 104.35(a) (evaluation and placement), 300.504(b)(i)–(ii) (1996) (parent consent).

246. *See, e.g.,* Fla. Admin. Code Ann. r. 6A-6.03011(3) (1994); Mass. Regs. Code tit. 603, § 28.309.0 (1994).

247. 20 U.S.C.A. § 1412(5)(C) (West 1996); 34 C.F.R. § 300.530(b) (1996); 34

C.F.R. § 300.532(a)(1) (1996) & 58 Fed. Reg. 13528 (1993); *see also Larry P. v. Riles,* 495 F. Supp. 926 (N.D. Cal. 1979), *aff'd in part and rev'd in part,* 793 F.2d 969 (9th Cir. 1984). For a discussion of racially biased testing in the context of Section 504 and Title VI of the Civil Rights Act 1964, *see Georgia State Conference of Branches of NAACP v. State of Georgia,* 775 F.2d 1403 (11th Cir. 1985).

248. 34 C.F.R. § 300.532(a)(2)(3) (1996); 34 C.F.R. § 104.35(b)(1) (1996).

249. 34 C.F.R. § 500.532(d) (1996); 34 C.F.R. § 104.35 (1996).

250. 34 C.F.R. § 300.532 (1996); 34 C.F.R. § 104.35(b) (1996).

251. *Id.*

252. *Id.* at § 300.532(f) (1996).

253. *Id.* at §§ 300.533(a), 104.35(c) (1996).

254. *Id.* at pt. 104, app. A, ¶ 25 (1996).

255. *Id.* at § 300.343(c) (1996).

256. 20 U.S.C.A. § 1415(b)(1)(A) (West 1996); 34 C.F.R. § 300.503 (1996).

257. 34 C.F.R. § 300.503(b) (1996).

258. *See, e.g., Chicago Public Schools, Dist. #299,* EHLR 353:214 (U.S. Dep't of Educ., Office of Civil Rights, Feb. 6, 1989) (use of monolingual speech therapists and untrained aides to provide speech therapy to Spanish-speaking students violated Title VI and Section 504).

259. 20 U.S.C.A. § 1415(b)(1)(D) (West 1996); 34 C.F.R. § 300.505 (1996).

260. 20 U.S.C.A. § 1415(b)(1)(B) (West 1996); 34 C.F.R. § 300.504(a)(1)–(2) (1996).

261. 34 C.F.R. § 300.505(a) (1996).

262. 20 U.S.C.A. § 1415(b)(1)(D) (West 1996); 34 C.F.R. § 300.505 (1996).

263. 20 U.S.C.A. § 1415(b)(1)(E) (West 1996); 34 C.F.R. §§ 300.504(a)(1)–(2), 300.506 (1996).

264. 20 U.S.C.A. § 1415(b)(2) (West 1996); 34 C.F.R. § 300.506 (1996).

265. 20 U.S.C.A. § 1415(b)(1)(E) (West 1996); 34 C.F.R. §§ 300.504(a)(1)–(2), 300.506 (1996).

266. 20 U.S.C.A. §§ 1415(b)(2), (c), (f) (West 1996).

267. 34 C.F.R. § 300.506(c) (1996).

268. *Id.* at § 300.512(a) (1996).

269. 20 U.S.C.A. § 1415(b)(2) (West 1996); 34 C.F.R. § 300.507 (1996).

270. 20 U.S.C.A. § 1415(d)(2)–(3) (West 1996); 34 C.F.R. § 300.508(a)(2)–(4) (1996).

271. 20 U.S.C.A. § 1415(d)(1) (West 1996); 34 C.F.R. § 300.508(a)(1) (1996).

272. 20 U.S.C.A. § 1415(d)(4) (West 1996); 34 C.F.R. § 300.508(a)(5) (1996).

273. 20 U.S.C.A. § 1415(e)(2) (West 1996).

274. *See, e.g., Pihl v. Massachusetts Dep't of Educ.,* 9 F.3d 184 (1st Cir. 1993); *Todd D. v. Andrews,* 933 F.2d 1576, 1584 (11th Cir. 1991); *Lester H. v. Gilhool,* 916 F.2d 865 (3d Cir. 1990), *cert. denied,* 499 U.S. 923 (1991).

275. 20 U.S.C.A. § 1415(c) (West 1996); 34 C.F.R. §§ 300.509, 300.510 (1996).

276. 20 U.S.C.A. § 1415(e)(2) (West 1996); 34 C.F.R. § 300.511 (1996).

277. 20 U.S.C.A. § 1415(e)(3)(A) (West 1996); 34 C.F.R. § 300.513 (1996). Section

1415(e)(3) was amended in 1994 in the limited circumstance when schools seek to change the placement of students with disabilities who bring firearms to school. 20 U.S.C.A. § 1415(e)(3)(B) (West 1996).

278. 20 U.S.C.A. § 1415(e)(4)(B), (C)–(F) (West 1996); 34 C.F.R. § 300.515 (1996).

279. 20 U.S.C.A. § 1415(e)(4) (West 1996); *see also Shelley C. v. Venus Ind. Sch. Dist.,* 878 F.2d 862 (5th Cir. 1989), *cert. denied,* 493 U.S. 1024 (1990).

280. 34 C.F.R. § 300.660–.662 (1996).

281. *Id.* at § 300.662 (1996).

282. *Id.*

283. 20 U.S.C.A. § 1415(b)(1)(A), (B) (West 1996); 34 C.F.R. §§ 300.13, 300.514 (1996).

284. 20 U.S.C.A. § 1415(b)(1)(B) (West 1996); 34 C.F.R. § 300.514(a)(1)–(3) (1996).

285. 34 C.F.R. § 300.514(c) (1996)(criterion for selecting surrogates).

286. 20 U.S.C.A. § 1415(b)(1)(B) (West 1996); 34 C.F.R. § 300.514(d) (1996).

287. 34 C.F.R. § 300.514(c) (1996).

288. *Id.* at § 104.36 (1996).

289. *Id.*

290. *Id.* at § 104.4(b)(4) (1996); 28 C.F.R. § 35.130(b)(3). (1996).

291. *See id.*

292. 34 C.F.R. § 100.7(b)(1996). 34 C.F.R. § 104.61 (1996) makes 34 C.F.R. § 100.6–.10 applicable to violations of Section 504.

293. *Id.* at § 100.7(b) (1996).

294. *Id.* at § 100.7(c)–(d) (1996).

295. *Id.* at § 100.8(a) (1996).

296. 29 U.S.C.A. § 794 (West 1996); 34 C.F.R. §§ 104.3(j), 104.4(b), 104.33, 104.35 (1996); 42 U.S.C.A. § 12132 (West 1996); 28 C.F.R. § 35.130(a)–(b) (1996) (implementing ADA). *See also* the following U.S. Dep't of Educ./OCR complaint decisions: *School Administrative Unit #38 (NH),* 19 IDELR 186; *Ohio Co. (KY) School Dist.,* 17 EHLR 528; *Compliance Review of Riverview (WA) School Dist.,* EHLR 311:103; and *Nash Co. (NC) School Dist.,* EHLR 352:37.

297. *Id.*

298. *Honig v. Doe,* 484 U.S. 305 (1988).

299. 20 U.S.C.A. § 1415(e)(3) (West 1996).

300. *See, e.g., Texas City Ind. Sch. Dist. v. Jorstad,* 752 F. Supp. 231 (S.D. Tex. 1990).

301. *See* 20 U.S.C.A. §§ 1415(e)(3)(B), 8921 (note) (West 1996). Amendments made by section 314 of Improving America's Schools Act of 1994, Pub. L. No. 103-382, 108 Stat. 3518 (1994), are codified as a note to 20 U.S.C.A. § 8921 (West 1996) and provide that they "shall be interpreted in a manner that is consistent with the Department's final guidance concerning State and local responsibilities under the Gun-Free Schools Act of 1994." The House Conference Report on the Improving America's Schools Act clarifies that "the Department's final guidance" is the U.S. Department of Education document printed in the Congressional Record of July 28, 1994 at S. 10017. *See* H.R. Conf. Rep. No. 761, 103d Cong., 2d Sess. 883. The guidance provides that if a student's action in bringing a firearm to school

is related to the student's disability, the school system may suspend for up to ten days and, where a longer exclusion from the current educational placement is believed to be necessary because the student is considered to be dangerous, seek a court order changing the placement. The forty-five day exception to "stay-put rights" created by 20 U.S.C.A. § 1415(e)(3)(B) (West 1996) therefore does not apply.

302. *See* Section 314(a)(2) of Improving America's Schools Act of 1994, Pub. L. No. 103-382, 108 Stat. 3518 (1994).

303. 20 U.S.C.A. §§ 1681–88 (West 1996); 34 C.F.R. § 106 (1996).

304. *See* Jacqueline A. Berrien et al., *Equal Educational Opportunities for Pregnant and Parenting Students: Meshing the Rights with the Realities* 3 (American Civil Liberties Union and American Association of University Women Educational Foundation, 1990).

305. *Child Care for Children of Adolescent Parents: Findings from a National Survey and Case Studies* (Wellesley College Center for Research on Women, Working Paper No. 184, 1989).

306. 20 U.S.C.A. § 1070a-13 (West 1996).

307. *Id.* at § 1070a-12 (West 1996).

308. *Id.* at § 1070a-13(b) (West 1996).

309. *See id.* at §§ 1070a-13(b), (c) (West 1996).

310. *Id.* at § 1070a-13(b)(8) (West 1996).

311. *Id.* at § 1070a-14 (West 1996).

312. *Id.* at § 1070a-12(b) (West 1996).

313. *Id.*

314. *Id.* at § 1070a-12(c)(2) (West 1996).

315. The information in this section is drawn largely from *Student Guide, 1994–1995: Financial Aid from the U.S. Department of Education* (U.S. Government Printing Office, 1993).

316. *See* National Center for Education Statistics, *National Post-secondary Student Aid Study: Estimates of Student Financial Aid 1992–93* iv (June 1995).

317. 42 U.S.C.A. § 12601 (West 1996).

318. 42 U.S.C.A. § 2753 (West 1996).

319. Pub. L. No. 104-193, 110 Stat. 2105, § 103 (1996)(adding new § 408(a)(6) (1996) to Title IV of the Social Security Act).

VI

Access to Justice

If an indigent is arrested and cannot afford a lawyer, does the government have to provide representation free of charge?

Yes. Under the Sixth Amendment to the federal Constitution, an indigent criminal defendant has a right to counsel if she or he faces incarceration upon conviction.[1] As the Supreme Court has explained, the ideal of "fair trials before impartial tribunals in which every defendant stands equal before the law . . . cannot be realized if the poor man charged with crime has to face his accusers without a lawyer to assist him."[2] Many state constitutions also guarantee counsel in criminal cases to indigents who cannot afford to hire a lawyer.[3]

The constitutional right to counsel applies whenever there is any risk that an individual will be sentenced to jail[4] and extends to children facing criminal charges in juvenile or family courts.[5] The right attaches not simply at trial, but also at any "critical stage" of the case, including arraignment, preliminary hearings, and sentencing.[6] A person accused of a crime also has a constitutional right to ancillary services needed to mount a defense at trial or for an appeal. These services may include experts, translators, and free transcripts.[7]

An accused's rights under the Sixth Amendment are not without limit. Thus, for example, the United States Supreme Court has held that it is constitutionally permissible for a state to refuse to appoint counsel to enable an indigent to take a discretionary appeal.[8] And the Court has refused to mandate free counsel for criminal defendants who face fines, rather than imprisonment.[9] Moreover, although an accused has a right to a lawyer, and the lawyer must be competent, the Constitution does not give an indigent the right to a lawyer of his or her choice.[10] An individual who is incompatible with an assigned lawyer can make a formal request for a change of counsel, but the court has broad discretion to deny the motion.[11]

States provide indigent defense services in a variety of ways. In the majority of counties, private lawyers are assigned to individual cases, either on an ad hoc basis or through a systematic program. A smaller but still significant number of counties provide indigent defense through a public defender system, which involves a public or private organization employing full-time staff. Finally, a minority of counties provide representation through lawyers or organizations that are hired on contract for a period of time.[12]

In recent years, virtually all indigent defense systems have faced severe fiscal pressures, leading to mounting caseloads, over-extended lawyer training, and case delay. The National Advisory Commission on Criminal Justice Standards and Goals recommends that yearly case assignments not exceed 150 felonies, 400 misdemeanors, 200 juvenile cases, or 25 appeals per attorney.[13] But because of inadequate funding, caseloads in many states and counties far exceed these guidelines. Caseloads for public defenders in Connecticut juvenile courts, for example, average 716 cases per year per attorney, ranging up to over 1,500 cases per year in the most congested court.[14] In-custody felony defendants in Jones County, Mississippi typically have had to wait three to four months before even being interviewed by part-time public defenders.[15]

Whether an assigned lawyer has provided effective counsel that meets constitutional standards is an issue that an appeals court considers on a case-by-case basis. To overturn a criminal conviction because of the ineffective assistance of counsel, one must show that the lawyer was incompetent and that it is likely that if competent counsel had been provided, the outcome of the case would have been different.[16] Federal courts have so far been unwilling to issue across-the-board performance standards in cases challenging the adequacy of indigent defense systems.[17] Some state courts, however, have entered orders to deal with the systemic problems that may result from inadequate funding of indigent defense systems. In a few of these cases, courts have ordered caseload relief and increased compensation as a way to improve the quality of representation in individual cases.[18]

What happens if an arrestee cannot afford to post bail?

Historically, the most common method to ensure that an arrestee would be present at trial was to require the posting of bail, which directed the accused to give the government a sum of money that would be returned when she or he appeared at trial. As the United States Supreme Court has explained, "[A] primary function of bail is to safeguard the courts' role in adjudicating the guilt or innocence of defendants."[19] The right to bail, however, is not absolute. Although the Eighth Amendment to the federal Constitution provides that in a criminal proceeding "[e]xcessive bail shall not be required,"[20] a court may refuse bail in a capital case or where the defendant presents a risk of flight. Under federal law, a federal court may now also refuse bail where "no release conditions 'will reasonably assure . . . the safety of any other person and the community.' "[21] Standards for setting amounts of bail also vary from state to state. If a judge finds there is a risk that an accused will not show up at trial, or there is any other statutorily authorized reason to justify pretrial detention, the judge can set bail and keep an accused in jail if the required amount of bail cannot be posted.[22]

Can the government imprison a person who is sentenced to a fine but cannot afford to pay it?

A person cannot be sent to jail simply because he or she cannot afford to pay a fine or court costs.[23] The United States Supreme Court has made clear, however, that poverty "does not insulate those who break the law from punishment."[24] The government can, therefore, impose other methods to compel payment, such as requiring payment of the fine on the installment system. And the court can imprison a person who can afford to pay a fine, but refuses to do so.

The United States Supreme Court has addressed this issue in a trilogy of cases. *Williams v. Illinois* involved a law imposing a maximum sentence of one year for petty theft and a $500 fine, plus $5 in court costs.[25] The defendant was unable to pay, and was ordered to remain in jail the length of time required to "work off" the obligation at the rate of $5 per day—an additional 101 days beyond the statutory maximum. The Court held that imprisonment beyond a statutory maximum was constitutionally impermissible when imposed on a defendant who was economically unable to pay the fine. "[T]he Fourteenth Amendment requires that the statutory ceiling placed on imprisonment for any substantive offense be the same for all defendants irrespective of their economic status."[26]

In *Tate v. Short*, the Court extended the reasoning of the *Williams* decision to bar imprisonment for nonpayment of a fine for an offense that is statutorily punishable only by fine. As the Court explained, "Since [the state] has legislated a 'fines only' policy for traffic offenses, that statutory ceiling cannot, consistently with the Equal Protection Clause, limit the punishment to payment of the fine if one is able to pay it, yet convert the fine into a prison term for an indigent defendant without the means to pay his fine."[27]

Finally, in *Bearden v. Georgia*, the Court held that a state cannot revoke probation that is conditioned on payment of a fine and restitution, where the defendant is unable to pay. The record showed that the defendant had borrowed money to pay part of the amount owed but subsequently lost his job. Despite repeated efforts to find work, he was unable to pay the balance and was ordered to jail for 100 days, to "work off" the obligation at the rate of $5 per day. The Court explained: "[I]f the probationer has made all reasonable efforts to pay the fine or restitution, and yet cannot do so through no fault of his own, it is fundamentally unfair to revoke probation automatically without considering whether adequate alternative methods of punishing the defendant are available."[28]

What happens if an indigent is sentenced to "30 days or 30 dollars" and cannot pay the fine?

The alternative sentence of "30 days or 30 dollars" is a common feature of many local ordinances that criminalize aspects of poverty, such as begging or sleeping in public. The United States Supreme Court has never addressed the specific question of whether alternative sentences of this sort violate principles of equal protection or due process. In *Williams v. Illinois*, the Court explicitly stated that its holding "does not deal with a judgment of confinement for nonpayment of a fine in the familiar pattern of alternative sentence of '$30 or 30 days.' "[29] An alternative sentencing scheme reflects a legislative decision that imprisonment is penologically appropriate for a particular kind of offense. Nevertheless, under the *Williams* trilogy of cases, it should be constitutionally impermissible for a state to erect an alternative sentencing scheme that allows the affluent to escape imprisonment yet condemns the indigent to jail.

Does it cost money to file a civil lawsuit in court?

Yes. Courts charge a "filing fee" for new lawsuits. But depending on the kind of case and the governing state law, a court may be obliged to waive the filing fee for a poor person who cannot afford to pay and is barred from bringing suit.[30] Under the federal Constitution, a court must waive a filing fee if an indigent would otherwise be unable to enforce a fundamental right and has no alternative means of redress. Thus, for example, the United States Supreme Court has held that a court must waive a filing fee for divorce because the right to marry is fundamental and marriage cannot be dissolved without judicial involvement.[31] As the Court explained,

> [G]iven the basic position of the marriage relationship in this society's hierarchy of values and the concomitant state monopolization of the means for legally dissolving this relationship, due process . . . prohibit[s] a State from denying, solely because of inability to pay, access to its courts to individuals who seek judicial dissolution of their marriages.[32]

By contrast, the Court found that due process is not violated if an indigent cannot pay a filing fee to declare bankruptcy and is prevented from discharging debts. No fundamental right is involved, and debts may be adjusted through private negotiation with creditors without court involvement.[33] Similarly, if an indigent wants to challenge a decision made by a welfare official, the court does not have to waive its fee to allow the filing of a lawsuit.[34]

Although the federal Constitution does not guarantee free access to the courts in all cases, almost all courts have a statutory or administrative procedure allowing an indigent to bring a lawsuit without first paying a filing fee. The procedure is called *in forma pauperis* or poor person's relief and, depending on the court, excuses or postpones the payment of judicial costs and fees.[35] The federal *in forma pauperis* statute, for example, provides:

> Any court of the United States may authorize the commencement, prosecution or defense of any suit, action or proceeding, civil or criminal, or appeal therein, without prepayment of fees and costs or security therefor, by a person who makes affidavit that he is unable to pay such costs or give security therefor. Such affidavit shall state the nature of the action, defense or appeal and affiant's belief that he is entitled to redress.[36]

Under this statute, an indigent does not have to show "absolute destitution,"[37] and at least one court of appeals has held that a a poor litigant should not "be made to choose between abandoning a potentially meritorious claim or foregoing the necessities of life."[38]

Generally, a person who is planning to file a lawsuit should contact the clerk of the relevant court and ask for information about how to apply for a waiver of fees and costs. A legal services or legal aid attorney can also provide this information. Most courts will generally require submission of an "affidavit," a document that is sworn to or affirmed, setting forth relevant financial information such as employment, other sources of income, assets, debts, and obligations. If the request is granted, courts in some states will waive not only the filing fee, but also litigation expenses such as the cost of a transcript for appeal and service of process.[39]

Does a poor person have a right to free representation in a civil lawsuit?

It depends on the rights that are at stake in the lawsuit. In general, an indigent litigant, whether a plaintiff or a defendant, does not have a right to free, appointed counsel in a civil lawsuit.[40] Such a right has been recognized only in those cases where a party "may lose his physical liberty if he loses the litigation."[41] Thus, children accused of delinquency[42] and individuals at risk of either civil commitment[43] or imprisonment for civil contempt[44] have been found as a matter of due process to have a right to free appointed counsel. By contrast, the Court has held that an indigent faced with termination of parental rights does not have an automatic right to counsel.[45] Many advocates believe that counsel should be provided to indigent tenants faced with eviction in state court housing proceedings.[46]

Although the federal Constitution has not been interpreted as creating a right to counsel in all civil lawsuits, state constitutions may establish such a right in particular kinds of cases. For example, a number of state courts interpreting their state constitutions have held that counsel must be appointed in parental termination proceedings for indigents who cannot afford representation.[47]

The court may also have discretion to appoint counsel under federal or state statutory law. Under federal law, the district court judge has authority to appoint a lawyer under the *in forma pauperis* statute if the complaint appears meritorious and representation would assist the court in its deliberation, given the complexity of the legal issues, the plaintiff's ability to present his or her case, and the need for cross-examination.[48]

Similarly, the granting of a motion to proceed *in forma pauperis* under many state laws authorizes the court to appoint counsel in appropriate cases. Thus, for example, under New York law, it has been held an abuse of discretion for a trial court to refuse to appoint counsel where an indigent presents a meritorious claim and cannot obtain free representation from a legal services office.[49] Laws in other states grant the court authority to appoint counsel in specific kinds of cases, such as divorce or parental neglect,[50] or for particular kinds of litigants, such as children or prisoners.[51] In some kinds of cases the right to counsel is mandatory, while in others the granting of

TABLE 6-1
1996 Federal Income Limits for Eligibility for Free Legal Services

Size of Family	48 Contiguous States	Alaska	Hawaii
1	$ 9,675	$12,075	$11,138
2	$12,950	$16,175	$14,900
3	$16,225	$20,275	$18,663
4	$19,500	$24,375	$22,425
5	$22,775	$28,475	$26,188
6	$26,050	$32,575	$29,950
7	$29,325	$36,675	$33,713
8	$32,600	$40,775	$37,475
Each additional person	$ 3,175	$ 4,100	$ 3,763

Source: 61 Fed. Reg. 12041 (March 29, 1996) (codified at 45 C. F. R. pt. 1611 (1996)).

representation is within the discretion of the court. The rules governing appointment of counsel vary from case to case, depending on state law, the nature of the claim, the kind of litigant, and other factors that the court has discretion to consider. Appendix E at the end of this book lists different statutory bases for a right to counsel under the laws of the fifty states.[52]

Even if a poor person does not have a right to assigned counsel, free representation may still be available from a legal services or legal aid office. Legal services offices are similar to legal aid, but receive most of their funding from the federal government and are subject to a number of restrictions.[53] To be eligible for free legal services, a litigant must meet federally defined income limits that are typically fixed at 125 percent of the federal poverty index. In 1996, eligibility levels were as shown in table 6-1.[54]

The telephone number of a neighborhood legal services or legal aid office should be listed in the local phone book. But even if income guidelines are met, the office may not be able to provide representation because of its own funding and resource limitations. Moreover, each legal services and legal aid office sets its own case priorities. Some offices, for example, focus only on housing; others on benefits and domestic matters.

If counsel is not available from legal services or legal aid, it may help to contact a local bar association, which in some communities keeps "referral lists" for persons in need of representation. In addition, some public interest organizations, like the NAACP Legal Defense and Educational Fund, Inc., and the American Civil Liberties Union, handle lawsuits for free if they raise issues that are expected to have a broad impact on large groups of people.[55] Finally, some private lawyers may agree to take on a poor person's case in the expectation that fees will be paid by someone other than the client because of the nature of the claim. In civil rights cases, for example, federal law provides for "fee shifting," which means that a losing defendant is required to pay the prevailing plaintiff's attorney's fees and costs.[56] In addition, in many kinds of accident or negligence cases, where an injured party is seeking damages for harm that was done, lawyers may agree to representation for a contingency fee, which means that the lawyer will receive a percentage of damages that the court awards if the plaintiff wins the lawsuit.

Do courts assign free interpreters in civil cases to indigent litigants who do not speak English?

Generally, no.[57] There is no federal constitutional right to a translator in a civil case. Although a court will typically provide translators for non-English speaking witnesses in civil cases, parties do not have an automatic right to this service for free.[58]

A court may nevertheless exercise its discretion to assign a translator if particularly significant interests are implicated in a poor person's lawsuit. Cases where translators are more likely to be assigned involve children and allegations of abuse and neglect. Finally, if a translator is needed because an indigent litigant has a disability, such as a hearing impairment, federal and state laws prohibiting discrimination against persons with disabilities may require the court to make reasonable accommodation through the assignment of a translator.[59]

Will the court provide free experts and special tests to indigent litigants in civil cases?

Some civil cases involve disputed factual issues that can be resolved only through the assistance of an expert or the use of a specialized test. The classic example of this kind of dispute is paternity, where a blood grouping test provides a unique form of exculpatory evidence. Expert evidence is implicated in many other kinds of cases, as well. For example, in a nonpayment eviction proceeding involving unsafe conditions in an apartment, testimony from an environmental expert on lead paint hazards could be useful. Similarly, a psychiatrist's testimony may be essential for a poor person to prove a disability for purposes of receiving SSI.

The United States Supreme Court has never recognized a general constitutional right to free experts and special tests in civil cases. The Court has, however, recognized that the withholding of specialized litigation services may violate due process in cases where the state is a party to the litigation and the denial of the service "operates to deprive an individual of a protected right."[60] Thus, for example, in *Little v. Streater*, the Court held that the state of Connecticut has a constitutional obligation to provide free blood-grouping tests to an indigent defendant in a paternity case.[61] By contrast, numerous lower courts have held that an indigent does not have an automatic right to a court-appointed psychiatrist in child custody and civil commitment proceedings.[62]

The Court has not addressed the issue of whether a trial judge has discretion to appoint expert witnesses in civil cases under the *in forma pauperis* statute, and lower courts so far have declined to exercise any such authority.[63] Moreover, the majority of courts have refused to advance or waive witness fees for *in forma pauperis* litigants.[64] Under certain circumstances, however, a federal court has authority to appoint an expert under the Federal Rules of Evidence, and a few courts have done this even where a party is indigent.[65] An indigent litigant who is unable to afford an expert can ask the court to appoint a court expert to assist in the resolution of complex and disputed factual matters.[66]

If a poor person loses a civil case and wants to appeal, is there a right to a free copy of the transcript of the trial?

It depends on the type of case and the court in which the case was heard. In federal court, federal law guarantees a free transcript if needed to appeal, so long as the litigant legitimately cannot afford to pay for a copy and if the appeal is taken in good faith.[67] In state court, the judge has discretion to order a free transcript as part of *in forma pauperis* relief.[68] Whether a court will make a transcript available is likely to turn on the nature of the lawsuit, the identity of the parties, and the kind of rights at stake.[69]

Notes

1. U.S. Const. amend. VI ("In all criminal prosecutions, the accused shall enjoy . . . the Assistance of Counsel for his defence.").
2. *Gideon v. Wainwright*, 372 U.S. 335, 344 (1963).

3. Examples of state analogues to the Sixth Amendment are collected in Jennifer Friesen, *State Constitutional Law: Litigating Individual Rights, Claims and Defenses,* ¶ 12.03 at 12–17 n.24 (1993).

4. *Powell v. Alabama,* 287 U.S. 45 (1932)(state capital felony prosecutions); *Johnson v. Zerbst,* 304 U.S. 458 (1938)(federal noncapital felony prosecutions); *Gideon v. Wainwright,* 372 U.S. 335 (1963)(state noncapital felony prosecutions); *Argersinger v. Hamlin,* 407 U.S. 25 (1972)(state misdemeanor prosecutions).

5. *In re Gault,* 387 U.S. 1 (1967)(juvenile cases).

6. *Coleman v. Alabama,* 399 U.S. 1 (1970)(preliminary hearing); *Mempa v. Rhay,* 389 U.S. 128 (1967)(sentencing); *White v. Maryland,* 373 U.S. 59 (1963) (pleading guilty).

7. *Ake v. Oklahoma,* 470 U.S. 68 (1985)(psychiatric expert); *Mayer v. Chicago,* 404 U.S. 189 (1971)(adequate record to appeal a conviction under a fine-only statute); *Douglas v. California,* 372 U.S. 353 (1963)(lawyer on first direct appeal); *Roberts v. LaVallee,* 389 U.S. 40 (1967)(transcript of preliminary hearing for use at trial); *Griffin v. Illinois,* 351 U.S. 12 (1956)(transcript on appeal).

8. *Ross v. Moffitt,* 417 U.S. 600 (1974); *see also United States v. MacCollom,* 426 U.S. 317 (1976)(provision of transcript conditioned on certification that challenge is not frivolous).

9. *Scott v. Illinois,* 440 U.S. 367 (1979).

10. *See Wheat v. United States,* 486 U.S. 153, 159 (1988). The right to effective counsel was established in *McMann v. Richardson,* 397 U.S. 759 (1970).

11. *E.g., United States v. Calabro,* 467 F.2d 973 (2d Cir. 1972), *cert. denied,* 410 U.S. 926 (1973).

12. *See* Richard Klein & Robert Spangenberg, *The Indigent Defense Crisis 1993,* A.B.A. Sec. Crim. Just. 3, *citing* Bureau of Justice Statistics, U.S. Dep't of Justice, *Criminal Defense for the Poor, 1986* (1988).

13. *Id.* at 11, *citing* The Nat'l Advisory Comm. on Criminal Justice Standards and Goals, *Task Force on the Courts,* Standard 13.12 (1973).

14. *See* complaint in *Rivera v. Rowland,* ¶¶ 24, 26, CV 95-0545629S (Conn. Super. Ct., Jud. Dist. of Hartford/New Britain at Hartford, Jan. 5, 1995).

15. *See The Indigent Defense Crisis 1993, supra* note 12, at 11.

16. *Strickland v. Washington,* 466 U.S. 668 (1984).

17. *See Luckey v. Harris,* 860 F.2d 1012 (11th Cir. 1988), *cert. denied,* 495 U.S. 957 (1990), *district court order vacated sub. nom. Luckey v. Miller,* 929 F.2d 618 (11th Cir. 1991); *Gardner v. Luckey,* 500 F.2d 712 (5th Cir. 1974), *cert. denied,* 423 U.S. 841 (1975); *see generally* Rodger Citron, *(Un)Luckey v. Miller: The Case for a Structural Injunction to Improve Indigent Defense Services,* 101 Yale L.J. 481, 486 (1991).

18. *See, e.g., Wilson v. State,* 574 So. 2d 1338 (Miss. 1990); *State v. Ryan,* 233 Neb. 151, 444 N.W.2d 656 (1989); *State ex rel. Stephan v. Smith,* 242 Kan. 336, 747 P.2d 816 (1987); *State v. Smith,* 140 Ariz. 355, 681 P.2d 1374 (1984); *Escambia County v. Behr,* 384 So.2d 147 (Fla. 1980); *Ligda v. Superior Court,* 5 Cal. App. 3d 811, 85 Cal. Rptr. 744 (Cal. Ct. App. 1970).

19. *United States v. Salerno,* 481 U.S. 739, 753 (1987).

20. U.S. Const. amend. VIII.

21. *Salerno*, 481 U.S. at 739 (*quoting* Bail Reform Act of 1984, 18 U.S.C. § 3142(e) (1982 Supp. III)).

22. *But see Stack v. Boyle*, 342 U.S. 1 (1951).

23. *See Bearden v. Georgia*, 461 U.S. 660 (1983); *Tate v. Short*, 401 U.S. 395 (1971); *Williams v. Illinois*, 399 U.S. 235 (1970).

24. *Bearden*, 461 U.S. at 675 (White, J., concurring, joined by Burger, C.J., Powell & Rehnquist, JJ.), 669 ("A defendant's poverty in no way immunizes him from punishment.").

25. *Williams v. Illinois*, 399 U.S. 235 (1970).

26. *Id.* at 244.

27. *Tate v. Short*, 401 U.S. 395, 399 (1971).

28. *Bearden*, 461 U.S. 660, 668–69 (1983).

29. *Williams*, 399 U.S. at 243.

30. *See* Frank I. Michelman, *The Supreme Court and Litigation Access Fees: The Right to Protect One's Rights—Part I*, 1973 Duke L.J. 1153.

31. *Boddie v. Connecticut*, 401 U.S. 371 (1971).

32. *Id.* at 374–75.

33. *United States v. Kras*, 409 U.S. 434 (1973).

34. *Ortwein v. Schwab*, 410 U.S. 656 (1973). The United States Supreme Court also affirmed a decision by a three-judge district court upholding a Louisiana law that defendants in a foreclosure action post security prior to resisting foreclosure. *Ross v. Brown Title Corp.*, 356 F. Supp. 595 (E.D. La.), *aff'd mem.*, 412 U.S. 934 (1973).

35. *See, e.g.*, 28 U.S.C.A. § 1915 (West 1996); Cal. Govt. Code §§ 26720.5, 68511.3 (West 1995); D.C. Code § 15-712 (1996); Fla. Stat. Ann. § 34.041(2) (West 1995); N.Y. CPLR § 1102 (McKinney's 1996).

36. 28 U.S.C. § 1915 (1995).

37. *Potnick v. Eastern State Hosp.*, 701 F.2d 243 (2d Cir. 1983).

38. *Id.* (citing *Adkins v. E.I. DuPont de Nemours & Co., Inc.*, 335 U.S. 331, 339 (1948)); *see also Fediuk v. State of New York*, 575 F. Supp. 233 (S.D.N.Y. 1983).

39. Annotation, *What Costs or Fees Are Contemplated by Statute Authorizing Proceeding in forma pauperis*, 98 A.L.R.2d 292 (1964).

40. Numerous scholars have tried to establish a right to counsel in civil cases under the federal Constitution, *see, e.g.*, Lester Brickman, *Of Arterial Passageways Through the Legal Process: The Right of Universal Access to Courts and Lawyering Services*, 48 N.Y.U. L. Rev. 595 (1973)(locating a right to counsel in civil cases in the First Amendment). For an international comparison, *see* Earl Johnson, Jr., *The Right to Counsel in Civil Cases: An International Perspective*, 19 Loy. L.A. L. Rev. 341 (1985); Francis William O'Brien, *Why Not Appointed Counsel in Civil Cases? The Swiss Approach*, 28 Ohio St. L.J. 1 (1967).

41. *Lassiter v. Dep't of Social Servs.*, 452 U.S. 18, 25 (1981).

42. *In re Gault*, 387 U.S. 1 (1967).

43. *Vitek v. Jones*, 445 U.S. 480 (1980).

44. *Walker v. McLain*, 768 F.2d 1181 (7th Cir. 1985), *cert. denied*, 474 U.S. 106 (1986); *see* Robert Monk, Comment, *The Indigent Defendant's Right to Court-Appointed Counsel in Civil Contempt Proceedings for Nonpayment of Child Support*, 50 U. Chi. L. Rev. 326 (1983).

45. *Lassiter v. Dep't of Social Servs.*, 452 U.S. 18 (1981); *see also* Regina M. Campbell, Comment, *No-Frills Due Process—Who Needs Counsel? Lassiter v. Department of Social Services*, 14 Conn. L. Rev. 733 (1982).

46. *See* Karl Monsma & Richard Lempert, *The Value of Counsel: 20 Years of Representation before a Public Housing Eviction Board*, 26 L. & Soc. Rev. 627 (1992); Andrew Scherer, *Gideon's Shelter: The Need to Recognize a Right to Counsel for Indigent Defendants in Eviction Proceedings*, 23 Harv. C.R.-C.L. L. Rev. 557 (1988).

47. *E.g., V.F. v. State*, 666 P.2d 42 (Alaska 1983)(stating that the Alaska Supreme Court was joining the "growing number of jurisdictions that have held that the right to counsel in termination proceedings exists under the state constitution").

48. 28 U.S.C.A. § 1915(d) (West 1996); *see also Whisenant v. Yuam*, 739 F.2d 160 (4th Cir. 1984); *Merrit v. Faulkner*, 697 F.2d 761 (7th Cir.), *cert. denied*, 464 U.S. 986 (1983); *Maclin v. Freake*, 650 F.2d 885 (7th Cir. 1981); *Gordon v. Leeke*, 574 F.2d 1147 (4th Cir.), *cert. denied*, 439 U.S. 970 (1978); Note, *The Civil Indigent's Last Chance for Meaningful Access to the Federal Courts: The Inherent Power to Mandate Pro Bono Publico*, 71 B.U. L. Rev. 545 (1991).

49. *E.g., Yearwood v. Yearwood*, 54 A.D.2d 626, 387 N.Y.S.2d 433, 434 (N.Y. App. Div. 1976); *Hotel Martha Washington Mgt. Co. v. Swinick*, 66 Misc. 2d 833, 835, 322 N.Y.S.2d 139, 141 (N.Y. App. Term. 1971).

50. *See, e.g.*, D.C. Code Ann. § 16-918 (1996) (divorce); Iowa Code Ann. § 232.89 (West 1996)(abuse and neglect); Mass. Gen. Laws Ann. ch. 209(c), § 7 (West 1996)(paternity).

51. *See, e.g., Tedder v. Fairman*, 92 Ill. 2d 216, 441 N.E.2d 311 (Ill. 1982)(prisoners).

52. The appendix is adapted from materials prepared by Steven Weller & David A. Price, *Representing Indigent Parties in Civil Cases: An Analysis of State Practices* (State Justice Institute, 1994).

53. 42 U.S.C.A. § 2996 (Wet 1996). Congress established the Legal Services Corporation in 1974. The federal government prohibits legal services lawyers from representing litigants in cases involving abortion and school desegregation. 42 U.S.C.A. §§ 2996f(b)(8) and (9) (West 1996).

54. 61 Fed. Reg. 12041 (March 29, 1996) (codified at 45 C.F.R. pt. 1611 (1996)).

55. *See In re Primus*, 436 U.S. 412 (1978); *NAACP v. Button*, 371 U.S. 415 (1963).

56. 42 U.S.C.A. § 1988(b) (West 1996).

57. *See, e.g., Jara v. Municipal Court*, 21 Cal. 3d 181, 578 P.2d 94 (Cal. 1978), *cert. denied*, 439 U.S. 1067 (1979).

58. *See* 28 U.S.C.A. § 1827(d) (West 1996); Cal. Evid. Code § 752 (West 1996).

59. 42 U.S.C.A. § 12132 (West 1996) prohibits discrimination by state or local governments; §§ 12131(2) and 12102(1) suggest that it is discrimination if the government fails to provide needed translator services. No court appears to have yet applied these statutes to private civil litigants, although one court has held that the Americans with Disabilities Act, 42 U.S.C.A. § 12132 (West 1996), requires prison officials to provide deaf and hearing-impaired inmates with translators or other accommodations that allow full participation in educational and rehabilitative programs and in disciplinary and grievance proceedings. *Clarkson v. Coughlin*, 898 F. Supp. 1019 (S.D.N.Y. 1995).

60. *Boddie v. Connecticut*, 401 U.S. 371, 379 (1971).

61. *Little v. Streater*, 452 U.S. 1 (1981). State courts in a number of jurisdictions have applied *Little* to mandate provision of free blood-grouping tests in those states' paternity proceedings. *See Pierce v. State*, 251 Ga. 590, 308 S.E.2d 367 (1983); *Shaw v. Seward*, 689 S.W.2d 37 (Ky. Ct. App. 1985); *Kennedy v. Wood*, 439 N.E.2d 1367 (Ind. Ct. App. 1982); *Anderson v. Jacobs*, 68 Ohio St. 2d 67, 428 N.E.2d 419 (1981). In Alabama, the supreme court found that while *Little* requires provision of free blood-grouping tests in paternity actions, the defendant does not have to receive the "seven systems" test ordered in that case by the United States Supreme Court. *See Ex Parte Calloway*, 456 So.2d 308 (Ala.1984), *cert. denied, Calloway v. Alabama*, 470 U.S. 1002 (1985).

62. *Goetz v. Crosson*, 41 F.3d 800 (2d Cir. 1994), 116 S.Ct. 80 (1995)(civil commitment); *In re Shaeffer Children*, 85 Ohio App.3d 683, 621 N. E.2d 426 (Ohio Ct. App. 1993) (child custody).

63. *See Pedraza v. Jones*, 71 F.3d 194 (5th Cir. 1995); *Boring v. Kozakiewics*, 833 F.2d 468 (3d Cir. 1987), *cert. denied*, 485 U.S. 991 (1988).

64. *See Aiello v. McCaughtry*, 92 F.3d 1187, 1996 WL 420456 (unpublished) (7th Cir. 1996); *Tedder v. Odel*, 890 F.2d 210 (9th Cir. 1989).

65. *See* Fed. R. Evid. 706(a)("The court may on its own motion or on the motion of any party enter an order to show cause why expert witnesses should not be appointed."); *McKinney v. Anderson*, 924 F.2d 1500, 1511 (9th Cir.), *vacated and remanded on other grounds*, 502 U.S. 903 (1991); *Webster v. Sowders*, 846 F.2d 1032, 1038–39 (6th Cir. 1988).

66. *See Beaver v. Board of County Comms. of Gooding County*, 1991 WL 350749 (D. Idaho 1991)(appointment of court expert in civil rights case involving conditions in county jail); *but see Mallard Bay Drilling v. Bessard*, 145 F.R.D. 405 (W.D. La. 1993)(conflicting expert opinions on medical condition did not require appointment of additional expert).

67. 28 U.S.C.A. § 1915(b) (West 1996).

68. *See, e.g., State ex rel Girouard v. Circuit Court*, 155 Wisc. 2d 148, 454 N.W.2d 792 (1990); N.Y. Civ. Prac. L. & R. § 1102(b) (McKinney's 1996); D.C. Code § 15-712 (1996).

69. *Compare* Colo. Rev. Stat. Ann. § 19-3-609(2)(West 1996)(right to transcript in termination of parental rights cases) *with Almarez v. Carpenter*, 183 Colo. 284, 477 P.2d 792 (1970)(no such right generally).

VII

Rights in Public Places

Do the poor and unemployed have a right to relocate to another state?

Yes. In 1941 in a case called *Edwards v. California*,[1] the United States Supreme Court invalidated a California statute that made it a crime to transport poor nonresidents into the state. Some version of the law had been on the books since 1860, but California did not begin vigorous enforcement until the Great Depression, when drought and economic collapse brought an unprecedented migration of poor people into the state.[2] Striking down the law under the Commerce Clause of the federal Constitution,[3] the Court held that a state cannot constitutionally "isolate itself from difficulties common to all [states] . . . by restraining the transportation of persons . . . across its borders."[4]

The *Edwards* decision marked an important new chapter in the history of poor persons. At the founding of the Republic, states and localities tried to block the migration of indigents into their jurisdictions on the view that poverty is a "moral pestilence" that might infect the rest of the community.[5] Exclusionary practices of this sort dated back at least to English laws of the fourteenth century, which, upon the break-up of feudalism, attempted to restrain the mobility of free laborers.[6] *Edwards* made clear, however, that "[p]overty and immorality are not synonymous"[7] and confirmed that indigents have the same rights of national citizenship as their more affluent neighbors. Under the Court's reasoning, a poor person who seeks a better life cannot and should not be prevented from establishing residence in a new state. Subsequent to *Edwards,* at least some lower federal courts have recognized that the federal Constitution protects not only the right to travel from state to state, but also the right to travel "within a state."[8]

Despite the clear holding of the *Edwards* decision, many cities and towns are currently trying to fence the poor out of their communities as a way to deal with the social consequences of hunger and homelessness.[9] Of forty-nine cities surveyed in 1994, more than 25 percent had enacted or begun to enforce local laws that restrict poor people's access to public places or that effectively criminalize the status of being poor.[10] Policies that seek to exclude the poor from entering a community or from participating in community life violate the spirit of the *Edwards* decision, as well as the bedrock principle of national citizenship.[11]

Do poor people have a right to "hang out" on the streets?

Yes, but cities and towns are increasingly ordering poor and homeless people to "move on" or face arrest. Streets, sidewalks, and parks have traditionally been regarded as open to the people and available for speech and association. As the United States Supreme Court has explained: "[W]herever the title of streets and parks may rest, they have immemorially been used for purposes of assembly, communicating thought between citizens, and discussing public questions. Such use of the streets and public places has, from ancient times, been a part of the privileges, immunities, rights, and liberties of citizens."[12] Until twenty years ago, however, it was a crime in most states and localities for a poor person—typically a beggar or vagrant—to stand on or wander the streets if he or she did not live in the community or have some visible means of support. Laws prohibiting vagrancy date back to the medieval period as a way to control the lives of the poor.[13] In their most extreme form, antivagrancy statutes historically imposed harsh and disproportionate punishment on people who had committed no crime other than their poverty. The Slavery Act of 1547, for example, branded vagabonds with a "V" and enslaved them for two years in their town of origin. Those who attempted to escape were branded with an "S" and enslaved for life.[14] Even in their less extreme form, vagrancy statutes functioned, as one respected scholar put it, as "weapons of the establishment for keeping the untouchables in line."[15]

During the 1960s, the Warren Court began to look skeptically at the constitutionality of loitering laws. In an early case, the Court made clear that a person who lingered on a sidewalk but did not obstruct passage could not be convicted of loitering for merely refusing to move on after a police request to do so.[16] Then, in 1972, the Court more broadly invalidated a Florida vagrancy statute that imposed criminal penalties on "persons wandering or strolling around from place to place." Among its constitutional failings, the Court explained, was the law's prohibition of activities that comprise a "part of the amenities of life as we have known them" even if "not mentioned in the Constitution or in the Bill of Rights."[17] An additional problem was the law's vagueness, in that a person of reasonable intelligence could not know that her or his behavior was illegal. Moreover, the statute gave the police unfettered discretion to stop and arrest individuals who were doing no more than lingering on the streets. For all of these reasons, the Court found that the law created the constitutionally impermissible situation "in which the poor and the unpopular are permitted to 'stand on a public sidewalk . . . only at the whim of any police officer.' "[18]

Despite the Court's clear ruling on this issue, many localities are again imposing criminal sanctions on poor people who linger or "hang out" on the public streets.[19] Some of these newer laws ban particular kinds of public behavior, such as sitting or lying on the street even if pedestrian traffic is not obstructed. The laws ought to be constitutionally impermissible if designed to exclude the poor from major sections of a community, such as the downtown area or parks, or to punish them for conduct that the affluent find aesthetically displeasing but is otherwise innocuous. Such laws are vague, overbroad, and infringe on a number of constitutionally protected rights.

On this view, a federal court in New York City issued a preliminary injunction to stop police at Pennsylvania Station from arresting the " 'homeless, pan handlers, ticket scalpers, and thieves' " who linger at the station.[20] And in Berkeley, California, a federal court preliminarily enjoined a local ordinance that more generally barred sitting or lying on a public sidewalk because the prohibition implicated state and federal constitutional speech rights.[21] But in Seattle, Washington, a federal court upheld an ordinance that prohibits sitting or lying on public sidewalks in commercial areas during specified hours, finding no evidence that the city council "was targeting homeless people in a hostile and discriminating fashion."[22] And in San Francisco, California, a federal court refused to enjoin a local "Matrix Quality of Life Program," which criminalized such conduct as sitting on the sidewalk and sleeping in public.[23]

The law in this area is thus mixed, and it is important to be aware of the restrictions that apply in a given community.

What if the police stop a poor person and demand identification papers?

In *Kolender v. Lawson*,[24] the United States Supreme Court invalidated a California law that allowed police to request identification or some other accounting from people who loiter or wander in public places. In the Court's view, the law was unconstitutionally vague because it gave police "virtually complete discretion . . . to determine whether the suspect has satisfied the statute."[25] Under the Court's decision, the police can ask the name of a person on the street, but cannot demand "credible and reliable" identification or require any other explanation.

Can the police arrest someone for begging or panhandling?

Courts are only beginning to consider the validity of laws that impose criminal sanctions on beggars and panhandlers. Begging and panhandling communicate a message about poverty in our society and ought to be constitutionally protected under the First Amendment. But most states impose criminal penalties on indigents who solicit alms on their own behalf.[26] At least some communities also ban "aggressive panhandling," to cover the situation where an individual is said to seek assistance through intimidation or unwarranted physical contact.[27] Like the related bans on loitering and vagrancy, antibegging ordinances are designed to cleanse the streets of so-called undesirables who offend or frighten the more affluent. The United States Supreme Court has not yet considered the constitutionality of begging laws, where the solicitation is by an indigent rather than by a charitable organization on behalf of the indigent. Lower court decisions in this area are mixed, and the constitutionality of any particular statute depends on its detail and scope.[28]

Can the police arrest someone for sleeping in a park or some other public place?

The law in this area is still evolving. Many localities have responded to the problem of homelessness by banning and even criminalizing sleeping or camping on the streets, in other public places, and in cars. Advocates for the homeless argue that antisleeping laws are vague, overbroad, and impose cruel and unusual punishment on the status of being poor. The Fourth Amendment protection against illegal search and seizure may also be implicated if the police seize a homeless person's possessions while evicting her or him from an abandoned building or park bench.[29]

Facial challenges to antisleeping laws have met with very mixed results. Some lower courts have found antisleeping laws to be unconstitutional.[30] Others have upheld them.[31] The Supreme Court has not yet decided a case involving sleeping in public where sleep is not expressive conduct protesting a lack of affordable housing.[32] Nor has the Court considered a ban on sleeping as applied to homeless people who have no place other than public spaces to perform daily living activities. At least one commentator has suggested that antisleeping laws ought to be subject to strict scrutiny because they impinge on a homeless person's right to travel and the correlative right to stay put.[33]

In *Pottinger v. City of Miami*, homeless people living in Miami, Florida sued the city to stop "a policy of arresting, harassing and otherwise interfering with homeless people for engaging in basic activities of daily life—including sleeping and eating—in the public places where they are forced to live."[34] Finding that the homeless in Miami "have no realistic choice but to live in public places,"[35] the district court held that it was a violation of the Eighth Amendment's prohibition on cruel and unusual punishment to criminalize their sleeping in public.[36] As the district court explained:

> To paraphrase Justice [Byron] White [of the United States Supreme Court], plaintiffs have no place else to go and no place else to be. . . . This is so particularly at night when the public parks are closed. As long as the homeless plaintiffs do not have a single place where they can lawfully be, the challenged ordinances, as applied to them, effectively punish them for something for which they may not be convicted under the eighth amendment—sleeping, eating and other innocent conduct.[37]

The district court further found that the city's policy was a form of banishment violating a homeless person's fundamental right to travel and to equal protection of the law.[38] Despite the *Pottinger* decision, the law in this area remains in flux.[39]

Can the police search or seize the belongings of a person who is sleeping in a park or some other public place?

Not without a warrant. Since the landmark decision in *Katz v. United States*, the United States Supreme Court has recognized that the Fourth Amendment protects "people—and not simply [places]" against unreasonable searches and seizures.[40] Courts currently employ a two-prong test to determine whether an individual has a reasonable expectation of privacy. Under this test, an individual has a constitutionally protected interest if she or he has exhibited an actual, subjective expectation of privacy and if that expectation is one that society is prepared to recognize as reasonable.[41]

A few courts have held that homeless individuals who live in parks or shelters have a reasonable expectation of privacy against warrantless police searches. The Connecticut Supreme Court held that the police violated a homeless person's right to privacy when they searched through a cardboard box and duffel bag left unattended in a state-owned area.[42] A Florida federal court held that police violated Fourth Amendment rights when they conducted warrantless searches of property left by homeless people in Miami public parks.[43] And a federal court in Washington, D.C., held that federal marshals looking for a fugitive acted unconstitutionally when they entered a shelter without a warrant and demanded identification from the homeless people sleeping inside.[44] A person whose belongings are taken by the police should contact a legal services lawyer for advice.

Can the police arrest someone for performing in public?

Generally, no. Performing—singing, dancing, miming, playing an instrument—is a form of expression and protected under the First Amendment.[45] Like any other form of speech, however, a public performance can be regulated to conform to reasonable time, place, and manner restrictions as long as the restrictions are content neutral. Thus, the government can set reasonable regulations concerning the acceptable times when a performance can take place, and the places where performance is permitted. In addition, the government can regulate certain specific problems that may arise with some performing, such as playing an instrument too loudly.[46] Many recent ordinances that restrict the public activities of poor people potentially infringe on the right to perform in public.[47]

What if a person who is performing also asks for money?

In the same way that begging and performing are protected, so should performing for money. Thus, the police should not be able to arrest a person who is performing on the street and also asking for money, unless the person is engaged in some prohibited activity.[48]

Can government charge marchers or demonstrators a fee for using public streets or other public areas?

A locality can charge the sponsor of a demonstration a "user fee" as long as the fee is genuinely related to the cost of processing a permit application; does not vary with the kind of demonstration; and is so small that it does not deter the exercise of free speech.[49] The government cannot impose a participation fee on someone who is simply attending a demonstration.

Many years ago, the United States Supreme Court upheld the imposition of nominal fees on the sponsors or organizers of a demonstration,[50] and the Court recently reaffirmed that holding.[51] Lower courts have recognized, however, that it would be unconstitutional to charge a fee that is not truly nominal, because it could deter the exercise of First Amendment rights.[52] In analogous contexts, lower courts have invalidated fee requirements, reasoning that "[i]ndigent persons who wish to exercise their First Amendment rights of speech and assembly and as a consequence of the added costs of police protection, are unable to pay such costs, are denied an equal opportunity to be heard."[53] A court should strike down any application fee that prevents an indigent from sponsoring a rally, but the United States Supreme Court has not yet addressed this issue.[54]

The government may also constitutionally require an individual who wants to stage a demonstration to obtain a permit. A permit system allows the government to anticipate and prepare for crowd control, street closings, and other consequences of the demonstration. It also ensures that there will not be two groups seeking to march or rally at the same time and place. Permit charges are imposed on the sponsors or organizers of a demonstration, and the permit application may request information needed to help the locality prepare for the event. It is questionable, however, whether the application can request personal information about the sponsor (such as questions about his or her income) that is unrelated to a legitimate administrative purpose.[55]

Permit systems raise other constitutional problems when they leave discretion in the hands of city officials to set the amount of a "user fee" or to waive it entirely. This is the case whether the charge is called an application fee, a clean-up fee, or an insurance fee. Within such a system, the government might be willing to waive the fee for the Boy Scouts but require it for a less popular group of homeless men. An official's arbitrary exercise of discretion may violate the First Amendment rights or abridge Due Process.

Can demonstrations be held in a welfare office?

The law in this area is in flux. Years ago, the courts were generally sympathetic to the idea of individuals handing out leaflets or having conversations with persons in the waiting room of a welfare office. A few lower courts found that speech activity of this sort was not disruptive of the business of the welfare office and was constitutionally permissible.[56]

More recently, however, the United States Supreme Court has seriously limited the permissible scope of First Amendment activity in places that are not traditionally available for public discussion and in this sense are not considered public forums.[57] The better view is that you have the right to hand out leaflets in the waiting room of a welfare office and to talk to welfare applicants. Certainly an individual has the right to demonstrate on the sidewalk in front of a welfare office or to hand out leaflets, as long as access to the office is not obstructed and use of the sidewalk is not impeded. And if the welfare office allows other groups to use a bulletin board or an internal mail system, poor people wanting to communicate should be given equal access.[58]

Can everybody use the public library?

Yes. Public libraries do not charge a fee for admission and most books may be borrowed for free if you have a current library card. An individual is allowed to remain in the library as long as his or her behavior does not violate library regulations that govern patron conduct. Library regulations typically ban behavior that interferes with another patron's reasonable use of the facility or is inconsistent with the library's purpose. Sometimes library regulations require patrons to conform their "dress and personal hygiene . . . to the standard of the community for public places."[59]

Communities throughout the country have begun to enforce "personal decorum" regulations as a way to bar the homeless from public libraries.[60] Advocates have challenged the application of these regulations as unconstitutionally vague, inconsistent with the First Amendment, and a violation of equal protection, but at least one federal appeals court has sustained their validity. While acknowledging that the regulations (especially those provisions that deal with dress and personal hygiene) "may disproportionately affect the homeless who have limited access to bathing facilities," the appeals court nevertheless found that "this fact . . . would not justify permitting a would-be patron, with hygiene so offensive that it constitutes a nuisance, to force other patrons to leave the library."[61]

Can a person who does not have a home address receive mail at the post office?

Yes. Homeless persons who do not have a fixed address can apply for post office box or general delivery service. In order to get a post office box, you have to file Form 1093, which is available at a local post office. An application may be approved if

- The applicant is personally known to the postmaster or clerk;
- The applicant submits valid identification, which includes a driver's license or some other credential that bears a signature and a number that can be traced; or
- The applicant provides a verifiable point of contact, such as a shelter or social services office.

An applicant who does not meet these conditions can still request general delivery service, which is granted at the discretion of the postmaster.[62]

Notes

1. 314 U.S. 160 (1941).

2. *See* Stephen Loffredo, *"If You Ain't Got the Do, Re, Mi": The Commerce Clause and State Residence Restrictions on Welfare,* 11 Yale L. & Pol'y Rev. 147, 175 (1993).

3. U.S. Const. art. I, § 8, cl. 3 (Congress shall have power to "regulate Commerce . . . among the several States").

4. *Edwards,* 314 U.S. at 173.

5. *Id.* at 177; *see City of New York v. Miln,* 36 U.S. 102, 142–43 (1837).

6. *See* Daniel R. Mandelker, *Exclusion and Removal Legislation,* 1956 Wis. L. Rev. 57, 58 (1956).

7. *Edwards,* 314 U.S. at 177.

8. *See Lutz v. City of York,* 899 F.2d 255, 268 (3d Cir. 1990); *King v. New Rochelle Mun. Hous. Auth.,* 442 F.2d 646, 648 (2d Cir. 1971), *cert. denied,* 404 U.S. 863 (1971).

9. Newspaper stories provide many examples of this trend, *see, e.g., Hartford Restricts Social Services to Stem Flow of Poor People,* N.Y. Times, Aug. 14, 1996, B2; Editorial, *Pushing Away the Homeless,* Wash. Post, Apr. 29, 1995, A16; Michael Janofsky, *Many Cities in Crackdown on Homeless,* N.Y. Times, Dec. 12, 1994, A34; Editorial, *A Lady in a Car,* N.Y. Times, Dec. 9, 1994, A31. *See generally* Maria Foscarinis, *Downward Spiral: Homelessness and Its Criminalization,* 14 Yale L. & Pol'y Rev. 1 (1996); Robert B. Reich, *Secession of the Successful,* N.Y. Times Magazine, Jan. 20, 1991, 16.

10. *See* National Law Center on Homelessness and Poverty, *No Homeless People Allowed: A Report on Anti-Homeless Laws, Litigation and Alternatives in 49 United States Cities* (1994).

11. *See* Loffredo, *supra* note 2.

12. *Hague v. CIO,* 307 U.S. 496, 515 (1939); *see also Perry Educ. Assn. v. Perry Local Educators' Assn.,* 460 U.S. 37, 45 (1983).

13. *See* Mark Malone, *Homelessness in a Modern Urban Setting,* 10 Fordham Urb. L.J. 749, 753–56 (1982); Jacobus tenBroek, *California's Dual System of Family Law: Its Origin, Development and Present Status,* Part I, 16 Stan. L. Rev. 257 (1964).

14. *See* Harry Simon, *Towns Without Pity: A Constitutional and Historical Analysis of Official Efforts to Drive American Persons from American Cities*, 66 Tul. L. Rev. 631, 676 n.37 (1992) (discussing Slavery Act, 1 Edw. 6 Ch. 3 (1547)(Eng.)).

15. Anthony G. Amsterdam, *Federal Constitutional Restrictions on the Punishment of Crimes of Status, Crimes of General Obnoxiousness, Crimes of Displeasing Police Officers, and the Like*, 3 Crim. L. Bull. 205, 233 (1967).

16. *Shuttlesworth v. City of Birmingham*, 382 U.S. 87 (1965); *see also Gregory v. City of Chicago*, 394 U.S. 111 (1969).

17. *Papachristou v. City of Jacksonville*, 405 U.S. 156, 164 (1972).

18. *Id.* at 170, *quoting Shuttlesworth*, 382 U.S. 90 (1976).

19. *E.g., Church v. City of Huntsville*, 30 F.3d 1332 (11th Cir. 1994) (vacating preliminary injunction against Huntsville, Alabama practice of removing homeless persons from the city for gathering in public places); *see* Malcolm Gladwell, *Honey, I Shrunk N.Y. Does Mayor Giuliani Have a Secret Plan to Drive the Poor Out of the City?*, Wash. Post, Mar. 19, 1995, C1.

20. *StreetWatch v. National Railroad Passenger Corp.*, 875 F. Supp. 1055 (S.D.N.Y. 1995).

21. *Community Health Project v. City of Berkeley*, 902 F. Supp. 1084 (N.D. Cal. 1995).

22. *Roulette v. City of Seattle*, 850 F. Supp. 1442, 1450 (W. D. Wash. 1994), *aff'd*, 78 F.3d 1425 (9th Cir. 1996).

23. *Joyce v. City and County of San Francisco*, 846 F. Supp. 843 (N.D. Cal. 1994).

24. 461 U.S. 352 (1983).

25. *Id.* at 358.

26. Begging and panhandling laws are collected and analyzed in Helen Hershkoff & Adam S. Cohen, *Begging to Differ: The First Amendment and the Right to Beg*, 104 Harv. L. Rev. 896 (1991). *See also* Paul G. Chevigny, *Begging and the First Amendment: Young v. New York City Transit Authority*, 57 Brook. L. Rev. 525 (1991). For a contrary view, *see* Robert C. Ellickson, *Controlling Chronic Misconduct in City Spaces: Of Panhandlers, Skid Rows, and Public-Space Zoning*, 105 Yale L. J. 1165 (1996).

27. *See, e.g.,* Seattle Mun. Code § 12 A.12.015(A)(1) (criminalizing begging with the intent to intimidate another person into giving money or goods). A federal district court upheld the facial constitutionality of this statute when interpreted to ban "only those threats which would make a reasonable person fearful of harm to his or her property." *Roulette*, 850 F. Supp. at 1453, *aff'd*, 78 F.3d 1425 (9th Cir. 1996).

28. The leading published cases are: *Loper v. New York City Police Dep't*, 999 F.2d 699 (2d Cir. 1993); *Young v. New York City Transit Auth.*, 903 F.2d 146 (2d Cir. 1990), *cert. denied*, 498 U.S. 984 (1990); *Blair v. Shanahan*, 775 F. Supp. 1315 (N.D. Cal. 1991), *vacated*, 919 F. Supp. 1361 (N.D.Cal. 1996); *C.C.B v. State*, 458 So.2d 47 (Fla. Dist. Ct. App. 1984). Unpublished decisions involving the constitutionality of begging and aggressive panhandling are collected in *No Homeless People Allowed, supra* note 10, at A1–16.

29. *E.g., Pottinger v. City of Miami*, 810 F. Supp. 1551 (S.D. Fl. 1992)(holding that seizure of homeless person's belongings from public area violated Fourth and Fifth Amendments); *but see Stone v. Agnos*, 960 F.2d 893 (9th Cir. 1992) (upholding constitutionality of seizure and destruction of homeless person's property during arrest for sleeping on park bench). Other cases include: *Commonwealth v. Gordon*, 433 Pa. Super. 157, 640 A.2d 422

(Pa. Super. Ct. 1994), *appeal granted,* 542 Pa. 632, 655 A.2d 467 (1995)(seizure of homeless person's belongs in abandoned building must comply with constitutional protections).

30. *Horn v. City of Montgomery,* 619 So. 2d 949 (Ala. Crim. App. 1993); *City of Pompano Beach v. Capalbo,* 455 So. 2d 468 (Fla. Dist. Ct. App. 1984), *cert. denied,* 474 U.S. 824 (1985); *United States v. Abney,* 534 F.2d 984 (D.C. Cir. 1976); *State v. Penley,* 276 So. 2d 180 (Fla. Dist. Ct. App. 1973), *cert. denied,* 281 So. 2d 504 (Fla. 1973).

31. *State v. Sturch,* 82 Hawaii 269, 921 P.2d 1170 (Hawaii App., June 25, 1996), *as amended* (June 27, 1996), *cert. denied,* 922 P.2d 973 (Hawaii July 8, 1996); *Whiting v. Town of Westerly,* 743 F. Supp. 97 (D.R.I. 1990), *aff'd,* 942 F.2d 18 (1st Cir. 1991); *Hershey v. City of Clearwater,* 834 F.2d 937 (11th Cir. 1987); *Joyce v. City and County of San Francisco,* 846 F. Supp. 843 (N.D. Cal. 1994); *People v. Davenport,* 176 Cal. App. 3d Supp. 10, 222 Cal. Rptr. 736 (Cal. App. Dep't Super. Ct. 1985), *cert. denied,* 475 U.S. 1141 (1986); *Seeley v. State,* 134 Ariz. 263, 655 P.2d 803 (Ariz. Ct. App. 1982); *City of Portland v. Johnson,* 59 Or. App. 647, 651 P.2d 1384 (Or. Ct. App. 1982).

32. If sleeping in public is part of a demonstration protesting the lack of housing for poor people, First Amendment rights are implicated. In that case, sleeping may be prohibited only if the prohibition is a reasonable restriction on the place or manner of speech and alternative means of expression remain available. *See Clark v. Community for Creative Non-Violence,* 468 U.S. 288 (1984).

33. *See Towns Without Pity, supra* note 14, at 654.

34. *Pottinger v. City of Miami,* 810 F. Supp. 1551, 1554 (S.D. Fla. 1992).

35. *Id.* at 1563.

36. *Id.* at 1564.

37. *Id.* at 1565.

38. *Id.* at 1581.

39. Relying on *Pottinger,* a federal court struck down an anticamping ban in Dallas, Texas, but its decision was later vacated on appeal, *see Johnson v. City of Dallas,* 860 F. Supp. 344 (N.D. Tex. 1994), *reversed and injunction vacated,* 61 F.3d 442 (5th Cir. 1995). *See also Roulette v. City of Seattle,* 850 F. Supp. 1442, 1448, *aff'd,* 78 F.3d 1425 (9th Cir. 1996)(distinguishing *Pottinger*); *Davison v. City of Tucson,* 924 F. Supp. 989 (D. Ariz. 1996)(upholding ban on encampment on city-owned property); *Joyce v. City and County of San Francisco,* 846 F. Supp. 843 (N.D. Ca. 1994)(refusing to enjoin law enforcement measures as part of anti-homeless program); *Tobe v. City of Santa Ana,* 32 Cal. App. 4th 941, 27 Cal. Rptr. 2d 386 (Cal. Ct. App. 1994), *rev'd,* 892 P.2d 1145 (Cal. 1995)(upholding anticamping law).

40. 389 U.S. 347, 353 (1967). *See* U.S. Const. amend. IV ("the right of the people to be secure in their persons . . . shall not be violated").

41. *See, e.g., Vernonia Sch. Dist. 47J v. Acton,* 115 S. Ct. 2386 (1995), *relying on Skinner v. Railway Labor Executives' Assn.,* 489 U.S. 602, 619 (1989).

42. *State v. Mooney,* 218 Conn. 85, 588 A.2d 145 (1991), *cert. denied,* 502 U.S. 919 (1991).

43. *Pottinger,* 850 F. Supp. at 1583.

44. *Committee for Creative Non-Violence v. Unknown Agents of the U.S. Marshals Service,* 797 F. Supp. 7 (D.D.C. 1992).

45. *Ward v. Rock Against Racism,* 491 U.S. 781 (1989); *Schad v. Borough of Mount*

Ephraim, 452 U.S. 61 (1981); *Goldstein v. Town of Nantucket*, 477 F. Supp. 606 (D. Mass. 1979). *But see Barnes v. Glen Theater, Inc.*, 501 U.S. 560 (1991)(city may ban nude dancing).

46. *See Ward*, 491 U.S. at 781; *Carew-Reid v. Metropolitan Transit Auth.*, 903 F.2d 914 (2d Cir. 1990).

47. E.g., *Roulette v. City of Seattle*, 850 F. Supp. 1442 (W.D. Wash. 1994), *aff'd*, 78 F.3d 1425 (9th Cir. 1996).

48. *See, e.g., Goldstein*, 477 F. Supp. at 606.

49. *See* Eric Neisser, *Charging for Free Speech: User Fees and Insurance in the Marketplace of Ideas*, 74 Geo. L.J. 257 (1985).

50. *Cox v. New Hampshire*, 312 U.S. 569 (1941).

51. *Forsyth County, Ga. v. The Nationalist Movement*, 505 U.S. 123 (1992).

52. *See, e.g., Eastern Conn. Citizen's Action Group v. Powers*, 723 F.2d 1050 (2d Cir. 1983).

53. *Central Fla. Nuclear Freeze Campaign v. Walsh*, 774 F.2d 1515, 1523 (11th Cir. 1985), *cert. denied*, 475 U.S. 1120 (1986).

54. *Forsyth County, Ga. v. The Nationalist Movement*, 505 U.S. 123 (1992), in which four Justices held that more than nominal charges may be assessed and five other Justices, in an ambiguous statement, appeared to hold that the constitutionality of a fee does not depend on whether it is nominal or not.

55. *See Fernandes v. Limmer*, 663 F.2d 619 (5th Cir. 1981), *cert. dismissed*, 458 U.S. 1124 (1982).

56. E.g., *Project Vote v. Ohio Bureau of Employm. Serv.*, 578 F. Supp. 7 (S.D. Ohio 1982); *Albany Welfare Rights Org. v. Wyman*, 493 F.2d 1319 (2d Cir. 1974), *cert. denied*, 419 U.S. 838 (1974); *Unemployed Workers Union v. Hackett*, 332 F. Supp. 1372 (D.R.I. 1971).

57. *See United States v. Kokinda*, 497 U.S. 720 (1990)(four-justice plurality concluding that the sidewalk in front of the U.S. Post Office is not a traditional or designated public forum, and cannot be used for expressive activity); *Perry Educ. Ass'n v. Perry Local Educators' Ass'n*, 460 U.S. 37 (1983).

58. *See Hazelwood School Dist. v. Kuhlmeier*, 484 U.S. 260, 267 (1988) (facility is deemed to be a public forum if the government " 'by policy or by practice,' opens the facility for 'indiscriminate use by the general public' . . . or some segment of the public" (quoting *Perry Educ. Ass'n. v. Perry Local Educators' Ass'n.*, 460 U.S. at 47).

59. *Kreimer v. Bureau of Police*, 958 F.2d 1242, 1247 (3d Cir. 1992) (quoting library rules of Morristown Township, N.J.).

60. *See, e.g.*, Madeleine R. Stoner, *The Civil Rights of Homeless People: Law, Social Policy, and Social Work Practice* 165 (1995)(discussing removal of homeless persons from public libraries in Las Vegas).

61. *Kreimer*, 958 F.2d at 1242.

62. U.S. Postal Bulletin D930 (June 23, 1990).

VIII

The Right to Vote

Does the federal Constitution guarantee a poor person's right to vote?

Yes. The United States Supreme Court has ruled in many cases that the federal Constitution guarantees poor people the same right to vote as other citizens and prohibits states from conditioning that right on property ownership, ability to pay poll taxes, or other criteria related to economic status.[1] Indeed, since the 1960s, the Court has repeatedly held that the right to vote is a "fundamental right" under the Constitution and that it must be dispensed equally, "without regard to race, sex, economic status, or place of residence within a state."[2] More generally, the Court has declared that "each and every citizen has an inalienable right to full and effective participation in the political processes" and that "any alleged infringement of the right of citizens to vote must be carefully and meticulously scrutinized" because "the right to exercise the franchise in a free and unimpaired manner is preservative of other basic civil and political rights."[3]

It has not always been this way. When the nation was founded, the right to vote was largely a matter of state concern, and state laws restricted the franchise to white men of property. As one historian explains, eighteenth-century limits on the right to vote reflected the prevailing ideology of the Founding Fathers, who believed that "[b]y and large, that element of the population which was relatively poor and lacked education and standing in the community was not likely to develop an active interest in the affairs of state."[4]

Over the last two hundred years, amendments to the federal Constitution, as well as the passage of federal statutory laws, have steadily expanded the vote to include all citizens, regardless of race, gender, or economic status. In 1870, the Fifteenth Amendment extended the vote in state and federal elections to all male citizens, regardless of "race, color, or previous condition of servitude."[5] Fifty years later, the Nineteenth Amendment extended the vote to women.[6] In 1924, the Citizenship Act extended the vote to Native Americans.[7] In 1964, the Twenty-Fourth Amendment guaranteed the right of all citizens to vote in federal elections, regardless of their ability "to pay any poll tax or other tax."[8] And in 1971, the Twenty-Sixth Amendment extended the right to vote to citizens 18 years of age or older.[9]

Well into the twentieth century, however, the Supreme Court remained generally unwilling to extend federal constitutional protection to the vote. Although the Court held that article I, section 4 of the Constitution, authorizing Congress to regulate federal elections, justified a ban on private discrimination in registering and voting for federal officials,[10] it refused to review the propriety of elections under article IV, section 6 of the Constitution, guaranteeing a republican form of government.[11]

Moreover, the Court consistently declined to locate the right to vote in the First Amendment, which guarantees freedom of speech, relying instead on the more narrow basis of the Fifteenth Amendment which protects the right of African Americans to vote as free citizens. In *Guinn v. United States*,[12] for example, the Court invalidated a grandfather clause of the Oklahoma Constitution, which required all voters to be able to read and write but provided an exemption for voters and descendants of voters who were "on January 1, 1866, or at any time prior thereto, entitled to vote under any form of government." The Court held that the clause violated the Fifteenth Amendment because its only purpose was to exclude racial minorities from voting. The same case, however, upheld literacy tests as a condition for voting.[13]

Beginning in 1927, in the "White Primary Cases," the Court allowed challenges to the exclusion of minorities from Democratic primary elections.[14] Then, in a series of cases,[15] the Court invalidated, again under the Fifteenth Amendment, the exclusion of blacks from voting in party primaries pursuant to party rule (as opposed to state law) or in primaries held by so-called private clubs that duplicated the functions of primaries held by parties. The full flowering of the right to vote as an equal protection concept occurred in the 1960s, with the Warren Court basing its jurisprudence on the Fourteenth Amendment.[16] As the Court later explained, "Once the franchise is granted to the electorate, lines may not be drawn which are inconsistent with the Equal Protection Clause of the Fourteenth Amendment."[17]

Is there a state constitutional right to vote?

Yes. State constitutions explicitly guarantee the right to vote to all citizens who are residents of the state.[18] Franchise rights under state constitutions have undergone a significant evolution since the eighteenth century, when they were restricted to white male property owners. After the Revolution and the founding of the Republic, many state constitutions eliminated an explicit property requirement from their franchise provisions, but in time imposed new restrictions that limited the vote to taxpayers. Many of these requirements were intended to bar African Americans and paupers from the ballot box. Under current doctrine, state constitutions can condition the vote in general elections only upon citizenship, upon age, and upon being a bona fide resident of the community in which a person seeks to vote.

Can a state require its citizens to pay a poll tax in order to vote?

No. The right to vote, whether in state or federal elections, cannot be conditioned on payment of a poll tax. Historically, requiring proof of payment of a poll tax was often a subterfuge for disenfranchising blacks.

In 1964, the Twenty-fourth Amendment to the federal Constitution prohibited the states and the United States from conditioning the right to vote in any federal election or primary on payment of "any poll tax or other tax." The amendment did not eliminate this condition from state elections, and the practice persisted in Alabama, Mississippi, Virginia, and Texas. In 1966, the Supreme Court in *Harper v. Virginia Board of Elections* invalidated Virginia's poll tax, a law that the Court had previously upheld fifteen years earlier.[19] Although the Twenty-fourth Amendment does not explicitly refer to state elections, such as those for election of the governor, the Court unequivocally held that states cannot use payment of a poll tax or any tax as an election requirement. As the Court explained, "[v]oter qualifications have no relation to wealth nor to paying or not paying this or any other tax."[20]

Do citizens who are unemployed or receiving welfare have a right to vote?

Yes. The Supreme Court has never considered the specific question of whether the right to vote can be conditioned on gainful employment. But the principle is well settled "that a State violates the Equal Protection Clause of the Fourteenth Amendment whenever it makes the affluence of the voter . . . an electoral standard."[21] As the Court has further explained, "there is no indication in the Constitution that . . . occupation affords a permissible basis for distinguishing between qualified voters within the State."[22] Based on this established doctrine, a poor person cannot be barred from the voting booth because he or she is unemployed or on welfare.

Can a state deny the vote to people who do not own property?

In general, no. The well-settled rule is that a citizen cannot be denied the right to vote in a general election simply because he or she does not own property in the district in which the voter resides. The United States Supreme Court first addressed this issue in 1969 when it considered a pair of cases that limited the franchise to property owners. In *Kramer v. Union Free School District No. 15*,[23] the Court struck down a New York statute that limited the vote in local school board elections to persons who owned or leased taxable real property in the school district or who had children enrolled in the district's public schools. And in *Cipriano v. City of Houma*,[24] the Court invalidated a Louisiana statute that limited the franchise in local revenue bond elections to "property taxpayers" of the district. In subsequent cases, the Court has repeatedly reaffirmed this principle, explaining that participation in general elections—including those for school boards—cannot be conditioned on the possession of property or the payment of taxes.[25]

In a few limited circumstances, however, the vote can constitutionally be restricted to property owners who have a "special interest" in the outcome of the election. Thus, for example, in *Salyer Land Co. v. Tulare Lake Basin Water Storage District*, the Court held that a water district can allocate votes in an election for board of directors according to the assessed value of each voter's land.[26] Because of the water district's "special limited purpose and . . . the disproportionate effect of its activities on landowners as a group," the election of the Board was considered by the Court to be of sufficient "special interest" to a limited class of property owners as to allow restriction of the franchise.[27] The circumstances under which a state can limit the vote to property owners, however, is extremely narrow.

Can an individual who has just moved to a community still vote in an upcoming election?

It depends on how long the individual has been living at the new place of residence. Residence requirements limit the vote to individuals who live in a particular community. The Supreme Court has recognized that an "appropriately defined and uniformly applied requirement of bona fide residence may be necessary to preserve the basic conception of a political community,"[28] and such requirements are constitutionally valid when applied to voting. Thus, if a citizen lives in Kansas, he or she cannot vote in a school board election in Texas where the voter happens to be on vacation.

Many communities, however, also traditionally conditioned the franchise on a durational residence requirement, which requires an individual to be a resident for a fixed length of time before participating in the political process. Such a requirement is unconstitutional, although election administrators are permitted to close the voter registration process for a brief period prior to the election in order to prepare the lists of registered voters that must be sent to the polling places on election day.[29]

The Court first addressed this issue in 1972 in a case called *Dunn v. Blumstein*, which involved a Tennessee law that conditioned the vote on one year of state residence.[30] Striking down the law, the Court explained that although a short waiting period may be needed to allow election officials to prepare voting rolls, mere administrative need cannot justify the exclusion of new residents for an entire year.[31] In presidential elections, federal law currently limits the waiting period to no more than thirty days,[32] and fifty days seems to be the longest period the Supreme Court would tolerate under the Fourteenth Amendment.[33]

A person who has recently relocated and is not able to vote in his or her current place of residence may have the right to vote by absentee ballot in the prior electoral district. This right is specifically protected in presidential elections under the Voting Rights Act.[34] Contact a local election agency or League of Women Voters for more information.

Can homeless people vote?

Yes. A citizen does not need a home to vote, but he or she does have to prove bona fide residence. Residence does not require a house or an apartment, as long as election officials can verify the district in which the voter lives. A voter can satisfy this requirement by living on a street grate, in a shelter, on a park bench, or at some other nontraditional place within the electoral district. In some states, election officials may also want to be able to contact the voter to verify residence. It should be sufficient for a homeless person who cannot supply a street address to designate a shelter or a post office box as a place to receive mail. Finally, a homeless person without any current place of residence may be able to vote—either in person or by absentee ballot—in the last district in which he or she resided.

The right of homeless people to vote is still evolving and has been hard fought in the courts.[35] Only a few states have official policies supporting the right of homeless persons to register and to vote. Nine states have enacted statutes dealing specifically with the registration of homeless persons (Arizona, Colorado, Illinois, Indiana, Iowa, Maine, Nebraska, Oregon, and West Virginia).[36] As a practical matter, a homeless person may face difficulty if he or she tries to vote. If the election registrar turns a homeless person away or denies access to the voting booth, contact a local election agency or League of Women Voters. A legal services or legal aid lawyer may also be able to provide advice.

Table 8-1 sets forth the right of homeless persons to vote in each of the fifty states, the District of Columbia, and the Virgin Islands. The first two columns of the chart tell whether a homeless person can vote if he or she lives in a shelter or on the street. The third column indicates whether a mailing address is needed to register (if a mailing address is needed, using a shelter address may be sufficient). The fourth, fifth, and final columns indicate whether there are state policies protecting the right of homeless persons to vote.

Can election officials deny the vote to citizens who cannot pass a literacy test?

No. Although the Supreme Court in the past upheld the constitutionality of literacy tests,[37] in 1965 it invalidated literacy tests used to exclude minorities from voting.[38] Congress has also enacted a permanent, nationwide ban on literacy tests because they were used to prevent African Americans and other minorities from exercising their right to vote,[39] and the Court has specifically upheld this exercise of congressional power.[40] Thus, a person does not have to prove that he or she can read or write in order to vote.

Can an individual vote even if English is not his or her primary language?

Yes. The Voting Rights Act, as amended in 1975, provides significant protection to the franchise rights of citizens who have only limited proficiency in the English language. Language-minorities are defined by the statute as Native Americans, Asian Americans, Alaskan natives, and those of Spanish background.[41] Finding that "voting discrimination against citizens of language minorities is pervasive and national in scope,"[42] Congress has not only prohibited voting discrimination against language minorities,[43] but also has imposed affirmative obligations on states and municipalities to con-

TABLE 8-1
Voting Rights of the Homeless

STATE	Homeless May Register & Vote — Living in Shelters	Homeless May Register & Vote — Living on the Street	Mailing Address Required to Register	State Policy Allowing Homeless to Register — Written	State Policy Allowing Homeless to Register — Verbal	State Has Enacted Homeless Registration Statute
Alabama	Yes	Yes	No	No	Yes	No
Alaska	Yes	No	Yes	No	Yes	No
Arizona	Yes	Yes	No	Yes	—	Yes
Arkansas	Yes	Yes	Yes	No	Yes	No
California	Yes	Yes	Yes	No	Yes	No
Colorado	Yes	Yes	Yes	Yes	—	Yes
Connecticut	Yes	Yes	No	Yes	—	No
Delaware	Yes	Yes	Yes	Yes	—	No
Florida	Yes	Yes	Yes	Yes	—	No
Georgia	Yes	Yes	Yes	Yes	—	No
Hawaii	Yes	Yes	Yes	No	Yes	No
Idaho	Yes	Yes	No	No	Yes	No
Illinois	Yes	Yes	Yes	Yes	—	Yes
Indiana	Yes	Yes	Yes	Yes	—	Yes
Iowa	Yes	Yes	No	Yes	—	Yes

TABLE 8-1 continued on next page

TABLE 8-1 continued

STATE	Homeless May Register & Vote		Mailing Address Required to Register	State Policy Allowing Homeless to Register		State Has Enacted Homeless Registration Statute
	Living in Shelters	Living on the Street		Written	Verbal	
Kansas	Yes	Yes	No	Yes	—	No
Kentucky	Yes	Yes	No	Yes	—	No
Louisiana	Yes	No	Yes	No	No	No
Maine	Yes	Yes	No	Yes	—	Yes
Maryland	Yes	Yes	Yes	Yes	—	No
Massachusetts	Yes	Yes	Yes	Yes	—	No
Michigan	Yes	Yes	No	No	Yes	No
Minnesota	Yes	Yes	No	Yes	—	No
Mississippi	Yes	Yes	No	No	No	No
Missouri	Yes	Yes	No	No	Yes	No
Montana	Yes	Yes	No	No	No	No
Nebraska	Yes	Yes	No	Yes	—	No
Nevada	Yes	Yes	No	No	Yes	No
New Hampshire	Yes	Yes	No	No	Yes	No
New Jersey	Yes	Yes	Yes	Yes	—	No

TABLE 8-1 continued on next page

TABLE 8-1 continued

STATE	Homeless May Register & Vote		Mailing Address Required to Register	State Policy Allowing Homeless to Register		State Has Enacted Homeless Registration Statute
	Living in Shelters	Living on the Street		Written	Verbal	
New Mexico	Yes	Yes	Yes	No	Yes	No
New York	Yes	Yes	Yes	No	No	No
North Carolina	Yes	Yes	No	No	No	No
North Dakota[1]	Yes	Yes	No	No	No	No
Ohio	Yes	Yes	No	Yes	—	No
Oklahoma	Yes	Yes	Yes	No	Yes	No
Oregon[2]	Yes	Yes	No	Yes	—	Yes
Pennsylvania[3]	Varies	Varies	Varies	No	No	No
Puerto Rico	Yes	Yes	No	Yes	—	No
Rhode Island	Yes	Yes	No	No	Yes	No
South Carolina	Yes	Yes	Yes	No	Yes	No
South Dakota	Yes	Yes	Yes	No	No	No
Tennessee[4]	Yes	Yes	No	Yes	—	No
Texas	Yes	Yes	No	No	Yes	No
Utah	Yes	Yes	Yes	No	Yes	No

TABLE 8-1 continued on next page

TABLE 8-1 *continued*

STATE	Homeless May Register & Vote		Mailing Address Required to Register	State Policy Allowing Homeless to Register		State Has Enacted Homeless Registration Statute
	Living in Shelters	Living on the Street		Written	Verbal	
Vermont	Yes	Yes	No	No	Yes	No
Virgin Islands	Yes	Yes	Yes	Yes	—	No
Virginia	Yes	No	Yes	No	Yes	No
Washington	Yes	Yes	No	No	Yes	No
Washington, D.C.	Yes	Yes	Yes	Yes	—	No
West Virginia[5]	Yes	Yes	Yes	Yes	—	Yes
Wisconsin	Yes	Yes	No	Yes	No	No
Wyoming	Yes	Yes	No	No	Yes	No

Source: National Coalition for the Homeless & National Law Center on Homelessness and Poverty, 1996 Voter Registration Packet, "You Don't Need a Home to Vote" (1996).

[1] North Dakota does not require residents to register to vote.

[2] In Oregon, the election clerk's office may be used as a mailing address. During mail elections, persons using such an address must go to the office to pick up their ballots.

[3] In Pennsylvania, each county elections clerk has discretion to allow a person who lives in a shelter or on the streets to register. The clerk also has discretion whether to require a mailing address.

[4] In Tennessee, a mailing address is needed only to register by mail. A mailing address is not needed to register in person.

[5] In West Virginia, each county elections clerk has discretion to allow a person to register even without a mailing address.

duct bilingual elections where 5 percent of the voting-age citizens of a single language minority cannot speak English.[44] The entire states of Alaska, Arizona, and Texas, as well as 280 counties in states across the country, are currently required to provide bilingual election procedures for one or more language minorities.[45] To find out whether your election district must conduct bilingual elections, you can call your local League of Women Voters or the U.S. Department of Justice, Civil Rights Division, in Washington, D.C.

Do citizens have to register in order to vote?

Yes. All states except North Dakota require individuals to register to vote before an election takes place. A few states allow registration on election day. In 1993, Congress enacted the National Voter Registration Act, which makes it much easier for poor persons and others to register to vote. Under the act, states must allow voter registration at the same time that a driver's license is renewed (in fact, registration is automatic unless a person chooses to opt-out). States must also allow voter registration by mail. In addition, the act requires states to offer voter registration assistance at any welfare agency that provides food stamps, WIC, public assistance, Medicaid, and services for the disabled (registering to vote is not, however, a condition of eligibility for public assistance). A state may also choose to designate other public agencies such as a library, unemployment office, or local school as sites where a person can register to vote. As of January 1995, all states were required to have adopted a plan putting the act into effect,[46] although a few states had failed to comply with the statute.[47] For more information about how to register, contact a local election agency or League of Women Voters.

Can election officials require payment of a filing fee in order to run for office?

No, if paying the fee would prevent you from running for office. The Supreme Court has held that it is permissible for election officials to limit the ballot to "serious" candidates. Election officials may not, however, screen out candidates by requiring them to pay a fee if they cannot afford to pay and if that is the exclusive method by which a candidate can secure access to the ballot. (Some states, however, including California, permit candidates to pay filing fees in lieu of petitioning their way onto the ballot.)[48] In limiting the use of filing fees, the Court has explained that "the process of qualifying candidates . . . may not constitutionally be measured solely in dollars."[49]

Do candidates have to own property in order to run for office?

No. In 1970, the United States Supreme Court struck down a Georgia law requiring candidates for a local school board to own property. Even though the law required only "one square inch" of property, the Court found that it lacked any valid state purpose and could not be imposed to keep landless candidates off the ballot.[50] Thus, an individual does not have to own property to run for office. As a practical matter, however, poor people who seek electoral office must hurdle extreme economic barriers in the political process.[51] The estimated cost of the 1996 Presidential election is $800 million, with another $800 million being spent on congressional races.[52] The skyrocketing cost of political campaigns, of public opinion polls, of special interest lobbying, and of media outreach has caused a leading commentator to conclude that "[t]he power of money in . . . [American] politics, long a scandal, has now become a disaster."[53]

Notes

1. *See, e.g., Harper v. Virginia Bd. of Elections,* 383 U.S. 663, 666 (1966)(invalidating poll tax on the ground that "a State violates the Equal Protection Clause of the Fourteenth Amendment whenever it makes the affluence of the voter or payment of a fee an electoral standard"); *Kramer v. Union Free School District,* 395 U.S. 621 (1969)(invalidating property qualification for vote in school board elections); *Cipriano v. City of Houma,* 395 U.S. 701 (1969)(invalidating property qualification for vote on public bond issue); *City of Phoenix v. Kolodziejski,* 399 U.S. 204 (1969)(same); *cf. Bullock v. Carter,* 405 U.S. 134 (1972)(invalidating ballot access fee on the ground that it discriminates against candidates "lacking both personal wealth and affluent backers" and "has a real and appreciable impact on the exercise of the franchise . . . related to the resources of the voters supporting a particular candidate"); *Lubin v. Panish,* 415 U.S. 709 (1974)(same).

2. *See, e.g., Reynolds v. Sims,* 377 U.S. 533, 561–62, 656–68 (1964); *Wesberry v. Sanders,* 376 U.S. 1 (1964); *Gray v. Sanders,* 372 U.S. 368 (1963).

3. *Reynolds,* 377 U.S. at 561–68.

4. Chilton Williamson, *American Suffrage: From Property to Democracy 1760–1860* (1960) 6–7.

5. U.S. Const. amend. XV, § 1 ("The right of citizens of the United States to vote shall not be denied or abridged by the United States or by any State on account of race, color, or previous condition of servitude.").

6. U.S. Const. amend. XIX ("The right of citizens of the United States to vote shall not be denied or abridged by the United States or by any State on account of sex.").

7. 8 U.S.C.A. § 1401 (West 1996).

8. U.S. Const. amend. XXIV, § 1 ("The right of citizens of the United States to vote in any primary or other election for President or Vice President, for electors for President or Vice President, or for Senator or Representative in Congress, shall not be denied or abridged by the United States or any State by reason of failure to pay any poll tax or other tax.").

9. U.S. Const. amend. XXVI, § 1 ("The right of citizens of the United States, who are eighteen years of age or older, to vote shall not be denied or abridged by the United States or by any State on account of age.").

10. *See Ex parte Yarbrough*, 110 U.S. 651 (1884); *United States v. Classic*, 313 U.S. 299 (1941).

11. *Luther v. Borden*, 48 U.S. 1 (1849).

12. 238 U.S. 347 (1915)

13. *See also Lane v. Wilson*, 307 U.S. 268 (1939) (invalidating under the Fifteenth Amendment a state statute allowing only twelve days for registration of voters disenfranchised by unconstitutional grandfather clause).

14. *See Nixon v. Herndon*, 273 U.S. 536 (1927); *Nixon v. Condon*, 286 U.S. 73 (1932).

15. *Smith v. Allwright*, 321 U.S. 649 (1944); *Terry v. Adams*, 345 U.S. 461 (1953).

16. *See Reynolds*, 377 U.S. 533 (1964)(establishing the principle of one person, one vote, as a matter of equal protection doctrine); *see also Gomillion v. Lightfoot*, 364 U.S. 339 (1960) (protecting the rights of minorities to vote under the Fifteenth Amendment).

17. *Harper*, 383 U.S. at 663.

18. *See* Ala. Const. art. 8, § 177; Alaska Const. art. 7, § 2; Ariz. Const. art. 7, § 2; Ark. Const. art. 3, § 1; Cal. Const. art. 2, § 2; Colo. Const. art. 6, § 1; Conn. Const. art. 6, § 1; Del. Const. art. 5, § 2; Fla. Const. art. 6, § 2; Ga. Const. art. 2, § 1; Haw. Const. art. 2, § 2; Idaho Const. art. 6, § 2; Ill. Const. art. 3, § 1; Ind. Const. art. 2, § 2; Iowa Const. art. 2, § 1; Kan. Const. art. 5, § 1; Ky. Const. § 145; La. Const. art. 1, § 10; Me. Const. art. 2, § 1; Md. Const. art. 1, § 1; Mass. Const. part of the second ch. 1, § 3, art. 4; Mich. Const. art. 2, § 1; Minn. Const. art. 7, § 1; Miss. Const. art. 12, § 241; Mo. Const. art. 8, § 2; Mont. Const. art. 4, § 1; Neb. Const. art. 6, § 1; Nev. Const. art. 2, § 1; N.H. Const. part of the first art. 11; N.J. Const. art. 2, § 3; N.M. Const. art. 6, § 1; N.C. Const. art. 6, § 1; N.D. Const. art. 2, § 2; Ohio Const. art. 5, § 1; Okla. Const. art. 3, § 1; Or. Const. art. 2, § 2; Pa. Const. art. 7, § 1; R. I. Const. art. 2, § 1; S.C. Const. art. 2, § 4; S.D. Const. art. 7, § 2; Tenn. Const. art. 4, § 1; Tex. Const. art. 6, § 2; Utah Const. art. 4, § 2; Vt. Const. ch. 2, §42; Va. Const. art. 2, § 1; Wash. Const. art. 6, § 1; W. Va. Const. art. 4, § 1; Wis. Const. art. 3, § 1; Wyo. Const. art. 6, § 2; *see generally* Carrie Hillyard, *The History of Suffrage and Equal Rights Provisions in State Constitutions*, 10 BYU J. Pub. L. 117 (1996).

19. *See Butler v. Thompson*, 341 U.S. 937 (1951); *see also Breedlove v. Suttles*, 302 U.S. 277 (1937)(upholding Georgia's poll tax).

20. *Harper*, 383 U.S. at 663, 666 (1966).

21. *Id.*

22. *Gray v. Sanders*, 372 U.S. at 380.

23. 395 U.S. 621 (1969).

24. 395 U.S. 701 (1969)

25. *See, e.g., Hill v. Stone*, 421 U.S. 289 (1975)(Texas requirement that voters "render" or list real or personal property for taxation violates equal protection); *Phoenix v. Kolodziejski*,

399 U.S. 204 (1970)(Phoenix law restricting vote to real property taxpayers violates equal protection).

26. 410 U.S. 719 (1973).

27. *Id.* at 728.

28. *Dunn v. Blumstein,* 405 U.S. 330, 343–44 (1972).

29. *Holt Civic Club v. Tuscaloosa,* 439 U.S. 60 (1978).

30. 405 U.S. 330 (1972).

31. *Id.* at 348.

32. 42 U.S.C.A. § 1973aa-1(e) (West 1996).

33. *See Marston v. Lewis,* 410 U.S. 679 (1973).

34. 42 U.S.C.A. § 1973aa-1(e) (West 1996).

35. The leading published cases are *Pitts v. Black,* 608 F. Supp. 696 (S.D.N.Y. 1984), and *Collier v. Menzel,* 221 Cal. Rptr. 110, 176 Cal. App. 3d 24 (Cal. Ct. App. 2d Dist. 1985). Unpublished cases and attorney general opinion letters include: Voter Registration of Homeless Persons, Formal Opinion No. 2 (Op. N.J. Att'y Gen., Apr. 17, 1991); *Board of Elections v. Chicago/Gary Union of the Homeless,* No. 86-29 (Ill. Cir. Ct. Sept. 26, 1986); *Committee for Dignity and Fairness for the Homeless v. Tartaglione,* No. 84-3447 (E.D. Pa. Sept. 14, 1984); *In the matter of: The Application for Voter Registration of Willie R. Jenkins* (D.C. Board of Elections and Ethics, June 7, 1984). *See* Patricia M. Hanrahan, *Homeless Are Often Denied That Most Basic Element of Democracy,* 21 Human Rights 8 (Winter 1994); Note, *Disenfranchisement of Homeless Persons,* 31 J. Urban and Contemporary L. 225 (1987); Robert W. Collin, *Voting Rights of the Homeless,* 15 Stetson L. Rev. 809 (1986); Suzie Turner, *Recognition of the Rights of the Homeless,* 3 J.L. & Politics 103 (Winter 1986).

36. National Coalition for the Homeless and the National Law Center on Homelessness & Poverty, "You Don't Need a Home to Vote," 1996 Voter Registration/Rights Campaign Packet (1996).

37. *Lassiter v. Northampton Co. Bd. of Elections,* 360 U.S. 45 (1959).

38. *Louisiana v. United States,* 380 U.S. 145 (1965).

39. 42 U.S.C. § 1973b (1988).

40. *Oregon v. Mitchell,* 400 U.S. 112 (1970); *South Carolina v. Katzenbach,* 383 U.S. 301 (1966).

41. 42 U.S.C.A. § 1973aa-1a(e) (West 1996).

42. *Id.* at § 1973b(f)(1) (West 1996).

43. *Id.* at § 1973b(f) (West 1996).

44. *Id.* and at 1973aa-1a (1988).

45. The states are California, Colorado, Connecticut, Florida, Hawaii, Idaho, Illinois, Massachusetts, Michigan, Mississippi, Montana, Nevada, New Jersey, New Mexico, New York, North Carolina, North Dakota, Oklahoma, Oregon, Pennsylvania, Rhode Island, South Dakota, Utah, and Wisconsin.

46. 42 U.S.C.A. §§ 1973gg through gg-10 (West 1996); *see* Burck Smith, *"Motor-Voter" Implementation* (Center for Policy Alternatives, 1993). An example of one state's procedures to enforce the act is set forth in N.Y.S. Dep't of Social Servs., Administrative Directive 95 ADM-1 (Jan. 6, 1995).

47. The act has spawned litigation to secure enforcement by a few recalcitrant states. *See*

Association of Community Organizations for Reform Now v. Miller, 912 F. Supp. 989 (W.D. Mich. 1996) (Michigan); *Association of Community Organizations for Reform Now v. Edgar*, 56 F.3d 791 (7th Cir. 1995)(Illinois); *Voting Rights Coalition v. Wilson*, 60 F.3d 1411 (9th Cir. 1995) (California); *see also U.S. Sues 3 States to Force Them to Obey Voter Registration Law*, N.Y. Times, Jan. 24, 1995, at A12.

48. *See Adams v. Askew*, 511 F.2d 700 (1975); *Matthews v. Little*, 498 F.2d 1068 (5th Cir. 1974); *Cassidy v. Willis*, 323 A.2d 598 (Del. 1974), *aff'd*, 419 U.S. 1042 (1974).

49. *Lubin v. Panish*, 415 U.S. 709, 716 (1974); *see also Bullock v. Carter*, 405 U.S. 134, 144 (1972)(filing fees imposed on potential candidates may "[t]end to deny some voters the opportunity to vote for a candidate of their choosing").

50. *Turner v. Fouche*, 396 U.S. 346 (1970).

51. *See, e.g.*, Burt Neuborne, *A Survey of Existing Efforts to Reform the Campaign Finance System*, (White Paper Prepared by the Brennan Center for Justice, New York University Law School, July 2, 1996); Debra Burke, *Twenty Years After the Federal Election Campaign Act Amendments of 1974: Look Who's Running Now*, 90 Dick. L. Rev. 357 (1995); David Adamany, *PAC's and the Democratic Financing of Politics*, 22 Ariz. L. Rev. 569, 571 (1980).

52. *See* Leslie Wayne, *Campaign Finance: Business Is Biggest Donor to Political Campaigns, Study Says*, N.Y. Times, Oct. 18, 1996, A27.

53. Ronald Dworkin, *The Curse of American Politics*, 43 N.Y. Rev. of Books 19 (Oct. 17, 1996).

Appendix A
Supplemental Security Income Worksheet

Appendix B
Physician's Report Form Samples

Appendix C
Explanation of the "Forty Quarters" Rule

Appendix D
Food Stamp Income Worksheets

Appendix E
State Guide to an Indigent's Right to
Counsel in Civil Cases

Appendix F
The Legal System

APPENDIX A

Supplemental Security Income Worksheet

The following instructions explain how to calculate your SSI grant amount. Calculations are done on a monthly basis. A worksheet is included at the end of these instructions.

STEP 1: Add together all of your *unearned* income for the month (exclude cash or goods listed under the question "What is not considered income?" in chapter 1). This is your *total unearned income* for the month.

STEP 2: Subtract from total unearned income for the month all of the following exclusions and deductions that apply to you:

1. *Income excluded by federal law.* There are many federal laws that provide income or benefits to individuals and specify that such income or benefits may not be considered for determining SSI eligibility and grant amount.[1] A complete list of federal income and benefits that are not counted as income for SSI purposes appears in Title 20 of the Code of Federal Regulations, pt. 416, subpt. K, appendix 1. The following are some examples of benefits that do not count as income:

   a. Food stamps.
   b. WIC (Women, Infants and Children) food coupons.
   c. Federally donated foods.
   d. Meals provided under the National School Lunch Program.
   e. Home Energy Assistance payments.
   f. Federal housing assistance.[2]
   g. Certain grants or loans to undergraduates made or insured through a program administered by the U.S. Secretary of Education.
   h. Distributions made to Native Americans from certain claim funds, judgments, and land trusts.
   i. Assistance (other than wages) to an individual under the Older Americans Act of 1965.
   j. Payments from the Agent Orange Settlement Fund.
   k. Payments made under section 6 of the Radiation Exposure Compensation Act.

2. *Assistance payments from a State or a Native American tribe.* Needs-based

assistance payments funded wholly by a state or local government or a Native American tribe are not considered in determining SSI eligibility or grant amount.[3] (Note: Temporary Assistance to Families (formerly AFDC) benefits are partially funded by the federal government and therefore *are* counted as income for SSI purposes. General Assistance programs are wholly funded by states and localities and so are not included in the calculation of SSI income.)[4]

3. *Any public agency's refund of taxes on real property or food.*[5]

4. *Scholarships, grants, and fellowships.* Any part of a scholarship, grant, or fellowship used for tuition, fees, or other educational expenses is not counted as income for SSI purposes.[6]

5. *Food raised by you or your spouse.* Food raised by you or your spouse and consumed by your household does not count as income.[7]

6. *Disaster relief.* Assistance received under the Disaster Relief and Emergency Assistance Act and any other federal assistance received under a presidential declaration of major disaster does not count as income.[8]

7. *Small and irregular income payments.* Unearned income of twenty dollars or less in a month is not counted if you receive it only once during a calendar quarter from a single source or "cannot reasonably expect it."[9]

8. *Interest on burial funds and burial space purchase agreements.* Interest accrued on and left to accumulate in a burial fund or burial space purchase agreement and any appreciation in value of the burial arrangement do not count as income.[10]

9. *Home Energy Assistance provided by state or certain private agencies.*[11]

10. *One-third of support payments made to you if you are a child.*[12]

11. *Income used to fulfill an approved plan to achieve self-support.* Any earned or unearned income that you receive and use to fulfill an approved plan to achieve self-support will not be counted as income if you are blind or disabled and under age 65 or if you received SSI as a blind or disabled individual the month before you reached age 65 and you continue to be blind or disabled.[13]

12. *Expenses for rental property.* If you receive rental payments, subtract the ordinary expenses of producing and collecting that income (e.g., interest on debts, taxes, utility payments).[14] Depreciation is not, however, allowed as a deduction. (Note: if you are "self-employed in the business of renting properties," net rental income is treated as "earned income," and different exclusions and deductions apply.)[15]

13. *The $20 General Deduction.* Subtract $20 from any unearned income remaining after application of the exclusions and deductions listed above.

STEP 3: Your total unearned income minus items one through thirteen is your *countable unearned income.*

STEP 4: Add together all of your *earned* income for the month (include gross wages and net self-employment income, but *exclude* cash or goods listed under "What is not considered income?" in chapter 1) This is your *total earned income* for the month.

STEP 5: Subtract from total earned income for the month all of the following deductions and exclusions that apply to you, *in the order listed below*.

1. *Income excluded by federal law.* Certain federal laws that provide income to individuals also direct that such income not be considered for determining SSI eligibility and grant amount.[16] A complete list of federal income that may not be counted as income for SSI purposes appears in Title 20 of the Code of Federal Regulations, pt. 416, subpt. K, appendix 1. The following are some examples of earned income that is not considered "countable income":

    a. Wages received by a handicapped person employed in a project under Title VI of the Rehabilitation Act of 1973.

    b. Compensation to volunteers in the foster grandparent program and other similar programs.

2. *Earned Income Credit.* Payments of the Earned Income Credit, whether made to you in advance by your employer or made to you as part of your federal income tax refund, do not count as income for SSI purposes.[17]

3. *Small and irregular income.* Earned income of $10 or less in a month is not counted if you receive it no more than once during a calendar quarter from any single source or "cannot reasonably expect it."[18]

4. *Student income.* If you are under age 22 and are regularly attending school, subtract up to $400 per month of your earned income—but not more than a total of $1,620 in a calendar year.[19]

5. *Any unused part of the $20 General Deduction.* If you did not use all of the $20 General Deduction on your unearned income in a given month, subtract the unused part from your earned income.[20]

6. *The $65 Monthly Earned Income Deduction.* Subtract an additional $65 per month of earned income.[21]

7. *Disability-related work expenses.* If you are disabled and (a) under age 65 or (b) received SSI as a disabled person for the month before you reached age 65, then subtract the cost of items and services you need to enable you to work despite your disability.[22]

8. *The 50 Percent General Deduction.* Subtract one-half of your remaining earned income.[23]

9. *Work expenses for the blind.* If you receive SSI as a blind person, subtract all work-related expenses.[24]

10. *Income used to fulfill an approved plan to achieve self-support.* If you are under age 65, or if you received SSI as a blind or disabled individual the month

before you reached age 65 and you continue to be blind or disabled, subtract any earned income that you use to fulfill an approved plan to achieve self-support.[25]

STEP 6: Your total earned income minus items one through ten is your *countable earned income.*

STEP 7: Add your countable unearned income (step 3) and your countable earned income (step 6): The total is your *countable income* for the month.

STEP 8: Calculate the maximum monthly SSI benefit for a person in your category. (The maximum SSI grant is equal to the federal monthly benefit (in 1997, $484 per month for an individual and $726 per month for an eligible couple) plus the state supplement for a person in your category.)

STEP 9: Subtract your countable income (step 7) from the maximum SSI grant for a person in your category (step 8): the result is your monthly SSI grant.

SSI WORKSHEET

Part I: Find Monthly Countable Income

1. **Enter** Gross Unearned Income for the Month
   (see Step 1) $_____ (1)
2. **Subtract** Exclusions and Deductions from
   Step 2, items 1–13   – $_____ (2)
3. Countable Unearned Income (1 minus 2)   = $_____ (3) ANSWER
4. **Enter** Gross Earned Income for the Month
   (see Step 4) $_____ (4)
5(a). **Subtract** Exclusions and Deductions
   from Step 5, items 1–5, if applicable   – $_____ (5a)
5(b). **Subtract** the $65 earned income deduction   – $_65___ (5b)
   Subtotal   = $_____ (5b) ANSWER

5(c). **Subtract** disability-related work expenses
   from Step 5, item 7, if applicable   – $_____ (5c)
   Subtotal   = $_____ (5c) ANSWER

5(d). **Subtract** one-half of the subtotal on line
   "(5c) ANSWER"   – $_____ (5d)
   Subtotal   = $_____ (5d) ANSWER

5(e). **Subtract** work expenses for the blind and
   income used for a PASS plan, from Step 5,
   items 9 and 10, if applicable   – $_____ (5e)
6. Countable Earned Income
   (4 minus 5(a)–(e))   = $_____ (6) ANSWER
7. **Add** line 3 _____ and line 6 _____
   to arrive at MONTHLY COUTABLE
   INCOME $_____ (7) ANSWER

continued on next page

SSI WORKSHEET *continued*

Part II: Find Monthly SSI Grant Amount

8. **Enter** Maximum SSI Benefit (see Step 8) $_____ (8)
9. **Subtract** Monthly Countable Income
    (from line 7)   − $_____ (9)
10. **MONTHLY SSI GRANT** (8 minus 9)   = $_____ (10) ANSWER

N O T E S

1. *See* 20 C.F.R. § 416.1124(a) and (b) (1996).

2. Assistance paid under the U.S. Housing Act of 1937, the National Housing Act, Section 101 of the Housing and Urban Development Act of 1965, Title V of the Housing Act of 1949, or Section 202(h) of the Housing Act of 1959. *See* 20 C.F.R. § 416.1124(c)(14) (1996).

3. *Id.* at § 416.1124(c)(2) (1996).

4. *Id.*

5. *Id.* at § 416.1124(c)(1) (1996).

6. *Id.* at § 416.1124(c)(3) (1996).

7. *Id.* at § 416.1124(c)(4) (1996).

8. *Id.* at § 416.1124(c)(5) ; *see also id.* at § 416.1150 (1996).

9. *Id.* at § 416.1124(c)(6) (1996).

10. *Id.* at § 416.1124(c)(9) & (15) (1996).

11. *Id.* at § 416.1124(c)(10); *see also id.* at § 416.1157 (1996).

12. *Id.* at § 416.1124(c)(11) (1996).

13. *Id.* at §§ 416.1112(c)(8), 416.1124(c)(13) (1996).

14. *Id.* at § 416.1121(d) (1996).

15. *See id.* at §§ 416.1110(b), 416.1121(d) (1996).

16. *See id.* at § 416.1112(a)–(b) (1996).

17. *Id.* at §§ 416.1112(c)(1) (1996).

18. *Id.*

19. *Id.* at §§ 416.1112(c)(2), 416.1856, 416.1861 (1996).

20. *Id.* at § 416.1112(c)(3) (1996).

21. *Id.* at § 416.1112(c)(4) (1996).

22. *Id.* at §§ 416.1112(c)(5), 416.976 (1996).

23. *Id.* at § 416.1112(c)(6) (1996).

24. *Id.* at § 416.1112(c)(7) (1996).

25. *Id.* at § 416.1112(c)(8) (1996).

Appendix B

Physician's Report Form Samples

SAMPLE 1:
**A Physician's Report for Claim of
Disability Due to Physical Impairment**

Patient's Name:
Patient's Address:
Patient's Social Security No.:

Dear Doctor:

Please answer each of the following questions about your patient. They concern your patient's claim of entitlement to disability benefits under the Social Security Act. The information provided will be used by the Social Security Administration to decide if your patient is disabled.

1. Give first and last dates of treatment and the average frequency of treatment.

2. Diagnosis(es).

3. a. Have any of the patient's medical conditions lasted at least 12 months? Yes___ No___
   b. If not, are any of the patient's medical conditions expected to last at least 12 months or result in death? Yes___ No___

4. State in detail the patient's symptoms (the patient's complaints and description of his or her impairments, including pain).

5. Describe in detail the patient's signs (your clinical findings).

6. List all medical and other tests given to the patient and the test results.

7. Does or could any medical condition cause the patient pain? Yes___ No__ If yes, explain.

8. Does the patient have to lie down during the day? Yes___ No___ If yes, state the period of time and the reason.

9. Describe the treatment other than medication the patient has received.

10. a. List all medications prescribed for the patient, including the dosage and frequency.

b. Do any medications have any side effects or limit the patient's activities? Yes___ No___ If yes, explain.

11. Please answer each question by *estimating* the degree of the patient's ability to do the following on a daily basis *in a work place setting:*

a. In an 8-hour workday, how many hours total can the patient sit in a normal position?

b. How long can the patient sit *continuously* in a normal position at a work station?

c. In an 8-hour workday, how many hours can the patient stand at a work station?

d. How long can the patient stand *continuously* at a work station?

e. In an 8-hour workday, how many hours can the patient walk?

f. How long can the patient walk *continuously?*

For questions (g)–(k), use the following key: N = never; O = occasionally; F = frequently; C = continuously

g. In an 8-hour workday, how often can the patient **lift** the following weight (in pounds)

Up to 5 ___; 6–10 ___; 11–20 ___; 21–50 ___; 51–100 ___

h. In an 8-hour workday, how often can the patient **carry** the following weight (in pounds)

Up to 5 ___; 6–10 ___; 11–20 ___; 21–50 ___; 51–100 ___

i. In an 8-hour workday, how often can the patient

Bend ___; Squat ___; Crawl ___; Climb ___; Reach ___

j. In an 8-hour workday, how often can the patient use hands for repetitive action, such as

Handling (gross manipulation): Right ___ Left ___

Fingering (fine manipulation): Right ___ Left ___

Pushing and pulling of arm controls: Right ___ Left ___

k. In an 8-hour workday, how often can the patient use feet for repetitive movements, such as pushing and pulling of leg controls

Right ___ Left ___ Both ___

12. a. Indicate whether the patient has restrictions involving the following activities (Use the following key: N = none; M = mild; Mod = moderate; T = total)

_____ Unprotected heights

_____ Being around moving machinery

_____ Exposure to marked changes in temperature and humidity

_____ Driving a motor vehicle

_____ Exposure to dust, fumes, gases, noxious odors, and poor ventilation

    b. Explain or add any restrictions.

13. The Social Security Administration has established a "Listing of Impairments," which is published in Title 20 of the Code of Federal Regulations, pt. 404, subpt. P, app. 1. If you are able to consult the Listing of Impairments, state whether your patient has an impairment that meets or is equal in severity to a listed impairment and set forth the section number(s) of the impairment(s).

14. Could the patient travel alone to work on a daily basis: By bus? Yes__ No__ By subway? Yes__ No__

15. Additional comments.

Physician (signature)_____ Date_____
Physician (print name)_____
Address_____ Telephone Number_____
Specialty_____

SAMPLE 2
A Physician's Report for Claim of
Disability Due to Mental Impairment

Patient's Name:
Patient's Address:
Patient's Social Security No.:

Dear Doctor:

Please answer each of the following questions about your patient. They concern your patient's claim of entitlement to disability benefits under the Social Security Act. The information provided will be used by the Social Security Administration to decide if your patient is disabled.

1. Give first and last dates of treatment and the average frequency of treatment.

2. Diagnosis(es) (using DSM IV terminology and axes).

3. State in detail the patient's symptoms (the patient's complaints and description of his or her impairments, including pain).

4. Describe in detail the patient's mental status, including general appearance; attitude and behavior; characteristics of speech; characteristics of thought; mood and affect; sensorium and intellectual functions; and insight and judgment.

5. Give name and results of any tests given to the patient.

6. Does the patient have to lie down during the day? Yes__ No__ If yes, for how long and for what reason.

7. Describe the treatment (other than medication) the patient has received.

8. a. Give the medications prescribed for the patient, including the dosage and frequency.
   b. Do any of the medications have any side effects or limit the patient's activities? Yes__ No__ If yes, explain.

9. The Social Security Administration publishes a "Listing of Impairments" in Title 20 of the Code of Federal Regulations, pt. 404, subpt. P, app. 1. If you are able to consult the Listing of Impairments, please state whether the patient's mental impairment is described in the listing and set forth the section number(s) of the listed impairment(s).

10. Could the patient travel alone to work on a daily basis: By bus? Yes__ No__ By subway? Yes__ No__

11. Please answer the following questions about the patient's mental residual functional capacity. *Each mental activity is to be evaluated within the context of the patient's capacity to sustain that activity over a regular workday and workweek on an ongoing basis.* Use the following scale: not significantly limited = 1; moderately limited = 2; markedly limited = 3; extremely limited = 4
   a. *Understanding and Memory*
   (1) can remember locations and work-like procedures
   (2) can understand and remember very short instructions
   (3) can understand and remember detailed instructions
   b. *Sustained Concentration and Persistence*
   (4) can carry out very short and simple instructions

(5) can carry out detailed instructions

(6) can maintain attention and concentration for extended periods

(7) can perform activities within a schedule, maintain regular attendance, and be punctual within customary tolerances

(8) can sustain an ordinary routine without special supervision

(9) can work in coordination with or proximity to others without being distracted by them

(10) can make simple work-related decisions

(11) can complete a normal workday and workweek without interruptions from psychologically based symptoms and can perform at a consistent pace without an unreasonably lengthy rest period

c. *Social Interaction*

(12) can interact appropriately with the general public

(13) can ask simple questions or request assistance

(14) can accept instructions and respond appropriately to criticism from supervisors

(15) can get along with coworkers or peers without distracting them or exhibiting behavioral extremes

(16) can maintain socially appropriate behavior and adhere to basic standards of neatness and cleanliness

d. *Adaptation*

(17) can respond appropriately to changes in setting

(18) can be aware of normal hazards and take appropriate precautions

(19) can travel in unfamiliar places or use public transportation

(20) can set realistic goals or make plans independently of others

12. Additional comments.

Physician (signature)_____ Date_____

Physician (print name)_____

Address_____ Telephone_____

Specialty_____

SAMPLE 3
Physician's Report for Child's Claim of Disability

Patient's Name:
Patient's Address:
Patient's Birth Date: Patient's Current Age:
Patient's Social Security No.:

Dear Doctor:

Please answer each of the following questions about your patient. They concern your patient's claim of entitlement to disability benefits under the Social Security Act. The information provided will be used by the Social Security Administration to decide if your patient is disabled.

1. Give first and last dates of treatment and the average frequency of treatment.

2. State in detail the child's symptoms (the child's complaints and description of his or her impairments, including pain).

3. Describe in detail the child's signs (your clinical findings).

4. List all medical or other tests given to the child and the results.

5. Diagnosis(es).

6. a. Have any of the child's medical conditions lasted at least 12 months? Yes__ No__
    b. If not, are any of the child's medical conditions expected to last at least 12 months? Yes__ No__

7. Does or could any medical condition cause the child pain? Yes__ No__ If yes, explain.

8. Does the child have to lie down during the day? Yes__ No__ If yes, state the period of time and the reason.

9. Describe the treatment (other than medication) the child has received.

10. a. List the medications prescribed for the child, including the dosage and frequency.
    b. Do any of the medications have any side effects or limit the child's activities? Yes__ No__ If yes, explain.

11. Has the child been hospitalized? Yes__ No__ If so, when and for how long?

12. The Social Security Administration publishes a "Listing of Impairments" in Title 20 of the Code of Federal Regulations, pt. 404, subpt. P, app. 1. If you are able to consult the Listings of Impairments, please state whether the child has an impairment that meets or is equal in severity to a listed impairment and set forth the section number(s) of the impairment(s).

13. Functional limitations might be in any area, including physical, mental, emotional, developmental, sensory, behavioral, or environmental. Does the child have any limitation or impairment of function:

DEVELOPMENTAL: Mild___ Moderate___ Severe___ Describe.

PHYSICAL: Mild___ Moderate___ Severe___ Describe.

MENTAL/INTELLECTUAL: Mild___ Moderate___ Severe___ Describe.

BEHAVIORAL: Mild___ Moderate___ Severe___ Describe.

SENSORY: Mild___ Moderate___ Severe___ Describe.

OTHER: Mild___ Moderate___ Severe___ Describe.

14. If the child is functioning *below* his/her age-appropriate level in any of the following areas, indicate how far below in years and months:

PERSONAL CARE (toileting, bathing, dressing, etc.)

COMMUNICATION (speaking, listening, understanding, etc.)

MENTAL ACTIVITY (thinking, planning, attention/concentration, etc.)

PHYSICAL ACTIVITY (running, jumping, playing, mobility, manipulating/handling, etc.)

ACADEMIC DEVELOPMENT (reading, writing, arithmetic, etc.)

SOCIAL DEVELOPMENT (relating, sharing, getting along with others, following directions, etc.)

OTHER (anything else not covered above)

15. Additional comments.

Physician (signature)_____ Date_____
Physician (print name)_____
Address_____ Telephone_____
Board Certified? Yes__ No__
Specialty_____

APPENDIX C

Explanation of the "Forty Quarters" Rule

Lawful permanent residents who meet the forty quarters rule are eligible for food stamps and Supplemental Security Income and may not be excluded from state Medicaid, Temporary Assistance for Needy Families, or General Assistance programs. A permanent resident satisfies this rule if he or she has done enough work in the United States to qualify for forty "quarters of coverage" in the Social Security system. The rule is also satisfied if work done by the permanent resident, added to work done by the resident's parents while he or she was a minor, and work done by the resident's spouse during an undissolved marriage, is—in total—equivalent to forty quarters of coverage in the Social Security system. (After 1996, work performed by a spouse or parent counts toward the requisite forty quarters of coverage only if the spouse or parent did not receive federal means-tested benefits in that quarter.)

An individual qualifies for "quarters of coverage" in the Social Security system by working and earning income. A worker can accumulate up to four quarters of coverage each year, depending on the amount of his or her employment income. In 1996, a worker earned one "quarter of coverage" for every $640 in wages regardless of when during the year the income was made. *See* 60 Fed. Reg 54751 (Oct. 10, 1995). Thus, workers who made at least $2,560 in 1996 earned four quarters of coverage ($640 × 4 = $2,560); workers who earned between $1,920 and $2,560 earned three quarters of coverage ($640 × 3 = $1,920); etc. The amount of income required for one quarter of coverage is recalculated each year in accordance with a statutory formula that accounts for changes in national wage levels, as shown below.

1995	$630	1990	$520
1994	$620	1989	$500
1993	$590	1988	$470
1992	$570	1987	$460
1991	$540	1986	$440

Source: 58 Fed. Reg 58004 (Oct. 28, 1993); 57 Fed. Reg. 48619 (Oct. 27, 1992): 56 Fed. Reg. 55325 (Oct. 25, 1991); 55 Fed. Reg. 45856 (Oct. 31, 1990); 54 Fed. Reg. 45801 (Oct. 31, 1989); 53 Fed. Reg. 43932 (Oct. 31, 1988); 52 Fed. Reg. 41672 (Oct. 29, 1987); 51 Fed. Reg. 40256 (Nov. 5, 1986); 50 Fed. Reg. 45558 (Oct. 31, 1985).

As this book goes to press, the Social Security Administration has yet to issue regulations describing how an immigrant can claim eligibility under the forty quarters rule. Many immigrants (and their parents and spouses) may have worked off the books, or their employers may have neglected to report wages to the Social Security Administration. The federal statute does not appear to require that an immigrant's employment has been reported or that Social Security taxes have been paid in order for the earnings to count toward the requisite forty quarters. All the statute seems to require is that the immigrant's employment earnings (together with those of his or her spouse and parents, as applicable) equal or exceed the amount that would entitle a worker to forty quarters of coverage, whether or not the quarters were actually credited in the Social Security system. By the time you read this book, the Social Security Administration may have published regulations explaining what an immigrant must do to establish eligibility under the forty quarters rule.

Appendix D

Food Stamp Income Worksheets

Worksheet 1 tells you how to calculate income for households with at least one elderly or disabled person. Worksheet 2 tells you how to calculate income for all other households. Benefit levels apply to 1996–1997.

Worksheet 1: Households with an Elderly or Disabled Member

A. Figure out your monthly wages because the food stamp office counts your income on a monthly basis. Depending on how frequently you get paid, you may have to convert a weekly or biweekly amount into a monthly figure. If you are paid every week, multiply your paycheck before payroll deductions by 4.3. If you are paid every two weeks, multiply your check before payroll deductions by 2.15. If you are paid twice a month, multiply the amount before payroll deductions by 2. (You are getting paid twice a month if you get your checks on the 1st and 15th; you are getting paid every two weeks if you get your checks on the same day of the week every second week.) The number you get is your **gross monthly earned income**. Put down this total next to (A). If you do not have any earned income, go to step D.

B. Take 20 percent of your gross monthly earned income.[1] To do this, divide (A), your gross monthly earned income, by five. The answer is your **work expense deduction**, (B).[2]

C. *Subtract* (B), your work expense deduction, from (A), your gross monthly earned income, to get (C).[3]

D. *Add* to (C) all other income, including unearned income, that your household received during the month (for example, AFDC, General Assistance, SSI, Social Security benefits, etc.), to yield (D).[4]

E. *Subtract* from (D) the current **standard deduction** to yield (E).[5]

F. *Subtract* from (E) monthly **medical costs** over $35 of anyone in your household who is elderly or disabled, to yield (F).[6] Medical costs include doctor, dentist, and hospital bills, prescription drugs and over-the-counter medicine prescribed by a doctor, Medicare and insurance premiums, payments, and deductibles, payments to someone to care for the elderly or disabled person in the home, transportation to and from the doctor or hospital, medical supplies that you need, payments to a nursing home for the care of someone who was in your household before she or he became sick, and other medical costs that you pay and are not reimbursed. You *cannot* deduct any part of medical costs that insurance, Medicare, medical assistance, or any other source will pay up front or reimburse. Subtract $35 from the total of these costs, and then subtract the resulting figure from (E), to get (F).

G. Now *subtract* from (F) your **dependent care costs** up to $175 per person or $200 per child up to age two.[7] Dependent care costs are what you pay for day care or a sitter to take care of children, or any adults that need watching, so that someone in your household can work, look for work, or take training or classes that will help get work. The answer, listed on line (G), is your **adjusted income** for the month.

H. Next, figure out your monthly **shelter cost** based on what you have been billed (even if you have not yet paid the bill).[8] Shelter costs include rent, mortgage payments, payments on a mobile home and rent for the space where it is parked, electricity, gas, heating oil, bottled gas, firewood, water, sewerage, garbage, taxes, insurance on your house, repairs to your house for damage caused by a fire, flood, storm, or other disaster, installation fees for utilities or telephones, and the basic charge for one telephone. You cannot count the unpaid balance on your bill from an earlier month. Some states add up exact monthly figures for each cost and then round off the total. Other states round each figure to the nearest dollar. Check with your food stamp office to find out how your state adds up these costs. The answer is your monthly **shelter cost**, (H).

NOTE: Most states use a **standard utility allowance (SUA)**. This worksheet shows how to figure your utility costs in a state that uses one SUA for all utilities including telephone charges. Many states let households deduct both the SUA and the basic telephone charge. Some states also have specific SUAs for each utility, while other states have SUAs for people who pay for heat separate and apart from their rent and for people who do not. Depending on your state's SUA, you may want to adjust this worksheet before making your calculations.

NOTE: States are now required to provide a **standard shelter allowance** for homeless households. The 1996 federal estimate for the homeless shelter deduction is $143. States have authority, subject to federal approval, to develop their own standards based on the actual costs of housing in the area. Households with higher actual shelter costs should deduct their actual costs instead of the standard shelter deduction.

I. Now divide (G), your adjusted income, in half. Adjusted income is your income after having subtracted your work expense deduction, the standard deduction, your medical cost deduction, and dependent care costs.[9] The answer is (I).

J. *Subtract* (I), half of your adjusted income, from (H), your shelter cost.[10] If your shelter cost (H) is more than half your adjusted income (I), the answer is your shelter deduction (J). If your shelter cost is less than half your income after other deductions, you do not get a shelter deduction. In that case, your adjusted income (G) is your monthly net income.

K. *Subtract* your shelter deduction (J) from your adjusted income (G).[11] The result is your **monthly net income** (K).

L. Now that you know your monthly net income, you can find out if you meet the income limits of the food stamp program. Find your household size at the top of the chart in part II of worksheet 1. Look at the number below the household size. That number is the largest net monthly income your household can have and still receive food stamps if you meet other program requirements.

M. To figure out the size of your monthly food stamp allotment (M), first multiply your net monthly income by three-tenths. This is because 30 percent of your net income counts against your food stamp allotment, in the sense that for every ten dollars of net income, the food stamp office will reduce your benefits by three dollars (M).

N. Round up (M) to the next whole dollar.[12] The result is your **adjusted food stamp income** (N). (Income limits are slightly higher in Alaska and Hawaii.)

O–Q. Look at the chart in part II of worksheet 1 to find out your food stamp allotment. Find your household size at the top of the chart. Look at the number below the household size. Subtract the number in (N) from the number below your household size. This number is your **monthly food stamp allotment**, or (O). If (O) is $1, $3, or $5 and there are at least three people in your household, round up to $2, $4, or $6, or (P). Your household is entitled to at least $10 of food stamps if it includes one or two people. If you are a one- or two-person household and (N) is greater than (O), your monthly food stamp allotment is $10 (Q). If (O) is less than $10, your monthly allotment is still $10 (Q).

R. Write down your monthly allotment in the space provided. Most of the time, you will not get a full month of food stamps for the month in which you apply. How many food stamps you receive for the first month will depend on how early in the month you turn in your food stamp application.[13] The earlier you sign your application and turn it in to the food stamp office, the more food stamps you will get because you get food stamps for the remaining days in the month. This is called prorating your benefits. Food stamp offices figure the exact allotment with a proration table; they must show you the table if you ask to see it. If you want to figure out yourself how the food stamp office will prorate your benefits for the first month, go on to steps S through V on the worksheet. Keep in mind that if you apply for food stamps so late in the month that your allotment for the remaining days will be less than $10, you will not get any food stamps for that month.[14]

Worksheet 2: Households with No Elderly or Disabled Members

A. Figure out your monthly wages because the food stamp office counts your income on a monthly basis. Depending on how frequently you get paid, you may have to convert a weekly or biweekly amount into a monthly figure. If you are paid every week, multiply your paycheck before payroll deductions by 4.3. If you are paid every two weeks, multiply your check before payroll deductions by 2.15. If you are paid twice a month, multiply the amount before payroll deductions by 2. (You are getting paid twice a month if you get your checks on the 1st and 15th; you are getting paid every two weeks if you get your checks on the same day of the week every second week.) The number you get is your **gross monthly earned income**. Put down this total next to (A). If you do not have any earned income, go to step D.

B. List on line (B) all other income, including unearned income, that your household received during the month (for example, AFDC, General Assistance, SSI, Social Security benefits, etc.).

C. *Add* (A), gross monthly earned income, to (B), monthly unearned income, to get (C), gross monthly income. Look at the chart in part I of worksheet 2 to see if your gross monthly income meets the food stamp program's gross monthly income limit. Compare the number listed on line (C) with the number on the chart listed for the number of people in your size household. If (C) is larger than the listed number, your household is ineligible, because its gross monthly income is higher than the amount allowed for this size household. If (C) is not larger, go on to the next step to determine your net monthly income.

D. Write (A), your gross monthly earned income, on line (D). If you do not have any gross monthly earned income, go on to step G.

E. Take 20 percent of your gross monthly earned income.[15] To do this, divide (D), your gross monthly earned income, by five. The answer is your **work expense deduction**, (E).[16]

F. *Subtract* (E), your work expense deduction, from (D), your gross monthly earned income, to yield (F).[17]

G. *Add* (B) your monthly unearned income, to (F), your remaining earned income, having subtracted the **work expense deduction**.[18] The result is (G).

H. Now *subtract* from (G) the current **standard deduction**.[19]

I. *Subtract* from (H) your **dependent care costs** up to $200 per child under age 2 and $175 for each other dependent.[20] Dependent care costs are what you pay for day care or a sitter to take care of children or any adults that need watching so that someone in your household can work, look for work, or take training or classes that will help get work. The answer is (I), your **adjusted income** for the month.

J. Now figure out your monthly **shelter cost** based on what you have been billed (even if you have not yet paid the bill).[21] Shelter cost includes rent, mortgage payments, payments on a mobile home and rent for the space where it is parked, electricity, gas, heating oil, bottled gas, firewood, water, sewage, garbage, taxes, insurance on your house, repairs to your house for damage caused by a fire, flood, storm, or other disaster, installation fees for utilities or telephones, and the basic charge for one telephone. You cannot count the unpaid balance on your bill from an earlier month. Some states add up exact monthly figures for each cost and then round off the total. Other states round each figure to the nearest dollar. Check with your food stamp office to find out how your state adds up these costs. The answer is your **monthly shelter cost** (J).

NOTE: Most states use a **standard utility allowance (SUA)**. This worksheet shows how to figure your utility costs in a state that uses one SUA for all utilities including telephone charges. Many states let households deduct both the SUA and the basic telephone charge. Some states also have specific SUAs for each utility, while others have different SUAs for people who pay for heat separate and apart from their rent and for people who do not. Depending on your state's SUA, you may want to adjust this worksheet before making your calculations.

NOTE: States are now required to provide a **standard shelter allowance** for homeless households. The 1996 federal estimate for the homeless shelter deduction is $143. States have authority, subject to federal approval, to develop their own standards based on the actual costs of housing in the area. Households with higher actual shelter costs should deduct their actual costs instead of the standard shelter deduction.

K. Now take (I), your adjusted income, which is your monthly income after subtracting your work expense deduction, the standard deduction, and your dependent care costs, and divide the figure in half.[22] The answer is (K).

L. *Subtract* (K), half of your adjusted income, from (J), your shelter cost.[23] If your shelter cost (J) is more than half your income after other deductions (K), the answer is your shelter deduction (L), unless it is more than the maximum for the **shelter deduction.** If the maximum shelter deduction for your area is less than the difference between your shelter cost and half your income after other deductions, the maximum is your shelter deduction (L).[24] If your shelter cost is less than half your income after other deductions, you do not get a shelter deduction. In that case, (I) is your monthly net income.

M. *Subtract* (L), your **shelter deduction**, from (I), your adjusted income.[25] The result is your **monthly net income**, (M).

N. Now that you know your monthly net income, you can find out if you meet the income limits of the food stamp program. Find your household size at the top of the chart in part III of worksheet 2. Look at the number below the household size. That number is the largest net monthly income your household can have and still receive food stamps if you meet other program requirements. (Income limits are slightly higher in Alaska and Hawaii.)

O. To figure out the size of your monthly food stamp allotment, first multiply your net monthly income by three-tenths. This is because 30 percent of your net income counts against your food stamp allotment, in the sense that for every $10 of net income, the food stamp office will reduce your food stamps by three dollars (O).

P. Round up (O) to the next whole dollar.[26] The result is your **adjusted food stamp income**, (P).

Q–S. Look at the chart in part III of worksheet 2 to find out your food stamp allotment. Find your household size at the top of the chart. Look at the number below the household size. Subtract (P) from the number below your household size. This number is your **monthly food stamp allotment,** or (Q). If (Q) is $1, $3, or $5 and there are at least three people in your household, round up to $2, $4, or $6, or (R). Your household is entitled to at least $10 of food stamps if it includes one or two people. If you are a one or two person household and the number in (P) is greater than the number in (Q), your monthly food stamp allotment is $10, (S). If (Q) comes out to less than $10, your monthly allotment is still $10, (S).

T. Write down your monthly allotment in the space provided. Most of the time, you will not get a full month of food stamps for the month in which you apply. How many food stamps you receive for the first month will depend on how early in the month you turn in your food stamp application.[27] The earlier you sign your application and turn it in to the food stamp office, the more food stamps you will get, because you will get food stamps for the remaining days in the month. This is called prorating your benefits. Food stamp offices figure the exact allotment with a proration table; they must show you the table if you ask to see it. If you want to figure out yourself how the food stamp office will prorate your benefits for the first month, go on to steps U through Y on the worksheet. Keep in mind that if you apply for food stamps so late in the month that your allotment for the remaining days will be less than $10, you will not get any food stamps for that month.[28]

FOOD STAMP WORKSHEET 1
Household with Elderly (Age 60 or Over) or Disabled Member

Part I: Find Net Income

A.	Gross Earned Income for Month		$_____	(A)
B.	**Subtract** Work Expense Deduction (20% of A)	−	$_____	(B)
C.	Net Earned Income (A − B)	=	$_____	(C)

continued on next page

FOOD STAMP WORKSHEET 1 *continued*

D.	**Add** Other Income			
	(SSI, GA, Social Security, etc.)	+	$_____	
	Subtotal	=	$_____	(D)
E.	**Subtract** Standard Deduction	–	$_____	
	Subtotal (D – Standard Deduction)	=	$_____	(E)
F.	**Subtract** Medical Costs over $35			
	Deduction = (Cost: $_____) – $35	–	$_____	
	Subtotal	=	$_____	(F)
G.	**Subtract** Dependent Care Costs	–	$_____	
	Adjusted Income	=	$_____	(G)

H. Find Excess Shelter Cost

1. Rent or Mortgage		$_____	
2. Fire Insurance on Home	+	$_____	
3. Property Tax	+	$_____	
4. Basic Telephone Charge (SUA if applicable)	+	$_____	
5. Electricity	+	$_____	
6. Gas and Kerosene	+	$_____	
7. Oil, Coal and Wood	+	$_____	
8. Water/Sewer	+	$_____	
TOTAL (4 through 8) $_____ *or* $_____ (SUA)	+	$_____	
TOTAL SHELTER COST	=	$_____	(H)

I.	**Subtract** 1/2 of Adjusted Income (1/2 × G)	–	$_____	(I)
J.	**EXCESS SHELTER COST** (H - I)	=	$_____	(J)
K.	Take the Figure for Adjusted Income (G)		$_____	(G)
	Subtract Excess Shelter Cost (J)	–	$_____	(J)
	MONTHLY NET INCOME (G - J)	=	$_____	(K)

Part II: Find Amount of Food Stamps

L. Compare Monthly Net Income to Chart. (*If Monthly Net Income is higher than figure on the chart, household is ineligible.*)

HOUSEHOLD SIZE	1	2	3	4	5	6	7	8	+1
MAXIMUM NET INCOME	$645	$864	$1,082	$1,300	$1,519	$1,737	$1,955	$2,174	+ $219

M.	Multiply the Household's *Net Income* (K) by 0.3		
	(K × 0.3)	$_____	(M)
N.	Round *up* to the next whole dollar to find		
	Adjusted Food Stamp Income	$_____	(N)

continued on next page

FOOD STAMP WORKSHEET 1 *continued*

O.   Subtract *Adjusted Food Stamp Income* (N) from the figures in the chart below:

HOUSEHOLD

SIZE	1	2	3	4	5	6	7	8	+1

MAXIMUM FOOD STAMP ALLOTMENT

	1	2	3	4	5	6	7	8	+1
MAXIMUM FOOD STAMP ALLOTMENT	$120	$220	$315	$400	$475	$570	$630	$720	+ $90

Maximum Food Stamp Allotment minus Adjusted Food Stamp Income: $_____ (O)

P.   If the number of people in the household is three or more, and (O) is $1, $3, or $5, round up to $2, $4, or $6. $_____ (P)

Q.   If the number of people in the household is one or two, the household is entitled to at least $10 of food stamps. If the *Adjusted Food Stamp Income* (N) is greater than the maximum food stamp amount, the allotment is $10. If (O) is less than $10, the allotment is $10. $_____ (Q)

R.   **MONTHLY FOOD STAMP ALLOTMENT:** Use the result from O (or from P or Q if applicable).   (R)

Part III: Prorate the First Month's Food Stamps

S.   Take the number your state uses to prorate food stamps. (This is either 31 *or* 1 + the number of days in the month).   _____ (S)

T.   **Subtract** the day of the month the household applied   −

   Subtotal   = _____ (T)

U.   **Divide** by 30   ÷

   Subtotal (T/30)   = _____ (U)

V.   **Multiply** by the household's Monthly Food Stamp Allotment (R)   × $_____ (R)

   Unrounded first month's food stamp allotment = $_____ (V)

W.   Round *down* to next whole dollar to find *First Month's Food Stamp Allotment* (if rounded amount is less than $10, household gets no allotment for the first month)   (W)

FOOD STAMP WORKSHEET 2
Household with No Elderly (Age 60 or Over) or Disabled Members

Part 1. Find Gross Income Eligibility

A.	Gross Monthly Earned Income	$_____	(A)
B.	**Add** Other Income		
	(AFDC, SSI, GA, Social Security, etc.)	+ $_____	(B)
C.	Gross Monthly Income	= $_____	(C)

If gross income is higher than maximum on this chart, household is ineligible.

HOUSEHOLD SIZE

+ 1	1	2	3	4	5	6	7	8	+1

MAXIMUM GROSS INCOME $839 $1,123 $1,407 $1,690 $1,974 $2,258 $2,542 $2,826 + $284

Part II: Find Net Income

D.	Gross Monthly Earned Income	$_____	(A)
E.	**Subtract** Work Expense Deduction (20% of A) −	$_____	(E)
F.	Net Earned Income (A − E) =	$_____	(F)
G.	**Add** Other Income		
	(AFDC, SSI, GA, Social Security, etc.) +	$_____	(B)
	Subtotal (B + F) =	$_____	(G)
H.	**Subtract** Standard Deduction −	$_____	
	Subtotal (G − Standard Deduction) =	$_____	(H)
I.	**Subtract** Dependent Care Costs −	$_____	
	Adjusted Income (H − I) =	$_____	(I)
J.	Find Excess Shelter Cost		
	1. Rent or Mortgage	$_____	
	2. Fire Insurance on Home +	$_____	
	3. Property Tax +	$_____	
	4. Basic Telephone Charge (or SUA) +	$_____	
	5. Electricity +	$_____	
	6. Gas and Kerosene +	$_____	
	7. Oil, Coal and Wood +	$_____	
	8. Water/Sewer +	$_____	
	TOTAL (4 through 8) $_____ or $_____		
	(SUA) +	$_____	
	TOTAL SHELTER COST =	$_____	(J)
K.	**Subtract** 1/2 of Adjusted Income (1/2 × I) −	$_____	(K)
L.	**EXCESS SHELTER COST** (J − K) =	$_____	(L)

continued on next page

FOOD STAMP WORKSHEET 2 *continued*

M.	Take the Figure for Adjusted Income	\$_____	(I)
	Subtract Shelter Deduction (Excess Shelter	− \$_____	(L)
	Cost up to \$247		
	MONTHLY NET INCOME (I − the lesser of		
	L or \$247)	= \$_____	(M)

Part III: Find Amount of Food Stamps

N. Compare Monthly Net Income to Chart. (*If Monthly Net Income is higher than figure on chart, household is ineligible.*)

HOUSEHOLD SIZE	1	2	3	4	5	6	7	8	+1
MAXIMUM NET INCOME	\$645	\$864	\$1,082	\$1,300	\$1,519	\$1,737	\$1,955	\$2,174	\$219

O.	Multiply the Household's *Net Income* (M) by 0.3 (M × 0.3)	\$_____	(O)
P.	Round *up* to the next dollar to find *Adjusted Food Stamp Income*	\$_____	(P)
Q.	Subtract *Adjusted Food Stamp Income* (P) from the figures in the chart below:		

HOUSEHOLD SIZE	1	2	3	4	5	6	7	8	+1
MAXIMUM FOOD STAMP ALLOTMENT	\$120	\$220	\$315	\$400	\$475	\$570	\$630	\$720	+ \$90

Maximum Food Stamp Allotment Minus Adjusted Food Stamp Income:		\$_____	(Q)
R.	If the number of people in the household is three or more, and (Q) is \$1, \$3 or \$5, round up to \$2, \$4 or \$6.	\$_____	(R)
S.	If the number of people in the household is one or two, the household is entitled to at least \$10 of food stamps. If the *Adjusted Food Stamp Income* (P) is greater than the maximum food stamp amount, the allotment is \$10. If (Q) is less than \$10, the allotment is \$10.	\$_____	(S)
T.	**MONTHLY FOOD STAMP ALLOTMENT:** Use the result from Q (or from R or S if applicable)	[ ]	(T)

continued on next page

FOOD STAMP WORKSHEET 2 *continued*

Part IV: Prorate the First Month's Food Stamps

U. Take the number your state uses to prorate
    food stamps. (This is either 31 *or* 1 + the
    number of days in the month.) _____ (U)

V. **Subtract** the day of the month the household
    applied   − _____
    Subtotal (U − V)   = _____ (V)

W. **Divide** by 30   ÷ _____
    Subtotal (V/30)   _____ (W)

X. **Multiply** by the household's Monthly Food
    Stamp Allotment (T)   × $_____ (T)
    Unrounded first month's food stamp allotment = $_____ (X)

NOTES

1. 7 C.F.R. § 273.10(e)(1)(i)(B) (1996).
2. 7 C.F.R. § 273.9(d)(2) (1996).
3. 7 C.F.R. § 273.10(e)(1)(i)(B) (1996).
4. 7 C.F.R. § 273.10(e)(1)(i)(B) (1996).
5. 7 C.F.R. § 273.10(e)(1)(i)(C) (1996).
6. 7 C.F.R. §§ 273.10(e)(1)(i)(D), 273.9(d)(3) (1996).
7. 7 C.F.R. §§ 273.10(e)(1)(i)(E), 273.9(d)(4) (1996).
8. 7 C.F.R. § 273.10(e)(1)(i)(F) (1996).
9. 7 C.F.R. § 273.10(e)(1)(i)(F) (1996).
10. 7 C.F.R. §§ 273.10(e)(1)(i)(F), 273.9(d)(5) (1996).
11. 7 C.F.R. § 273.10(e)(1)(i)(G) (1996).
12. 7 C.F.R. § 273.10(e)(2)(ii)(A)(1) (1996).
13. 7 C.F.R. § 273.10(a)(1)(ii) (1996).
14. 7 C.F.R. § 273.10(e)(2)(ii)(B) (1996).
15. 7 C.F.R. § 273.10(e)(1)(i)(B) (1996).
16. 7 C.F.R. § 273.9(d)(2) (1996).
17. 7 C.F.R. § 273.10(e)(1)(i)(B) (1996).
18. 7 C.F.R. § 273.10(e)(1)(i)(B) (1996).
19. 7 C.F.R. § 273.10(e)(1)(i)(C) (1996).
20. 7 C.F.R. §§ 273.10(e)(1)(i)(E), 273.9(d)(4) (1996).
21. 7 C.F.R. § 273.10(e)(1)(i)(F) (1996).
22. 7 C.F.R. § 273.10(e)(1)(i)(F) (1996).
23. 7 C.F.R. §§ 273.10(e)(1)(i)(F), 273.9(d)(5) (1996).

24. 7 C.F.R. § 273.10(e)(1)(i)(G) (1996).
25. 7 C.F.R. § 273.10(e)(1)(i)(G) (1996).
26. 7 C.F.R. § 273.10(e)(2)(ii)(A)(1) (1996).
27. 7 C.F.R. § 273.10(a)(1)(ii) (1996).
28. 7 C.F.R. § 273.10(e)(2)(ii)(B) (1996).

Appendix E

State Guide to an Indigent's Right to Counsel in Civil Cases

State	Type of Case	Procedure or Standard to Determine Indigency	Court Obligation To Appoint Counsel
Alabama	Guardianship for Minor [§ 12-15-8, § 12-15-90]	Financial affidavit	Discretionary
	Involuntary Commitment [§ 22-52-4–§ 22-52-14]		Mandatory
	Paternity [§ 26-17-11]		Mandatory for minor
	Parental Consent to Abortion [§ 26-21-4(b)]		Mandatory for minor
	Dependency [§ 12-15-63, § 12-15-8]		Mandatory for minor and parent; *but see Morgan v. Lauderdale Cty. Dep't of Pensions*, 494 So. 2d 649 (Ala. Civ. App. 1986) (due process does not require counsel for parents in dependency & temporary custody proceeding)
	Involuntary Commitment of Minor [§ 12-15-90(d)(2)]		Mandatory for minor
Alaska	Incapacitated Persons [§ 13.26.106–§ 13.26.112]	Annual income may not exceed maximum established by legal services. If income exceeds maximum, trial court may make specific finding of indigency based on sworn statement of person's income, assets, debts, dependents and monthly expenses for necessaries.	Mandatory

State	Type of Case	Procedure or Standard to Determine Indigency	Court Obligation To Appoint Counsel
Alaska *(continued)*	Child in Need [§ 47.10.050]		Mandatory
	Child Custody [§ 44.21.410]		Mandatory if one party represented by public agency
	Involuntary commitment of minor [§ 47.30.775]		Mandatory
	Adoption under Indian Minor Welfare Act [25 U.S.C. §§ 1901 *et seq.*]		Discretionary
	Child Guardianship		Discretionary
	Protective Proceedings [A.S. § 13.26]		Discretionary, except where appointment of Office of Public Advocacy mandated
	Paternity		Discretionary for putative father
	Involuntary Alcohol Commitments [A.S. § 47.37]		Discretionary
	Representation of Minor: Custody, Support, Visitation [§ 25.24.310] and Removal of Disabilities of Minor [§ 9.55.590]		Discretionary
	Adoption [§ 25.23.180]		Mandatory
	Involuntary commitment of adults & voluntary commitment of adults & minor [§ 47.30.700]		Mandatory, except for voluntary commitment of adults
	Involuntary commitment [§ 18.85.100]		Mandatory
	Civil Contempt for Non-Support		Mandatory
Arizona	Alcoholics—involuntary commitment [§ 36–2026.01]	Varies by county. Statute provides that a person claiming indigent status must complete sworn affidavit. Some counties require only statement in open court.	Mandatory
	Housing Discrimination [§ 41-1491.32]		Discretionary

State	Type of Case	Procedure or Standard to Determine Indigency	Court Obligation To Appoint Counsel
Arizona *(continued)*	Termination of Parental Rights [§ 8-535]		Mandatory if mentally incompetent or guardian ad litem otherwise needed
	Involuntary Commitment [§ 36-503.01]		Mandatory
	Incapacitated Persons [§ 14-5303] or Infants [CRP § 17(g)]		Mandatory
	Insanity Hearing [§ 13-4013]		Mandatory
Arkansas	Family in Need of Services and Termination of Parental Rights [§ 9-27-316]	No uniform criteria	Mandatory
	Guardian to defend infant, insane, or prisoner [§ 16-61-108, § 16-61-109; ARCPR 17]		Mandatory
	Guardianship of Incapacitated Persons [§ 28-65-319]		Mandatory
	Involuntary Commitment [§ 20-47-212, §§ 5-28-301 to 305]		Mandatory
California	Termination of Parental Rights, Adoption, Dependency [FC § 7851, § 7861, § 7862]	Not specified	Mandatory
	Paternity [W&I § 11350.1, § 11475.1]		Mandatory where state appears as party or on behalf of minor or mother
	Involuntary Commitment [W&I § 5111, § 5302, § 6500]		Mandatory
	Indigent Prisoner sued in civil case		Discretionary
	Probate—Guardian Ad Litem [Probate § 1003]		Mandatory
	Nonpayment of Child Support—Contempt [W&I § 11350, CCP § 1209(a)(5), Pen. § 987.2, Court Rule § 1285.60]		Mandatory
	Minor Custody [Civ. Code § 4606—*Repealed Jan. 1, 1994*]		Discretionary for minor
Colorado	Representation of Minor [§ 15-14-207]	Public Defender form (essentially financial affidavit). Requires pay stub, W-2 form.	Discretionary

State	Type of Case	Procedure or Standard to Determine Indigency	Court Obligation To Appoint Counsel
Colorado *(continued)*	Incapacitated Person [§ 15-14-303]		Discretionary ("if rights & interests not otherwise adequately protected, then court shall appoint")
	Paternity [§ 19-4-110]		Discretionary
	Involuntary Commitment—Mentally Ill [§ 27-10-106(10), § 27-10-107(5), § 27-10-108, § 27-10-109(3)]		Mandatory
	Sterilization of Developmentally Disabled [§ 27-10.5-129(4)]		Mandatory
	Custody, Support, Visitation [§ 14-10-116]		Discretionary
	Nonpayment of Child Support [§ 14-10-117(4); *see Padilla v. Padilla*, 645 P.2d 1327 (Colo. App. 1982)]		Discretionary
	Discriminatory Housing Practice [§ 24-34-307 (1990)]		Discretionary appointment of guardian ad litem
	Dependency and Neglect [§ 19-3-203(1), § 19-3-312(3)]		Mandatory appointment of guardian ad litem
	Termination of Parental Rights [§ 19-3-602]		Discretionary for parents; mandatory for minor
	Involuntary Commitment—Alcoholism [§ 25-1-310(6), § 311(3)(10)]		Mandatory
	Protective Services for Developmentally Disabled [§ 26-3-104(2)]		Mandatory
Connecticut	Probate—Minor or Incapacitated Person [§ 45a-620]	Determined on case-by-case basis depending on statute and subject matter involved	Mandatory
	Representation of Incapacitated or Mentally Retarded Persons [§ 45a-649(b)(2), § 45a-673]		Mandatory
	Sterilization [§ 45a-694]		Mandatory
	Termination of Parental Rights [§ 45a-716]		Mandatory
	Paternity		Mandatory if state-initiated and possibility of incarceration

State	Type of Case	Procedure or Standard to Determine Indigency	Court Obligation To Appoint Counsel
Connecticut *(continued)*	Child Welfare [§ 17a-101]		Mandatory
	Commitment Proceedings [§ 17a-498, § 17a-698]		Mandatory
	Civil Contempt—Nonpayment of Child Support		Mandatory
	Child—Family Relations [§ 46b-62]		Mandatory for certain proceedings
	Abused or Neglected Minor—Appointment of Guardian Ad Litem (P.B. § 484)		Mandatory
	Juvenile Matters [§ 46b-136, P.B. § 1045] All proceedings concerning neglected or dependent minor, termination of parental rights of minor committed to state agency, matters concerning families with service needs and contested termination of parental rights transferred from probate court; does not include guardianship, adoption or property rights		Mandatory (a) upon request, or (b) in the case of counsel for minor in which custody is at issue or if in the opinion of the court the interests of parent & minor conflict, or (c) if a fair hearing necessitates such an appointment
Delaware	Involuntary Commitment [Title 16 §§ 5006–5008]	*In forma pauperis* affidavit	Mandatory
	Sterilization [Title 16 § 5710]		Mandatory
	Custody [Title 13 § 721]		Discretionary
	Paternity [Title 13 § 814]		Discretionary
	Divorce [Title 13 § 1516(c)]		Discretionary
	Family Court [Fam. Ct. Civ. R. 204]		Discretionary
District of Columbia	Divorce, Support, Custody [§ 16-918]	In general, financial inability to afford counsel	Discretionary
	Infants [§ 13-332]		Discretionary
	Involuntary Commitment [§ 6-1942, § 21-543; SCR-MR § 11, § 11-2601]		Mandatory
	Probate [SCR-PD § 308]		Discretionary
	Termination of Parental Rights [§ 16-2304, § 11-2601 *et seq.*]		Mandatory for parent, guardian or custodian

State	Type of Case	Procedure or Standard to Determine Indigency	Court Obligation To Appoint Counsel
Florida	Juvenile—Dependency, Termination of Parental Rights [§ 39.415, § 39.467, § 39.474]	Financial affidavit and/or respond to court's questions	Mandatory for parent
	Involuntary examination & treatment, hospitalization, placement & isolation of persons infected with tuberculosis [§ 392.55–.56]		Mandatory
	Involuntary admission of mentally retarded [§ 393.11]		Mandatory
	Family in Need of Services [§ 39.447]		Mandatory
	Involuntary Treatment of Alcoholics [§ 396.102(9)]		Mandatory
	Involuntary Commitment—Mentally Ill [§ 394.467]		Mandatory
	Involuntary Treatment—Drug Abuse [§ 397.052]		Mandatory
	Non-Consent Protective Services for Abused, Aged Persons or Disabled Adults [§ 414.105]		Mandatory
Georgia	Termination of Parental Rights [§ 15-11-85]	In general, not specified	Mandatory for minor [*but see Arlington v. Hand*, 193 Ga. App. 457, 388 S.E.2d (1989) (adoption statutes do not require appointment of attorney for minor, therefore court is not required to appoint in adoption proceedings)]; mandatory for parents if requested
	Juvenile Proceedings—Custody, Support & Deprivation [§ 15-11-30]		Mandatory
	Unemancipated Minor Seeking Abortion [§ 15-11-114]		Mandatory
	Involuntary Commitment [§ 37-3-62, § 37-3-147, § 37-3-148, § 37-3-150]		Mandatory

State	Type of Case	Procedure or Standard to Determine Indigency	Court Obligation To Appoint Counsel
Georgia *(continued)*	Habilitation of Mentally Retarded [§ 37-4-43]		Mandatory if requested
	Treatment of Alcoholics & Drug Users—Court-ordered evaluation [§ 37-7-62, § 37-7-147]		Mandatory
	Guardianship for Incapacitated Adults [§ 29-5-6(b)(2)]		Mandatory
Hawaii	Civil Contempt [§ 802-1]	Not specified	Mandatory
	Involuntary Commitment [§ 802-1; Chapter 334]		Mandatory
	Family Court [Chapter 571]		Mandatory
	Incapacitated Persons [Chapter 551A]		Mandatory
	Prisoners [§ 353-34]		Discretionary
	Paternity—Minor [§ 584-9]		Mandatory
Idaho	Involuntary Commitment [§ 19-854, § 18-212, § 18-214, § 66-322, § 66-326, § 66-329, § 66-409]	Not specified	Mandatory
	Termination of Parental Rights [§ 16-2009]		Mandatory
	Involuntary Sterilization [§ 39-3903(b)]		Mandatory
Illinois	Paternity [750 ILCS § 45/18]	Financial inability to pay fee	Discretionary
	Probate—Disabled Persons [755 ILCS § 5/11a-10]		Discretionary; mandatory if respondent takes position adverse to guardian ad litem
	Civil Rights [775 I.L.C.S. § 5/10-102]		Discretionary
	Civil Contempt		Mandatory
	Adoption [750 ILCS § 50/13]		Mandatory for minor adoptee, named minor, defendant under legal disability, & parent if allegedly "unfit"
	Indigent Prisoners		Discretionary

State	Type of Case	Procedure or Standard to Determine Indigency	Court Obligation To Appoint Counsel
Illinois *(continued)*	Involuntary Commitment— Mentally Ill & Developmentally Disabled [405 ILSC § 5/3-805]		Mandatory
	Abortion—Parental Notice [720 ILCS § 520/5(b)]		Mandatory if requested; mandatory guardian ad litem for minor
Indiana	Abortion—Minor [§ 35-1-58.5-2.5]	Any relevant information relating to inability to pay	Mandatory
	Child—Family [§ 31-6-7-2]		Discretionary
	Parents—Family [§ 31-6-7-2]		Mandatory for termination of parental rights; otherwise, discretionary
	Probate—Incapacitated Person [§ 29-3-4-4]		Discretionary; mandatory guardian ad litem
	Involuntary Commitment [§ 12-26-2-2]		Mandatory for mentally ill; otherwise, discretionary
	Civil Contempt		Mandatory
Iowa	Termination of Parental Rights [§ 232.113]	Financial affidavit. Also consider age, competency and whether incarcerated	Discretionary
	Dissolution of Marriage—Alimony, Minor Support & Custody Determination [§ 598.12]		Discretionary for minor
	Civil Contempt		Mandatory
	Probate—Incapacitated Person [§ 633.561]		Mandatory for adult who is not petitioner & discretionary for minor
	Minor in Need of Assistance— Abuse, Neglect, Abandonment [§ 232.89]		Mandatory for parent, guardian, custodian and minor
	Family in Need of Assistance [§ 232.126]		Mandatory counsel or guardian for minor; mandatory for parent if requested
	Involuntary Hospitalization of Mentally Ill Persons [§ 229.8]		Mandatory

State	Type of Case	Procedure or Standard to Determine Indigency	Court Obligation To Appoint Counsel
Iowa *(continued)*	Indigent Civil Defendants—Incompetent, Prisoner, Minor, Confined to State Hospital [IRCP § 13]		Mandatory guardian ad litem
	Incompetent to Stand Trial/ Commitment [§ 812.2]		Mandatory
Kansas	Involuntary Commitment pursuant to KSA § 22-3428 (insanity defense) or § 59-2917 (mentally ill) [§ 22-4503]	Financial inability to pay fees. Consider assets, income, expenses, costs of representation, complexity of proceeding	Mandatory for habeas corpus proceedings
	Involuntary Commitment [§ 59-214, § 59-2914, § 59-2914a, § 59-2917]		Mandatory for certain proceedings
	Minor Custody & Minor in Need of Care—Abuse, Neglect [§ 38-1505]		Mandatory guardian ad litem for parent if minor or mentally ill; otherwise discretionary for parents
	Termination of Parental Rights [§ 38-1582]		Mandatory for parent who fails to appear
	Relinquishment and Adoption [§ 59-2115, § 59-2136]		Mandatory for minor parent contesting adoption
	Guardianship [§ 59-3010, § 59-3011]		Mandatory
Kentucky	Involuntary Hospitalization [§ 202A.121]	Unable to pay for representation and other expenses	Mandatory
	Mental Retardation Admission [§ 202B.210]		Mandatory
	Termination of Parental Rights [§ 625.080]		Discretionary
	Civil Contempt—Nonpayment of Support		Mandatory
	Incompetents [§ 387.560]		Mandatory
	Dependency, Neglect, & Abuse [§ 620.100]		Mandatory for minor & parent with custodial control or supervision; discretionary for non-parent with custodial control or supervision

State	Type of Case	Procedure or Standard to Determine Indigency	Court Obligation To Appoint Counsel
Kentucky *(continued)*	Discriminatory Housing Practice [§ 344.655, 344.675]		Discretionary
Louisiana	Minor in Need of Care—Abuse, Neglect [LSA-CJP Art. 13(14)(b); Art. 114A; Ch. C. Art. 607–608]	Consider ability to pay (income, property, outstanding obligations, dependents)	Mandatory for minor if commitment may result; mandatory for parent
	Termination of Parental Rights [Ch. C. Art. 1016, RS § 15:147]		Mandatory for minor and parent
	Child—Custody [C.J.P. Art. 95]		Mandatory
	Voluntary Surrender of Parental Rights [Ch. C. Art. 1146]		Mandatory for permanent placement of minor
	Commitment/Competency Hearing [§ 28:64 (1992) and Ch. C. Art. 1442]		Mandatory
	Voluntary and Involuntary Mental Health Treatment [Ch. C. Art. 1405]		Mandatory
	Mentally Retarded & Developmentally Disabled— Involuntary Admission [R.S. § 28:404]		Mandatory
	Divorce [C.C.P. § 1201, § 5091]		Mandatory for absent defendant
	Paternity [C.C.P. Art. 5091.1]		Mandatory for minor if parent disavows parentage
Maine	Child Protection [Title 22 § 4005]	Inability to afford counsel	Mandatory for parents and custodians if requested & indigent, except for preliminary protection orders or petition for medical treatment
	Termination of Parental Rights [Title 22 § 4052]		Mandatory
	Involuntary Commitment [Title 34-B § 3864(5)(D)]		Mandatory
	Sterilization [Title 34-B § 7008, § 7013]		Mandatory
	Emancipation—minor 16 years or older who refuses to live at home [15 M.R.S.A. § 3506-A]		Mandatory for minor if requested

State	Type of Case	Procedure or Standard to Determine Indigency	Court Obligation To Appoint Counsel
Maine *(continued)*	Abortion—Minor's consent [22 M.R.S.A. § 1597-A]		Mandatory for any party, within 24 hours of hearing
	Judicial Consent—HIV test [Title 5 § 19203-C]		If requested
Maryland	Adoption and Guardianship [FL § 5-323 and Rule D75]	In general, not specified	Mandatory for parent if involuntary termination; for adoptee if consent is requested & individual is disabled; for disabled biological parent; and for minor parent
	Custody, Visitation, Support [FL § 1-202]		Discretionary for minor
	Guardian in Divorce [Rule S72]		Mandatory
	Child in Need of Assistance—Abuse, Neglect, Mentally Disabled [Courts § 3-821 & § 3-834; Rule 906(b)(2)]		Mandatory for petitioner, minor, and indigent custodial parent or guardian
	Civil Contempt		Mandatory
Massachusetts	Adoption [§ 210.3]	In general, receiving public assistance or income after taxes of 125 percent poverty level	Mandatory for minor unless petition not contested by any party
	Minor—general right to counsel [Supreme Judicial Court Rule 3:10]		Discretionary
	Abuse, Neglect, Removal of Minor/Custody [§ 119:29]		Mandatory for minor; mandatory for parent or custodian if Dep't of Social Services or minor placement agency is party to action
	Voluntary/Involuntary Commitment [§ 123:5, § 123:10]		Mandatory
	Paternity [§ 209C:7]		Discretionary
	Divorce [§ 208:16]		Discretionary
Michigan	Paternity [§ 772.714(3)]	Financial affidavit	Mandatory
	Incapacitated Person [§ 700.443a]		Mandatory
	Minor [§ 700.427]		Discretionary
	Guardianship for Developmentally Disabled [§ 330.1615]		Mandatory

State	Type of Case	Procedure or Standard to Determine Indigency	Court Obligation To Appoint Counsel
Michigan *(continued)*	Civil Commitment [§ 330.1517, § 330.1454]		Mandatory
	Civil Contempt [§ 552.631, § 552.633, § 552.635]		Mandatory
Minnesota	Termination of Parental Rights [§ 260.155]	*In forma pauperis*	Discretionary for minor, parents or guardian
	Custody, Support, Legitimacy [§ 257.69]		Mandatory
	Paternity		Mandatory for defendant
	Adoption [§ 259.33]		Discretionary for adoptee
	Civil Contempt for Nonpayment of Minor Support		Mandatory if incarceration real possibility
	Involuntary Commitment [§ 253B.03]		Mandatory
	Guardianship [§ 525.5501]		Mandatory if involuntary petition for guardianship
Mississippi	Involuntary Commitment—Drug & Alcohol [§ 41-30-27]	Financial affidavit	"Shall have opportunity to be represented"
	Involuntary Commitment—Mental Illness [§ 41-21-67]		Mandatory
Missouri	Minor—Abortion [§ 188.028]	Each court has individual discretion	Discretionary
	Incapacity/Disability [§ 475.075]		Mandatory
	Termination of Parental Rights [§ 211.462]		Discretionary for minor; mandatory for parent or guardian
	Involuntary Commitment [§ 632.415]		Mandatory
	Minor Custody [§ 452.490]		Mandatory guardian ad litem for minor
Montana	Termination of Parental Rights [§ 41-3-607]	In general, not specified	Mandatory for parents
	Abuse, Neglect, Dependency [§ 41-3-401(12)]		Discretionary
	Support, Custody, Visitation [§ 40-4-205]		Discretionary for dependent minor

State	Type of Case	Procedure or Standard to Determine Indigency	Court Obligation To Appoint Counsel
Montana *(continued)*	Paternity [§ 40-6-119]		Mandatory
	Involuntary Commitment—Alcoholics [§ 53-24-302]		Mandatory
	Involuntary Commitment—Developmentally Disabled [§ 53-20-125]		At request of parent or guardian
	Involuntary Commitment—Mentally Ill [§ 53-21-116]		Mandatory
	Incapacitated Person/Minor [§ 72-5-225, § 72-5-315, § 72-5-408, § 72-5-322]		Discretionary
Nebraska	Involuntary Commitment [§ 83-1049, § 29-3915]	Financial affidavit or testimony that person cannot afford counsel	Mandatory
	Termination of Parental Rights [§ 42-364]		Mandatory for parents
	Dependency [§ 43-272]		Mandatory on request of parent, guardian or minor
	Paternity		Mandatory
Nevada	Paternity, Support [§ 126.201]	Not specified	Discretionary for parent; mandatory guardian or guardian ad litem for minor
	Termination of Parental Rights [§ 128.100]		Discretionary for parent & minor
	Abuse & Neglect [§ 432B.420]		Discretionary for parent, custodian and minor
	Involuntary Commitment [§ 433A.270]		Mandatory
	Mentally Retarded—Involuntary Admission [§ 435.126]		Mandatory
New Hampshire	Minor—Divorce, Custody, Visitation [§ 458:17]	Financial affidavit	Discretionary appointment of guardian ad litem
	Minor Protection Act—Neglect or Abuse [§ 604-A:1a; § 169-C:10]		Mandatory for minor; discretionary for parents
	Domestic Violence [§ 173-B:5]		Discretionary guardian ad litem for minor

State	Type of Case	Procedure or Standard to Determine Indigency	Court Obligation To Appoint Counsel
New Hampshire *(continued)*	Termination of Parental Rights [§ 170-C:10, § 170-C:7]		Mandatory if requested
	Placement—Developmentally Disabled [§ 171-A:10]		Mandatory
	Involuntary Commitment [§ 135-C:22]		Mandatory
	Civil Contempt		Discretionary
New Jersey	Out of Home Placement—Minor [§ 2A:4A-89]	Financial affidavit	Mandatory for parent & minor
	Developmentally Disabled [§ 30:4-165.13]		Discretionary for individual or class
	Mentally Ill—Admission, Retention, Release [§ 30:4-27 *et seq.*; R. 4:74-7]		Discretionary
	Protective Services—Abuse, Neglect [§ 9:6-8.23, § 9:6-8.43]		Mandatory guardianship ad litem for minor; parent may apply to Dep't of Public Advocacy
	Termination of Parental Rights [§ 30:4C-12]		Discretionary for parents; mandatory for minor in termination and dependency hearings
	Medical Guardianship [Rule 4:83-12 & § 44:1-140]		Mandatory
	Guardianship of Incompetent [Rule 4:86-4(b)]		Mandatory
	Involuntary Civil Commitment [Rule 4:74-7]		Mandatory guardian ad litem for minor
	Paternity		Mandatory
New Mexico	Adoption [§ 40-7-48]	Financial affidavit	Discretionary for adoptee, minor or incompetent, but if contested then mandatory
	Paternity [§ 40-11-19]		Discretionary
	Voluntary/Involuntary Commitment [§ 43-1-16, § 43-1-16.1]		Mandatory
	Involuntary Commitment— Developmentally Disabled [§ 43-1-13]		Mandatory

State	Type of Case	Procedure or Standard to Determine Indigency	Court Obligation To Appoint Counsel
New York	Commitment of Mentally Ill, Mentally Defective or Narcotic Addict; Commitment of Guardianship & Custody to Agency Due to Parental Mental Illness or Retardation; Consent to Adoption of Minor by Mentally Ill Parent [JUD § 35 & CPLR § 1101]	Financial inability established by affidavit setting forth employment status, income, assets, etc.	Mandatory
	Minor—Family Court Proceedings [FCA § 241 et seq.]		Mandatory for minor protection proceedings; discretionary in other proceedings
	Termination of Parental Rights; Family Offenses, Custody; Contempt; Adoption; Paternity [FCA § 262, § 1120]		Mandatory for termination of parental rights & where custody of minor may be given to an agency; discretionary in all other cases
	Civil Actions generally [CPLR § 1101]		Discretionary
North Carolina	Termination of Parental Rights [§ 7A-289.23, § 7A-451(14)]	Financial affidavit	Mandatory
	Dependency, Neglect, Abuse [§ 7A-587]		Mandatory for parent; discretionary for minor, but mandatory guardian ad litem
	Sterilization [§ 35-45, § 7A-451(10)]		Mandatory
	Incompetency/Guardianship [§ 35A-1107, § 7A-451(13)]		Mandatory—attorney as guardian ad litem
	Involuntary Commitment [§ 122C-224, § 112C-264, § 122C-267(d), § 7A-451(6)]		Mandatory for minor, discretionary for adult
	Minor Support [§ 50-13.9(f)]		Mandatory for party who is owed support
	Civil Contempt		Mandatory
North Dakota	Family/Parentage [§ 14-17-15(1)]	Not specified	Mandatory
	Termination of Parental Rights [§ 14-17-18]		Mandatory if parent requests
	Involuntary Commitment [§ 26-03.1-13]		Mandatory

State	Type of Case	Procedure or Standard to Determine Indigency	Court Obligation To Appoint Counsel
North Dakota *(continued)*	Neglect, Abuse, Dependency [§ 27-20-26]		Mandatory for parent & minor, if minor is not represented by parent, guardian or custodian
Ohio	Hospitalization of Mentally Ill [§ 5122.15, § 5122.43(7)]	Financial affidavit	Mandatory
	Involuntary Commitment— Developmentally Disabled and Mentally Retarded [§ 5123.71]		Mandatory
	Adult in Need of Protective Services (incapacitated, abused) [§ 5101.70]		Mandatory when Dep't of Human Services petitions for protective services
	Paternity		Mandatory for defendant when State is adversary and mother/minor receive public assistance
	Abuse, Neglect, Dependency [Juv. R. 4; § 2151.352]		Mandatory
	Civil Contempt—Nonpayment of Child Support		Discretionary
Oklahoma	Parentage, Custody, Support [Title 10 § 24; 22 OS § 1355.8]	Not specified	Mandatory upon request of parent, minor or guardian
	Termination of Parental Rights, Dependent & Neglected Minor [Title 10 § 1109; 22 OS § 1335.8]		Mandatory for minor; mandatory for adult, if possibility of termination of parental rights; otherwise only if requested
	Child Abuse [Title 21 § 846(G)]		Mandatory for minor
	Civil Contempt [Title 12 Ch. 2 App. Rule 29]		Mandatory if hearing may result in incarceration
	Incapacitated Person [Title 30 § 3-107]		Discretionary
	Detention—Mentally Ill [Title 43A §§ 5-210, 5-401]		Mandatory
	Protective Services for Elderly or Incapacitated [Title 43A § 10-108]		Mandatory
Oregon	Involuntary Commitment by Psychiatric Security Review Board [§ 161.346(6)(d)]	Financial affidavit, including bank accounts, real and personal property	Mandatory

State	Type of Case	Procedure or Standard to Determine Indigency	Court Obligation To Appoint Counsel
Oregon *(continued)*	Civil Commitment—Alcohol, Drug Abuse, Mentally Ill & Sexually Dangerous [§ 426.307(3), § 426.100, § 426.135]		Mandatory
	Civil Contempt [§ 33.035]		Mandatory
	Involuntary Commitment for Mentally Retarded [§ 427.265(3), § 427.245(2)]		Mandatory
	Dependency [§ 419.498]		Discretionary for minor; discretionary for parent depending on nature of proceeding
	Involuntary Sterilization [§436.265]		Mandatory if requested by respondent
Pennsylvania	Termination of Parental Rights [23 Pa. CSA § 2313]	*In forma pauperis* affidavit	Mandatory for minor if contested by parent; mandatory for parent
	Civil Commitment [50 PS § 4406, § 7304]		Discretionary
	Custody, Visitation [RCP § 1915.11(a)]		Discretionary for minor only
	Paternity		Mandatory
	Protective Services—Elderly [35 PS § 10220(c)]		Mandatory
	Dependency [42 Pa. CSA § 6337]		Mandatory
Rhode Island	Abuse, Neglect, Dependency [§ 40-11-14; Juv. Rule 15]	Financial affidavit	Discretionary guardian ad litem or special advocate for child; mandatory for parent
	Termination of Parental Rights [Juv. Rule 18(4)]		Mandatory for parent or custodian
	Mentally Ill [§ 40.1-5-17]		Mandatory
South Carolina	Abuse & Neglect [§ 20-7-110]	Not specified	Mandatory
	Adult Protective Custody [§ 44-35-45]		Mandatory
	Judicial Commitment—Mentally Ill [§ 44-17-530, § 44-17-510]		Mandatory
	Involuntary Admission—Mentally Retarded or Disabled [§ 44-20-450]		Mandatory

State	Type of Case	Procedure or Standard to Determine Indigency	Court Obligation To Appoint Counsel
South Carolina *(continued)*	Abortion—Judicial Bypass [§ 44-41-32]		Mandatory for minor if requested
	Involuntary Admission—Alcohol & Drug Abuse [§ 44-52-110, § 44-22-30]		Mandatory
South Dakota	Abuse & Neglect [§§ 26-8A-9, 8A-18]	Current assets and income, sources of financial support and dependents	Mandatory
	Mentally Ill—Noncompliance with treatment or unsuccessful treatment [§§ 27A-11A-21, 22]		Mandatory
	Involuntary Commitment— Mentally Retarded [§§ 27B-7–11, 12]		Mandatory
	Involuntary Commitment— Mentally Ill [§§ 27A-11A-7, 12]		Mandatory
Tennessee	Involuntary Commitment [§ 33-3-608]	Indigency not required	Mandatory
	Abuse, Neglect, Dependency, Termination of Parent-Minor Relationship [§ 37-1-147, § 37-1-149–150]		Mandatory guardian ad litem for minor if parent or custodian do not appear on minor's behalf, conflict of interest, or minor's interests warrant; discretionary for all other parties
Texas	Termination of Parent-Minor Relationship [Fam. § 11.10, § 51.10]	Financial affidavit, including income, property, bank accounts, dependents, debts, and monthly expenses	Discretionary for any party to protect interests of minor; mandatory for minor and each parent who opposes termination
	Mental Health [H&S § 571.017, § 571.018, Texas Const. Art. 1 § 15-a]		Mandatory
	Treatment of Chemically Dependent Persons [H&S § 462.063, § 462.064]		Mandatory
	Suits Affecting the Parent-Minor Relationship (minor support, custody, visitation order violations) [TRCP § 308a]		Discretionary appointment of attorney to investigate alleged violation of court order for support, custody or visitation

State	Type of Case	Procedure or Standard to Determine Indigency	Court Obligation To Appoint Counsel
Texas *(continued)*	Contempt—Nonpayment of Minor Support [Fam. § 14.32(f)]		Mandatory if incarceration possible
Utah	Protective/Termination of Parental Rights [§ 78-39-35]	Financial affidavit, including employment status, any state or federal public assistance, and borrowing capacity	Mandatory on request if county or State is party; discretionary if not requested, but in best interest of minor
	Involuntary Commitment [§ 62A-12-234(9)]		Mandatory for adults
Vermont	Child Support/Divorce [Title 15 § 594]	Financial affidavit	Discretionary for minor; mandatory if minor called as witness
	Involuntary Commitment [Title 18 § 7613]		Mandatory
	Sterilization [Title 18 § 8710]		Mandatory
Virginia	Involuntary Commitment [§ 37.1-67.3, § 37.1-67.6]	Generally, presumption if receiving public assistance	Mandatory
	Involuntary Commitment— Criminal [§ 19.2-182]		Mandatory
	Abuse, Neglect & Termination of Parental Rights [§ 16.1-266]		Mandatory attorney as guardian ad litem for minor; mandatory for parent
	Sterilization [§ 54.1-2975]		Mandatory for minor & adult incapable of consent
	Persons with Disability (confined, infant, mentally retarded or mentally ill, drug addict or alcoholic, incompetent or aged) [§ 8.01-2; § 8.01-9]		Mandatory guardian ad litem
	Supplemental Security Income Claims [§ 63.1-89.1]		Discretionary referral of local department of social services
Washington	Involuntary Commitment [§ 71.05.460, § 71.05.110]	Each county superior court establishes financial standards; consider financial capability	Mandatory
	Paternity—Parentage [§ 74.20.350, § 26:26]		Discretionary

State	Type of Case	Procedure or Standard to Determine Indigency	Court Obligation To Appoint Counsel
Washington *(continued)*	Adoption/Termination of Parental Rights [§ 26.33.110]		Mandatory if nonconsenting parent or alleged father; mandatory guardian ad litem for minor parent or minor alleged father; discretionary guardian ad litem for minor
	Abuse, Neglect, Dependency [§ 13.34.030, § 13.34.090, § 13.34.100]		Mandatory for parent, guardian or custodian; mandatory for minor in contested proceedings unless court finds good cause that appointment unnecessary; discretionary for minor in all uncontested proceedings
	Civil Contempt		Discretionary if imprisonment is immediate threat
West Virginia	Paternity/Minor Support [§ 48A-6-5]	Financial affidavit; determination is within judge's discretion	Mandatory for defendant; mandatory advocate for minor
	Dependency [§ 49-5-8(c), § 49-5-9, § 49-5-1]		Mandatory for minor
	Involuntary Commitment [§ 27-5-4]		Mandatory
	Abuse/Neglect which may result in Termination of Parental Rights [§ 29-21-2, § 29-21-9]		Mandatory for parent
	Contempt with risk of incarceration [§ 29-21-2, § 29-21-9]		Mandatory
	Sterilization of Incompetent [§ 27-16-1]		Mandatory
Wisconsin	Involuntary Commitment—drug addict, developmentally disabled, mentally ill or mentally deficient [§ 51.20(3)]	Financial affidavit setting forth assets less reasonable living expenses	Mandatory
	Transfer or Discharge of Mentally Ill Patients [§ 51.35(1)(e)2.c]		Mandatory
	Protective—Minor [§ 48.23]		Discretionary for minor; mandatory for parent; if contested adoption or involuntary termination of parental rights then mandatory counsel or guardian ad litem for minor

State	Type of Case	Procedure or Standard to Determine Indigency	Court Obligation To Appoint Counsel
Wisconsin *(continued)*	Paternity [§ 977.05(4)(i)(7)]		Mandatory if state is petitioner
	Contempt—Nonpayment of Minor Support [§ 977.05(4)(h)]		Mandatory
	Termination of Parental Rights [§ 977.05(4)(i)(6)]		Mandatory
	Protective—Mentally Ill, Developmentally Disabled & Aged [§ 55.06, § 880.33(2), § 757.48(1)]		Mandatory guardian ad litem who is attorney or counsel if requested
Wyoming	Probate—Minor [§ 2-2-310]	Financial affidavit stating that person is without sufficient funds to employ counsel	Discretionary
	Abortion—Minor [§ 35-6-118]		Discretionary
	Protective [§ 14-6-222]		Mandatory if requested; otherwise discretionary in "interest of justice"
	Abuse, Neglect, Dependency [§ 14-6-222, § 14-6-235]		Mandatory for minor; discretionary for parents
	Paternity/Minor Support [§ 14-2-116]		Mandatory
	Involuntary Commitment [§ 25-10-109, § 25-10-110]		Mandatory
	Termination of Parental Rights [§ 14-2-318, § 14-2-319]		Discretionary

Appendix F

The Legal System

For many persons, law appears to be magic—an obscure domain that can be fathomed only by the professional initiated into its mysteries. People who might use the law to their advantage sometimes avoid the effort out of awe for its intricacies. But in fact the main lines of the legal system, and of the law in a particular area, can be explained in terms clear to the layperson. The purpose of this appendix is to outline some important elements of the system.

What does a lawyer mean by saying that a person has a legal right?

Having a right means that society has given a person permission—through the legal system—to secure some action or to act in some way that she or he desires. For example, a woman might have a right to an abortion, a minority person the right to employment free from discrimination, or a person accused of a crime the right to an attorney.

How does one enforce a legal right?

The concept of *enforcing* a right gives meaning to the concept of the right itself. While the abstract right may be significant because it carries some connotation of morality and justice, enforcing the right yields something concrete—the abortion, the job, the attorney.

A person enforces her or his right by going to some appropriate authority—often, a judge—who has the power to take certain action. The judge can order the people who are refusing to grant the right to start doing so, on pain of going to jail if they disobey. The judge can also order the people to pay money to compensate for the loss of the right. Sometimes other authorities, such as federal and state administrative agencies or a labor arbitrator, can take similar remedial action.

The problem with the enforcement process is that it will often be lengthy, time-consuming, expensive, frustrating, and may arouse hostility in others—in short, it may not be worth the effort. On the other hand, in some cases you may not need to go to an enforcement authority in order to implement your right. The concerned persons or officials may not have realized that you have a right and may voluntarily change their actions once you explain your position. Then, too, they may not want

404

to go through the legal process either—it can be as expensive and frustrating for them as it is for you.

Where are legal rights defined?

There are several sources. Rights are defined in the statutes or laws passed by the U.S. Congress and by state and city legislatures. They are also set forth in the written decisions of judges, federal and state. Congress and state and local legislatures have also created institutions called administrative agencies to enforce certain laws, and these agencies interpret the laws in written decisions and rules that further define people's rights.

Are rights always clearly defined and evenly applied to all people?

Not at all, although this is one of the great myths about law. Because so many different sources define people's rights, and because persons of diverse backgrounds and beliefs implement and enforce the law, there is virtually no way to enforce uniformity. Nor do statutes that set forth rights always do so with clarity or specificity. It remains for courts or administrative agencies to interpret and flesh out the details; and in the process of doing so, many of the interpreters differ. Sometimes, two courts will give completely different answers to the same question. Whether or not a person has a particular right may depend on which state or city he or she lives in.

The more times a particular issue is decided, the more guidance there is in predicting what other judges or administrative personnel will decide. Similarly, the importance of the court or agency deciding a case or the persuasiveness of its reasoning will help determine the effect of the decision. A judge who states thoughtful reasons for a decision will have more influence than one who offers poor reasons.

Law, then, is not a preordained set of doctrines, applied rigidly and unswervingly in every situation. Rather, law is molded from the arguments and decisions of many persons and institutions. It is very much a human process of trying to convince others—a judge, a jury, an administrator, the lawyer for the other side—that your view of what the law requires is correct.

What is a decision or case?

Lawyers often use these words interchangeably, although technically they do not mean the same thing. A *case* means the lawsuit started by one person against another, and it can refer to that lawsuit at any time from the moment it is started until the final result is reached. A *decision* means the written opinion in which the judge declares who wins the lawsuit and why.

What is meant by precedent?

Precedent means past decisions. Lawyers use precedent to influence new decisions. If the facts involved in the prior decision are close to the facts in the present case, a judge will be strongly tempted to follow the former decision. The judge is not, however, bound to do so and, if persuasive reasons are presented to show that the prior decision was wrong or ill-suited to changed conditions in society, the judge may not follow precedent.

What is the relationship between decisions and statutes?

In our legal system, most legal concepts originally were defined in the decisions of judges. In deciding what legal doctrine to apply to a case, each judge kept building on what other judges had done before. The body of legal doctrines created in this way is called the *common law*.

The common law still applies in many situations, but increasingly state legislatures and the Congress pass laws ("statutes") to define the legal concepts that judges or agencies should use in deciding cases. The written decisions of individual judges are still important even where there is a statute because statutes are generally not specific enough to cover every set of facts. Judges have to interpret the meaning of statutes, apply them to the facts at hand, and write a decision; that decision will then be considered by other judges when they deal with these statutes in other cases. Thus it is generally not enough to know what a relevant statute defines as illegal; you also have to know how judges have interpreted the statute in specific situations.

What different kinds of courts are there?

The United States is unique for its variety of courts. Broadly speaking, there are two distinct court systems: federal and state. Both are located throughout the country; each is limited to certain kinds of cases, with substantial areas of overlap. Most crimes are prosecuted in state courts, for instance, although there are a number of federal crimes prosecuted in federal court. People must always use state courts to get a divorce (except in the District of Columbia and other federal areas), but they must sue in federal court to establish rights under certain federal laws.

In both federal and state court systems one starts at the trial court level, where the facts are "tried." This means that a judge or jury listens and watches as the lawyers present evidence of the facts that each side seeks to prove. Evidence can take many forms: written documents, the testimony of a witness on the stand, photographs, charts. Once a judge or jury has listened to or observed all the evidence presented by each side, it will choose the version of the facts it believes, apply the applicable legal doctrine to these facts, and decide which side has won. If either side is unhappy with the result, it may be able to take the case to the next, higher-level court and argue that the judge or the jury applied the wrong legal concept to the facts, or that no reasonable jury or judge could have found the facts as they were found in the trial court and that the result was therefore wrong.

What are plaintiffs and defendants?

The *plaintiff* is the person who sues—that is, who *complains* that someone has wronged him or her and asks the court to remedy this situation. The *defendant* is the person sued—the one who *defends* against the charges of the plaintiff. The legal writing in which the plaintiff articulates her or his basic grievance is the *complaint*, and a lawsuit is generally commenced by filing this document with the clerk at the courthouse. The defendant then responds to these charges in a document appropriately named an *answer*. Some states use different names for these documents.

One refers to a particular lawsuit by giving the names of the plaintiff and defendant. If Mary Jones sues Smith Corporation for refusing to hire her because she is a woman, her case will be called *Jones v. Smith Corporation* (*v.* stands for versus or against).

What is an administrative agency?

Agencies are institutions established by either state or federal legislatures to administer or enforce a particular law or series of laws and are distinct from both courts and legislatures. They often regulate a particular industry. For example, the Federal Communications Commission regulates the broadcasting industry (radio and television stations and networks) and the telephone and telegraph industry, in accordance with the legal standards set forth in the Federal Communications Act; and the Interstate Commerce Commission regulates trucking and railroads.

These agencies establish legal principles, referred to as rules, regulations, or guidelines. Rules are interpretations of a statute and are designed to function in the same way as a statute—to define people's rights and obligations on a general scale, but in a more detailed fashion than the statute itself. Agencies also issue specific decisions in particular cases, like a judge, applying a law or rule to a factual dispute between particular parties.

How does one find court decisions, statutes, and agency rules and decisions?

All these materials are published and can be found in law libraries. In order to find the item desired, one should understand the system lawyers use for referring to, or citing, these materials. Some examples will help clarify the system. A case might be cited as *Watson v. Limbach Company*, 333 F. Supp. 754 (S.D. Ohio 1971); a statute, as 42 U.S.C. § 1983; a regulation, as 29 C.F.R. § 1604. 10(b). The unifying factor in all three citations is that the first number denotes the particular volume in a series of books with the same title; the words or the letters that follow represent the name of the book; and the second number represents either the page or the section in the identified volume. In the examples above, the *Watson* case is found in the 333rd volume of the series of books called *Federal Supplement* at page 754; the statute is found in volume 42 of the series called the *United States Code* at Section

1983; the regulation is in volume 29 of the *Code of Federal Regulations* at Section 1604.10(b).

There are similar systems for state court decisions. Once you understand the system, all you need to do is find out from the librarian where any particular series of books is kept, then look up the proper volume and page or section. It is also important to look for the same page or section in the material sometimes inserted at the back of a book, since many legal materials are periodically updated. A librarian will tell you what any abbreviations stand for if you are unfamiliar with that series.

Given this basic information, anyone can locate and read important cases, statutes, and regulations. Throughout the book, such materials have been cited when deemed particularly important, and laypersons are urged to read them. Although lawyers often use overly technical language, the references cited in this book can be comprehended without serious difficulty, and reading the original legal materials will give citizens a deeper understanding of their rights.

What is the role of the lawyer in the legal system?

A lawyer understands the intricacies and technicalities of the legal system, can maneuver within it efficiently, and is able to help other people by doing so. Thus the lawyer knows where to find out about the leading legal doctrines in any given area and how to predict the outcome of your case, based on a knowledge of those doctrines. A lawyer can advise you what to do: take the case to an administrative agency; sue in court; make a will; and so on. The lawyer then can help you take the legal actions that you determine are necessary.

How are legal costs determined and how do they affect people's rights?

The cost of using the legal system is predominantly the cost of paying the lawyer for his or her time. Since this has become prohibitive even for middle-class individuals, many people are not able to assert their rights, even though they might ultimately win if they had the money to pay a lawyer for doing the job.

Is legal action the only way to win one's legal rights?

By no means. Negotiation, education, consciousness raising, publicity, demonstrations, organization, and lobbying are all ways to achieve rights, often more effectively than through the standard but costly and time-consuming resort to the courts. In all these areas, it helps to have secure knowledge of the legal underpinning of your rights. One has a great deal more authority if one is protesting illegal action. The refrain "That's illegal" may move some people in and of itself; or it may convince those with whom you are dealing that you're serious enough to do something about the situation—by starting a lawsuit, for instance.